D1327722

Back to the Present Forward to the Past

Irish Writing and History since 1798
Volume II

COSTERUS NEW SERIES 162

Series Editors:
C.C. Barfoot, Theo D'haen
and Erik Kooper

Back to the Present Forward to the Past

Irish Writing and History since 1798
Volume II

Edited by
Patricia A. Lynch,
Joachim Fischer and
Brian Coates

Rodopi   Amsterdam-New York, NY 2006

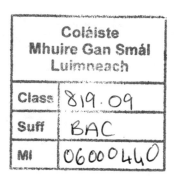
Cover image by courtesy of Prof. Mary Helen Thuente of North Carolina
State University and Eoin Stephenson, Photographic Unit of the University
of Limerick.

Cover design: Aart Jan Bergshoeff

The paper on which this book is printed meets the requirements of
"ISO 9706:1994, Information and documentation - Paper for
documents - Requirements for permanence".

ISBN-10: 90-420-2038-5
ISBN-13: 978-90-420-2038-2

Volume I and II
ISBN-10: 90-420-2036-9
ISBN-13: 978-90-420-2036-8

CONTENTS

OUT OF LIMERICK:
KATE O'BRIEN – FRANK McCOURT

KATE O'BRIEN AS A "HERSTORICAL" WRITER:
THE PERSONAL STORY OF WOMEN

MARÍA DE LA CINTA RAMBLADO MINERO

For Adele Dalsimer, *in memoriam.*

Kate O'Brien has been studied from different angles, and the most frequent has been the socio-historic approach. From this point of view she has been said to portray a social milieu that had not been represented before in Irish literature, that of the Catholic bourgeoisie.[1] Until recently, she had never been deeply studied from a feminist point of view because almost every critic seemed to have followed Reynolds's statement that Kate O'Brien was not a feminist, or at least, not explicitly.[2] It is true that O'Brien never manifested any tendencies towards feminist trends; however, it is possible to be a woman writer without being what we understand as feminist, that is, a radical feminist which, for the people on the streets, means fighting against the patriarchal system. However, O'Brien does not do this explicitly; she is better defined as a female writer. This can be explained in relation to Elaine Showalter's historical division of women's writing. According to Showalter, there are three stages in the tradition of women's literature:[3]

> *feminine*: characterized by the imitation of male models;
> *feminist*: reaction against patriarchy, emphasizing women's victimi-
> zation in a male-dominated environment;
> *female*: writing about women and their history, experiences and per-
> ceptions from a female point of view.

---

[1]   Adele M. Dalsimer, *Kate O'Brien: A Critical Study*, Dublin, 1990, xi.
[2]   Lorna Reynolds, *Kate O'Brien: A Literary Portrait*, Gerrards Cross, 1987, 128.
[3]   Elaine Showalter, "The Female Tradition", in *Feminisms: An Anthology of Literary Theory and Criticism*, eds R. R. Warhol and D. P. Herndl, New Brunswick, 1991, 269-88.

It is this third type of women's writing that seems to suit Kate O'Brien, because, although she may have been considered to imitate male models, she manipulates them to her own advantage; because she does not victimize her characters, and because she writes about the experiences of Irish women in and outside of Ireland:

> What her writing gives us is a perspective which is firmly woman-centred, which will accept nothing less for women than the unquestioned (but always questing) right for women to live their lives as they will, without constraint and without opprobrium. Kate O'Brien does not ... write about the experience of women's oppression; she does not, on the whole, linger with the victim. Rather, she strikes out, ventures for and charts a way towards freedom. [4]

At this point, the term used in the title can be introduced: "herstory". "Herstory" is defined as the history of women, as the perception of history from a female point of view, as an alternative to history that is male-oriented. Kate O'Brien offers a panoramic view of bourgeois women's history in Ireland, showing the obstacles that they may find in achieving self-fulfilment, the prices they may have to pay. However, there is something else in her work, which a little play with the term can explain: "herstory" is not only the history of women, it is also "her" history, her story, the story of her life, the progression of her self in that quest for self-fulfilment, independence and individuality. Thus, her fiction accomplishes two main objectives: the insertion of women in history, producing a female testimony of women's experience throughout relevant periods of national history; the recreation of the writer's own identity through the act of writing, which enables her to discover her own self.

Kate O'Brien's work has sometimes been labelled as autobiographical, but there has never been a study in detail of this phenomenon which seems to dominate her fiction. Kate O'Brien's work is based on the autobiographical, on her experience; and an overview of her work as a whole will prove that her fiction is exactly that, a fictionalization of the development of her own personality. However, first of all, it would be better to look at the herstorical

---

[4]   Ailbhe Smyth, "Counterpoints: A Note (or Two) on Feminism and Kate O'Brien", in *Ordinary People Dancing: Essays on Kate O'Brien*, ed. Eibhear Walshe, Cork, 1993, 34.

elements of her work from a general point of view, that is, in relation to the presentation of female characters, their circumstances and the obstacles they find in their quest for self-fulfilment. Then it will be time to look at these issues in relation to her own story, that is, Kate O'Brien's personal herstory.

The herstorical aspect of O'Brien's fiction is a complex matter. She seems to embark upon a journey from the woman of yesterday towards the new woman, from the woman subjected to patriarchy, who is witness to history, towards the new independent woman who becomes protagonist and interpreter of herstory.[5] In her novels, O'Brien sets in motion a process of reconstruction of history from a woman's point of view, analysing the way in which the historical background of her country conditions and affects women's development. Her fiction is a revision of history that culminates in the appearance of the new woman, who attempts to find a combination of origins and independence which will allow her to be herself either at home or abroad. According to Da Cunha-Giabbai, there are three main stages in this process of development:[6] subjection to the patriarchal order; realization of patriarchal limitations on her self-fulfilment; consciousness-raising by means of the reassessment of the two previous stages.

These stages are related to the development of the individual and are reflected and represented in O'Brien's fiction. The result of this process is the appearance of an individual who, after realizing the limitations imposed on her development, attempts to confront the situation and accept the responsibility of her own life, that is, accept her own authority to rule her own life.[7] In the first stage of the process, the woman of yesterday is represented as a conformist in the

---

[5]   Gloria Da Cunha-Giabbai, "La Mujer Hispanoamericana hacia el nueve milenio", in *La Nueva Mujer en la escritura de autoras hispánicas: Ensayas críticos*, eds Juana Alcira Arancibia and Yolanda Rosas, Montevideo, 1995, 27-39. Although Da Cunha-Giabbai's essay deals with Latin American women, it is possible to find a parallel with Irish women in relation to the different stages in the development of women's identity. A more thorough comparison is developed in the present author's dissertation, "'Notebooks that B[ear] Witness to Life': The Autobiographical as a Source of Literary Inspiration in the Fiction of Isabel Allende and Kate O'Brien" (Ph.D. dissertation, University of Limerick, 1999).

[6]   Da Cunha-Giabbai, "La Mujer Hispanoamericana", 30-37.

[7]   Heide Schmidt, "La Risa: etapas en la narrativa femenina en México y Alemania: Una aproximación", *Escritura: Teoría y Crítica Literarias*, XVI/31-32 (1991), 249.

sense that she accepts the patriarchal order and helps to perpetuate it. Thus, her own virtues of dedication, strength and enthusiasm are used by patriarchy to maintain the *status quo*. In the second stage, she becomes conscious of this fact, that she is helping in feeding the patriarchal rules, and that this dedication to the world of men "le impide desplegar un destino acorde con sus necesidades y deseos".[8] She recognizes her condition as an exile from herself, not being herself but what the phallic order wants her to be. In this second stage of consciousness raising, the woman starts to feel a strong sense of unhappiness, which leads her to rebel against the rules. Yet, this rebellion is too spontaneous, disorderly and confused, which causes almost immediate failure.[9] However unsuccessful these attempts may be, they still have a very important meaning, for they are the antecedent of future accomplished attempts. These characters that rebel and fail serve to show that in fact there are "limitaciones que la sociedad impone a la mujer [y al individuo]", that there are "conflictos de índole racial, religioso y económico que contribuyen a sujetarlas [/los] firmemente a los patrones sociales establecidos".[10]

Finally, in stage three, the new woman appears. She is born from "los escombros de la de ayer"[11] because she becomes conscious of herself by means of reflection upon the two previous stages. She discovers her own identity through a reassessment of the past that leads to a re-creation of the self. The new woman is defined as "aquella capaz de controlar su destino y de insertarse en la sociedad de acuerdo a su *talento* y *habilidades individuales*".[12]

In connection to the above, O'Brien's characters, especially the females, come across a series of obstacles in their fight for the self. These obstacles are the product of the background in which they live: a patriarchal system. In fact, the main topic of her novels is the exploration of women's position in society, their quest for individuality, their challenge to patriarchy. She presents the conflict between the social imposition upon her characters and their personal

---

[8]   Da Cunha-Giabbai, "La Mujer Hispanoamerica", 30: "prevents her from fulfilling a destiny according to her own needs and wishes" (my translation).

[9]   *Ibid.*, 32.

[10] *Ibid.*, 33: "limitations that society imposes on women [and the individual]", that in fact there are "racial, religious and economic conflicts that contribute to hold them tightly to the established social patterns" (my translation).

[11] *Ibid.*,38: "the rubble of the [woman] of yesterday" (my translation).

[12] *Ibid.*, 37: "the one who is able to control her own destiny and to integrate herself in society according to her own individual talents and abilities" (my translation).

freedom; the opposition between convention and free choice, subjection and independence.[13] In this sense, it can be observed that a series of characters in her works find a number of limitations when trying to develop themselves. There are many examples of this: Denis and Caroline in *Without My Cloak*, Agnes in *The Ante Room*, Mary in *Mary Lavelle*, Anna Murphy in *The Land of Spices*, Fanny in *The Flower of May*, among others. The main limitations that these characters have to face are closely related to their environment. In all of them, the obstacles and limitation have their origin in tradition and education. According to the patriarchal tradition in which they live, the supreme patriarchal institution, the family, has almighty control over its members, and the Church informs the rules of this collective. Thus, the characters are limited or constrained by a series of rules that dictate their future and their choices. In *Without My Cloak*, Denis must enter the family business and marry an equal; Caroline must cope with her marriage and be a model wife and mother; Mary Lavelle must go back to Ireland and face the consequences of her adulterous behaviour which has "stained" her reputation as an Irish Catholic bourgeois woman; Anna, in *The Land of Spices*, must get a suitable job, wait for Prince Charming, and forget educational expectations; and Fanny, the heroine in *The Flower of May*, must return home and wait, with her family, for a suitable husband. The characters are not free, they are possessed by their family and the Church; hence the conflict of interests between the individual and her or his background. These obligations imposed by family and religion make the characters react.

Due to the presentation of women in their fight against the limitations of patriarchy, we can consider Kate O'Brien a herstorical writer, because she offers a picture of the situation of women of her own class, of women's conflicts within a heteroreality dominated by male power. It is possible to observe a progression in the types of limitations and the types of goals of women in her novels which can be identified with women's advancement in their socio-historical environment.

The first obstacle that women must conquer is the family bond which limits their own expectations. In O'Brien's first novel, there is a woman who tries to do so but fails, Caroline Considine. Agnes

---

[13]   Eavan Boland, Introduction to Kate O'Brien, *The Last of Summer*, London, 1990, viii.

Mulqueen in *The Ante-Room* is another character who confronts the
same type of problem, and it is again the family background that holds
her back, family bonding, family affection. Thus, for the woman to
succeed, it is necessary to break, or at least, attenuate, this "terrible
family affection ... [this] cowardly inability to do without each
other"[14] because "they [are] tradition, conformity, conservatism – they
[are] values that are not [hers], they [are] pride and funny pomp and
the will of others – but they [are] home too, h[er] history and h[er]
guardians. They [are] [her] enemies and [s]he love[s] them."[15]

Once the female character is able to soften these bonds, she can try
and look for herself and find self-fulfilment. Mary Lavelle and Anna
Murphy are the first to attempt this. Mary goes away from Ireland and
Anna enters another community: the boarding school, a female
community ready to foster her goals in life as an individual and to
educate her in self-independence. In fact, the female community in
The Land of Spices (1941) is the starting point for an emphasis on
female bonding that is going to recur in Kate O'Brien's novels with
the exception of *Pray for the Wanderer* (1938).

The issue of female collaboration and female friendship is of great
importance in her fiction. Women will help one another in order to
achieve their goals. The best example of this is *The Flower of May*
(1953). In this novel, the friendship between Fanny and Lucille is
extraordinary, and in many cases it has been considered as a shy
representation of lesbianism.[16] The homosexual nature of the
relationship is not straightforward in the text, for the occasions of
physical contact could be interpreted as friendship tenderness.
However, it could be said that the nature of this relationship in which
Fanny and Lucille are central to each other is "in some way lesbian-
defined",[17] because "they are the central figures, are positively
portrayed [in the novel] and have pivotal relationships with one
another".[18] The relationship between these two women is the genuine
representation of gyn/affection, which is defined by Janice Raymond
as "woman-to-woman attraction, influence, and movement".[19] This

---

[14]   Kate O'Brien, *Without My Cloak* (1931), London, 1984, 244.
[15]   *Ibid.*, 248.
[16]   Dalsimer, *Kate O'Brien*, 99-102.
[17]   Janice Raymond, *A Passion for Friends: Towards a Philosophy of Female
       Affection*, London, 1986, 15.
[18]   Barbara Smith, "Toward a Black Feminist Criticism", *Conditions,* 2 (1977), 33,
       quoted in Raymond, *Passion for Friends,* 16.
[19]   Raymond, *Passion for Friends*, 7.

could explain why Fanny and Lucille as characters have often been perceived as lesbians, because "Many perceive any intense relationship between women as lesbian".[20] However, the relationship would be better classified as lesbian-defined because it does not offer clear sexual implications, and, still, as Adrienne Rich states, it "embrace[s] many more forms of primary intensity between and among women, including the sharing of a rich inner life, the bonding against male tyranny, the giving and receiving of practical and political support".[21]

Throughout her work, we see how her later female characters have earned the freedom of choice that the previous ones were looking for: Ana de Mendoza in *That Lady* (1946) chooses to defend her right to privacy, Fanny can pursue a career, and Clare Halvey in *As Music and Splendour* (1958) accepts her own emotional and sexual inclinations. All these characters take responsibility for their actions and defend their right to find themselves according to their own ideology, not according to patriarchal imposition.

The question now is, what relevance do these issues have to O'Brien's own experiences? A close look at Kate O'Brien's work in relation to her own life will show that all of her fiction seems to represent a personal *Bildung*, "a path to adult womanhood, to knowledge and self-knowledge, to passion and desire. She provides a perspective, a vocabulary for exploring what it can mean to be a woman and what one can become if we embrace freedom, with all the risks and uncertainties it brings."[22] Looking at her fiction as a whole will show that it follows a four-stage progression towards self-definition: search for origins – family, religion; education and female bonding; social political consciousness; individuality and the self (including sexuality).

It can be argued that all these elements are only part of her fiction and have nothing to do with her own story. However, a series of elements found in her non-fictional works suggest the opposite: that the basis for O'Brien's fiction is the autobiographical, the reflection upon experience, an attempt to understand the past and to find her own identity. This is not done in a straightforward manner though, but

---

[20] *Ibid.*, 15.
[21] Adrienne Rich, "Compulsory Heterosexuality and Lesbian Existence", *Signs: Journal of Women in Culture and Society*, 5 (1980), 648, quoted in Raymond, *A Passion for Friends*, 16.
[22] Smyth, "Counterpoints", 33.

through a series of distancing strategies that separate the writer from the work: artistic, temporal, geographical, psychological or ideological distance.

If we withdraw all these types of distance, it is possible to see that all the fictional trajectory of the Limerick writer is a never-ending *Bildungsroman*. Let me explain this further. The traditional definition of *Bildungsroman* labels it as "a novel about the moral and psychological growth of the main character",[23] or as "a novel which describes the protagonist's development from childhood to maturity".[24] This definition, though, is very restrictive, for it determines the content of a work by its form. Many critics, especially Germanists, have devoted their time to this matter, and more of them seem to come to the conclusion that the concept of *Bildung* is thematic rather than a question of genre.[25] In fact,

> the *Bildungsroman* can hardly be isolated as a specific "literary" genre with formal structural laws applying solely to it; it is rather determined by prerequisites that have to do with content, theme, and ideology and with its intended effect and function. It appears not as a categorical aesthetic form, but as a historical form deriving from specific and limited historical conditions in the understanding of the world and the self.[26]

Expanding even more this thematic concept, it could be argued that the *Bildung* theme can appear in several works, resulting in a progressive development through fragmentary selves which, if we withdraw all the distance, lead back to the author, a process in which the individual self is shaped "from its innate potentialities through acculturation and social experience to the threshold of maturity".[27]

Following this idea, Kate O'Brien's work can be seen as a process of evolution of the self. This process of individual development, as mentioned above, is achieved in several stages: realization; fight for individuality; self-acceptance and responsibility. These stages can also

---

[23] Jeffrey L. Sammons, "The *Bildungsroman* for Nonspecialists: An Attempt at Clarification", in *Reflection and Action: Essays on the Bildungsroman*, ed. James Hardin, Columbia, 1991, 26.
[24] Martin Gray, *A Dictionary of Literary Terms*, 2nd edn, London, 1992, 43.
[25] Sammons, "The *Bildungsroman* for Nonspecialists", 33.
[26] Fritz Martini, "*Bildungsroman*: Term and Theory", in *Reflection and Action*, ed. James Hardin, 24.
[27] Sammons, "The *Bildungsroman* for Nonspecialists", 41.

be applied to women's writing when its aim is self-consciousness,[28] that is, the understanding of the self: from understanding of the environment, through analysis of the interaction between society and the individual, towards self-definition.

These two elements, evolution and understanding, appear in a fragmentary way, as the writer fragments her self into different characters in different novels – which may not follow a fictional or real chronological order in relation to the author's life – with the purpose of exploring various aspects of her identity (background, education, personal, social and political ideology). This fragmentary insertion does not affect the writer herself only; it can also produce characters that are the result of a combination of people that the writer has known, friends, relations, etc. However, what is of relevance in this paper is concerned with characters that lead back to the writer herself, as these characters are there for a reason: to help in the construction of the woman writer's identity, to show the different stages in the development of such an identity, to act as testimony to the *Bildung* of the woman who writes. Fragmentary characterization has its origin in the writer's difficulty in saying "I", that is, in the inability to portray herself directly in her work of fiction, for it would not be fiction any more, it would be pure autobiography in the sense understood by canonical criticism: "I write about myself and name myself because I am unique." Kate O'Brien's intention is not so individualistic in this sense, for although her experiences belong to her, the use of personal experiences at the moment of writing fiction does not result in personal fiction only, but in a body of work that includes women in history, giving an example of "herstory".

There are four main types of distance that a writer may use in order to blur autobiographical reference:

Artistic:	fictionalization of events multiplicity of voices
Geographical:	settings change of landmarks place of writing
Temporal:	time of the setting reflection upon the past
Psychological/ ideological:	the past from the present in order to understand it.

---

[28] Schmidt, "La Risa", 249.

As to fictionalization, it is possible to observe that an event from the past or from the author's experience is taken as the basis for the plot of a novel. There are many examples of this in Kate O'Brien's fiction: *The Ante Room*, with the dying mother, the sick son, and the two daughters in love with the same man. The dying mother is a constant motive in O'Brien's fiction, probably inspired by her own mother's death; the sick son, Reggie, seems to be modelled on O'Brien's own maternal uncle, who "was to die of [tuberculosis] in his thirties, hurrying it on with alcoholism";[29] and the love triangle could be a speculation about O'Brien's mother's sister Mary, who became a nun shortly before Katty (O'Brien's mother) got married;[30] *Mary Lavelle* (1936), based on Kate's own experience as a governess in Spain; *The Land of Spices*, a fictional development of Kate's education in Laurel Hill. In all these cases, a fact from the experience or perception of the writer is adorned through fiction. Therefore, the fictionalization of events is the result of a combination of experience, subjectivity and imagination.

The multiplicity of voices is a very important feature of the artistic distance maintained by O'Brien, especially when compared to her non-fictional works. In her travelogues and memoirs, the narrator and the focalizor (the one that perceives the action) coincide, only varying in narrative types, whether the perceptions are reflections upon the past or the present. However, in her fiction, the focalizor and the narrator do not coincide; furthermore, we may find more than one focalizor, giving a complete picture of the action without dictating to the reader what to think, who is right and who is wrong. Through this Bakhtinian heteroglossia, O'Brien is able to transmit her own ideology in a fragmentary way, through a multiplicity of characters, for it is conceived as "another's speech in another's language serving to express authorial intentions but in a refracted way".[31] It is possible to observe an evolution in her narrative, especially in relation to the concept of focalization. Progressively, she seems to be freeing her characters so that they can express themselves directly to the reader. We could also consider that the narrative techniques in O'Brien's

---

[29]   Kate O'Brien, *Presentation Parlour*, Dublin, 1994 [first published 1963], 43.
[30]   *Ibid.*, 61.
[31]   Mikhail Bakhtin, "Discourse in the Novel", in Mikhail Bakhtin, *The Dialogic Imagination: Four Essays*, trans. Michael Holquist, Caryl Emerson and Michael Holquist, Austin: TX, 1981, 324-26.

novels are very traditional,[32] with the typical omniscient narrator. However, the narrator's position as an external observer allows her to offer different points of view from a non-judgemental position because, apparently, the narrator is also trying to understand the events and their effects on the characters:

> Kate O'Brien's novel[s] offer ... more than one perspective. Her conscious textual quotations and references are not reinforcements of a dominant patriarchal position but multiple questionings".[33]

Even allowing for the predominance of omniscient narration in her novels, there may be an objective character who seems to act as judge of the situation, and who may reflect the author's own ideas. Some other characters can also transmit O'Brien's ideology, but this is so because of the fragmented feature of her characterization. I shall illustrate this with some examples. In *Without My Cloak*, it is possible to observe how only Christina is able to elucidate the nature of the conflict which is at the bottom of her relationship with Denis Considine. She is the one who acknowledges the social boundaries that separate them, recognizing the snobbery of the Considines and the impossibility of her entering such a closed circle, although she is dismissed before the end of the novel in favour of Denis and his environment. In *The Ante-Room*, Dr Curran seems to be the one character who is able to perceive the type of environment in which the characters live, being capable of identifying its paralysis, although he may even enter it. Sometimes, it will be the main character who identifies the limitations of the milieu, as in the case of *Mary Lavelle*, *Pray for the Wanderer*, *The Flower of May* and *As Music and Splendour*. In these cases, the main characters' voices are filtered through the narrator in order to present ideas that lead back to the writer herself.

Finally, some other characters may also represent the author's ideology, as happens with Mary Helen Archer in *The Land of Spices*, where the English nun seems to reflect O'Brien's own ideas about Irish insularity in a manner that had been previously emphasized in *Pray for the Wanderer* by the character of Matt Costello. In this novel, there is also a secondary character who seems to transmit the same

---

[32] Eibhear Walshe, "How Soon is Now?", *Graph*, 4 (1988), 5.
[33] Anthony Roche, "*The Ante Room* as Drama", in *Ordinary People Dancing*, ed. Eibhear Walshe, 92.

views, Tom Mahony, who criticizes Irish society very bitterly in his conversations with Matt. The representation of different views and perceptions also implies an avoidance of judgement. Furthermore, it is obvious that the narrator expresses some type of preference for some characters. The reason for this phenomenon must be looked for in the equation narrator = author: "The closeness between narrator and character also creates an intimacy between author and reader, so that each of Kate O'Brien's works seems a mirror to her inner and outer experience. We see her reflection on the pages of each of her novels."[34]

The geographical distance is very obvious in her work, as she changes the names of the Limerick, Clare and Spanish places when she writes about Irish women discovering their identities in continental Europe. Also, most of her work was written outside Ireland or at least away from Limerick, which may have given her the necessary space to reflect upon the themes she wanted to examine.

Temporal distance is also obvious in most of her work, as many of her works are set in the past in relation to the time of writing, which allows for an analysis of past events and experiences from the present moment of literary creation; and in relation to this, the psychological distance also allows her to explore a series of past issues that must be understood in order to arrive at a definition of the self.

These types of distance are used in very different degrees in her works, as the following example will prove. I intend to give two extreme examples, one in which the distance is very strong, and one in which the distance is minimal. The first example is *That Lady*. The artistic distance is very strong because the plot of the novel is based on historical facts that are then developed fictionally. Geographically and temporally, the text is very far from the present too, because the setting is sixteenth-century Spain. However, the autobiographical reference is located in the ideological aspect of the work, as this novel is a forceful statement about the right to privacy, something in which O'Brien believed very strongly. In fact, the historical/patriarchal dimension is attenuated in favour of the female dimension: what matters is the woman herself and what she represents and fights for.[35]

The other example is *Pray for the Wanderer*, in which the distance is kept to a minimum. In fact, the main type of camouflage is artistic,

---

[34] Dalsimer, *Kate O'Brien*, xvii.
[35] Biruté Ciplijauskaité, *La Novela Femenina Contemporánea (1970–1985): Hacia una Tipología de la Narración en Primera Persona*, Barcelona, 1988, 124-25.

as the main character is male. Geographically, there is also distance for the setting is the Limerick of O'Brien's imagination, that is, Mellick. However, there is no temporal or psychological/ ideological distance, for O'Brien is writing about her position as a banned writer in Ireland, exploring her feelings in relation to De Valera's Ireland and its restrictive rule.

By withdrawing the distance we can observe that Kate O'Brien's fiction is a representation of her own development as an individual within a system that was very restrictive for her gender. The stages observed in the portrayal of women's situation reflect her own, and in this respect the most important factor seems to be female relationships, which may hint at the controversial issue of Kate O'Brien's lesbianism.

I am not going to enter that discussion now, but a very important point to make is that her defence of the alternative female community has a double meaning. First, it emphasizes the importance of female alternative worlds, in which women "resist the bondage of patriarchy and all its paraphernalia ... [and] come to knowledge, if not sweet and lasting joy, through experiences which are not defined or controlled by men".[36] Secondly, this is only the tip of the iceberg in relation to her belief in tolerance and self-acceptance. From her very first novel, she presents "unnatural loves", but she does not condemn them. In Kate O'Brien's work, the lesbian, homosexual or "unnatural" loves are not unsuccessful because of a series of circumstances directly related to the otherness of the affection; the cause for their failure is determined by factors that are common to all love bonds, like infidelity, unrequited love, social boundaries, etc.

To conclude, I would like to stress the point that I have attempted to make throughout the pages of this essay: Kate O'Brien's fiction is, from a thematic point of view, a never-ending *Bildungsroman*. Her fiction presents the development of the different aspects of the woman's personality, of her self. The description of this development is done by the writer; she considers herself from an external point of view; hence the retrospective nature of the novels, thus manifesting that split between the woman and the writer. She seems to be looking at herself in the mirror, and what she sees is what she writes about, but discarding the fact that the reflection is herself. Finally, there may be a moment of acceptance, and the writer and the woman become one, but

---

[36]   Smyth, "Counterpoints", 31.

this does not seem to happen very clearly in O'Brien's fiction. However, this lack of recognition of the self should not be considered as O'Brien's failure to assert herself, far from it; it is part of that personality that she has been examining, it is part of that great sense of privacy that critics like her friend Lorna Reynolds and Adele Dalsimer have already noticed, it is part of what is stated in *That Lady*: the right to privacy and freedom, the right to choose whether to remain silent or speak up. Her fiction acts as *Bildung*, not because it shows the progression of her own self only, but also because of the open-endedness of her novels and her career as a writer, as she never finished her last novel. Perhaps she was meant to write her memoirs, or her autobiography, but she did not need to because, as she said to Lorna Reynolds once, all she wanted to say about herself, she had already said in her novels;[37] she preferred to "convey her convictions obliquely".[38] Her work is "herstory", her story, my story, your story.

[37] Reynolds, *Kate O'Brien*, 133.
[38] Lorna Reynolds, "The Image of Spain in the Novels of Kate O'Brien", in *Literary Interrelations: Ireland, England and the World, III: National Images and Stereotypes*, eds Wolfgang Zach and Heinz Kosok, Tübingen, 1987, 187.

JUDGEMENT IN KATE O'BRIEN'S *THE LAND OF SPICES*

CLARE WALLACE

> And be the judge of your own soul; but
> never for a second, I implore you, set up
> as the judge of another. Commentator,
> annotator, if you like, but never judge.[1]

Mère Marie Hélène's parting advice to her surrogate daughter, Anna
Murphy, might be considered a synopsis of Kate O'Brien's preferred
ethos, an ethos which though ostensibly of a spiritual nature,
predicates individual judgement, impartiality and detachment. Mère
Marie Hélène's philosophy of "detachment of spirit" in *The Land of
Spices* gains a rather ironic dimension when one considers the book's
troubled history – clearly trust in citizens' capacity for judgement and
detachment of spirit were not among the Irish Censorship Board's
fortes. However, this ethos also gives rise to several conflicts within
the text in regard to the prerogatives and role of community structures
such as the church, state and family and individual rights and
responsibilities, as well as ambivalences within the narrative structure
of the text itself.

The interplay between the role of the individual and the community
has given rise to several quite divergent readings of *The Land of
Spices*. Among the most compelling of these are Ann Owens Weekes'
"Kate O'Brien: Family in the New Nation",[2] and Mary Breen's
"Something Understood? Kate O'Brien and *The Land of Spices*".[3] The
former deals with the novel as a "non traditional Irish Catholic female

---

[1] Kate O'Brien, *The Land of Spices*, London, 1973, 284.
[2] Ann Owens Weekes, *Irish Women Writers: An Uncharted Tradition*, Lexington:
     KY, 1990, 108-32.
[3] Mary Breen, "Something Understood? Kate O'Brien and *The Land of Spices*", in
     Ordinary People Dancing: Essays on Kate O'Brien, ed. Eibhear Walshe, Cork,
     1993, 167-89.

bildungsroman", with particular reference to Joyce's *Portrait of the Artist*.[4] The latter posits the novel as "a radical, if veiled, attack on everything that the Constitution of Ireland considered 'natural' or 'special' – the State, the family, the position of women in the home and marriage", while offering

> alternatives to each of these: an outward-looking European perspective ... presented as an alternative to Irish nationalism, the family replaced by a successful community of women ... [and] autonomy and agency outside the home and marriage.[5]

Both these readings have served usefully to emphasize the subversive elements of the novel, especially with regard to feminism and, clearly, feminist approaches to O'Brien's work are presently very popular among students and scholars.

However, as has been acknowledged by Breen, the subversive aspects of the text are tempered by ambivalences. These, I would contend, arise from the problematic bourgeois and hierarchical values of the closed world of the convent and from notions of detachment and judgement. Both these issues inform the text on several levels, primarily thematically, but also in terms of narrative structure and characterization. This essay examines the development of Mère Marie Hélène's ethos of "detachment of spirit", how this is debated within the text and the ambivalences that arise from its ideals.

The problematic of judgement has perhaps been most focused upon in relation to Helen Archer's rejection of her father. The implications of that infamous sentence, censorship and its arbitrariness and the effects of such judgements on O'Brien's work have been subjected to much analysis.[6] The question of judgement is also subtly inscribed within the text and is enacted in an episode which is less frequently explored. Anna Murphy's first crisis in the convent school takes place

---

[4]   Weekes, *Irish Women Writers*, 121.
[5]   Breen, "Something Understood?", 188.
[6]   Although the novel contains no advocacy of homosexual relationships, the implication of homosexuality in the text led to its being banned in 1942 by the Irish Censorship Board. In fact, the only reference to homosexuality in anything approaching a direct manner is the denouement of Henry Archer's affair with his student: "She saw *Etienne* and her father, in the embrace of love." (157) Not only is the sentence notable for its coyness, but it is in addition the explanation for Helen Archer's rejection of her father and entry into the convent.

when she succeeds in the Emulation test but is later cruelly disqualified by Mother Mary Andrew. In conjugating the French verb *finir*, Anna mistakenly writes *finant* instead of *finissant* as the present participle, hence the tenses derived from the stem of the present participle follow incorrectly. This apparently minor event is heavily laden with implications. On one level, Mother Mary Andrew's harsh judgement of Anna's error emanates from her dislike of the child whom she believes is a favourite of Reverend Mother and therefore is not impartial, but emotional and vindictive. On another level, the episode reveals a difference in perspective that is germane to the question of judgement throughout the novel. Mother Mary Andrew castigates Anna according to an absolutist logic:

> Certainly [she concedes] they're not all wrong.   But in one conjugation you made a mistake so silly as to show that you have no understanding of what you are doing, and so cannot receive marks like an intelligent schoolgirl.[7]

For Mother Mary Andrew the first error leads to the others and sabotages the whole exercise. Anna, in contrast, while understanding the "foolishness" of her first mistake argues that she nevertheless has obeyed the rules of grammar by conjugating the verbs that followed according to the original error:

> It is only one mistake. How silly .... Because you see, when I put *finant* I had to put the others. It would be sillier even if I didn't.

Nevertheless Anna's contention of the relativity of her error does not sway Mother Mary Andrew and "She knew that she was in the grip of omnipotence, that there was no Emulation ...".[8] The outcomes of this lesson are both endings – Anna's hopes for success and childish naïveté about fairness are quite literally finished, ironically by her error with a verb meaning to finish – and beginnings. As a result of this lesson Anna develops a meticulousness which eventually wins her a scholarship. She also, it seems, learns the futility of quarrelling with authority as is evidenced by her meekness towards the end of the novel. If the text is regarded as a *Bildungsroman*, then Anna is a rather

---

[7]   O'Brien, *Land of Spices*, 106.
[8]   *Ibid.*, 107.

ambivalent heroine; she is intelligent and sensitive but is also naïve, asexual and frequently unassertive.

As a metaphor of the dangers of false premises this episode may serve to illuminate other events and conflicts in the text. Following the logic of this grammar, an error in the present may affect not only how the past is perceived (the imperfect tense) but also emotional perception (the subjunctive tense). Within a closed system of reasoning as typified by grammar in this instance, but which may also include Christian thinking or nationalist ideology, it is necessary to return to and deal with the original mistake be it a grammatical error, sin, an historical grievance or flawed logic.

It is largely through the character of Helen Archer, later Reverend Mother, that problems of judgement, spiritual and moral, and convictions regarding detachment are confronted and explored. She emerges as a complex character whose perspective is pivotal to the novel, especially to its subversive aspects. The origins of her attitudes are to be found in her early experiences of family life. Her values, although Christian, are inherently liberal, middle-class and, ultimately, conservative. As the only child of attentive and intellectual parents, she was schooled in the "choice of cultures" she so actively defends in the Compagnie de la Sainte Famille convent school she now governs.

Her especially devoted relationship with her father is stressed in the descriptive passages which construct the character of the now middle-aged nun. She found in him:

> an accidental delight which had no necessary spring in filial feeling, but rose from the privilege of intimacy with someone whom she found pleasing and satisfactory far beyond what was necessary in a father, or in any fellow creature ...[9]

In the course of the narrative she recalls his dedication to endowing her with a rounded education, his love of the English poets of the seventeenth century, his atheism yet tolerance, even admiration, of Christian mysticism. Although her mother's early death leaves little impression upon her, the sudden discovery of her father's homosexuality devastates her belief in human love and radically changes the course of her life. Just as Anna's mistake with the present participle lead her further conjugations astray, Helen Archer's belief

---

[9]   *Ibid.*, 141.

in her father as the ultimate model of goodness and love lead her to "worship as perfect the author of her disillusion".[10]

In her jealousy and anguish at not being at "the centre of her father's heart" and, to a lesser extent, her revulsion towards what she sees as his sin and deception, she judges him absolutely and mercilessly as morally and spiritually detestable. In psychoanalytic terms, Helen Archer's psycho-sexual development is arrested. Traumatized by the revelation that her father's sexuality excludes her, she rejects sexuality *in toto*. She renounces human love as "devilry" and enters the convent out of hatred for him. Interestingly, the transition from the world to the convent involves a transfer of dependence from a human, sexual and fallible father figure to a spiritual, asexual and therefore infallible one, whose characteristics she may then attempt to emulate or identity with. As has been remarked by Breen, the language used to describe her state of mind at the time she discovers her father's secret is that of extreme psychological upheaval – madness, stupefaction, blindness, insanity, frenzy, trance. Just as in the conjugation exercise, her false, emotionally biased premise in believing her father first to be perfect, then to be evil, then impulsively rejecting all she thinks he represents involves an increasingly tangential path away from a balanced or detached judgement.

Mère Marie Hélène is forced, in the years that follow, to acknowledge the flaws in the reasoning that led her to become a nun. Through reunion with her father and under the gentle guidance of her mentor, Mère Générale, she realizes the arrogance of her emotional and falsely pious judgement of his life. While she had accepted the abstracts of the Augustinian teachings on God's grace, she is compelled, by the physical presence of her father, to apply abstract principles to the realities of her life. She recognizes the false presumption of her previous judgements and how, according to her youthful logic:

> [she] had decided that [God] was equity, detachment, justice, purity .... Anything good that was cold and had definition – of which love, it seemed, had none.[11]

---

[10]   *Ibid.*, 20.
[11]   *Ibid.*, 28.

Through the acknowledgement of her own previous mercilessness,
Mère Marie Hélène is driven, paradoxically, toward a much more
Protestant faith of personal interpretation of Christian doctrine and
individual accountability before God. Like Anna, Mère Marie Hélène
learns a lesson which shapes her future. She has lost a life in the world
but has acquired apparently "detachment of spirit". This detachment
hinges on an othering, seeing herself from the outside. This takes
places explicitly in the text through the child Anna, in whom
Reverend Mother perceives a trace of her old self mirrored "she saw
[the] baby in herself, herself in those tear-wet eyes".[12]

As Reverend Mother of the Sainte Famille convent in Ireland,
Mère Marie Hélène's preference for detachment and her liberal
values, especially with regard to the role of education, lead her into
conflict with her sisters in the convent and the prerogatives of Church,
State and family. In the context of the school she upholds the traditions and practices, an "education in Christian virtues and graces"
which will, she hopes, equip each girl for adult life. Her basic premise,
that education should offer students a "choice of cultures" and that the
Order, while "adapt[ing] the secular side of [its] curriculum to the
needs ... in [its] different foundations", ultimately should not concern
itself "with national matters", is directly at odds with the logic of the
Bishop who believes in the power of educationalists and the need "for
a truly national education".[13] The characters who espouse Irish nation-
nalism in the novel, namely the Bishop and Father Conroy, are
portrayed without sympathy. They are constrained by their suspicion
of Reverend Mother as an outsider, doubly offensive to their politics
because she is, in their eyes, primarily an English woman, and
therefore "cold" and "enigmatic".

The demands of Irish nationalism are considered reductive and
negative by Reverend Mother because she is able, as an outsider, to
see the Irish as they fail to see themselves and this is clearly another
instance where othering produces a perceptiveness associated with
"detachment of spirit". With comic cruelty we see the Irish from the
perspective of the outsider:

> They were an ancient martyred race, and of great importance to
> themselves – that meagre handful of conceptions made a history,
> made a problem – and made them at once unconquerable and a little

---

[12]   *Ibid.*, 82.
[13]   *Ibid.*, 15.

silly .... [it would be] [u]seless to explain the "silly" aspects of
England, Scotland, France or Greece. They would be conceded
freely, but the original point would remain a prejudicial insult and a
lie. About Ireland there was no appeal to the comparative method;
no detachment was regarded as just.[14]

Irish nationalism she perceives as ill-argued, emotional and ultimately
restrictive of the individual and these features are anathema to her.

While Mère Marie Hélène's perspective is inherently endorsed by
the narrative, the Bishop finds her politically naïve. The Bishop's
canvassing, in the opening chapter, to introduce the Irish language to
school curricula may also be viewed through the metaphor of Anna's
French test. According to his argument, educating the people of
Ireland to speak Irish is "a key question" so that they "do not merely
feel the ancient grievance, but see why it *is* a grievance, see its cultural
and historic reality".[15] Thus he addresses the question of "national
character" in the present through perceptions of the past and emotional
response, and the need to return to what he understands as a first
principle. Ironically, he cannot speak the language which he asserts
may facilitate a true understanding of Irish colonial history. Reverend
Mother, however, is multilingual and is therefore capable of
interpreting other discourses that are not held important by the Irish
nationalist ideology.

Her refusal to allow the education of children to become a
"political weapon", though idealistic, is nevertheless somewhat
disingenuous, as it fails to take into account the already political
nature of a prestigious upper middle-class school which is supported
financially by a class rife with snobbery and pretensions to grandeur.
The tradition of the Order is resolutely "stiff, polite and pious".[16] Mère
Générale, mentor to Reverend Mother, most clearly articulates their
creed, which is remarkable for its concentrated conservatism and the
bourgeois values and assumptions upon which it rests. She is
determined that the order must withstand the

assault of progress ... new fevers of theory and experiment, in
nationalism, in education, in social science which, threatening the

---

[14]   *Ibid.*, 75.
[15]   *Ibid.*, 15-16.
[16]   *Ibid.*, 56.

institutions of the Church with extinction, might force them in self-defence to unpredictable adaptions and vulgarities.[17]

Greater ambivalences as to the role of the Compagnie de la Sainte Famille, in the larger context of Europe, are gestured toward briefly at the end of the novel. Reverend Mother has just been called to lead the order and contemplates the future of Europe on the brink of the First World War:

> Germany, Austria, the Balkans all were seething – and in Ireland too there were fear and passion in the air. No one could guess how war would come to Europe, but it was visibly on its way ... whatever *was* to come, the Church was One, Holy, Catholic and Apostolic, and must ride, with its militant faithful, above mere temporal storms. The training of the Christian mind would go on, Reverend Mother reflected, however many wars barbarians wage.[18]

Detachment of spirit and tolerance in this context suddenly become much more problematic. Emphasis on the convent and the Catholic church in general as an enclave beset upon from without by multicultural barbarians (and this time not only the "ancient martyred race") steeped in modern nationalistic ideologies is hardly what the reader has come to expect from the character of Mère Marie Hélène.

Significantly her favourite place in the grounds of the convent is Bishop's Walk, an elm-lined path: "she liked the limited, urban formality of [it] ... its peaceful disassociation from the scenic splendours around ...."[19] Within the convent itself, the limitations of her notions of judgement are also evident. Amidst its lush gardens, tinkling chandeliers and the smell of good French coffee she can practise detachment and fairness as she sees fit, but this alternative to the rather inferior family structures within the novel, is as Breen notes, a strict hierarchy with little or no power in the world outside and only a temporary way of life for the girls who study there.[20]

In addition, the most powerful nuns after Mère Marie Hélène, Mother Mary Andrew and Mother Eugenia, do not share her values. In fact, they are rather humorously rendered caricatures of Irish snobbishness. Mother Mary Andrew is a vigorous and viperous Ulster

---

[17]   *Ibid.*, 57.
[18]   *Ibid.*, 279.
[19]   *Ibid.*, 274.
[20]   Breen, "Something Understood?", 188-89.

woman and Mother Eugenia originates from the Anglo-Irish gentry. They too misunderstand her detachment as coldness. Although it is not explicitly stated, it may be assumed that the Order itself will soon be dominated by Irish and American nuns who will most probably not respect the principles of its French foundress, and that after the departure of Mère Marie Hélène the convent will slip from the ethos of detachment she espouses to "psychological chaos" and bacon and cabbage dinners upon which the Irish in the novel seem to thrive.

In addition to such considerations, one of the chief ironies of *The Land of Spices* occurs at a narrative level. Although impartiality and objectivity are explicitly lauded, these principles are repeatedly undermined by the narrative voice within the text. As Breen has noted, Kate O'Brien strongly favoured "professional detachment" as the writer's position to his or her text.[21] Significantly, *The Land of Spices* is largely structured around the voice of an omniscient narrator and this voice determines much of the characterization which takes place. Although Breen acknowledges the unevenness of the treatment of the minor characters in the novel, she argues that the presentation of Mère Marie Hélène, Henry Archer and Anna Murphy is ostensibly unbiased. I would contend, in contrast, that the characters of Mère Marie Hélène and Anna Murphy are relentlessly championed by the omniscient narrator, with the result that in spite of their flaws, they are idealized.

In particular, the second chapter demonstrates the propensity of the narrator to over-determine the character of Mère Marie Hélène. The history of her life as a nun is traced in such a manner that, in spite of the fact that she entered convent life for very misdirected reasons, she becomes a figure almost beyond reproach. One is informed of how "ordinary life had lost a young woman of gifts and rippling sensibilities and the Compagnie de la Sainte Famille had gained a successful, over-disciplined nun". Yet even the mild taint of over-discipline is soon softened for upon her return to Brussels and reunion with her father:

> she had undergone in secret a salutary humiliation, a bewilderment never entirely dispersed, and by its impingement on her rigidity beneficial ... so that from an efficient, accomplished nun she was subtilised into an exceptional one.[22]

---

[21] *Ibid.*, 171.
[22] O'Brien, *Land of Spices*, 20-21.

And if this were not sufficient, the development of her character is laboriously referenced through the glowing reports of her superiors at Cracow.   Detachment of spirit is apparently absent in the non-focalized narrator, who in emphasizing all the desirable qualities of Mère Marie Hélène slips from description to adulatory admiration at the expense of those very qualities.

To conclude, judgement and detachment remain problematic concepts in *The Land of Spices*. Explicitly detachment is a key thematic element in the text, favoured by its author. Irish nationalism is undesirable as it is portrayed against wider European perspectives but the questions it introduces in regard to the role of institutions and individuals in a political context are elided by an insistence on the primacy of the individual and, more significantly, the highly questionable assumption of the objective value of common Christian principles.

"EXTERNAL IMPRESSIONS OF LIFE":
THE PARADOXICAL AUTOBIOGRAPHIES OF KATE O'BRIEN

TAURA S. NAPIER

Kate O'Brien, whom the American critic Mary Colum named in 1942 as "the best of the post-1914 Irish novelists",[1] believed that fiction writing represented the apex of literary ability; explicitly autobiographical writing was to her an inferior species. In *English Diaries and Journals,* a short monograph published in 1943, she comments that "Women diarists ... very likely would not have been diarists if they could have been something more directly self-expressive". Fanny Burney, for example, "should have been training herself to be a great novelist and had not enough decisiveness for that"; others were "obscure and lost, half-mad with a sense of frustration, and the need to say something, somehow".[2] Because O'Brien attained the status of being an acclaimed fiction writer during her career, she was at liberty and perhaps also at pains to write of herself through her fictional characters and created situations. As a result, her autobiographical voice is often deflected; instead of remaining confined within a formal autobiographical mode, it appears pluralistically throughout her fiction.

Yet Kate O'Brien's first-person writings, though not declared as autobiography and diverse in terms of subjects, themes, and time frames, comprise a coherent self-narrative that allows for her privacy-oriented nature to be expressed while providing a complex and challenging public disclosure of self. She repeatedly emphasizes that her autobiographies are impressions, rather than first-person-centred self-contemplations, but the picture that emerges from these shows both what O'Brien is and what she is not; what surrounds her and how

---

[1] Mary M. Colum, "Do We Learn From History?", *Saturday Review of Literature*, 5 September 1942, 3.
[2] Kate O'Brien, *English Diaries and Journals*, London, 1943, 48.

she assimilates with or remains separate from it. Her creative non-fiction, in the form of travel-autobiographies and a family memoir, is at least as important as her "autobiographical fiction" to an understanding of O'Brien as a writer and Irishwoman; to an understanding of what she thought of herself within these identities it is far more significant.

The self-writings O'Brien produced are *Farewell Spain* (1937), *My Ireland* (1962), *Presentation Parlour* (1963), and a collection of autobiographical pieces that would have become her *Memoirs* had she completed them before her death in 1974. Although little of this final self-narrative made its way into print,[3] she was likewise firm upon its not being labelled autobiography. The only published fragment, entitled "Memories of a Catholic Education", concentrates on her convent school, highlighting the English-born Reverend Mother whom O'Brien, as a student, venerated. Its most explicitly auto-biographical section centres on the moment in which O'Brien's lack of belief is revealed to her mentor:

> I told her a lie on that day when she forced me to speak about my non-belief and my private sins ... she accepted my lie and said she expected it and went on talking as if I had not uttered it. She never smiled; she said none of the bright things that one came to read later from English Catholics. She spoke, I think, in grief – and I was not able to help her. And she knew that. After twelve years I was going out from her house an unbeliever.[4]

In an RTÉ radio interview in 1966, O'Brien spoke of her projected *Memoirs*, maintaining her stance as an objective chronicler of personal reflection: "I'm writing another book which is a bit difficult to describe – sort of memories of people who influenced me, or people I was interested in and impressions that remain ... not autobiography, but impressions, external impressions of life."[5] The paradoxical nature of this statement reveals an important aspect of O'Brien's style of autobiography: every self-aspect is deflected onto another, ostensibly less personal, experience. Bullfights in Spain, the Irish countryside

---

[3]   The most substantial portion is found in *The Stony Thursday Book*, 7 (1977) which contains a three-page fragment from this work.

[4]   Kate O'Brien, "Memories of a Catholic Education", *The Stony Thursday Book*, 7 (1977), 30-31.

[5]   Kate O'Brien, *Personal Choice*, interview with Francis Russell, Radio Telefís Éireann sound archives, Dublin (5 March 1966), Tape A–3329.

and its stereotypes, her aunts, parents and teachers, become the channels through which O'Brien articulates her psychological landscape.

This is characteristic of Irishwomen's autobiography of the early and middle twentieth century. Lady Gregory charts the history of forming the Abbey Theatre with Yeats, Edward Martyn and John Synge in *Our Irish Theatre* (1913) and personally narrates the stories of her son, husband, nephew and estate in various self-writings without referring to herself directly. A significant portion of her six-hundred-page "declared" autobiography, *Seventy Years* (1974), is written in the third person. Elizabeth Bowen gives a detailed history of her family home and those who occupied it from 1776 to her own lifetime in *Bowen's Court* (1942), which ends just as it reaches the period of Bowen's adulthood. Mary Colum, Katharine Tynan, Edith Somerville and Violet Martin use similar techniques of deflecting personal experience.

Mary Jean Corbett has observed, in a study of Victorian women's literary autobiographies, that women writers "master their anxiety about being circulated, read, and interpreted only by carefully shaping the personae they represent, and more especially, by subordinating their histories of themselves to others' histories".[6] James Olney writes of literary autobiographers, who "would put down 'writer' when asked for a profession", that their tendency in producing both creative and autobiographical works is "to produce autobiography in various guises and disguises in every work and then – this being the other side of the coin – to seek a unique form in a work properly called 'an autobiography' that may express the life and the vision of this writer alone".[7] Irish women autobiographers, especially those who are also writers, do not appear to exhibit anxiety so much as the need to problematize and lend complexity to their narratives. Moreover, their status as public women confers upon them the necessity of writing the personal as a public declaration that entertains and illumines as it reveals aspects of the private life. Yet they too seek a first-person expression of their unique visions.

---

[6]   Mary Jean Corbett, "Literary Domesticity and Women Writers' Subjectivities", in *Women, Autobiography, Theory: A Reader*, eds Sidonie Smith and Julia Watson, Madison, 1998, 255.

[7]   James Olney, "Some Versions of Memory / Some Versions of *Bios*: The Ontology of Autobiography", in *Autobiography: Essays Theoretical and Critical*, ed. James Olney, Princeton: NJ, 1980, 236.

O'Brien's personal life remains "tantalisingly secret" even today, as Katie Donovan observes in a recent *Irish Times* article.[8] Adele Dalsimer postulates that "so many details in her novels have their roots in her past that *Presentation Parlour* seems to give the reader license to recognize the author in her adult characters and creations".[9] But this "license" remains purely speculative on the part of the reader. Even when considering O'Brien's alleged lesbianism, Dalsimer concedes that the novels *Mary Lavelle* and *As Music and Splendour,* in which there are overt expressions of homosexual love between female characters, do not necessarily attest to O'Brien's own preferences. It is therefore necessary to turn to her works of non-fiction in order to determine the nature of her autobiographical voice, as well as the ways in which it is manifested within her fictional works.

Farewell Spain, published when O'Brien was forty years old, is a witty and incisive travel memoir, but also a self-searching and self-interpretive cultural study. Throughout the book O'Brien wryly observes the activities of "13-day trippers" on summer vacations from Britain and Ireland, who move in querulous, sunburned packs searching for their bilingual Consul. But alongside this observation is O'Brien's own journey toward remembering her adopted country as she had experienced it, and coming to terms with the changes it was undergoing in the mid 1930s. This is less a travelogue than a highly personal account wherein lives become characters – the Spaniards, tourists, and the writer herself – which are interpreted, enjoyed, and criticized in equal measure as they form the substance of O'Brien's written life. With *Mary Lavelle*, O'Brien had already introduced the idea of "the real Spain" as perceived by English and other foreign visitors. She structures this novel on the diverse manners in which Spain exists for the "trippers", for the "Misses", who come from Britain and Ireland to work there as governesses, and, where her own voice is most evident, for the seasoned foreign traveller intimately familiar with Spain, yet still culturally removed from it and aware of this distance.

Dalsimer cites a passage from *Farewell Spain* in which O'Brien fuses the national and the sexual in describing her attraction to the adopted country:

[8]   Katie Donovan, "Giving a Voice to Forbidden Love" (review of *Ordinary People Dancing*), *The Irish Times*, 23 June 1993, 11.
[9]   Adele Dalsimer, *Kate O'Brien: A Critical Study*, Dublin, 1990, xvii.

> Fatal attraction between persons is an old poets' notion that some of us still like to believe is possible and occasional, though not probable – and Spain seems to be the *femme fatale* among countries .... One does not mix up the love one feels for a parent with the infatuations of adult life. And with Spain I am once and for all infatuated.[10]

This passage is used by Dalsimer to elucidate Mary Lavelle's experience at a bullfight, where she learns, from the "death and horror presented theatrically and really, both at once ... as symbolical and suggestive and heartrending as the greatest poetry, and ... as brutal and shameless as the lowest human impulse" that "passion and beauty can both charm and maim".[11] It is true that O'Brien discusses the aesthetics of a bullfight and the contrary responses it evokes in *Farewell Spain*:

> I believe it to be impossible for anyone of northern blood to sit through a *corrida* with an easy conscience, or without moments of acute embarrassment and distress. Nevertheless, the thrill and the beauty can seduce; more than that, can be remembered with longing.[12]

Both the novel and the travel-autobiography are personal and creative as well as public and political. But *Farewell Spain* is not merely a legend for reading the literary map of *Mary Lavelle*; it is a retrospective of O'Brien's life in Spain and a self-narrative that elucidates the personal experiences whose intensity inspired her Spanish novels.

O'Brien devotes one chapter, "Blondes and Fountains", to the ways in which modern culture has invaded "Spain's native taste, grave, common-sense, individual" and caused women, in their rage for blonde hair à la Marlene Dietrich and Jean Harlow, to sport "striped heads, black and gold like a football shirt; platinum surfaces with solid mid-brown underneath; olive-green *coiffures*; middle-aged pates of iron-gray with honey-coloured haloes".[13] O'Brien relates an incident in which she and her blonde companion, Mary O'Neill, who illustrated *Farewell Spain*, are mobbed by admiring young women as they sit in a café in Villalba:

---

[10]   Kate O'Brien, *Farewell Spain* (1937), London, 1985, 227.
[11]   Kate O'Brien, *Mary Lavelle* (1936), London, 1984, 140.
[12]   O'Brien, *Farewell Spain*, 135.
[13]   *Ibid.*, 176.

Girls simply swarming on us, smiling, gentle, but implacably fascinated by that head of hair. I must say I've seldom felt a greater fool in my life, and I've seldom disliked an inoffensive crowd of people as much as I did those sweeties of Villalba. But I don't honestly think the *rubia* [blonde] minded very much .... Our departure was a triumph – all the girls yelling "*adios*" and the *rubia* waving back at them, like a film star leaving Waterloo.[14]

O'Brien's distaste for this spectacle suggests her general aversion to the worship of an alien and superficial ideal, rather than one that is spiritual and culturally intrinsic. It is helpful to recognize this distinction, since O'Brien obviously relishes the spectacle of the bullfight but enjoys it precisely because it is an integral part of Spanish culture to which Spaniards are fiercely dedicated.

Throughout *Farewell Spain* Mary O'Neill functions as a hyper-feminine antagonist to O'Brien's austere, veteran traveller who speaks with village men and smokes alone in cafés. She is blonde and therefore embodies the 1930s female beauty paradigm; she enjoys attention in a way that O'Brien implies is superficial and somewhat vapid; she befriends sundry small beggar-boys in every town, buying them treats and clothing. O'Neill is vociferously squeamish about bullfights, although not so squeamish that she wants to stop attending them. She is also repulsed by insects, which, in spite of O'Brien's protests to the contrary, she insists have infested the entirety of Spain. O'Neill is not so much representative of the foreign tourist as of the reality of the feminine aesthetic that inevitably proves less attractive than its ideal embodiment. She serves as an illustration of the superficiality of the Spanish beauty ideal that, like the "radio as big as a bathing-hut ... and flashier strip-lighting than you've ever seen"[15] in O'Brien's hotel, inhibits development of the intrinsic Spanish way of life.

In *My Ireland,* O'Brien is similarly critical of stereotypical femininity, not only among women but also within the expectations of men who come to the West of Ireland seeking versions of the "dewy-eyed colleen ... tied up in a shawl of Galway grey, who is always somehow, by some trick, seduced". Such women, O'Brien asserts, do not exist in folklore or reality, but are a figment of the prurient Victorian imagination:

---

[14] *Ibid.,* 177-78.
[15] *Ibid.,* 180.

> It is an infantile fantasy of the not-so-infantile-as-all-that Victorians; and it is amusing to find it perversely sustained even now by men descended from princes who had to endure the realistic hells created for them by such women as Niamh, Gráinne, and the terrifying Máire Rua O'Brien. For let the uninformed believe me that in Irish recorded literature, the colleen is missing .[16]

O'Brien's objective, "an odd one for the 1960s", is to dispel the tourist-brochure notion that Irish women are pliable and naïve: "I suggest to exploratory Don Juans that ... they will be happier for listening to [my advice], in that they will be able to leave Ireland with their vanity intact."[17] The Stage Irish colleen, with her head shawl and sentimental songs, is banished from O'Brien's landscape as decisively as incarnations of the bottle-blonde beauty culture of Spain.

Patricia Coughlan writes in an essay on feminine beauty, feminism and sexuality in O'Brien's fiction:

> Her near-obsession with what almost seems an abstract, essentialized quality of beauty in women sharply conflicts with the process of representing the achievement of freedom and individual thought by the women in the fictions, because fully interiorized autonomous subjectivity becomes the property of the male viewer, whose appreciation gives him ... the kind of originality of creative perception attributed to an artist .... In O'Brien's aesthetic discourse beauty is always thrown back to an earlier ideal.[18]

The alleged lesbianism in Kate O Brien's writings, as remarked by Dalsimer, Emma Donoghue, and Ailbhe Smyth, while it is not a monolithic feature of her literary voice, may help to resolve the "sharp conflict" that Coughlan finds between images of feminine beauty and the achievement of freedom for O'Brien's female characters. As a woman ambivalent toward the received identity and role of her gender in early twentieth-century Ireland, O'Brien sought to challenge and disrupt the sovereignty of this aspect of the patriarchal tradition. As an artist sexually oriented towards women, it is conceivable that she would have represented them scopically, as objects of desire seen

---

[16]   Kate O'Brien, *My Ireland*, London, 1962, 54.

[17]   *Ibid.*, 57.

[18]   Patricia Coughlan, "Kate O'Brien: Feminine Beauty, Feminist Writing, and Sexual Role", in *Ordinary People Dancing: Essays on Kate O'Brien*, ed. Eibhear Walshe, Cork, 1993, 63.

from the point of view of both creator of the fictional and connoisseur of the actual. In *Mary Lavelle*, when Agatha Conlon says to Mary, "I like you the way a man would",[19] this may be taken literally, with its attendant voyeurist and connoisseurist implications. This species of desire resonates, albeit less directly, throughout her non-fiction. O'Brien's "I" in *Farewell Spain* is the possessive, ardent voice of a lover who falls at the feet of her *femme fatale*, defending and desiring even as she recognizes imperfections.

The title of O'Brien's other travel-autobiography also suggests possession, but rather than possession of the lover by her beloved, it is instead the more accustomed, if no less problematic, affection of the parent-child relationship. In *My Ireland,* written twenty-five years after *Farewell Spain,* O'Brien returns to the country that had fomented its religious and legal forces against her creative talents, to speak of it, if not with love, with something akin to understanding, as that which a grown child might have for an capriciously judgemental parent. Where she had identified herself as a sentimental traveller in *Farewell Spain,* revisiting the country with which she was "once and for all infatuated", O'Brien writes in this case from the standpoint of the "accidental national", relating her ideas about the country that engendered and, later, rejected her. But in spite of this rejection, and O'Brien's implicit references to it throughout *My Ireland,* there is a distinct air of loyalty to her homeland. Although O'Brien had not dedicated a book in nearly thirty years,[20] she made an exception for Limerick, which she paternalistically calls "my dear native place" in the inscription to *My Ireland.*

This final travel-autobiography contains various anecdotes about the people of Ireland, as well as extensive summaries of Irish history and mythology pertinent to every area that O'Brien visited. But her most moving stories, the ones that reveal her own personality most clearly, are about the women whose lives are connected with hers by her travels, including Lady Gregory, Maria Edgeworth and Maud Gonne. Her eulogy of Lady Gregory while travelling through County Galway is a notable example:

> We must go back to Coole. Only briefly, to look enviously down the rides of the seven woods; to taste silence and consider the nettles

---

[19]   O'Brien, *Mary Lavelle*, 285.
[20]   Michael O'Toole, "Kate O'Brien's Limerick", *The Stony Thursday Book,* 7 (1977), 27.

and fallen stones that Yeats foresaw; and to decipher a few of the carvings on the beech-tree ... they are not easy to decipher from beyond the wire netting, but all of them together are the Irish Literary Movement – and it moved from Coole. For the Old Lady did not say NO, either at the beginning of her groping purpose, or when the road was clear. She taught herself to be an artist and to serve and drive artists – and there is no better thing to do, never mind the mistakes, the rows or the ingratitude.[21]

By chance in Cushendall, O'Brien meets a ninety-year-old shopkeeper, "Mrs Stone", with whom she strikes up a conversation about literature that becomes a friendship. Her account of this friendship dominates her chapter on Antrim, and her description of their last evening together is particularly expressive of the connection between the two women as mutually supportive creators and thinkers:

> I talked over Mrs Stone's fire until half-past one in the morning. And then she insisted on walking the length of the street with me to my hotel. It was a clear, cold night, very still; we could hear the gentle voice of the sea off to the left. At the hotel door […] she thrust a great roll of paper into my hands. "It's foolscap," she said, "hard to get now. Do you write on it?"
>
> I told her that indeed I always did, […] but that I could not take that great roll from her.
>
> "You must," she said. "It's a present. Cover it with good words."[22]

As with James Joyce, O'Brien's removal from the quotidian activities of Irish middle-class life allowed her to see her country and city with a greater purity of vision: certainly not an objective view, but instead a fusion of what she had known while in the midst of her lived life in Limerick and her perceptions of this life as an exile from it.

O'Brien's last full-length work, completed when she was sixty-six, reflects the spirit of her travel-autobiographies in its stated objective of personal reflection. But it differs from them in that it does not result from its author's desires to inform and illuminate readers who might benefit from her own experiences, but from a need, as she writes, "to refresh and amuse myself".[23] As an "out of fashion" and

---

[21] O'Brien, *My Ireland*, 49-50.
[22] *Ibid.*, 92.
[23] Kate O'Brien, *Presentation Parlour*, London, 1963, 5.

financially troubled writer approaching old age, O'Brien begins to identify with the five aunts on whom her narrative is centred; as she identifies with them, she remembers her childhood and young adulthood spent in their care and company after the death of her mother. Although O'Brien's narrative reaches further than the hours spent with her family in this parlour to comment on the lives of her aunts, the room itself serves as a portal through which O'Brien can re-observe and detail interactions, and not always fortuitous ones, between her aunts and the rest of her family.

It is evident when reading *Presentation Parlour* that it is intended to be more than an affectionate memorial. As O'Brien charts the personality of each aunt, she retells many of her own lived and fictionalized stories. Her description, in the portrait of her Aunt Mary, of the romantic attraction between her father and mother, which fortunately happened to coincide with her grandfather's arrangement of their marriage, provides insight into O'Brien's ambiguity regarding the family romance.[24] Typically presented in her novels as detrimental to the individual desires of her characters, family obligations could not have been irrefutably so for O'Brien, since she and her siblings were the successful products of the "romantic" domestic contract. Yet this success had its problems: Aunt Mary's sudden flight to the Presentation convent the day before her sister's marriage may, as Michael O'Toole suggests, indicate "the possibility that ... she felt attracted to her future brother-in-law, or, indeed, he to her".[25]

In illustrating the family's concern for community, O'Brien identifies with each of her aunts' personalities: Annie's lack of respect for persons, mocking even bishops and Black and Tan soldiers audaciously and dangerously; Fan's piety combined with a need to be pampered and indulged; Mary's grave intelligence, striking beauty, and complete devotion to her religion, so that she became the Reverend Mother of her convent; and Aunt Hickey's elegance and desire for worldly adventure. O'Brien respects her Auntie Mick's intelligence and zeal to educate, but rejects her parsimony and cruelty; she regards having been Mick's "favourite" as a childhood stigma. In proving how unlike Auntie Mick she was, O'Brien would almost

---

[24] For a complete discussion of the family romance in O'Brien's novels, see Anne Fogarty, "'The Business of Attachment': Romance and Desire in the Novels of Kate O'Brien", in *Ordinary People Dancing*, 101-20.

[25] Michael O'Toole, "Foreword", in Kate O'Brien, *Presentation Parlour*, Dublin, 1994, 6.

bankrupt herself later in life through her generosity to other writers at her large estate in County Wicklow, which she was eventually forced to sell. But she is never unfair; she points out that Auntie Mick had "An unhappy temperament – because in some directions so expressively intelligent and just",[26] and finds reasons to admire her, and to criticize the beautiful, brilliant, and pious Aunt Mary for her "wilfully indulgent" act of self-mortification before her sister's wedding, which placed her among "the tiresome and self-centred saints".[27] She also illustrates Mary's and Fan's ruthless vicarious social climbing through O'Brien and her siblings, so that "One too often went home in tears ... from the Presentation Parlour".[28]

Though O'Brien is "earnest to avoid picturesque foreground presentation of that 'touching small figure' which most 'I' narrators of family chronicles become",[29] she shows that her life has absorbed and reflected these lives and their characteristics. *Presentation Parlour* may indeed give licence for acknowledging O'Brien's adult life within those of her fictional characters, but it more importantly becomes a key to her articulation of self. Her childhood is revealed, the structure and nature of her family at the apex and decline of its prosperity is paralleled with that of the Catholic middle class to which she belonged, as she searches for identities for these five women as products of their society and individual lives within it. *Presentation Parlour* does not fill the gnomon of O'Brien's written life created by her other writings, but it merges the diverse points of view from which she had composed literature throughout her life.

For Kate O'Brien, the articulation of an authentic self-narrative was a gradual process that would continue throughout her career. As Colette writes in *La Naissance du jour*: "Patience. I am not making my portrait. This is only my model." Nicole Ward Jouve replies:

> Spell it out: I am not giving you anything fixed, present or past, to theorize. [...] I am creating something ahead of me, something I can work towards, something that may help you work towards your own model.[30]

---

[26] O'Brien, *Presentation Parlour*, 112.

[27] *Ibid.*, 65.

[28] *Ibid.*, 125.

[29] *Ibid.*, 5.

[30] Nicole Ward Jouve, *White Woman Speaks With Forked Tongue: Criticism as Autobiography*, London, 1991, 11.

That O'Brien achieved partial expression of the autobiographical in
her novels is evident, but that such an expression precluded her
writing autobiography *per se* is not; to call O'Brien's fictional *oeuvre*
"her autobiography" imposes an erroneous identity on this body of
work. Her non-fictional writings not only provide undistorted points
of entry into her individual autobiographical mode, but also indicate
how O'Brien's personality and development as a writer were affected
by a tradition that encouraged her silence and self-imposed obscurity.

As Ailbhe Smyth remarks, finding the revolutionary qualities of
O'Brien's writing involves reading against the conventional surfaces
of the stories, noting O'Brien's creation and observation of female
characters, why they fail or succeed in their purposes:

> The "song pointed against" is difficult not to hear when you are
> reading for it, which is as pointed a way of reading a text, I agree, as
> deciding not to hear it. But why not read for the "other" melody, the
> counterpoint? ... *Can a woman read otherwise? Can she write
> otherwise?*[31]

What O'Brien writes about herself in her autobiographies, either as
what she is not by way of others, or as a self deflected on to her
external impressions, also requires a counter-reading. O'Brien is not
the naive, squeamish tourist in Spain or the insipid colleen of British
Victorian fantasy; she is not her tediously self-sacrificing Aunt Mary,
her spoiled Aunt Fan, or her parsimonious and vulgar Auntie Mick.
Her autobiographies comprise an aesthetic sphere removed from her
fundamental emotions and desires, yet as she casts off the personae of
those who surround her, she emerges as herself: a mature woman who
has escaped the constraints of others and is a foil to all of them. Her
1966 radio interview ends with her response to Russell's question of
where she is going next: "Home to Kent, to my little house and cats,
home to hard work, I hope." She never finished this work – either her
final novel or her final autobiography – before her death. But in what
remains of her self-writings, O'Brien has left a carefully-shaped, self-
representative space: an autobiographical persona that succeeds in

---

[31] Ailbhe Smyth, "Counterpoints: A Note (or Two) on Feminism and Kate O'Brien",
in *Ordinary People Dancing*, 24.

remaining intensely private but shares more than external qualities of a life endowed with diverse and illuminating impressions.

TRANSCENDING BORDERS – LIMERICK, IRELAND, EUROPE: KATE O'BRIEN AS CRITIC AND NOVELIST

KARIN ZETTL

Martin Heidegger has defined the border or boundary as a productive site. The boundary, he points out in "Building, Dwelling, Thinking", is not that at which something stops but "that from which something begins its presencing".[1] Kate O'Brien located herself in a border zone between her native Ireland and the outside world and that border position shaped her narrative perspective. The border between the native and the foreign is the point of origin of O'Brien's work.

The first part of my essay will focus upon O'Brien's autobiographical and critical writings. O'Brien's literary and social criticism, published in such magazines as *University Review* and the *Spectator*, forms a comprehensive corpus which has received little recognition. Yet it is her criticism as much as her fiction which shows O'Brien as a political individual and writer. She urged Irish society to open its borders towards Europe. As a literary critic, she warned Irish writers against sealing themselves off from other traditions. In the second part of my essay I want to show how O'Brien's fiction challenges the border of the Irish nation. The migration from Ireland to Europe is a movement characterizing O'Brien's fiction. Her protagonists cross the border of the home country, yet they remain concerned about their Ireland within Europe.

Limerick, Dublin, London, Bilbao, Roundstone, Rome, Boughton (Kent) – the numerous stations of O'Brien's biography show that she crossed and re-crossed the border of her home country while around the same time her Ireland was at pains to fortify its national border. While the official Ireland was asserting the separateness of its native

---

[1] Martin Heidegger, "Building, Dwelling, Thinking", in Martin Heidegger, *Basic Writings*, ed. David Farrell Krell, London, 1993, 356.

culture, O'Brien was developing a vision that rested upon her intimacy with a number of different cultures.

Salman Rushdie, a literary migrant like O'Brien, defined it as the responsibility of the writer-out-of-country not to let his home country forget that there is a world beyond the community to which we belong.[2] It was always O'Brien's concern to remind Ireland that there is a larger world outside its borders. O'Brien, who persistently connected Ireland to Europe, remained unheard at a time when Ireland's self-imposed isolation in cultural and political terms was most intense.

Her travel writings – *Farewell Spain* (1937) and *My Ireland* (1962) – show us that O'Brien wrote from an intriguing position in between cultures and nations. She never sees Spain and Ireland – the two countries most important to her imagination – as contrasts. Rather, she regards Spain as the "other" of Ireland and keeps spotting parallels and points of contact. In *My Ireland*, O'Brien approaches her home country as an individual who is familiar with other cultures. For instantce, she comments on the sisterhood of Ireland, Spain and Palestine or compares Limerick to Bilbao and Milan. The native is placed side by side with the foreign so that the border between them becomes blurred.

O'Brien's family background placed her in a position of difference to the Ireland of post-independence times. The secure status of her middle-class family of merchants with their close links to England and the Continent had little in common with the frugality of De Valera's inward-looking nation. Unlike the cultural nationalists of her time, she never experienced the English and continental cultures as antagonistic to her Irishness. O'Brien's boarding school education at Laurel Hill, a French convent school in Limerick, accentuated her outlook of cultural complexity. At Laurel Hill the Irish language and literature were being taught side by side with the French and the English tradition. In "Memories of a Catholic Education", O'Brien for instance remembers school productions of Irish Renaissance dramas as well as of plays by Racine or Schiller.

Limerick was the point of origin and departure for O'Brien. A beloved place which continued to haunt her imagination, it recurs as provincial Mellick in her fiction. Yet Limerick was the place from which to venture into the world, a locus where neither the author nor

---

[2]   Salman Rushdie, *Imaginary Homelands: Essays and Criticism 1981–1991*, London, 1991, 19.

her fictional daughters could feel restful. After years in self-chosen exile, O'Brien asserted that "it was still from Limerick that she looked out and viewed the world".[3] In the same way, it was always from the world, from the Europe outside, that O'Brien reviewed her Ireland. In her critical writings, twentieth-century Europe and Ireland's position within that Europe was O'Brien's most urgent concern. Long before Ireland began to re-establish links to Europe in the 1970s, O'Brien approached nationalist Ireland from a transnational perspective and censured her country's isolationist politics, as, for instance, in her essay "The Irish Novel Now":

> Some of the shapers or would-be-shapers of our new Ireland, tended either to ignore or actively ban the word European. But in general affairs their mistake is already becoming apparent ... Ireland has always been European ... if no man is an island, all the more is no island an island ...[4]

Already in 1934 in her essay "Changing Ireland", O'Brien challenged De Valera for:

> leading Ireland away from progress into isolation. The Irish national character has always excelled , not in isolation but in the stream of full life. The Irish are an extrovert nation who need a big sounding board ... to develop their most characteristic powers.[5]

O'Brien's political views differed so fundamentally from the official politics of her Ireland that her contributions remained unrecognized. The politicians and thinkers of the new nation were preoccupied with the question of a separate national identity and asked what distinguished the Irish. O'Brien, however, argued that it was not enough to be Irish. Great Irishmen such as St Patrick or Joyce, she pointed out in "Irish Writers and Europe", had always been Irish and European. She urged her countrymen and women "not to have their sight on the Parish hall but on the world and on the century".[6] O'Brien herself indeed had a keen perception of twentieth-century Europe. While her Ireland saw nationalism as the ideology that had liberated

---

[3]   Kate O'Brien, *My Ireland*, London, 1962, 148.
[4]   Kate O'Brien, "The Irish Novel Now", Tuairim lecture, Limerick (6 June 1962), 1-13 (typescript).
[5]   Kate O'Brien, "Changing Ireland", *Spectator*, 18 May 1934, 770f.
[6]   O'Brien, "The Irish Novel Now", 2.

the Irish from British rule, O'Brien set Irish nationalism in relation to the nationalist and fascist movements rising on the continent. Her critique of Irish nationalism resulted from her view of the Spanish Civil War and the Second World War, which she witnessed with great distress. In her essay "De Gaulle: And He Was and Remains Incorruptible", she pointed out, "Patriotism is an attribute in people which I, for one, never welcome overmuch. The idea that it is particularly wonderful to be, say, Irish or Spanish or Indonesian or whatever, always tires me."[7] Nationalism, she continues, "is a dangerous pride". In *Farewell Spain*, her manifesto against fascist regimes, she argues that the root of fascist thinking is the "glorification of one silly nationalism above another".[8] While her home country remained neutral during the Second World War, O'Brien experienced the war as a European trauma that demanded everybody's commitment. "All of us have helped to make the situation which Europe now confronts", she pointed out in a *Spectator* review in 1940. "It is our collective responsibility which we must face and examine as well as we can .... The ivory towers have all been bombed away."[9]

Kate O'Brien's refusal to identify with the Irish nation may be connected to her specifically female perspective. Virginia Woolf, who was equally distressed by the events of the Spanish Civil War and the Second World War, asserted in *Three Guineas* that "as a woman she has no country, as a woman her country is the whole world".[10] She cannot share the pride in a nation in which men only have power, in which women can merely be a society of outsiders. Woolf insists that the fascist dictator can be found not only abroad but also at home in the person of the nationalist patriarch who "dictates to other human beings how they shall live".[11] In a similar way, O'Brien's femininity distanced her from an Irish nationalism that had again and again excluded women. She connected nationalism to a "dangerous celebration of virility"[12] and also spotted the dictator within the home country. In *Farewell Spain* and "Changing Ireland", she suggests that,

[7] Kate O'Brien, "De Gaulle: And He Was and Remains Incorruptible", *Creation* (June 1969), 47.
[8] *Ibid.*, 221.
[9] Kate O'Brien, review of Jeffrey Dell, *Nobody Ordered Wolves* (1940), *Spectator*, 5 January 1940, 24.
[10] Virginia Woolf, *Three Guineas*, London, 1938, 125.
[11] *Ibid.*, 61.
[12] Kate O'Brien, review of Robert Greenwood, *Mr Bunting* (1940), *Spectator*, 18 October 1940, 398.

like the fascist leaders who "claim to patronise ... the destinies of millions without the faintest reference to their egos and their claims", De Valera "imposed a certain way of life on the Irish".[13]

As an Irish woman, O'Brien remained at the margin of a country whose politics she could not share but which she continued to view as her home. As an Irish writer with a culturally complex outlook, she was displaced from the canon of a national literature that was concerned with Irish matters only. Her critical works show that she did take part in the debate around a national literature and commented upon the question of what Irish literature should be like. In the 1930s, Daniel Corkery demanded that Irish literature must cease to go out from Ireland, it must "creep back to the native hearth".[14] O'Brien, however, urged Irish writing "to go back into Europe on its best strength".[15] Young Irish writing must form part of the European stream, she asserts in "Irish Writers and Europe". O'Brien represented Ireland in the European Community of Writers and saw it as imperative that "Irish writers help establish free and continuous dialogue between ... writers of all the countries of Europe, East and West".[16]

Edna Longley has characterized Irish literature as "writing which overspills borders and manifests a web of affiliations that stretches beyond any heartland – to ... Britain and Europe".[17] Similarly, O'Brien located the Irish novel in such a web of affiliations. Irish novelists, she argues in "The Irish Novel Now", must "examine the form of the novel in relation to themselves and must see how they are shaping in it, in contemporary European terms".[18]

In post-independence Ireland, eminent critics such as O'Connor and O'Faolain saw the short story as the genre of prose fiction most suitable for the representation of the Irish experience. O'Brien, however, focused on the novel in her fictional as well as her critical work. It was the very hybridity of the novel, the fact that it owed elements to a variety of traditions, which O'Brien found intriguing. She aligned herself with a tradition which is distinctly European. Salman Rushdie has also appreciated the novel as an "international

---

[13] Kate O'Brien, *Farewell Spain*, London, 1986, 221; O'Brien, "Changing Ireland", 770.

[14] Daniel Corkery, *Hidden Ireland*, Dublin, 1924, 100.

[15] Kate O'Brien, "Irish Writers and Europe", *Hibernia* (May 1965); repr. in *The Stony Thursday Book*, Limerick, 1980, 37.

[16] Kate O'Brien, "Avantgardism", *The Irish Times*, 21 October 1965.

[17] Edna Longley, *From Cathleen to Anorexia*, Dublin, 1995, 5.

[18] O'Brien, "The Irish Novel Now", 1.

form" which allows the novelist to "choose his parents from a polyglot family tree".[19] That was indeed what O'Brien did. She saw such novelists as Jane Austen, George Eliot, Henry James, Joyce, Flaubert, Proust, Turgenev as her literary ancestors. She emphasized the interdependence of the Irish and English tradition. In "The Irish Novel Now", she reminds Irish novelists that they are also heirs to a tradition shaped by Jane Austen, Charles Dickens, the Brontës and Eliot. Her European perspective made her appreciate the genius of Joyce and Beckett long before they were generally recognized in Ireland. In 1944, she praised Joyce as "the first Irish writer of genius who has related Ireland to the world ... and planted his country, and his town, not only in the very heart of European tradition but also ... in the vanguard of the tradition's twentieth century progression".[20] She deplored that "while Joyce's influence has been strong and formative in Europe ... it is not very evident in Irish writing".[21] O'Brien's comments on Joyce's and Beckett's Irishness tell us a lot about her own sense of nationality. In "The Irish Novel Now", O'Brien points out that "Joyce could not help being Irish, and so a living part of whatever we as Irish and in the Catholic inheritance with him, might ever want to say".[22] Similarly, she says about Beckett that "he is no conventional, traditional Irish novelist, but he is Irish ... with his very Irish, very recognizable fanaticism".[23]

Like Gertrude Stein, O'Brien was one of the writers who had to have two countries, one where she belonged and one in which she really lived. In "Return in Winter", an RTÉ feature, O'Brien points out that the most memorable fiction writers "made themselves remembered because ... they found a *pays* which analogized nearly and deeply to the hidden country of themselves".[24] Some of them, like Joyce, "could not have their *pays* underneath their eyes, they had to fly from it in order to find a place outside from where they could best relate this pays".[25] That Ireland which O'Brien recreated in her

[19]   Rushdie, 20.
[20]   Kate O'Brien, review of George Baker, *Fidus Achates, Spectator*, 4 August 1944, 112.
[21]   Kate O'Brien, "Imaginative Prose by the Irish – 1820-1970", in *Myth and Reality in Irish Literature*, ed. Joseph Ronsley, Waterloo, 1977, 312.
[22]   O'Brien, "The Irish Novel Now", 8.
[23]   *Ibid.*, 12.
[24]   Kate O'Brien, "Return in Winter", in *Contemporary Essays*, ed. Sylvia Norman, London, 1933, 30.
[25]   *Ibid.*, 27.

fictional Limerick remained her "hidden country", yet for her evocation of that place she needed the perspective of displacement. The "other place", the "other culture" from which she re-approached her Ireland was a necessary filter. O'Brien was one of George Steiner's "writers *enraciné*". What Steiner finds so intriguing about such writers as Beckett or Nabokov is that "the pressure of more than one language is perceptible in their texts, an other language always shines through".[26] Similarly, the pressure of more than one culture invigorates O'Brien's writing. An "other culture" always shines through O'Brien's Irish novels.

Like O'Brien, the protagonists of her novels are border crossers, migrants between Ireland and the outside world. They are transculturators, to use a concept developed by M. L. Pratt in her study of travel writing.[27] Through their wandering, O'Brien's protagonists mediate between Ireland and the world, they bring the native into contact with the foreign. Deliberately exiling themselves from their home country, they bring Ireland into the world. By their return to Ireland, whether it be imaginary or real, they bring the foreign back home.

From Ballykerran to Rome and Milano, from Mellick to Bilbao or Paris, from Ireland to Great Britain or Belgium – these movements described in O'Brien's texts make clear that she was always anxious to establish connections between Ireland and Europe. A mood of sadness prevails in those of her texts which suggest that the links to Europe have been broken by the Irish. For instance, Denis Considine, O'Brien's first protagonist in *Without My Cloak*, feels with regrets that his Mellick is cut off from such places as "Paris, Rome, Heidelberg ... with their books and learned men and their free familiarity with beauty's progress and tradition",[28] although Ireland is only three days away from that Europe. Irritated by the nationalist perspective of the Irish clergy, the Reverend Mother in *The Land of Spices* argues that the Irish must feel part of a larger Europe: "Certainly Ireland helped in impressing Christianity on Europe. So why should the Irish not go back now, and reclaim for Ireland some of

---

[26] George Steiner, *Extraterritorial: Papers on Literature and the Language Revolution*, London, 1972, 6.

[27] Mary Louise Pratt, *Imperial Eyes: Travel Writing and Transculturations*, London, 1992, 4.

[28] Kate O'Brien, *Without My Cloak*, London, 1986, 283.

the cultivated thing it planted."[29] In *Pray for the Wanderer,* O'Brien does not hide her anger about an Ireland that refuses to absorb the riches of European culture, a nation which does not know of Picasso and thinks Don Quixote "a deadly book". Perturbed by the "general European plight" in 1938, Matt Costello, the wandering Irishman in *Pray for the Wanderer,* condemns his home country for pretending to be a "floating lotus land when the floods rise".[30] Angèle Maury in *The Last of Summer* is one of Ireland's lost daughters who tries to recapture home. Yet she grows impatient with an Ireland which makes a point of not listening to the news at a time when Europe is on the brink of war in 1939.

For O'Brien's protagonists who feel Irish and European, the "non-existence of Europe" in Ireland is exasperating. The Ireland depicted in *The Last of Summer* is a nation which insists that the impending war will not be "our war" and that "Danzig is a far way from Drumaninch".[31] It ignores the warnings of its young generation that "it's 1939 even in Drumaninch". In *The Flower of May,* it is again the young daughter who reminds her parents that Ireland "isn't the only country" when they tell her that her French baccalaureate will be of no use to her at home. Fanny Morrow in *The Flower of May* knows that her departure from her Irish home is inevitable: "Her mind would not long be contained between the two bridges that span the canal at either end of Mespil Road."[32]

Mary Lavelle travelling on a train somewhere between Spain and Ireland, two Irish opera singers in Paris about to leave for the United States and Germany – these scenes conclude O'Brien's novels *Mary Lavelle* and *As Music and Splendour.* They evoke the sense of motion which characterizes O'Brien's texts. Having crossed the border of their Ireland, homecoming becomes impossible, however much O'Brien's wanderers might yearn for it. The homecoming artist can no longer belong, he or she is a mere visitor, as Matt Costello's Mellick insists in *Pray for the Wanderer.* O'Brien's texts plead for the necessity of departure from Ireland. At the same time they despair about the impossibility of homecoming. As O'Brien's last two exiled Irishwomen realize in *As Music and Splendour,* "there is no return to

---

29   Kate O'Brien, *The Land of Spices,* London, 1988, 13-14.
30   Kate O'Brien, *Pray for the Wanderer* (1938), Harmondsworth, 1951, 307.
31   Kate O'Brien, *The Last of Summer* (1941), London, 1990, 179.
32   Kate O'Brien, *The Flower of May,* London, 1953, 32.

Ireland in the old and simple sense", they must continue to "wander the world".[33]

Again and again O'Brien evokes the breakdown of communication between Ireland and the world. In *As Music and Splendour,* the Irish opera singers who have succeeded in the world fail to receive recognition in Ireland. When the grandmother of one of the singers dies, the only Irish person who was interested in the stories from the world can no longer listen. In *Mary Lavelle,* the protagonist's Irish family cannot comprehend the young woman's accounts of her life in Spain. The Ireland in *Pray for the Wanderer* refuses to read the works of its exiled writer. O'Brien and her protagonists did cross the border of their native culture and brought Ireland into the world. Yet they did not have the chance to bring the world back to Ireland in order to make it a different place.

---

[33] Kate O'Brien, *As Music and Splendour*, London, 1958, 128, 63.

TO HEAL AND BE HEALED:
READING FRANK MCCOURT'S *ANGELA'S ASHES*

M. CASEY DIANA

A Swiss professor of geology introduced me to Frank McCourt's work by presenting me with the 10 June 1996 edition of the *New Yorker* magazine, which contained "Sorry for your Troubles", a fragment of *Angela's Ashes*.[1] Half-way through, I was moved to tears. In it, I discovered a story coinciding with my own – Limerick youngster leaves for America's shores – and so forth. I resisted reading the book, however, because after that first bitter-sweet bite I realized the whole would be awfully traumatic. Notwithstanding, Americans who knew me as an Irish native kept prompting: "have you read *Angela's Ashes*, have you read *Angela's Ashes*?"[2] An English professor of Jewish descent articulated: "my mother just sent me that book for my birthday; it's luminous, you must read it." But it was not until the book was actually put into my hands by another friend (this one a concentration camp survivor) who pronounced: "this book is magic" that I read it. And, since reading it, at least once a week I hear "what do you make of *Angela's Ashes*?".

These insistent, repetitive inquiries, coupled with the fact that the memoir emerged as the biggest selling book of the 1990s, prompts me to question: just what is it about *Angela's Ashes* that makes it so incredibly popular, not just to the Irish and their descendants, but by now, literally, to the world? Just two years after its publication, the hardback edition has been reprinted nine times, the paperback edition twenty-six times, having sold more than four million copies worldwide. The memoir has been translated into at least nineteen languages, including Turkish and Croatian. In fact, the hardback

---

[1] Frank McCourt, "Sorry for Your Troubles", *The New Yorker*, 10 June 1996, 47-52.
[2] Frank McCourt, *Angela's Ashes*, New York, 1996.

edition continued as one of the best-selling books in the United States, remaining for ninety weeks on top, or near the top, of the *New York Times Book Review* best-seller list. The memoir earned for McCourt the Pulitzer Prize for biography, and the Hollywood motion picture has been filmed in Limerick, Cork and Dublin by director Alan Parker.[3] When I researched Frank McCourt on the World Wide Web, I discovered Scribner's "Simon Says" webpage, devoted by the publisher for general readers to review its publications. One reader had this to say about *Angela's Ashes*:

> All the reviews that rave about this book being unique and one of a kind and a treasure are grossly understated. McCourt speaks to the reader on an entirely different level.[4]

This different "level" is what concerns me.

McCourt's work is not one of a kind, or indeed at all atypical. In what follows, I demonstrate that beyond McCourt's powerful writing as a reason for *Angela's Ashes* phenomenal worldwide success lies the reader's response to its familiarity, to the deeply conventional, and therefore inherently satisfying configuration of the text. Structural analysis reveals the memoir's ageless episodic mythological configuration, employed in such autobiographical chronicles as St Augustine's *Confessions*, the Puritan conversion narratives, and even the American slave narratives. The inherent "level" in the author's work constitutes the Judeo-Christian mythic movement from innocent Edenic childhood into the wilderness, the struggle for survival, providential help, and finally, deliverance into the Promised Land. Originating with the loss of childhood innocence in depression-era Brooklyn, young Frankie McCourt is cast into a wilderness of poverty and pain, only to be attended by guardian Angels in various guises who aid him in his quest to return to the Promised Land, in this instance – America.

Is Ireland a wilderness and America an Eden? Absolutely not, no more than we could say, in the case of the slave narratives, that the American South is a wilderness and the North, a Paradise. It is the

---

[3]   Paul Gray, "Raking Up the Ashes", *Time Magazine*, 15 June 1998, 78; Nuala O'Faolain, "Ashes That Keep Burning", *The Sunday Times*, 1 November 1998, 12-13.

[4]   Simon and Schuster, "Simonsays.com", online at http://www.simonsays.com/ reviews/ reader/cfm?isbn0684874350.

dynamic process that is at issue here. In addition, I take this idea one step further and reveal how, in the creation of such a mythically grounded work, McCourt, the Writer, attempts to heal himself – his bruised psyche, his alienation and shame – his pain! Obversely, and it is this intersection that concerns me most, the Reader, by reading and integrating McCourt's revealing experiences, indirectly apprehends a similar and powerful personal healing sense of renewal. Thus, *Angela's Ashes* invokes a timeless universal sense of classic catharsis which accounts in great part for the popularity of the memoir. Now, by no means do I want to shove the author's writing style onto the back burner. Certainly, McCourt's penetrating but lyrical Irish voice is truly marvellous. But many brilliant writers have came out of Ireland in the past and continue to conceive, what I think of as, anyway, the world's finest literature. They just don't have nearly the popular appeal and impact of McCourt.

When we juxtapose such disparate works as St Augustine's *Confessions* (400), Puritan preacher John Bunyan's *Grace Abounding to the Chief of Sinners* (1666), the most popular American slave narrative, Frederick Douglass' *My Bondage and My Freedom* (1848) and Frank McCourt's *Angela's Ashes* (1996), we can observe parallel plots.[5] All invariably follow a negative to positive progression originating with the loss of Edenic childhood innocence, and the resultant migration into the real-world wilderness. Subsequently, all the narrators resolve to escape their unhappy state, endure failed attempts to flee their predicaments and, through providential encounters, undergo conversion and thus finally attain deliverance into the promised land.

At this point, the term conversion needs to be addressed. Am I claiming that Frank McCourt undergoes the wrenching Christian conversions reminiscent of St Augustine and John Bunyan? No. However, no one will argue that many times *Angela's Ashes* reads like a confessional narrative, and that the narrator indeed experiences a conversion, or if you will, a transformation, a metamorphosis, a transmutation, an evolution, or perhaps rebirth is the word, wherein emerges a new, enlightened self strong enough even to block out the "nay sayers" of Limerick, and return to the United States. William Butler Yeats' unadorned sentence, "it is myself that I remake",

---

[5] Augustine, *Confessions*, London, 1998; John Bunyan, *Grace Abounding to the Chief of Sinners*, eds John Stachniewski and Anita Pacheco, London, 1998; Frederick Douglass, *My Bondage and My Freedom*, Urbana: IL, 1987.

regarding his own autobiography illuminates this idea.[6] As Roy Pascal
in *Design and Truth in Autobiography* succinctly states: "one does not
need to be a Christian to recognize the profound truth of this mode of
expression."[7]

There has been scholarly debate lately about the idea of
Autobiography *vs.* Memoir; as McCourt said in an interview in *The
Quill*: "Obviously, you have to fill in the blank spaces, to color a bit.
We're memoirists, not journalists – I recall the essence." In the same
interview, McCourt notes that "the legitimacy of memoirs dates from
St Augustine's *Confessions*".[8]

Augustine, born in 354 in Northern Africa, launches his
introspective analysis by recalling his idyllic childhood spent at the
knee of his mother, St Monica, "amid the caresses of [his] nursery and
jests of friends, smiling and sportively encouraging".[9] Although he
doesn't elaborate, John Bunyan, son of a travelling tinker, makes
similar positive remarks about his childhood. And, in the same vein,
the former nineteenth-century American slave Frederick Douglass
discourses primarily on the free and idyllic innocence of his early
youth:

> Freed from all restraint, the slave-boy can be, in his life and conduct,
> a genuine boy, doing whatever his boyish nature suggests .... He
> literally runs wild ... he is, for the most part of the first eight years of
> his life, a spirited, joyous, uproarious, and happy boy.[10]

While Brooklyn does not constitute a bucolic state, the site of
McCourt's earliest memory is a playground. And, although food on
Classon Avenue, Brooklyn, is scant, the children are indeed fed, if not
by their parents, then by the likes of mighty neighbours from different
lands. In McCourt's earliest memories, people are kind-hearted, and
from this early era the author never has a bad word for anyone.

The subsequent phase in the dynamic mythic paradigm chronicles
forfeiture of innocence, and the advent into a real-world wasteland.
Augustine confesses youthful minor thefts and carnal corruption: "in

[6]   William Butler Yeats, *Collected Works of William Butler Yeats, III:
      Autobiographies*, eds William H. O'Donnell and Douglas N. Archibald, New
      York, 1999, 54.
[7]   Roy Pascal, *Design and Truth in Autobiography*, Cambridge: MA, 1960, 97.
[8]   Bill Kirtz, "Out of the Mouths of ... ", *The Quill* (April 1998), 8-9.
[9]   Augustine, Confessions, I, 14, 1.
[10] Douglass, *My Bondage and My Freedom*, 32.

that sixteenth year of the age of my flesh, when the madness of lust ... took over me ... I resigned myself wholly to it." He remarks: "I became a wasteland to myself."[11] Bunyan reminisces over his delight to be "taken captive by the devil at his will" and mentions that his "descent ... was ... of a low and inconsiderable generation" and that he "took much delight in all manner of vice", having had few equals at "cursing, swearing, lying, and blaspheming".[12] Douglass' loss of childhood innocence transpires through the realization of his enslaved state:

> It was a long time before I knew myself to be a slave ... but as I grew larger and older, I learned by degrees the sad fact ... I was quite too young to comprehend the full import of the intelligence .... It was intolerable.[13]

McCourt's narrator loses innocence, one could say, very early on when he encounters his Irish relatives. Although not evil, the McCourts are vindictive, harsh, and just plain downright nasty folks. Biblically speaking, there is no room for the American family at the inn. In an effort to rid themselves of this "clather of Angela's", the Northern grandparents loan them the bus fare out. But these kin cannot compare to their Limerick Grandma, scurrying about in her black shawl, constantly complaining, and Aunt Aggie, a harsh Irish Harpie, if ever there was one. The young Yank finds himself at the mercy of life, and experiences starvation in the Limerick slums. On the cold sodden banks of the River Shannon, to which McCourt alludes as "the River Hades", that poisonous "river of death", staying warm and dry is futile. Ferocious fleas, persecuting ruffians and tyrannical rod-wielding schoolmasters replace mythic beasts. Young Frankie intuits his status as a sinner prior to his first communion. His hunger many times necessitates stealing apples from orchards (reminiscent of Augustine's theft of pears), milk from cows, and even fish and chips from a drunken man. In his early teen years, he suffers agony over his sexual stirrings and endures severe mental anguish over young Theresa Carmody, who dies of consumption.

The struggle to survive the wilderness, and the declaration or oath to escape, comprises the next chronological phase in the Augustinian

---

[11] Augustine, *Confessions*, II, 4, 4.
[12] Bunyan, *Grace Abounding*, 4.
[13] Douglass, *My Bondage and My Freedom*, 82.

confessional prototype. Young Augustine continues in his quest for spiritual progress and seeks relief from his wretched life: he "at once ... loathed exceedingly to live and feared to die". In desperation, "sinking into the lowest pit", the young man looks to others for answers.[14] Bunyan, who chronicles his spiritual journey in prison, looks back upon his exertions to free himself from his days squandered in sin and his "apprehensions of devils and wicked spirits ... bound down with the chains and bonds of eternal darkness".[15] The Puritan also calls out for deliverance. In *My Bondage and My Freedom,* Douglass excludes no horrific event: the separation of relatives, the beatings, the whippings, the loss of identity, the sexual abuse of women, the lack of nourishment, proper bedding and housing, of education, of love, comfort, respect and dignity. By the time he reaches sixteen, the youngster encounters such a hell, day after day through continued beating and starvation, that he comes to cry out in anguish the declaration to flee, and to be free at any price:

> I will run away. I will not stand it. Get caught or get clear, I'll try it ... I have only one life to lose. I might as well be killed running as die standing ... one hundred miles straight north, and I am free! Try it? Yes! I will. It cannot be that I shall live and die a slave.[16]

McCourt suffers metaphoric enslavement, many times working like a slave hauling sacks of coal, and bundles of newspapers on rainy evenings for an uncle who would not give him even a chip for his troubles. And he endures beatings until tears are brought on, under leather straps, canes, ash and blackthorn sticks. The youngster's sense of despair increases gradually. He survives the unexplained loss of three siblings, the deprivation of his parents through drink and grief, a mother demented with worry forced into begging for bread and the employment of her body to provide a roof over her family's head, an extended stay in a typhoid ward at age eleven, and so forth, and so on. As he gets a bit older, Frankie sinks further into desperation, especially when his father leaves. The agonized youngster cries out: "he's not coming, Mam. He doesn't care about us. He's just drunk over there in England." Totally dejected, after Laman Griffin beats

---

[14]   Augustine, *Confessions*, IV, 15, 27.
[15]   Bunyan, *Grace Abounding*, 5.
[16]   Douglass, *My Bondage and My Freedom*, 136.

him and he realizes fully the true nature of his mother's relationship with his assailant, he declares loudly, "I'll go to America".[17]

Next, the mythological pattern progresses to the freedom attempt. At this phase of the escape, the providential appearance of a friend, a Good Samaritan figure, provides the key to freedom. In an effort to escape the pleasures of the body and his intense mental anguish, in his twenty-ninth year Augustine abandons Manichaean philosophy and moves closer to Christianity. Although he takes "pains to learn" the Christian creed, he remains filled with doubts, and still "shaken by worldly pursuits" defers daily "to turn to the Lord", until he meets Simplicanus and hears of the conversion of others to the Catholic faith.[18] But he continues to struggle between his carnal will and his spiritual calling. Finally, through the intervention of his devout mother, he encounters St Ambrose, "the only teacher capable of relieving his yearnings".[19]

Similarly, Bunyan finds in his wife, who reads to him from Arthur Dent's *The Plain Man's Pathway to Heaven* (1640) and Lewis Bayly's *The Practice of Piety* (1611), a modicum of redemption but like Augustine continues to struggle between true conversion and continued temptation of "the lusts and fruits of the flesh in his poor soul".[20] Time after time, he attempts to escape the invasion of evil thoughts and is continually buffeted between calm acceptance of Christ and stormy encounters with his tempter, Satan. Throughout his tempestuous journey he encounters others, like the poor people of Bedford who sit in the sunny beams of true conversion, and Mr Gifford who "made it much his business to deliver the people of God".[21] Try as he might, however, the young man constantly flounders and cannot escape his sinful state: "my desires for heaven and life began to fail."[22] Likewise, in the company of five other men, Douglass plans to escape north by water but endures betrayal and discovery. After a particularly rough whipping, at the slave's lowest point, he literally buries himself in the forest. The intervention of a fellow-slave, a Good Samaritan-like comrade, provides him with the

---

[17] McCourt, *Angela's Ashes*, 269, 295.
[18] Augustine, *Confessions*, V, 14, 24; VI, 11, 20.
[19] *Ibid.*, IX, 5, 13; IX, 12, 32.
[20] Bunyan, *Grace Abounding*, 15.
[21] *Ibid.*, 117.
[22] *Ibid.*, 77.

strength of mind necessary to make good his intention to achieve freedom.

Like Augustine, Bunyan and Douglass, young Frankie McCourt aspires to flee his lamentable life. Living with his demented uncle Pat, he is forced to steal bread to survive. He becomes obsessed with escaping to America: "I'll have no money to put back all that bread ... and no way of saving to go to America and if I can't go to America I might as well jump into the River Shannon." Constantly he agitates about how to save his fare: "I'll have to save a few shillings from my pound because if I don't I'll be in Limerick forever." Mrs Finucane's collection job provides the answer. As Frankie puts it, "I'll have my escape money to America".[23]

While we uncover more primary providential encounters in the autobiographies of Augustine, Bunyan and Douglass, McCourt's narrator faces throughout a more subtle series of guardian angels who provide him with the fortitude necessary to succeed: Mr Timoney, who introduces him to reading literature; young Patricia, who gives him the book wherein he first discovers Shakespeare; Mr O'Halloran, who encourages him to cultivate his mind: "it is your house of treasure and no one in the world can interfere with it ... your mind is a palace", he preaches. The headmaster also paints positive pictures of America and encourages him to leave Limerick: "you must get out of this country .... Go to America, McCourt. Do you hear me?" And, although no one could call his father Malachy a dependable parent, the scoundrel does indeed encourage his child to learn:

> he tells me ... I should be good in school and some day I'll go back to America and get an inside job .... He says you can do anything in America, it's the land of opportunity.

It is Uncle Pa who persuades him finally to escape the night before he is scheduled to take the post office examination: "you'll be dead in your mind before you're thirty", if you don't leave Limerick, the positive father figure warns.[24]

The final step in the Augustinian confessional model transpires at the moment of conversion. Augustine progresses slowly, and although he conceives of the "Lord Christ, as a man of excellent wisdom, to whom no one could be equalled", he doesn't truly believe until 386,

---

[23]   McCourt, *Angela's Ashes*, 300, 314, 332.
[24]   *Ibid.*, 178, 208, 335.

when one day in the midst of an agonizing inner struggle, "he calls out
to God for relief", and hears a chanting voice from heaven telling him
to "take up and read". While reading in the Bible of St Paul's
conversion, Augustine's "difficulties vanished away" and he experienced a spiritual awakening and emancipation, or as he puts it, a
freedom from the scratching "itch of lust" and the "anxiety for the past
life".[25] Bunyan, instead, undergoes a series of enlightenments. Time
after time, when he finds himself in the "miry bog", when he begins
"to sink greatly in [his] soul, and beg[ins] to entertain such
discouragement in [his] heart", he calls out and finds comfort in his
Bible. He also experiences deliverance in spiritual voices: "what relief
came to my soul ... it was a release to me from my former bonds."[26] In
complete despair and abject despondency, Douglass experiences a
similar leap of faith wherein he is able to confront and fight the tyrant
Covey:

> I was a changed being after that fight. I was nothing before. I WAS A
> MAN NOW. It recalled to life my crushed self-respect and my self-
> confidence, and inspired me with a renewed determination to be a
> FREEMAN.[27]

For McCourt, release, rebirth, redemption – conversion, if you will –
does not occur until the evening of his sixteenth birthday when the
youngster enters the Franciscan Church to intercede with his
namesake, St Francis, for the salvation of Theresa Carmody's soul.
Here, he experiences his most providential encounter yet with Father
Gregory, in whom he confides the depth of his despondency. The kind
father bestows upon the adolescent the ability to forgive, and most
important, to love himself. Dreaming of America day and night, from
this point, Frank quickly amasses the money necessary to reach his
dream. McCourt himself claims that he "escaped to America at age
19".[28]

Personal memoir and healing
At this point, I will return to my earlier suggestion concerning the
healing process involved in writing personal memoir. In his 1588

---

[25]   Augustine, *Confessions*, VIII, 12, 29.
[26]   Bunyan, *Grace Abounding*, 82, 78, 188.
[27]   Douglass, *My Bondage and My Freedom*, 186.
[28]   Kirtz, "Out of the Mouths of ...", 19.

autobiographical essay "Of Solitude", French essayist Michel de Montaigne reveals that

> if a man does not first unburden his soul of the load that weighs upon it, movement will cause it to be crushed still more .... Our illness grips us by the soul and that soul cannot escape from itself.[29]

McCourt, as forthright as possible, composes his autobiographical narrative, unburdens his soul, and experiences the death of the old conflicted self and the emergence of a new healthy self. Indeed, there is nothing too personal for McCourt to write about, and through this intense searing away of sorrow, he heals his inner self. When asked in a live interview by Kate Tentler on the WebChat Broadcasting System, "for whom did you write *Angela's Ashes*?" the author responded: "I didn't write it for anybody in particular. I started to write it for myself. To get it out of my system." And, in the same interview, replying to, "do you return much to Ireland?" McCourt retorted:

> Yes, lately I have been going back more than I did in the past because I feel easier about it .... I used to go back with a chip on my shoulder but now that I wrote the book and I've got this toxic stuff out of my system.

An audience member queried: "How did you overcome the bitterness and pain of your childhood? Was writing this book therapeutic, and if so, how?" And McCourt replied:

> First the bitterness and the pain .... Well, I carried it for a long time .... And writing the book was therapeutic but it was hard therapy because there were days when I did not want to go to that desk ... there were days I almost decided to give it up and go back to teaching. But in the long run ... I had to get it out of my system, and it's very satisfying.[30]

If McCourt finds a vehicle for spiritual transformation and healing in the act of writing *Angela's Ashes*, then is this enlightenment shared or

---

[29] Michel de Montaigne, *The Autobiography*, New York, 1999, I, 39.
[30] Kate Tentler, WebChat Broadcasting System online at http://www.groupweb.com/wbs.htm.

transmitted to the Reader? Undoubtedly, yes. A Simon and Shuster internet participant reported:

> Without being trite, this book changed my life. If Frankie can go through his life with love, humor, adventure and compassion, why can't we all?

It is the self-searing honesty expressed in McCourt's work that seems instrumental in providing a sensation of healing. As American psychotherapist Carl Rogers writes in *On Becoming a Person* (1961):

> There have been times when ... I have expressed myself in ways so personal that I have felt I was expressing an attitude which probably no one else could understand .... In these instances I have almost invariably found that the very feeling which has seeemd to me most private, most personal, and hence most imcomprehensible by others, has turned out to be an expression for which there is a resonance in other people.[31]

It is this "resonance" with which McCourt's reader identifies. By the act of reading the autobiographical narrative, the Reader comes to identify personally with the Writer.

Tradition associates the act of reading autobiography with spiritual transformation. Time after time, conversion results during or after reading of similar sufferers. Immediately before his moment of conversion, Augustine read of St Paul's spiritual rebirth. Ignatius Loyola underwent an intense spiritual conversion during his reading of works on the lives of Jesus Christ and the saints. John Calvin was reading about David in the *Book of Psalms*, John Wesley about Luther, and Thomas Merton about Gerard Manley Hopkins. St Teresa experienced conversion upon reading Augustine's *Confessions*. Simply, spiritual healing follows the act of reading the lives of others. Seemingly, however, these are all instances of Christian modelling that lead to spiritual transcendence and enlightenment. But can one compare accounts of the experiences of "saints" to those of Frank McCourt? Indeed, while reading *Angela's Ashes*, readers do experience a sense of personal identification with the author. One Simon and Shuster website respondent reports:

---

[31] Carl Rogers, *On Becoming a Person: A Therapist's View of Psychotherapy*, Boston, 1961, 2.

> Mr McCourt was telling the story of my life growing up poor in America. It was very painful to read at first, but then I remembered my sense of humor about having grown up poor, Irish and Catholic; it was then I could relax and read Frank McCourt's ANGELA'S ASHES .... I thank Mr McCourt for helping me to get over my fear of poverty.

Another reader responds:

> I am neither Irish nor as poor as Frank McCourt ever was (bless his loving, tolerant and forgiving heart!), but I could identify with the entire gamut of emotions so vividly evoked by Mr McCourt.[32]

The immense popularity of *Angela's Ashes* goes beyond McCourt's powerful writing style. Its mythological episodic structural configuration invokes in the reader a profoundly satisfying sense of familiarity. While perusing the author's autobiographical effort to heal himself, readers indirectly apprehend a similar and powerful personal restorative sense of renewal, and this contentment and joy they pass on to others, and others. Thus, one reason behind the phenomenal worldwide success of *Angela's Ashes*.

---

[32]   Simon and Schuster, "Simonsays.com".

ANGELA'S ASHES:
MYTH AND THE MEMOIR OF AN IRISH SURVIVOR

ALEXANDRA HENDRIOK

Frank McCourt's memoir *Angela's Ashes* tells the harrowing story of the author's childhood in poverty-stricken Limerick and his return to America, the country where he was born. Yet the book hardly needs any introduction, as it shot to the top of best-seller lists in America, the United Kingdom and Germany shortly after its publication in 1996 and received considerable media attention. This success, overwhelming for a first publication by an unknown author, merits some investigation in its own right. Here this is approached through genre. Though *Angela's Ashes* is a memoir and therefore typically associated with "telling a story from the heart", it also follows a clear and deliberate structure, that of the quest and initiation. The aim of this article is twofold: to outline the structural elements that connect this memoir to the quest-tales, and then to investigate what consequence this structure has for the depiction of Irish and American society within the memoir and for its readership.

Angela's Ashes is the story of a survivor, a confessional story of endurance, suffering and guilt. As readers' responses show, the attraction lies in accounts with which a lot of people can identify, whether it is the overcoming of guilt indoctrinated by the Catholic church, the experience of a first confession or the encounters of an emigrant in a foreign country. Not only do the genres of the mythic quest and memoir blend well but it is their fusion that creates a sense of universal appeal within a personal narrative. McCourt's novel provides the reader with many mirrors in which to find one's own reflection. Reading *Angela's Ashes* thus becomes a healing and identification process for many.

According to Frank McCourt,[1] the title of his memoir *Angela's Ashes* was chosen because he intended to tell the story of his life up to the burial of his mother, Angela, with her ashes being brought back to the graveyard in her hometown, Limerick. Yet though the plot changed, and the memoir now finishes with Frank's return to America, the title still remains. Within the altered framework it acquires a new meaning. The title sums up Angela's life which is dead, grey and cold like proverbial ashes due to the daily struggle for survival for herself and her family in the lanes of Limerick. Like the Cinderella of fairy-tale Angela spends her rare spare time huddled up close to the fire to find warmth and comfort, looking into the ashes. Yet her story reads like an anti-fairy-tale; the fairy godmother never appears and instead of changing into new clothes that would signify a new life and hope, Angela's clothes turn into rags and with them her life and that of her family disintegrates. Significantly, the only good piece of clothing, a bright red coat she brought back with her from America, cannot be worn in Limerick as it would class her as an outsider, but is kept like a treasure together with the hope for better times.

The title sets the tone for the enfolding story, a story of poverty and hardship. At the close of the memoir, Frank is the only one who manages to escape the downward spiral of poverty by emigrating to America. The narration, as well as the life of the protagonist, has come full circle at this stage, as both started in the States. Frank returns, literally, to the beginning. This circular structure, with the protagonist leaving one place and, after struggles and hardship, returning to it as a man, suggests the structure of the circuitous quest, that is, the return to the beginnings but at a higher level. The superimposed frame sets up a dialectic between America and Ireland portraying one as the place of possibility and hope, the other as the manifestation of trial and hardship.

Although the America of the protagonist's youth is far from being depicted as an Eden, it is still better than Ireland, though in the beginning of the novel this is difficult to imagine as the New York of the 1930s is marked by the hardships of the Depression. This is exchanged for poverty-stricken and claustrophobic Belfast and, mainly, Limerick. The changes for the worse are signalled by comparison with similar situations in New York. A foreboding of

---

[1]   Barbara Dimmit, "Frank McCourt: The Interview", *Reader's Digest Online Interviews*, 16 September 1998:   http://www.readersdigest1.com/rdmagazine /specfeat/archi ves/fmccourt.htm.

worse things to come is achieved when the father, who used to charm the children with his stories in New York, raises his voice and hands against them on arrival in Ireland. The loving neighbours who protected and cared for the family in America are replaced by cold relatives who cannot communicate their feelings. Even the American grocery shop owner, a friendly Italian who used to give them credit and leftovers as he knew of their plight, is now replaced by a selfish shopkeeper who cheats even the poorest of her customers. Most remarkable is a loss of community. Whereas in America the McCourts belonged to the vast Irish immigrant community, Ireland with its stringent class and identity awareness casts them as outsiders. Because of their American accent the children are marked as "Yanks" and expected to conform to the stereotypes of America as portrayed in the movies. Their outsider status becomes clear on the first day at school:

> The boys in Leamy's want to know why we talk like that. Are ye Yanks or what? And when we tell them we came from America they want to know, Are ye gangsters or cowboys? A big boy sticks his face up to mine. I'm asking ye a question, he says. I tell him I don't know.[2]

They are separated not only by their language but also by different customs. Limerick society is portrayed as being ruled by the Church which infiltrates every aspect of people's lives and thus is alien to the children who were not brought up as devout Catholics. Their ignorance in religious matters is looked down upon and confirms their outsider status. Frank and his brothers do not really belong to any society – they have left America, but their new home is not yet ready to accept them. Limerick is depicted as a place where it is easy to become an outsider. Frank's aunt, for instance, is ignored simply because she is from Galway and has, allegedly, the look of a Spaniard. Thus it is not astonishing that Frank's father, Malachy, is not accepted either, as he is from the North, in itself a sin in Holy Limerick. His Northern accent renders looking for a job more difficult. The myth of America as the big melting pot where achievement matters more than class is affirmed by juxtaposing it with the image of a priest and class-ridden Ireland, where movement out of the preordained place decided by birth becomes impossible.

---

[2]   Frank McCourt, *Angela's Ashes*, London, 1997, 83.

The first description of Limerick given on the opening page of the novel sets the tone for any further development:

> Above all – we were wet. Out in the Atlantic Ocean great sheets of rain gathered to drift slowly up the river Shannon and settle forever in Limerick. The rain dampened the city from the Feast of the Circumcision to New Year's Eve. It created a cacophony of hacking coughs, bronchial rattles, asthmatic wheezes, consumptive croaks.[3]

Even the weather seems to obey the Church calendar, turning Limerick into a place afflicted by the deluge as it rains unrelentingly.[4] This obvious allusion to the Flood turns Limerick into a place punished by God with floods of rain, and more than once Limerick is directly associated with illness and death. Here Frank's two brothers and several of his classmates die because of respiratory diseases, the causes of which are connected with the Shannon.[5] Whereas in most cultures water is a symbol of life, here it has the opposite meaning. The Shannon is directly identified as the harbinger of death and the bringer of disease and is described as "a river that kills",[6] alluding to the mythical river Styx from Greek mythology which formed the border between the world of the living and the underworld. The McCourts seem to have crossed the threshold between the world of the living and the dead when they left America, and exchanged it for a metaphorical Hades, a place where disease and death abound.

Limerick is also associated with death in a metaphorical way, insofar as there is no progress, everything seems to lead to a dead-end. For example the McCourt family is doomed to embark on an odyssey around the city. Every move is motivated by the death of a child, as Angela wants to escape the memories which the familiar environment evokes. Yet every move represents a step downward, into greater poverty and misery. From sharing a tiny house with the parents' relatives, they move into their own tiny room with a flea-ridden bed, and ultimately into a house. The initial joy of having more than one room turns stale when they discover that the ground floor floods every winter, which forces the family to move upstairs. The division of space

---

[3] *Ibid.*, 1
[4] The Feast of the Circumcision is on 1 January.
[5] This association with death is by no means uniform in Irish literature. James Joyce, in the story "The Dead" in *Dubliners*, calls the Shannon "mutinous", whereas Edna O'Brien associates the Shannon with "life" in many of her novels.
[6] McCourt, *Angela's Ashes*, 238.

is especially interesting, as the upstairs is called "Italy" where it is warm and dry, whereas downstairs is the wet, cold and smelly Limerick. When the McCourt family cannot pay the rent any longer they are evicted. This time the move downward is marked by a situation of dependency. The McCourts lose their own space and move in with cousin Laman. As there is no money, the mother has to exchange sexual favours for the rent.

In the same way work, normally the means of earning a living, is here connected with illness and death. An example to illustrate this is the character of Mr Hannon, who earns his living delivering coal. The strain of the hard work proves too much for him, yet he cannot give it up as the alternative would be to condemn his family to starvation. Instead of sustaining his life, his job is destroying it. Multiple aspects of working-class life in Limerick are associated with death.

Limerick is depicted as the antithesis of America, but the novel's circular structure also implies that it is the place where the protagonist/hero has to prove himself before he can return again. The voyage across Limerick seems to suggest the narrative structure of the picaresque novel in which the hero, more often than not a child[7] like Frank, has to undergo a voyage during which various trials occur and adverse situations have to be overcome until the hero/ine is restored to his/her rightful place in society. This is reminiscent of the quest narratives, dating back to the twelfth century, which in turn can be related back to fertility myths.[8] One important example of a quest narrative is Chrétien de Troyes' *Ivayn*, the prototype of the Arthurian novel.

The general structure of the courtly quest novels is very schematic: the hero has to leave the idealized world of the court either to prove himself or to restore order to the court. To do this, he has to venture out on a journey on which various trials pose themselves and tasks have to be fulfilled. The places visited during the voyage are always significantly "other" and are therefore often introduced by describing them as everything that the court is not. A dialectic between court and adventure is set up which resembles strongly the dialectic between New York and Limerick in *Angela's Ashes*. The quester has to identify

---

[7] Henry Fielding's *Tom Jones* and Mark Twain's *Tom Sawyer* and *Huckleberry Finn*, as well Charles Dickens' *Oliver Twist*, seem to fit especially well in this context.

[8] This was argued first by Jessie Weston in her book *From Ritual to Romance*, London, 1920; cited in Lawrence Coupe, *Myth*, London, 1997, 26-28.

suitable role models and reject unsuitable ones, he/she has to undergo rites of passage and many adventures to prove him/herself, so that he/she can return in the end to the place of departure as a whole person, grown in spirit, and ready to enter a new world. The geographic structure of the quest is easily recognizable in Frank's odyssey across Limerick, as in both quest and novel each place is associated with new tasks and adventures.

One of Frank's earliest memories is of sitting on his father's knees listening to stories about Cuchulain. Cuchulain is the archetypal Irish hero, used by poets such as Yeats to represent the spirit of the new, independent Ireland. He became the icon of the nationalist spirit in the aftermath of the 1916 Uprising. First of all, the exchange of Irish myths between father and son helps to express the strong bond between the two. Frank, as the first born, listens enraptured to his father's stories about the Irish hero. They become "his" stories and he jealously guards them: "That's my story. Dad can't tell that story to Malachy or any other children down the hall."[9]

In addition, these tales take on a symbolic meaning, as they come to represent Ireland to him in the absence of any real experience of Ireland. In the same way Malachy McCourt clings on to stories about nationalism, like the songs about Kevin Barry, Roddy McCorley or Cuchulain. Malachy had to leave Ireland because of his claimed involvement with the IRA. In America, the only tangible images left of his past and of himself as a nationalist are Cuchulain – as the embodiment of the nationalist spirit – and stories of the men who died for Ireland. He clings on to these like a drowning man to the plank and makes even his children swear to die for Ireland. How far removed from the real Ireland this romantic notion is becomes obvious on the McCourts' return to their mother country. Once in Dublin, Malachy McCourt wants to show his son the statue of Cuchulain in the Dublin General Post Office. There he has to accept that he is the only one who still cares or even understands the image. The driver who takes them there has a far more pragmatic approach to politics and life:

> The driver says he has no notion of who this Cuchulain was .... Now what in God's name is this all about? What's this fellow doin' with the long hair and the bird on his shoulder? And will you kindly tell me mister what this has to do with the men of 1916? Dad says, Cuchulain fought to the end like the men of Easter Week. His

---

[9]   McCourt, *Angela's Ashes*, 13.

enemies were afraid to go near him till they were sure he was dead
and when the bird landed on him and drank his blood they knew.
Well, says the driver, 'tis a sad day for the men of Ireland when they
need a bird to tell them a man is dead. I think we better go now or
we'll be missing the train to Limerick.[10]

Life in the South has moved on, and like Cuchulain himself Malachy
McCourt seems like a relic from times past.[11] These stories of
nationality and identity, so important to Frank's father as they shape
and to a certain extent are his identity, are only important to Frank
until he is able to find his own identity. Tellingly, in the latter part of
the memoir, once Frank is grown-up, the ghost of Cuchulain seems
exorcized; the Irish hero is not mentioned any more.

For Frank, the hero of the memoir, life in Limerick holds numerous
tribulations. Apart from the fact that it is more difficult for him to find
his niche in a society that classes him as a Yank, an outsider, and that
his family is existing on the verge of starvation, he has to undergo a
serious illness, typhoid, and only just escapes death. Yet this episode
with its connotations of death and rebirth – as he does survive his
illness – can be interpreted as his spiritual awakening. Before, he
unquestioningly believed the political and religious indoctrination in
school and Church alike. During his recovery in hospital he comes in
contact with English literature and develops a deep love for it. He
reads bits of Shakespeare, and also an English history book is added to
the list of Irish myths and literature. It is significant in this respect that
the first line of Shakespeare Frank reads is: "I do believe, induced by
potent circumstances, that thou art mine enemy."[12] Though he does not
understand the meaning of this sentence, he is fascinated by it and
repeats it again and again.

This experience can be read as a parallel to his political
indoctrination at school, where the relationship between Ireland and
England is depicted as one of unfairness, cruelty and domination,
though the historical background is never given. This establishes a
binary axis of victims and victimizers that leads to a self-perpetuating
stereotyping of everything English without explaining or questioning

---

[10] *Ibid.*, 55.

[11] This recalls the character of Michael Moran in McGahern's *Amongst Women* (John McGahern, *Amongst Women*, London, 1990). Like Malachy, Moran clings to the past and is disappointed by it at the same time.

[12] McCourt, *Angela's Ashes*, 222.

any further the "potent circumstances" that led to it. The result of this indoctrination is made clear in an episode when Frank comes across the word "perfidy" in his English history book. Although he does not know its meaning, he immediately concludes that "if it's something the English do it must be terrible".[13] However, Frank is able to break this cycle of stereotyping as he finds himself drawn to Shakespeare's writing. The bard's lines, though written by an Englishman, feel "like having jewels in my mouth when I say the words".[14]

After Frank is released from hospital his new teacher, Mr O'Halloran, encourages a critical approach when he questions the biased version of history Frank had encountered before:

> It's a shock to everyone when he [O'Halloran] says, the battle of Kinsale in sixteen nought one was ... a close battle with cruelty and atrocities on both sides. Cruelty on both sides? The Irish side? How could that be? All the other masters told us the Irish always fought nobly, they always fought the fair fight.[15]

In the absence of Frank's real father, O'Halloran can be seen as a guide-figure. He is the one to reaffirm Frank's intention to leave Ireland for America:

> He [O'Halloran] is disgusted by this free and independent Ireland that keeps a class system foisted on us by the English, that we are throwing our talented children on the dungheap. You must get out of this country, boys. Go to America, McCourt. Do you hear me, McCourt? I do, Sir.[16]

The role of the teacher in *Angela's Ashes* is very similar to the character of Master Boyle in Brian Friel's play *Philadelphia, Here I Come!*.[17] McCourt played the role of Master Boyle in a 1990[18] production of Friel's play which probably accounts for the similarities. Both play and memoir are about emigration from Ireland to America and the teachers play a crucial role in the life of both protagonists.

---

[13] *Ibid.*, 226.
[14] *Ibid.*, 222.
[15] *Ibid.*, 236.
[16] *Ibid.*, 338.
[17] Brian Friel, *Philadelphia, Here I Come!*, London, 1965.
[18] Robert Simonson, "The Irish ... and how they got that way", http://www.backstagecasting, com/reviews/ny/irishandhow.asp (30/07/98).

They are portrayed as guides who help the spiritual development of the main characters, thereby substituting for emotionally unstable or distanced fathers.[19] Boyle and O'Halloran alike express their great enthusiasm for America and thus affirm the protagonists' decision to go there. The most telling difference between play and memoir is that whereas in Friel's play America is seen as one alternative, in McCourt's memoir it is portrayed as the only possibility, reaffirming again the binary axis between Limerick and New York.

At the age of fourteen, after higher education has been denied to him, Frank starts looking for a job. This is the time of passing from childhood to adolescence and is marked by leaving his family and finding a future for himself. What follows now can be regarded as different stages of initiation, or rites of passage. According to Laurence Coupe[20] and Mircea Eliade,[21] initiation is the signal for belonging to a society, as it reveals to the initiate intimate knowledge about this society. Yet the three different incidents where he has to prove himself and which are thus presented as initiations and rites of passage are not imbued with positive values; they do not lead to personal growth.

Firstly, the context of initiation is evoked by the ritualistic manner in which "drinking one's first pint" is described. The first time Frank is told about pubs, the pint is mentioned in a way that evokes a religious context by playing with the vocabulary of the Eucharist:

> Dad and Uncle Pa drink their glass of black stuff and have another. Uncle Pa says, Frankie, this is the pint. This is the staff of life.[22]

According to McCourt, sixteen is the age when boys are traditionally given their first pint. This event is described in terms of a ritual. A grown-up, normally the father, has to introduce the initiate, and order the pint for him. Then he introduces the initiate formally to society, that is, the men in the pub:

> The barman brings the pints, Uncle Pa pays, lifts his glass, tells the men in the pub, This is my nephew, Frank McCourt, son of Angela

---

19   The role of the spiritual guide figure is well established in literature. One only has to think about Merlin in many of the Arthurian romances, or of Arthur and Lancelot as role models for the younger knights.

20   Laurence Coupe, *Myth*, London, 1997.

21   Mircea Eliade, *Myths, Dreams and Mysteries*, New York, 1957.

22   McCourt, *Angela's Ashes*, 78-79.

Sheehan, the sister of my wife, having his first pint, here's to your
health and long life.[23]

Drinking is associated with destruction in the memoir, for example the
father's alcoholism keeps the family in poverty. Frank's first drink
leads to an argument with his mother and eventually to violence.
Instead of enabling personal growth, his initiation is accompanied by
violence and destruction.

Secondly, when at the age of fourteen the protagonist starts
working, he frequently describes himself as a "man".[24] Yet the work
offers no possibilities for advancement, and without secondary
schooling his possibilities in Ireland are limited. The depiction of this
stagnant situation is reinforced by the association between Limerick
and death. Thirdly, there is his sexual initiation, a rite of passage
episode. Yet again this is accompanied by negative connotations. The
girl he loves and is seduced by, Theresa Carmody, is terminally ill and
dies within weeks of starting the affair. Because of his Catholic
upbringing, Frank feels guilty for condemning her to eternal
damnation. Although initiations and rites of passage take place, they
are linked with stagnation, guilt, violence or death.

After Theresa's death, Frank becomes obsessed with his guilt and
the idea of going to America to find his salvation grows even more
pressing. From this time onwards he is alone; he has left his family
home and is solely responsible for his own life. The Frank McCourt
character seems to be modelled on the role of the silent and lonesome
cowboys of the Hollywood movies he used to watch in the cinema. In
the absence of real role models, he imitates the screen characters. This
creation of the self is evident in the episode with Mrs Finucane, a loan-
shark. In order to make ends meet and achieve his goal to save enough
money to go to America, he becomes an "outlaw".

From being Mrs Finucane's accomplice, a position that forces him
to blackmail friends and family members, he stoops even lower and
even steals from Mrs Finucane after her death. His outlaw status is
remedied by the fact that after her death he destroys all evidence of her
debtors, thereby establishing himself as the Robin Hood of the lanes of
Limerick. Yet this refashioning of the self is not entirely successful, as
he is only imitating role models without having found his own identity.
The first step towards finding his real self is accomplished when he

---

[23]   *Ibid.*, 398.
[24]   *Ibid.*, 363.

learns how to accept himself. This lesson is taught to him by a Franciscan priest, after a confession in which he is able for the first time to tell his whole story. A healing process is activated and Frank is able to exchange his old, conflicted self that was a creation of the society he lived in for a new, healed self:

> He tells me God forgives me and I must forgive myself, that God loves me and I must love myself for only when you love God in yourself can you love all God's creatures.[25]

These episodes mark the end of his trials in Limerick. After having saved enough money Frank is able to board a ship and leave for America. That he goes by ship and therefore has to cross the ocean is interesting when read in context of symbolism and myth, as already pointed out in connection with the river Shannon. Water often symbolizes rebirth, and Frank's arrival in America can be seen as such. He has escaped the slums of Limerick and undergone various trials and tribulations in order finally to return to the beginning, the place where he was born, New York. There are signs that this time his life will not be marked by poverty, but success.

The very first time he steps on American ground, he is immediately seduced by an American girl, an episode that mirrors closely his first sexual experience. This time there is no hint of guilt, but elation and a sense of freedom from the former restraints, signifying a successful rite of passage. Both times the women's bodies seem to represent the country and society, thereby attaining a symbolic quality that expresses Frank's relation with the two societies. Whereas in Limerick Frank wedded death he is now wedding life. Although Frank has found acceptance in Ireland, as symbolized by the episode with Theresa, there is no possibility for growth or development, the only result being guilt and death. After his odyssey across Limerick and after enduring various hardships on a journey that is reminiscent of the roving hero of the quest and picaresque novels, Frank has finally found his niche and identity in a society into which he fits, and which will allow him to grow.

The dialectic between America and Ireland set up by the circular structure makes for a rather stereotypical depiction of Ireland. America during the Depression is bad, but Limerick is even worse.

---

[25] *Ibid.*, 403.

Easily recognizable are all the common stereotypes of Ireland: it always rains; the men drink too much; the women suffer; and, decades before *Riverdance* made it sexy, the only outlet was rigid, unsensual Irish dancing. Irish dancing as a pastime harks back to the era of De Valera, who encouraged dancing as the ideal expression of the bucolic and innocent in Irish culture. Frank McCourt, who cannot see the value his father and mother attribute to it, prefers to spend the money for the dancing lessons on American movies – yet another example of the juxtaposition of Irish and American culture. At home Frank makes up patriotic names for dances to cover up the fact that he never went to class: "The Siege of Dingle" and "The Walls of Cork"[26] are born. McCourt's treatment of Irish dancing renders De Valera's notion of it as an expression of Irish spirit absurd by setting it against the background of poverty-stricken, urban Limerick.

Yet although the stereotypes are all there, they are not necessarily reinforced. Angela is the long-suffering mother, but she has also got other sides to her. She is arguably the central character of the memoir, and would go to any length to hold her family together. Malachy also is not portrayed only as the absent and alcoholic father. His knowledge and ability to tell stories draw the children to him, and in one scene he is even established as a wise character. When Frank asks him about the meaning of nationality – "What's Jewish?" – he replies, "Jewish is people with their own stories".[27]

What makes the memoir so readable, despite this obvious stereotyping of Irish society, is the introduction of the voice of the child, a narrative technique that was, according to Phillip Lejeune,[28] first introduced by Jules Valle in 1869 in his autobiographical novel *Le Testament d'un blageur*. By employing this technique McCourt manages to give his depiction an innocent immediacy. The child-narrator does not evaluate or question circumstances but recounts the situations with a guileless and moving directness that can be at once extremely funny and heartbreaking. However, towards the end of the novel, McCourt can no longer sustain this voice. When the narrator

26 *Ibid.*, 159-60.
27 *Ibid.*, 28.
28 Phillip Lejeune, *On Autobiography: Theory and History of Literature*, Minneapolis, 1998. Though Lejeune's observation is correct for autobiographical writing, there are earlier examples of an adult narrator managing, by way of retrospective vision, to adopt a tone of childlike immediacy, e.g. Charles Dickens' *Great Expectations* (1860).

reaches puberty, the child's voice becomes less convincing. The reader might prefer on some occasions a more questioning and searching portrayal of Irish society.

By making Ireland the central location for the quest, it is presented as "other" in both temporal and spatial terms. The place where the quest takes place is always outside the subject's community and also a place of the past, as the present happens within the new community and on a higher level. In McCourt's narrative this spatial/temporal division is clearly visible. When the protagonist leaves Ireland his trials are over, he has proven himself worthy to enter America again. Ireland, on the other hand, becomes a location of the past.

McCourt's memoir is a reflection of the exile. The new home and the old society together create the self as a hybrid of two communities. The self belongs in this case more to the American frame, which is signified by the circular structure that has Frank begin and end his personal story in America. As the place of present and future, America is of greater importance. Thus, the frame of the circular quest marginalizes Ireland. At the same time, however, the circular structure secures Ireland a central place, as the plot unfolds here. This ambiguity is particularly apt to express the situation of the exile, which is the reason why the mythic structure of the quest is so suitable to explore the personal history of an emigrant.

McCourt's more unifying vision, which results from his chosen narrative style, is reinforced by the structural frame of the quest. This has the effect of contrasting Ireland with America, thereby glorifying the American dream of a meritocratic society in which everything can be achieved. At the age of nineteen Frank leaves his old life behind him and starts into a promising future. This promise is packed into a single word: "'Tis".[29] The last chapter of the novel consists of only this one word, which provides the answer to the question: "Isn't this [America] a great country altogether?"[30] This prominent placing of the affirmative answer leaves the reader free to guess at the implied wonderful things to come. As in a Hollywood romance that stops with the happy married couple before the altar, here the narration stops at the turning point in the protagonist's life, his arrival in America. *Angela's Ashes* is an ultimately American story, even if it recounts a

---

[29] McCourt, *Angela's Ashes*, 426.
[30] *Ibid.*, 425.

childhood in Limerick. The memoir becomes the myth of the survivor, the one who has found his way out of the ashes. It is a Cinderella story in more ways than one.

ANGELA IN AMERICA:
FRANK MCCOURT'S MEMOIR

PAUL ROBINSON

> It was a book for bad times as well as
> good, which in spite of literary critics,
> was the test of any book.[1]

When Frank McCourt writes about the famine in Ireland in the 1840s, he speaks of *Angela's Ashes* as a book on the subject of physical hunger.[2] The temptation is to read hunger as the governing metaphor of the experience of growing up in the slums of Limerick from 1934 to 1950. But that can be left to those literary critics McGinley alludes to. It would be a far more helpful theme than that found in the review of the *Irish Literary Supplement* that appeared in the issue of Fall 1996: "There's a market for this somewhere." Thus the review of *Angela's Ashes* and Greg Dalton's *My Own Backyard* comes to a close with the faintest praise for McCourt's efforts.[3] The review in a recent publication of the *IASIL Newsletter* trivializes the book beyond recognition. The time frame of the book is placed in "the self-punishing Puritanism of the age of de Valera". Reference is made to another review by a well-known Irish man of letters who finds the book a "strange combination of the remembered with the stereotypical"[4] as both the source of the book's appeal and its problems. I ask here: What problems? If the purity of a literary genre is assaulted by McCourt's efforts, so be it!

---

[1] Patrick McGinley, *The Trick of the Ga Bolga*, London, 1985, 287.
[2] Frank McCourt, "Scraps and Leftovers: A Meditation", in *The Irish in America*, ed. Michael Coffey, New York, 1997, 12.
[3] Robert G. Lowery, "Miserable and Flawed Childhoods", *Irish Literary Supplement* (Fall 1996), 31
[4] "Gardeloo", *IASIL Newsletter* (March 1998), 17.

At this present stage, the immense popularity of the book is
unassailable. A very recent article in *Time Magazine* places the sales
of the book, world wide, at four million.[5] Publishers Clearing House
allows for the calculation of one hundred weeks on the bestseller list
and still counting.[6] Why is *Angela's Ashes* so popular in America and
why is its popularity so lasting?

The experience of being Irish Catholic in America has something
to do with it. The time frame of the Great Depression is an obvious
start. When the McCourt family departed New York for Ireland in
1934, the healing process to the problems of desperate unemployment
had only just begun to ease the crisis under Roosevelt. The Supreme
Court would soon shoot down some of his New Deal solutions. But
the spectre of unemployment, dire poverty, loss of dignity and pride
was measurable throughout the US. There were soup lines and apple
pedlars, clothes unfit to wear, a whole culture of hobos travelling the
rails throughout the land looking for work of any kind. All this in
abundance from the Wall Street crash of 1928 until the war economy
appeared in 1939. Poverty is a relative term, but the degradation in
America was as real, though not as intense, as in the slums of
Limerick.

Another area of common ground, in many instances ignored by the
critics, is the role and place of the Catholic Church in the memoir and
in the lives of Irish Catholic Americans. In what may well be the most
quoted sentence from the book, the author describes his topic as
follows: "Worse than the ordinary miserable childhood is the
miserable Irish childhood, and worse yet is the miserable Irish
Catholic childhood."[7] What the IASIL review refers to as "the self-
punishing Puritanism of the age of de Valera"[8] is the Catholic Church
in action, in both Ireland and the USA during the time frame of the
book. The term, Irish Catholic, in Ireland was very close to being
redundant. The same term used in America is a distinctive description
and represents, depending on the area, anything from zero to forty per
cent of the population. The home diocese where this writer grew up

[5]   Paul Gray, "Raking Up the Ashes", *Time Magazine*, 15 June 1998, 78.
[6]   *Publishers Weekly*. On 26 January 1998, *Angela's Ashes* had been on the best-
      seller list for hardback non-fiction for sixty-nine weeks, and for about one
      hundred weeks by summer 1998.
[7]   Frank McCourt, *Angela's Ashes*, New York, 1996, 11.
[8]   "Gardeloo", 17.

was named by a late archbishop as the least Catholic of any major city outside the South. Only ten per cent of the area's population is Catholic, still a veritable mission for those called to go forth and bring the good news. Did the Irish seminaries and convents respond to the call?

A few Irish facts for an answer: first of all, Irish immigration to America between 1820 and 1920 is estimated at three and a half million people. This same authority observes that by 1920 two-thirds of the American hierarchy were Irish, and the numbers of priests, nuns and brothers exceeded their proportion of the Catholic population.[9] The archivist of the local diocese made it possible to localize and bring up to date the influence of the Irish hierarchy and clergy on the Catholic population hereabouts.[10] Present census figures find forty-five million American are Irish born or of Irish descent.

Here are the names of four bishops and archbishops who have presided since the founding of the Seattle diocese in 1902: O'Dea, Shaughnessy, Connolly and Murphy. None of them was Irish born, by the way, but it is not possible to lose sight of their roots. Coming all from good Irish stock, they did not hesitate to draw on their heritage to school and guide their flocks. Murphy may be the exception, since his time of taking staff in hand and herding the flock came after Vatican II and in the midst of the New Age and after the time-frame of McCourt's book. Vocations to the priesthood and convent dried up, and the original font of spiritual guidance seems to have fallen on very hard times, if figures on vocations and ordinations in Ireland and America are in any way accurate. But that is a problem outside the subject of this paper.

The reader of *Angela's Ashes* who is Irish Catholic in America and has lived within the time frame of the book, *c.* 1932 to 1950, has encountered little about the Catholic Church in the book that is not familiar. And the basis of this is the hierarchy and clergy and their roots at the time. The criticism of the Church in the book is at times stringent, to say the least, but not unfamiliar nor unfair. The myth of the strictness of the Catholic Church in Ireland as a result of

[9]   Laurence McCaffrey, "Irish Catholics in America", in *The Encyclopedia of American Catholic History*, eds Michael Glazier *et al.*, Collegeville: MN, 1997, 696-98.
[10] J. Norman Dizon, Assistant Archivist, Catholic Archdiocese of Seattle; telephone interview, early July 1998.

Jansenism in the French seminaries where the Irish clergy were trained in penal times does not hold up under scrutiny. The puritan strain, if you will, was caused by the good behaviour of the Anglo-Irish Protestants whom the native sons and daughters were forced to emulate lest their behaviour did not measure up to their doomed neighbours. If one wants to transfer such an attitude to Irish Catholicism in America, a path can be found. In the far reaches of the Northwest, for instance, the system called for a separation. Almost all parishes had a school that taught the children to the end of eight grades, and the teachers were nuns. If McCourt attended a school of boy students with men teachers, the subject matter and the values were the same as in the schools in America run by the nuns under the pastor's guidance.

In reading through the memoir, the American Irish Catholic connects with the Limerick experience. At times, the similarity is startling as common methods of teaching religious customs and practices that reflect common values are linked to Frank McCourt's burden: growing up poor and Irish and Catholic.

Here are a few more facts about the Catholic Church in the Northwest. Religious orders of priests, nuns and brothers contributed to stabilizing the Church in this part of the world. There was no Irish national parish in the diocese, but other nationalities such as German, Italian and Polish had their own. But throughout the diocese, priests from Ireland and of Irish descent were ubiquitous. The hierarchy, such as O'Dea, Shaughnessy and Connolly, recruited directly from the Irish seminaries. As late as 1966, Archbishop Connolly submitted a list of fifty-two Irish-born diocesan priests to the Irish American Cultural Institute in St Paul, Minnesota.[11] If one chose to hazard a guess about first-generation Irish in the diocesan ranks, and the number of Irish and first-generation American Irish serving the diocese in religious orders, the number is not insignificant.

The Irish Catholic in America had a very good chance of being schooled and guided in his religion by Irish-born or first-generation Irish American clergy and nuns. Even in areas most remote from Ireland, such as Seattle, Irish seminaries and convents sent their products past the ports of entry to minister to the spiritually needy. The fact that many of the needy were Irish Catholic did not bring

---

[11]   J. Norman Dizon, telephone interview.

anything but a special Irish impact. To this day, the Irish-born clergy
of the diocese meet on St Patrick's Day to celebrate their Irishness and
the history of their ministry to the souls of the Catholics in the
Northwest. One of their group reads the Mass in Irish, the language
referred to as Gaelic by anyone not Irish (something not allowed
during the pre-Vatican II times), to add an emphatic Irish flavour to
the festivities. If this group has a model in McCourt's book, the priest
in the last chapter, who tries to thwart the on-shore party in
Poughkeepsie, serves us well. He is the Irish-born priest serving out
his clerical ministry in America, and not losing the clerical attitude he
was given in the Irish seminary that trained him. Here we concede to
the term "stereotype".

Vestiges of ties to the Catholic Church are found throughout the
book. From a choice of examples, those connected to the Sacrament
of Penance, surrounded by guilt and repentance and their
ramifications, readily relate to the experience of the Irish Catholic in
America and sound the bell of memory for those who made that first
confession and a few thereafter in the process of coming of age.

There is always a problem with the first confession, the nature and
substance of sin. The sins recited in that first trip to the confessional
do not amount to much. Frank O'Connor's short story about such an
experience makes the classic statement. In Frank McCourt's account,
he shares in a competition with his classmates over who committed
the worst transgression. He had listened to the story of Emer winning
the heart of Cuchulain, this in yet another contest. But the priest
assures him, in response to Frank's question at the end of his
confession, that he does not win the "worst sin" award. Not much
guilt, little need of repentance. No waste of time trying to explain
sanctifying grace at this stage. That will come with the preparation for
confirmation. As for the Sixth Commandment, Frank's friend
Clohessy, is equal to the task. When the master asks about the
meaning of adultery, he has the answer. "Impure thoughts, impure
words, impure deeds, sir."[12] Guilt and remorse can come later.

When Frank is sent off to Saturday morning dancing class (is
Riverdance somewhere on the horizon?), with money in his pocket to
pay the fee, the outcome is predictable. He falls in with an evil
companion and the two of them take the fee money and spend it more

---

[12]   McCourt, *Angela's Ashes*, Chapter 4.

wisely, on candy and the cinema. Justice, of course, will out and Frankie's valiant efforts to hide the truth from his parents by making up songs and dances that he "learned" at the dance session come to naught. Included also is that grand old Irish tradition of the informer, one of the members of the dancing class, who hurries the bad news along to the parents. When confronted by them with his dastardly deeds, Frankie tells the shameful truth. The solution to the problem: off to confession! His father takes Frankie to the Redemptorist confessor. The Redemptorist finds going to films bad, dancing almost as bad, but the good father escapes the quandary by zeroing in on "taking my mother's sixpence and lying and there's a hot place in hell for the likes of me, say a decade of the rosary and ask God's forgiveness for you're dancing at the gates of hell itself, child".[13] The confessional has now become a source of guilt and shame rather than release from such feelings.

When our hero at a later time steals the fish and chips off a drunken man, he feels he is in the state of sin for stealing. But, he notes, it is Saturday and the priests are still in the confession boxes: "I can clear my soul after I feed." At his confession, Frank gets the priest's reaction to hearing the sins of the poor: "I should be on my knees, washing their feet. Do you understand me, my child?"[14] He does not understand the priest now, but later he will.

The role of the confessional is ongoing. Quasimodo's mother recommends it for Frank when he is caught in the intent of watching his friend's sisters take their Friday night bath.[15] When he is in the hospital with typhoid, the nun captures and reads the poem that Patricia Madigan has been "feeding" him through the neighbouring wall. Sister Rita's advice to the ne'er-do-well: "I'd be well advised to tell the priest in Confession."[16] When the household is again without food, Frankie steals some lemonade and bread, with the promise to tell everything to the priest in the confessional because it's easier.[17] After a hell-fire and brimstone sermon by the Redemptorist, whose order is famous for its preaching from the pulpit, Frank goes on the lookout

---

[13]   *Ibid.*, 140-45.
[14]   *Ibid.*, 184, 185.
[15]   *Ibid.,* 190.
[16]   *Ibid.*, 198.
[17]   *Ibid.*, 236.

for an easy priest for confession.[18] Nothing new here! One of
Chaucer's priest confessors gained his popularity by giving out light
penances. There comes a stage in the memoirs when the sins pile up.
No comfort, no shortage of guilt. All that is about to change in an
episode before Frank departs for America.

At the Franciscan church with the statue of his patron saint, Frank
is still carrying spiritual burdens that he must set down. After berating
St Francis for not solving his problems, he still dreads the millstone
around his neck. A Franciscan priest comes and sits by his side and
gives Frank courage and a less threatening method of confession.
Frank talks to the statue while Father Gregory listens to Frank's
version of his family history and problems: deaths of his brothers and
sister, the father who did not support the family, sins of self-abuse, the
tears of his mother whom he had slapped that day. Frank kneels for
absolution, is assured that Theresa Carmody was not sent to hell for
her "affair" with Frank the Messenger Boy. Father Gregory's words
capture the essence of the sacrament: "He tells me God forgives me
and I must love myself for only when you love God in yourself can
you love all God's creatures."[19] If Irish Catholics in America are
looking for something profound in their religious heritage from these
memoirs, Frank McCourt responds with these words of Father
Gregory, telling them what growing up Irish Catholic, in Ireland or
America, is all about.

The book's appeal in America is the result of sundry causes, with
the Irish Catholic amidst it all. Frank McCourt has placed the reader in
the time warp of the Great Depression and the wartime economy that
brought both Ireland and America out of it. The abject poverty of his
Limerick childhood is framed in the spiritual values of the Catholic
Church, the same values that Irish hierarchy and clergy and convent
were guarding and projecting in Frank McCourt's land of birth. Critics
have recognized the book's distinguishing quality of presenting the
viewpoint of the child and the young man growing up amidst the
paradoxes and contradictions around him. Should he die for Ireland at
his father's urging or for the Church, as his preparation for
confirmation calls for? The pendulum swings between the ineffable
sadness of childhood death (his brothers and sister, his hospital mate

---

[18] *Ibid.*, 292.
[19] *Ibid.*, 344.

who "will never live to see a gray hair") and the exultant joy of unexpected accomplishment (scoring the winning goal for the Red Hearts of Limerick). Some critics heap mighty praise upon the book and others give it faint praise at best. But if one is waiting for another memoir about an Irish childhood that attains such a popular response, patience and longevity will be strained. The reader who grew up Irish Catholic in America will surely agree.

REGIONALISM

REGIONALISM AND REALISM IN *THE BELL*

MALCOLM BALLIN

In this article I seek to demonstrate how the monthly magazine, *The Bell*, produces its age and its readership as well as reflecting them and how regionalism and realism are related in this process. *The Bell* is unique among contemporary periodicals in English. Other magazines centred themselves around the cultural interests of an educated elite in Dublin or London, but *The Bell* self-consciously incorporates inclusiveness as a value within a "realist aesthetic" which informs the decision-making of its two editors, Sean O'Faolain (1940-46) and Peadar O'Donnell (1946-54).[1] My research into *The Bell*'s place in periodical history, including close examination of its style and content, shows how this magazine created a regional audience for itself. In reaching out beyond the metropolitan centre, it resembled the Irish performative texts of the eighteenth and nineteenth centuries, designed to instigate radical changes in perceptions across the country as a whole, aspiring to speak to and for all classes.[2] This radical stream of periodical writing defines itself in terms of such areas of difference as location, readership and ideology.

The *Bell's* realism, in the historical context of post-revolutionary Ireland, constructs viable political alternatives to the backwards-looking politics of the government of Éamon de Valera. De Valera's picture of the nation is powerfully underwritten by populist sentiment, and stresses the antiquity of Ireland, the Gaelic tradition, the historic links to the saints and the scholars. It asserts the moral superiority of Ireland's rural poverty, especially over the materialism of English

---

[1] Gerard Smyth, "Decolonization and Criticism: A Study of the Relationship between Political Decolonization and Literary Criticism in Ireland, with special reference to the period 1948–58" (Ph.D. dissertation, Staffordshire University, 1994), 87.

[2] Terry Eagleton, *Heathcliff and the Great Hunger: Studies in Irish Culture*, London and New York, 1995, 148.

industrial society.[3] Realism in *The Bell* is about the projection of an alternative, modernizing vision. The ideological position of the magazine can be related to its insistence on realism as an aesthetic imperative. Erich Auerbach, also writing in the 1940s, reasserts the survival of the European humanist tradition in the face of Fascism. In *Mimesis* he sets off realism against fantasy, seeing realism as an inclusive style, mixing genres and opposed to instinctual manifestations of irrationality.[4] *The Bell's* miscellany style is built on similar allegiances to inclusiveness and variety and it underscores O'Faolain and O'Donnell's political opposition to the fantasy images of Ireland projected by the government of the day. O'Faolain is seen by Luke Gibbons as mounting "a strategic shift of the blame for the failure of the revolution from *external* sources – British imperialism – to inherent deficiencies in the native tradition".[5]

A comparable note of cultural aspiration is struck in 1842 when Thomas Davis, in his first editorial for *The Nation*, declares that "journals with all their means and appurtenances were and are to be for many a day the stimulating power in Ireland". Benedict Anderson persuasively asserts the power of print culture in the creation of imagined national communities and in the processes of decolonialization; this theoretical analysis is validated by my examination of journals and their reception.[6] *The Nation's* claimed circulation of thirty-five thousand copies, each, according to Davis, seen by at least ten readers, comprised a newly created audience among "the country people". The development of Daniel O'Connell's reading rooms "encouraged literacy and made it possible for the press to reach people even in the remotest parts of the country".[7] This audience, like that later addressed by *The Bell*, was to be there for other inflammatory successors later in the century, such as the *Irish Felon* or the *United Irishman*. A more direct influence on the editors

---

[3]   Michele Dowling, "'The Ireland that I Would Have': De Valera and the Creation of a National Image", *History Ireland*, 2 (Summer 1997), 37.

[4]   Erich Auerbach, *Mimesis: The Representation of Reality in Western Culture*, Princeton: NJ, 1974, 247.

[5]   Luke Gibbons, "Challenging the Canon: Revisionism and Cultural Criticism", in *The Field Day Anthology of Irish Writing*, ed. Seamus Deane, Derry, 1991, III, 566-68.

[6]   Benedict Anderson, *Imagined Communities: Reflections on the Origin and Spread of Nationalism*, London, 1990, 26.

[7]   Malcolm Brown, *The Politics of Irish Literature: From Thomas Davis to W. B. Yeats*, London, 1972, 67.

of *The Bell*, however, was that exerted by two periodicals edited by
George Russell (AE). *The Irish Homestead* (1905–23), was the voice
of the co-operative movement. It "visualised forms of collective
identity fostered by active citizenship at local level".[8] Its immediate
successor, the *Irish Statesman* (1923–30), for which Sean O'Faolain
wrote his first published work in 1926, was later described by him as
"a paper of an excellence never before or since equalled in Irish
journalism".[9] According to Terence Brown, it "waged strenuous war
against the Irish Irelanders' conception of Gaelic civilization with the
Irish language as the matrix of Irish life" and fought to open Ireland
up to external influences.[10] I would now like to argue that Sean
O'Faolain deliberately placed *The Bell* in this interventionist, radical
tradition.

Sean O'Faolain drew a direct comparison in his second editorial, in
1940, with *The Nation*'s successful first-day reception. His later claim,
in 1944, that each of *The Bell*'s thirty thousand copies is seen by ten
people, and his emphasis on the magazine's appeal to "the country
people", constitute further conscious echoes of Thomas Davis' first
editorial.[11] O'Faolain emphasizes *The Bell*'s achievement of becoming
"the only native periodical open to *everybody*".[12] But who are "the
country people" in 1944? And how does *The Bell* construct a
particular appeal to them? The magazine's outward style, with its
relatively low production values, poor paper (even for the period) and
an accessible price (1s. 6d.) demonstrates its intention to recruit
outside literary and metropolitan circles. Sean O'Faolain's personal
commitment at the time was expressed in a letter to his daughter:

> I was fully integrated because I was on the attack. I had accepted
> responsibility as a citizen and thought of myself as speaking for a
> great silent majority.[13]

[8]   Catherine Nash, "Visionary Geographies: Designs for Developing Ireland",
      History Workshop Journal, No. 45, 73.
[9]   Seán O'Faoláin, *Vive Moi: An Autobiography*, London, 1965, 186; Maurice
      Harmon, *Sean O'Faolain: A Life*, London, 1994, 69 and Alvin Sullivan, *British
      Literary Magazines, III: The Modern Age, 1914–1984*, New York and London,
      1986, 41.
[10] Terence Brown, *Ireland: A Social and Cultural History 1922–1985*, London,
      1985, 121.
[11] *The Bell* I/2 (November 1940), 5; IX/2 (November 1944), 95f.
[12] *The Bell*, I/5 (February 1941), 6.
[13] Harmon, *Sean O'Faolain*, 149.

Realism, in itself, was calculated to make a particular claim on the attention of those thus instantiated as being of themselves the *real* people of the nation. This invocation of the country people, essentially making up a regional audience, attracted the attention of Flann O'Brien, who gently satirizes "the Bellman's" sentimental appeal to "The Plain People of Ireland" from the sophisticated vantage point of his column in *The Irish Times*.[14]

There is further internal evidence of the magazine's relationship to a newly created readership in *The Bell*'s own interrogation of its audience. Responses to a questionnaire included in the May 1945 edition, and reported on in August 1945, confirm impressions of the readership which appear elsewhere in the magazine, in articles by Vivian Mercier and Donat O'Donnell (the pen-name of Conor Cruise O'Brien). These suggest, in Mercier's words, that the magazine had a special appeal to "small town intellectuals", more precisely identified by O'Donnell as typically "teachers, librarians, junior civil servants, the lettered section of the Irish petty bourgeoisie".[15] These readers were caught in the wide-angle lens of O'Faolain's vision of a modernizing Ireland. Peter Denman supports this view, saying that:

> the unremitting focus on Ireland as a whole was *The Bell's* great strength. It was a truly Irish magazine rather than a Dublin one. Its reach extended into the towns and villages throughout Ireland, particularly among those such as national schoolteachers who at the time constituted a cadre of lower-middle-class intellectual meritocracy in the provinces.[16]

Dermot Foley recalls the subversive way in which the magazine was sold under the counter in Ennis when it first appeared in 1940, being privately circulated among friends, eluding censorious eyes.[17] It is clearly actively creating a solidarity among a self-selected minority.

The content and the style of the magazine confirm a range of interest calculated to appeal to a regional readership. Michael Farrell's

---

[14]   Flann O'Brien, *The Best of Myles: A Selection from "Cruiskeen Lawn"*, London, 1993, 79.

[15]   *The Bell*, X/2 (May 1945), 187 (questionnaire); X/5 (August 1945), 431-37 (responses); X/2 (May 1945), 159; XI/6 (March 1946), 1030.

[16]   Peter Denman, "The Little Magazines", in *300 Years of Irish Periodicals*, eds Barbara Hayley and Edna McKay, Dublin, 1987, 134.

[17]   Dermot Foley, "Monotonously Rings the Little Bell", *Irish University Review: A Journal of Irish Studies*, VI/1 (1976), 54.

series of articles on Country Theatre demonstrate the characteristic mix of realism and regionalism. They speak of cultural activities in Dundalk, Wicklow and Kerry. Farrell documents in detail the theatres' finances and administration, as well as the quality of the drama. He records the generosity (or the illiberality) of the local council, and the temerity (or the timidity) behind the choice of play, in the light of the censorship exercised by the local churches. He celebrates, for example, the "remarkable urban standard of co-operation, enterprise and business-man's courage" needed to mount "a torrent of dramatic activity" in the Donegal Festival of October 1944. This included such "strong plays" as *Riders from the Sea, Cathleen ni Houlihan* and Lennox Robinson's *The White Headed Boy,* presented by teams which together, he claims, constitute "a University of North Irish Drama".[18] This claim echoes *The Bell*'s more general ambition to become a kind of academy which turns its readers into writers, active participants in building a discourse of cultural alliance.

Hubert Butler, at one time *The Bell*'s review editor, pays tribute to O'Faolain's generous inclusion of Ulster, in contrast to the centripetal forces within Ireland which tend to concentrate cultural life in the capital so that, as he says, "the whole island was tilted eastwards". Butler planned a successor to *The Bell* to be called the *Bridge*, with an overt policy of eliminating the cultural border with Ulster.[19] *The Bell* actively seeks a redistribution of interest across previously designated cultural boundaries, negotiating a new recognition of the significance of regional populations. Richard Furze notes how *The Bell* worked to break down barriers between North and South; Geoffrey Taylor, the poetry editor, asserts that more than half the poems published come from Ulster.[20] The Ireland of the North found frequent expression in *The Bell,* for example in the work of John Hewitt and in the prose and poetry of Louis MacNeice, who also became, for a time, the poetry editor.

The variety of the South is also widely represented in short stories, poems and documentary, ranging from the verse of an unknown lighthouse-keeper from Donegal, and from Patrick Kavanagh's "stony grey soil of Monaghan" to Frank O'Connor's Cork. Sean O'Faolain

---

[18]   *The Bell*, IX/1 (October 1944), 67; 70.
[19]   Hubert Butler, *Escape from the Anthill*, Mullingar, 1986, 3, 86.
[20]   Richard A. Furze, Jnr, "A Desirable Vision of Life: A Study of 'The Bell': 1940–1954" (Ph.D. dissertation, University College Dublin, 1974), 234; *The Bell*, III/5 (February 1942), 403.

describes in detail the history and the present-day geography of Graignamanagh on the River Barrow, on the borders of County Kilkenny and County Carlow. This romantic evocation of a timeless pastoral scene valorizes a national and cultural landscape, centred in the rural midlands of Ireland, whilst warning that "our wildest fancies about the future of any thing or any place in Ireland are likely to be wrong".[21] Seamus Deane, opposing the concepts of nation and community to those of the mob and the crowd, speaks of the need felt by writers of the Irish Revival to "preserve traditional community values in an era of modernization".[22] Privileging of country values in this context might be read as situating *The Bell* in a debate about the relationship of tradition to modernity, the relation of past and present reality to future possibilities. It also places a distinctive emphasis on regional rather than metropolitan values. *The Bell*, despite being published in Dublin, always displayed more regional interest than other contemporary periodicals, such as David Marcus's *Irish Writing* or *Poetry Ireland,* both of which, although based in Cork, "were never regional publications".[23]

This recourse of *The Bell* to the periphery was not only a matter of geography however. The choice of topics probed into many hitherto unexplored corners of Irish life. The lives of orphans, of tuberculosis sufferers in sanatoria, of schoolteachers under training, the voices of the unemployed and the slum dwellers are all encompassed in *The Bell*'s journalism of record. The realism of *The Bell*'s fiction insists upon the harsher facts of country life, in advance excerpts from Kavanagh's *Tarry Flynn* or Eric Cross' *The Tailor and Ansty.* The life of the jazz club, the dance hall or the dog track is given significance in the life of the modern nation as is the experience of a prisoner, in "I did Penal Servitude" by a writer only identified as D83222. These lives, in the telling of them, become the signifiers of a new linguistic community, celebrated in print and converted into subjects of readerly interest. Adapting Italo Calvino's words, *The Bell* "gives a voice to what as yet has no name, especially to what the language of politics excludes or attempts to exclude".[24]

---

[21]   *The Bell,* X/2 (May 1945), 118.
[22]   Seamus Deane, *Strange Country: Modernity and Nationhood in Irish Writing since 1790,* New York and Oxford, 1997, 119.
[23]   Denman, "The Little Magazines", 135.
[24]   Italo Calvino, *The Uses of Literature: Essays,* trans. Patrick Creagh, San Diego, New York and London, 1993, 98.

O'Faolain mounted a sustained critique of what he termed "the thin society", throughout a post-revolutionary period marked by Ireland's isolation from a global conflict which was further neutralized by being called "The Emergency". This period was one of poor economic performance, high emigration rates, and low living standards, making the Ireland of the 1940s into what Joseph Lee has termed "the most stultifying society in Northern Europe".[25] This isolation of Ireland had a direct effect on *The Bell* and other periodicals of the day. The British Board of Trade order of 1947, preventing the importation of magazines into the UK, both cut Ulster off from Irish publications and, by sealing Irish writers off from a wider public, increased a tendency to introversion in Ireland. This alone probably decided the fate of more literary publications, such as *Envoy,* which nursed greater ambitions for international recognition.[26] Sean O'Faolain's editorials insist as a high priority on the articulation of a clear vision of Ireland's society and on the recognition of regional responses, the realization of which represents some of *The Bell's* most effective writing.

There is however some tension in *The Bell* between regionalism, nationalism and internationalism. O'Donnell's contributions spell out his concerns with the Irish abroad and emphasize the need to "Bring the Exiles Home". O'Faolain's "One World" editorials speak of the need to look outwards to the wider post-war world, with the creation of the European Community and the redefinition of the Common-wealth.[27] *The Bell*, under O'Donnell's editorship, tries to open Ireland to European cultural influences, for example through the writings of François Mauriac or the paintings of Jaroslav Pavelka. One of his later editorials, perhaps reflecting his personal commitment to international socialism, places De Valera's Ireland in the context of what he calls "Our Mythical Fascism".[28] *The Bell* here encounters some of the problems faced by AE's *Irish Homestead*, which, according to Catherine Nash (writing in 1998), "prefigured today's efforts to rethink Irish nationhood or 'postnationalism' through European federalism or the global community of the Irish diaspora".[29]

---

[25] Joseph Lee, *Ireland 1912–1985: Politics and Society*, Cambridge, 1989, 263.
[26] Denman, "The Little Magazines", 136.
[27] See, for example, *The Bell*, IX/1 (October 1944), 1-10 and IX/4 (January 1945), 277-87.
[28] *The Bell,* XV/1 (October 1947), 1-4.
[29] Nash, "Visionary Geographies", 69.

Edward Said has written about how the processes of resistance and decolonization persist beyond the achievement of political independence and how nationalist rhetoric can actually prevent a new state from coming to terms with economic realities. He says that "neither Yeats nor Fanon offers a prescription for making a transition after decolonization to a period when a new political order achieves moral hegemony".[30] Sean O'Faolain was well aware of the transitional state of Irish society in his era, when an abstract and fantasizing idea of Ireland dominated political debate. He argued that "the outstanding thing about the development of a national intellect is the amazing slowness, difficulty and complexity of what we once thought about as a simple process".[31] He recognized the need, in the process of state formation, to redefine national symbolism and to abandon "any of the old symbolic words" which are "as dead as Brian Boru".[32] The complexity and ambivalence of nationalism's construction has been addressed by David Lloyd, who draws attention to the tensions between modernity as a necessary prerequisite for nationalism and the atavism of emotive appeals to a nation's cultural history. He shows how, particularly in the case of Ireland, this led to uneasy relationships between nationalism and "subaltern" discourses such as those of feminism or class.[33] These temporal tensions between modern and ancient models of nationhood generate an area of high energy within which *The Bell* manoeuvres, creating a space for both realist writing and regional interests.

The linked powers of realism and regionalism are both marked by the desire to create a new cultural community in post-revolutionary Ireland, concentrating on what Seamus Deane has called "the creation of a possible future rather than the recreation of an impossible past".[34] This future is firmly rooted in a pluralist vision of the present, in all its variety, extending to all classes and to all areas of the nation. Its emphasis on variety, inclusiveness and the celebration of difference is radically and deliberately opposed against De Valera's singular vision of Ireland, which concentrates on unifying similarities and seeks to elide diversity. Luke Gibbons, in *Transformations in Irish Culture,*

30 Edward Said, *Culture and Imperialism*, London, 1994, 284.
31 Lee, *Ireland 1912–1985*, 629.
32 *The Bell*, I/1 (October 1940), 5.
33 David Lloyd, "Nationalisms against the State", in *Gender and Colonialism*, eds Timothy P. Foley *et al.*, Galway, 1995, 265.
34 Seamus Deane, *A Short History of Irish Literature*, London, 1986, 208.

describes the frontiers beyond which culture does not have a perceptible existence and points out that "to engage in cultural activities where the culture is in the process of being obliterated is to make a political statement". He goes on, later, to suggest that Sean O'Faolain is seeking, in the words of Stephen Daedalus, "to escape from the nightmare of history".[35] Sean O'Faolain created readers in the regions and deflected the conventional stance of the literary magazine in order to command their attention and their loyalty. He had to balance the dangers of cultural isolationism against the need to define the universal in terms of the regional.[36] *The Bell* was successful to the degree that it turned a silent majority into an audience of active readers.

"Reading", says Jonathan Culler, "is not an innocent activity. It is charged with artifice."[37] An editor, whether it is Thomas Davis or Sean O'Faolain, who envisages ten people reading each copy of his magazine is himself creating an imagined audience, a fictive readership. The charged activity of reading *The Bell* in Ireland during the 1940s and 1950s represented an endorsement of a particular aesthetic, a commitment to pluralism, enquiry and to the inclusion of all classes and regions within Ireland's national community. *The Bell*'s journalism of record insists, in Foucault's phrase, upon "writing the history of the present".[38] This represents an engagement with what David Lloyd calls "the contemporaneity of the people".[39] Intervening at a critical juncture between Ireland's dominant past and her newly created present, *The Bell* helped the nation to escape from preoccupation with the effects of colonialism and revolution and envisioned, together with a newly created and culturally influential readership spread through every region of the country, a range of alternative possibilities for Ireland's future.

---

[35]   Luke Gibbons, *Transformations in Irish Culture*, Cork, 1996, 8, 82.
[36]   Furze, "A Desirable Vision of Life", 51.
[37]   Jonathan Culler, *Structuralist Poetics: Structuralism, Linguistics and the Study of Literature*, London, 1975, 129.
[38]   Michel Foucault, *Discipline and Punish*, trans. Alan Sheridan, New York, 1977, 33.
[39]   Lloyd, "Nationalisms against the State", 261.

PUTTING BENEDICT KIELY IN HIS PLACE

THOMAS O'GRADY

Writing in 1966, in a poem entitled "Yeats", Patrick Kavanagh ranges
(typically enough) far enough from his ostensible subject to evoke
(coincidentally enough) Benedict Kiely's image of local poet Andy
McLoughlin, the last bellringer and town crier in Omagh, County
Tyrone, who reportedly "claimed a 'poetic licence' (much as if he had
bought it like a dog licence or, more aptly, a gun licence) to call
everybody names":[1]

> I mean to say I'm not blind really
> I have my eyes wide open as you may imagine
> And I am aware of our boys such as Ben Kiely
> Buying and selling literature on the margin.[2]

Reflective, perhaps, of his own magnanimity, Benedict Kiely never
returned the favour of such a dismissive evaluation – and three
decades after that malignant aside he remains one of Kavanagh's great
apologists.

Reflective, however, of a variety of forces and factors, Kiely's
place relative to the Irish literary pantheon seems truly to be "on the
margin" – his reputation defined by the benign neglect that trends and
tendencies in the market-place and in academia can effect. In part,
this neglect may be attributed to Kiely's public profile: to his being
best known in Ireland as a "personality" in both print and broadcast
media – to his being thought of more as a diverting raconteur than as a
serious littérateur. In the last three decades of this century, however,
this neglect may also be attributed in part to the readerly and scholarly

---

[1]   Benedict Kiely, "The Whores on the Half-Doors", in *Conor Cruise O'Brien
      Introduces Ireland*, ed. Owen Dudley Edwards, New York, 1969, 148.
[2]   Patrick Kavanagh, "Yeats", in Patrick Kavanagh, *The Complete Poems*, ed. Peter
      Kavanagh, Newbridge, 1984, 348.

attention demanded by the emerging chorus of Northern Irish poetic voices – Seamus Heaney, Kiely's fellow Tyroneman John Montague, Derek Mahon, Michael Longley, Paul Muldoon, Medbh McGuckian – which, collectively, effectively drowned Kiely's singular (if not quite solitary) fictional voice out of Ulster. Engaging variously with the North – especially with the contemporary "Troubles" – the poets have individually and collectively composed a literary construct over-shadowing not only competing but also complementary constructions of Ireland north and south.

Obviously, in more immediately recent years a new generation of writers – poets, dramatists, writers of fiction and memoir – have begun to alter the literary landscape of Ireland once again, expanding the notions of Irish experience not only beyond the literal or metaphorical bog (or, perhaps closer to the point, the Bogside), and not only beyond the Pale, and indeed not only beyond the Irish Sea as the island goes "global", but also into previously uncultivated thematic territory: the Irelands left "outside history" by social, cultural and political convention or intention as well as "the hidden Irelands" of domestic discord, of urban squalor, of rural lives of quiet desperation which give the lie to De Valera's vision of "fields and villages ... joyous with the sounds of industry, with the romping of sturdy children, the contests of athletic youths and the laughter of comely maidens".[3] Not quite paradoxically, the accommodating inclusiveness of this recent expansion into the rocky headlands (as it were) traditionally thought of as "on the margin" of the field of Irish literary interests may actually help to put the fiction of Benedict Kiely back on the map – indeed may help to redefine Kiely's "place" closer to the widening "centre" of Irish literary concerns.

The parish and the universe

For while Patrick Kavanagh's complaint against Kiely certainly has its merits, the poet may yet have a blind spot regarding the extent to which the novelist actually embodies the prevailing spirit of another of Kavanagh's unequivocal observations on Irish literature which remains current many decades after its first articulation. Advancing in his short essay "The Parish and the Universe" that "Parochialism and provincialism are opposites", Kavanagh elaborates:

---

[3]   Éamon de Valera, "The Ireland that We Dreamed Of", in *Speeches and Statements by Éamon De Valera*, ed. Maurice Moynihan, Dublin, 1980, 466.

The provincial has no mind of his own; he does not trust what his eyes see until he has heard what the metropolis – towards which his eyes are turned – has to say on any subject .... The parochial mentality on the other hand is never in any doubt about the social and artistic validity of his parish.[4]

Reflecting specifically on his own work, Kavanagh observes, "I realize that throughout everything I write there is this constantly recurring motif of the need to go back"[5] – to return to his own literal parish and literary universe of Iniskeen, County Monaghan; to revisit in his imagination "that first, best country", as Kiely himself has put it, "that ever is at home".[6]

"Whether it is merely the natural result of our being islanders", Kiely mused in his study *Modern Irish Fiction* (1950), "or whether it is the result of decades of compulsory emigration, or for whatever reason, the strongest force in the Irish soul is centripetal".[7] No less than Kavanagh, his fellow Ulsterman like himself transplanted permanently to Dublin by the early 1940s, Kiely has responded to the gravitational pull of place throughout his career as prolific man of letters, returning repeatedly both in person and in his writing to his boyhood territory of Omagh, County Tyrone and environs. In fact, in virtually all of Kiely's writing –whether fiction or non-fiction – one of the most distinguishing characteristics is the potent confluence of the literal and the literary, of the personal and the persona in the spirit he described in his essay "A Sense of Place" in 1982: "the interweaving of love and imagination with locality is something that our ancestors were particularly good at, back to the days of the earliest written records and beyond."[8]

In the early 1990s, Kiely revisited "Omey" through affectionate reminiscence in his memoir *Drink to the Bird*, an anecdotal portrait of the character – and the characters – of the locality which so shaped his remarkably fertile imagination. As he writes in the Introduction: "It has taken me the length of this book and the most of one hundred thousand words to say au revoir to Omagh Town in the County

---

[4] Patrick Kavanagh, "The Parish and the Universe", in Patrick Kavanagh, *Collected Prose*, London, 1967, 282.

[5] *Ibid.*, 283.

[6] Benedict Kiely, "A Sense of Place", in *The Pleasures of Gaelic Poetry*, ed. Seán Mac Réamoinn, Harmondsworth, 1982, 105.

[7] Benedict Kiely, *Modern Irish Fiction: A Critique*, Dublin, 1950, 129.

[8] Kiely, "A Sense of Place", 96–97.

Tyrone, and to the verdant land around that Town and to the people,
therein and thereon, living and dead, that I knew."[9] The fact is that it
has taken Kiely upwards of twenty books – more than a dozen of
fiction and another half-dozen of non-fiction – written over fully half
a century to begin to say that fond farewell to his "first, best country";
and it is his subtle engagement with that specific place as an
affirmation of the parish as the universe that may ultimately locate
Kiely among Ireland's more enduring writers. Indeed, in light of
Kavanagh's dismissive judgement of Kiely – a judgement presumably, and plausibly (if not altogether fairly), based on his five novels
published between 1950 and 1960 – Kiely's return to the townscape of
and the landscape around Omagh at telling points, early and late, in
his career, seems particularly illustrative of Kavanagh's argument that
"Parochialism is universal" because "it deals with fundamentals".[10]

In fact, while individually interesting and ambitious in both theme
and narrative, those five novels – *Call for a Miracle, Honey Seems
Bitter, The Cards of the Gambler, There Was an Ancient House,* and
The Captain with the Whiskers – have in common not only their being
set outside Kiely's native Tyrone but also a stylistic liability
manifested in Kiely's second novel, *In a Harbour Green,* based like
his first, *Land Without Stars,* in and around Omagh. Eventually – that
is, with the publication of the collection *A Journey to the Seven
Streams* in 1963 – Kiely emerged as a compellingly original writer of
short stories, and two subsequent collections – *A Ball of Malt and
Madame Butterfly* and *A Letter to Peachtree* – have ensured him
permanent prominence within that sub-genre of the Irish literary
tradition. Significantly, however, Kiely's narrative method in his
short stories resembles the technique of the fireside *seanchaí* much
more than the sanitized voice associated with modern realist fiction,
and in a typical Kiely story the self-evident pleasure the author takes
in *telling a story* acquires an importance possibly greater than the
thematic impetus of the story itself.[11]

When this same pleasure dominates a novel – as it tends to during
Kiely's writing of the 1950s – the result may be mixed. In *The Cards
of the Gambler,* for example, based in part on the Faust legend and in

[9]   Benedict Kiely, *Drink to the Bird,* London, 1991, 1.
[10] Kavanagh, "The Parish and the Universe", 283.
[11] I have discussed this aspect of Kiely's short fiction at greater length in "Echoes of
      William Carleton: Benedict Kiely and the Irish Oral Tradition", *Studies in Short
      Fiction,* XXVIII/3 (1991), 321-30.

part on a folk-tale Kiely heard in the Rosses Gaeltacht of Donegal, the voice of the *seanchaí* seems altogether appropriate: a *tour-de-force* elaboration on the universal themes of literature (and life) – good versus evil, faith versus doubt, mortality versus eternity –featuring along the way cardsharping, soul-selling, adultery, lashings of drink, and death-defying acts of bravery, this novel acknowledges transparently Kiely's unabashed belief in the virtues of a good tale well told. In contrast, while *Call for a Miracle* presents an intriguing glimpse inside a hidden Ireland – or at least a hidden Dublin, a world of broken bodies and damaged souls (devout believers, jaded journalists, jejune college students, displaced rural innocents) – the intricate web of connections among the characters is too convenient to be entirely plausible (even in Dublin); and despite the narrative frame which allows the first-person narrator to become a third-person protagonist, this conventionally realistic novel becomes a casualty of its internal stylistic conflict between storytelling and novelistic impulses.

Topophilia or topophobia?
In this respect, *Call for a Miracle* both resembles *In a Harbour Green* and highlights a crucial aspect of that earlier novel which might redeem it even by Patrick Kavanagh's critical standards. From one perspective, *In a Harbour Green* seems to embody Jane Austen's famous advice on novel-writing that she gave to her niece:

> You are now collecting your People delightfully, getting them exactly into such a spot as is the delight of my life; – 3 or 4 Families in a Country Village is the very thing to work on – & I hope you will write a good deal more, & make full use of them while they are so favourably arranged.[12]

Assembling a diverse cast of characters – the restless May Campbell, her more easily contented sister Dympna, the worldly solicitor Bernard Fiddis, the disreputable Scots divorcée Alice Graham, the patient and good-hearted Pat Rafferty – Kiely composes a darkly Austen-esque narrative centred around several romantic and social entanglements within this essentially closed circle of acquaintances. And no less than Austen, Kiely cannot resist the urge to resolve the novel's conflicts in altogether tidy fashion, having the manipulative

---

[12]   Jane Austen, *Jane Austen's Letters*, ed. Deirdre Le Faye, Oxford, 1995, 275.

May, pregnant with Pat's child, marry the equivocal Bernard – that potentially delicate matter conveniently de-complicated by Pat joining the British Army and becoming the first casualty from the community in the Second World War. What distinguishes *In A Harbour Green* from Kiely's next few novels, however – and what helps it transcend the neat resolution of its central thematic conflicts – is its firm grounding in Kiely's boyhood town of Omagh. Obviously intrinsic to the novel, this specific setting yet operates as an almost autonomous dimension of the novel, in effect allowing plot to recede into the background while place moves to the foreground as a powerful entity existing quite independently of the lives of the characters.

As such, the setting – or Kiely's recording of the setting – truly transforms this relatively transparent "novel of provincial life" (with all due respect to Flaubert) into a narrative defined by a persuasively "parochial" vision. In his essay "*Genius Fabulae*: The Irish Sense of Place", Patrick Sheeran echoes Kiely's earlier speculation concerning the role of exile in the Irish imagination, observing that Irish "topomania" – truly "a product of the native tradition" – "may well be fostered by displacement":

> The awareness of place *qua* place is especially acute in those who have left it as is shown by Joyce's Dublin, Yeats' Sligo, O'Flaherty's and Ó Direáin's Aran, Ó Cadhain's Iar Chonnacht, Kavanagh's Monaghan, Montague's Tyrone and Heaney's County Derry. It is a quality of awareness that occurs at a fracture point; between being rooted and being alienated, being an insider and an outsider.[13]

Initially, *In a Harbour Green* may seem to exemplify John Wilson Foster's counter-notion that "topophobia", not topophilia, is the dominant impulse behind the literary re-creation of place. Preoccupied with "place as an unseverable aspect of self", Irish literature, Foster argues, has as a recurring theme the phenomenon of

> place transformed into memory of place and therefore transportable. When this theme is conscious, we have that recurring Irish topophobia, hatred of the place that ensnares the self.[14]

---

[13]   Patrick Sheeran, "*Genius Fabulae*: The Irish Sense of Place", *Irish University Review*, XVIII/2 (1988), 198.

[14]   John Wilson Foster, "The Geography of Irish Fiction", in *The Irish Novel in Our Time*, eds Patrick Rafroidi and Maurice Harmon, Lille, 1975-76, 89-90.

Yet as much as Kiely literally exposes in *In a Harbour Green* the claustrophobic texture of life in the 1930s in a provincial town (additionally a British garrison town) – the shallowness, the pettiness, the posturing, the backbiting, the rumor-mongering – and thus seems to be celebrating his own topophobic escape from that town, he does so with such care, with such attention to the warp and weft of the fabric of the world that he knew there so intimately, that the novel ultimately affirms (perhaps for better and for worse) that crucial social and artistic validity of the parish that Kavanagh describes.

Of course, Foster might challenge such an affirming reading of place in *In a Harbour Green*, arguing that even when the theme of escape is not conscious, even when a writer seems to be expressing a love of place, he or she is really expressing

> a love of self which only in the short run contravenes the theme of self-escape. Ultimately, the Irish writer's concern with place is evidence of a subjectivity he is unwilling or unable to transcend. The richer the imagination the more expansive and decorative the captivity.[15]

The fact that Kiely would shortly abandon his native Omagh as valid – or at least viable – novelistic territory and set his next half-dozen novels elsewhere (in or around Dublin, in the Midlands, in the composite landscape of *The Captain with the Whiskers*) would seem to support Foster's argument.

Yet the spirit prevailing in Kiely's first novel – a spirit of proud authorial proprietorship toward Omagh and its surrounding countryside – seems still to hover over *In a Harbour Green*. Involving a more integrated sense of plot and place than his second novel – a less apparent distinction between foreground and background – *Land Without Stars* also features a more integrated sense of storytelling simplicity and novelistic weightiness. Focusing centrally on two brothers, Davy and Peter Quinn, and their competitive pursuit of the lovely Rita Keenan, the novel incorporates into their narrative a detailed depiction of life – domestic life, personal life, social life, political life – in Omagh at the start of the Second World War.

---

[15]   *Ibid.*, 90-91.

In a "Retrospect" written for the novel's reissue in 1990, forty-four years after its first publication, Kiely wonders about the innocence that permeates the life he records; and perhaps with literal retrospect that very innocence is what is at stake in the novel. For while the world of Davy and Peter – the streets of the town, Rita Keenan's dance parlour, the squalid hut shared by a pair of filthy hermits, the Rosses area of Donegal where Gaelic enthusiasts holiday and study Irish – is presented with veristic scrupulosity, the novel actually reads as a prophetic parable of forces much more powerful than sibling rivalry. In short, the drama involving the cerebral spoiled priest Peter and the earnest IRA man Davy vying for the affections of Rita Keenan embodies Kiely's projection of how the forces – essentially, intellectual-cultural and militant-political – within the Catholic nationalist community in post-Partition Northern Ireland are aligned in their competition to woo and win the elusive spirit of Ireland, conventionally feminized.

Presumably, the resolution of this drama also reflects Kiely's own bias in this matter; for while he casts Davy the revolutionary in a sympathetic light, as well-intentioned though misguided, he also has him killed by the Constabulary at the end of the novel, thus permitting Peter to claim Rita unopposed.

Yet the novel closes somewhat ambiguously, with Davy's more ruthless partner Dick Slevin still on the run and with Peter relocating to Dublin, leaving Rita to wait for his summons. Significantly, for Peter – as for Benedict Kiely himself – Dublin seems to represent the future; or perhaps it just represents the vantage point from which to gauge the future of Ulster, that "land without stars".

"That first, best country" revisited
In the decades following the publication of *Land Without Stars* and *In a Harbour Green*, Kiely continued to write specifically and evocatively about Omagh and vicinity in his short fiction, seemingly substantiating the premise he advanced in 1947 concerning his acknowledged literary forefather William Carleton. Musing on Carleton's "record of the joys and the desolation of the Irish" in *Poor Scholar*, his book-length study of Carleton published a year after the publication of *Land Without Stars*, Kiely makes an observation that may begin to illuminate his own intermittent engagement with their common "first, best country" in his longer fictional narratives:

Always the writing of that record, at its best and most vivid and most colourful moments, involved a certain return to the boy lost for ever in the Ulster valley that the young man abandoned for ever when he went recklessly on the world. He said that something always drew him back to the scenes of his youth, to his native hills and glens, to the mountains and lakes and the precipices that turned his memory into "one dreamy landscape, chequered by the clouds and sunshine of joy and tears". The mountains remained unchanged, made always the same appeal to the returning heart. The river that ran twisting through the hazel glen could never hurt him as the world could hurt him.[16]

In his retrospective Introduction to *Land Without Stars*, Kiely comments on how a particular scene in the novel "reads now even to me, like a fragment from William Carleton and, perhaps, I myself am a figment of Carleton's imagination, or he mine".[17] Certainly, a Carleton-esque temper continues to inform Kiely's short stories – both stylistically, in their adopting and adapting elements of the oral tradition of Irish storytelling, and thematically, in their affectionate rendering of the social and physical landscape of south-east Ulster. Indeed, "A Journey to the Seven Streams", the title story of Kiely's first collection, takes considerable licence from the peripatetic style and the essentially grotesque humour of Carleton.[18]

The account of a comically ill-fated family excursion – an attempt to "circumnavigate the globe" of southern Tyrone to indulge the "mild and gentle air of proprietorship"[19] of the narrator's father concerning his native territory – proceeds as unpredictably as the journey itself, the incessant and discursive "raconteuring" of the father aptly mimetic of an itinerary constantly revised by the humours of Hookey Baxter's crossbreed of an automobile hired by the narrator's family. There are "few places that day Hookey's motor machine did not honour with at least some brief delay",[20] and finally a punctured tyre deflates the remains of the family's expedition; but as the tangential or trivial

---

[16] Benedict Kiely, *Poor Scholar: A Study of the Works and Days of William Carleton*, New York, 1948, 46.

[17] Benedict Kiely, *Land Without Stars*, Dublin, 1990, iii.

[18] I have discussed this dimension of Kiely's fiction at greater length in "'A Ball of Malt and Madame Butterfly': Benedict Kiely's *Opéra Grotesque*", *Recorder*, VII/1 (1994), 124-34.

[19] Benedict Kiely, "A Journey to the Seven Streams", in Benedict Kiely, *The State of Ireland: A Novella and Seventeen Stories*, Boston, 1980, 84.

[20] *Ibid.*, 95.

minutiae of this tour-guide commentary at Clanabogan typify, the narrator's father remains equal to the various diversions, digressions, and disruptions of the afternoon:

> – Clanabogan planting, he said.
> The tall trees came around us and sunlight and shadow flickered so that you could feel them across eyes and hands and face.
> – Martin Murphy the postman, he said, who was in the survey with me in Virginia, County Cavan, by Lough Ramor, and in the Glen of Aherlow, worked for a while at the building of Clanabogan Church. One day the vicar said to him: "What height do you think the steeple should be?" "The height of nonsense like your sermons", said Martin, and got the sack for his wit. In frosty weather he used to seal the cracks in his boots with butter and although he was an abrupt man he seldom used an impolite word. Once when he was aggravated by the bad play of his wife who was partnering him at whist he said: "Maria, dearly as I love you there are yet moments when you'd incline a man to kick his own posterior."
> – There's the Church, my father said, and the churchyard and the haunted gate and the cross-roads.[21]

Crucially, however, as Kiely intimates in *Drink to the Bird*, the landscape which he once shared with Carleton has changed utterly since his boyhood in the 1920s and 1930s. For while virtually all of Kiely's reflections in his memoir originate in recollections of Omagh town during those decades, many of them culminate with a painful glance toward the euphemistically-called "Troubles" of contemporary Northern Ireland. Typically, a humorous anecdote involving the backwater village of Plumbridge concludes in unexpected fashion:

> My father, who had soldiered on far foreign fields, would say when he looked on some poor fellow who was particularly awkward in his ways: "They wouldn't have him in the Plumbridge militia."
> There never was a Plumbridge militia.
> Plumbridge, he meant, was in the heart of the wilderness. Or in the garden of Eden. Same thing?
> Yet not so long ago the Provos had a bomb there.
> Plumbridge had joined the world. And the new Ireland.[22]

---

[21] *Ibid.*, 94.
[22] Kiely, *Drink to the Bird*, 100.

In Kiely's case, then, unlike Carleton's, the "hurt" that ultimately compelled him to return in an extended narrative to "the river that ran twisting through the hazel glen" – to his native province, county and town – was the terrorist desecration of a place that he, like his fictionalized father in "A Journey to the Seven Streams" and (perhaps more symbolically) like Peter Quinn in *Land Without Stars*, still held a proprietary claim on. Indeed, published in 1977, more than a quarter-century after *In a Harbour Green*, *Proxopera* is infused from start to finish with a truly righteous anger not only expressed by the heroic protagonist Mr Binchey but embodied by the novella in its entirety. "To have your own stream on your own lawn is the height of everything" the third-person limited narrative proposes,[23] the broken tranquillity of a retired schoolteacher's golden years serving as a vital trope for the violation of place – of the sanctity of place – that the descendants not of Davy Quinn but of Dick Slevin have perpetrated. "These morons," Mr Binchey thinks, "have blighted the landscape, corrupted custom, blackened memory, drawn nothing from history but hatred and poison."[24]

Holding Mr Binchey's family hostage to his completing a "proxy operation" – the delivery to the nearby town of a bomb hidden in a milk can – the IRA men are cast as far from idealists; in Kiely's mind – as articulated through Mr Binchey's mind – the militant aggression of these cowardly pseudo-patriots becomes as much a personal as a moral transgression: "The world is in wreckage and these madmen would force me to extend that wreckage to my town below, half-asleep in the valley, my town, asleep like a loved woman on a morning pillow, my town, my town, my town."[25] Not just rightly but righteously, Mr Binchey balks at completing the proxy bombing, and though the terrorists burn down his house in their wake, by his rightful action which saved his town – and thus an essential part of his self – he is nonetheless left with "the most beautiful thing of all, cutting across a corner of the lawn, a small brook tumbling down to join the lake".[26]

---

[23] Benedict Kiely, *Proxopera: A Tale of Modern Ireland*, Boston, 1987, 10.
[24] *Ibid.*, 60.
[25] *Ibid.*, 76.
[26] *Ibid.*, 94.

Genius loci

Using Mr Binchey as the centre-of-consciousness for this remarkably lyrical narrative, Kiely composes in *Proxopera* an unabashedly nostalgic engagement with place which yet registers true to the present as well as the past. In 1978, the year after his novella appeared, Kiely published an altogether satisfying travelogue, *All the Way to Bantry Bay – and Other Irish Journeys*, which traces – with plausible detours along the way – a very practicable itinerary from his birthplace in Dromore, County Tyrone to Bantry Bay and the Ring of Kerry on the far south-western coast of Ireland. But as the foreword to the book portends in announcing that "These journeys or revisits begin in the north in the spring of 1969 before the horrors began in that part of Ireland",[27] many of Kiely's reflections on place in this book are ultimately affected by the exacerbated climate of sectarian differences and paramilitary terrorism which would define Northern Ireland over the next three decades. As numerous glances toward or digressions about contemporary Ulster suggest, Kiely is seeking through revisiting "places that have always pleased" him some sort of solace from "the Troubles" of "home": "Will holy Ireland ever," he asks, gazing meditatively into the River Bann at Toomebridge, "or should she ever, forget the story of the young girl who went shopping for her trousseau and brought her sister along with her, and met with gelignite upon the way, and the bride-to-be lost both legs and one arm and one eye? Her sister merely lost both legs."[28]

Obviously, this story would continue to haunt Kiely all the way into his novel *Nothing Happens in Carmincross*, published in 1985. Reworking the real-life village of Killeter into the fictional Carmincross, Kiely employs a quasi-picaresque narrative centred on an Irish-born American college professor returning to the North for his niece's wedding to reflect once again on the loss of innocence as a major by-product of the Troubles. Generally dissipated, disappointed in his domestic life, and now suddenly involved with Deborah, a woman from his past who is also unhappily married, Mervyn (who sometimes refers to himself facetiously as Merlin) sets out for Carmincross as if on a magical quest. For Mervyn, anticipating the reunion with his mother, his sister, and especially the bride-to-be Stephanie, Carmincross is the earthy equivalent of Carleton's "river that ran

27   Benedict Kiely, *All the Way to Bantry Bay – and Other Irish Journeys*, London, 1978, 11.
28   *Ibid.*, 34.

twisting through the hazel glen" or Mr Binchey's "small brook tumbling down to join the lake" – a backwater retreat from the hurtful world. Imagining himself and Deborah as Diarmuid and Grainne, and Deborah's husband as the jealous Finn, Mervyn longs for the serenity and the security that he clearly associates with the familiar place in a former time. Of course, in life (or in this case, in literature) as in legend, Diarmuid fails in his quest. For – for Kiely – Carmincross is another Plumbridge; and almost needless to say, the planned wedding never takes place as, posting the last of her wedding invitations, the intended bride gets blown to pieces by a bomb planted in a mailbox: like Plumbridge, Carmincross "had joined the world. And the new Ireland."

In other words, in a perverse inversion of Patrick Kavanagh's notion, the universe has become the parish. Yet through the very act of bearing righteous witness to this change, in refusing to stray from what Kavanagh calls "fundamentals", Kiely locates himself in the good company of those many Irish writers who continue to keep faith in "that first, best country" of the parish. "Which came first: the place or the poet?" he asks in *Yeats' Ireland*[29] in 1989 – like the earlier *Ireland from the Air*, a place-centred pictorial compilation that he wrote the commentary for. Coincidentally enough, he had already provided the answer to that question in (typically enough) the form of another question posed in *All the Way to Bantry Bay*. Reflecting on Donegal, a region of Ireland only newly discovered by "the world" – in this case relatively benign tourists – but long famous for its writers (most recently playwright Brian Friel) who, without succumbing to mere regionalism, have truly responded to its distinctive regional character, Kiely wonders:

> But will all the summer people respect the genius of the place: that is the *genius loci*, not Brian himself, nor Peadar O'Donnell even, nor the brothers O Grianna, Seamus, Seosamh and Sean Bán of the sweet voice, nor that courageous wanderer Patrick MacGill, but the thing that makes them all what they are: the spirit that lives in and the voice that speaks from rock, and from thornbush twisted and thwarted by the wind, and in evening by lonely little lakes with the gulls crying around them; the ghosts of memories at the corners of

---

[29] Benedict Kiely, *Yeats' Ireland: An Enchanted Vision*, New York, 1989, 9.

roads and old homesteads, small fields and gardens walled stoutly against the Atlantic wind? That's a long question.[30]

It is also a rhetorical question, one clearly implying Benedict Kiely's confidence in his own response not just to the *genius loci* of his place but as the *genius loci* – as the tutelary spirit of that place, his parish as universe.

---

[30] Kiely, *All the Way to Bantry Bay*, 89.

IRELAND AND THE SEA:
WHERE IS "THE MAINLAND"?

KRISTIN MORRISON

Despite her ancient nautical heritage, contemporary Ireland is not
thought of as a significant seafaring nation. This puzzling phenomenon raises many questions. I have time here to explore only one: how
does the fact that Ireland is surrounded by water manifest itself in
contemporary fiction, in those published narratives by which we tell
ourselves about ourselves (whether wrongly or rightly) and indulge
the fantasies that provide patterns for belief and action?[1] In particular,
how does this fiction conceive of a "mainland"? What is the relation
between various islands and that mainland? In playing with these
questions, I will consider two recent but quite different prose
narratives: Bernard MacLaverty's novel, *Grace Notes* (with its
interest in Ireland and Scotland, mediated by the Hebridean island of
Islay) and Jerome Kiely's tales of Inishbofin, *Isle of the Blest* (with its
echoes of ancient stories such as *The Voyage of Mael Dúin*).

But first a few general observations. When we begin to examine
the very broad topic of Ireland and the sea, two opposing phenomena
present themselves: the early Irish as seafaring pioneers, and the
contemporary Irish as supposed landlubbers. The marine historian G.
J. Marcus, in his book *The Conquest of the North Atlantic*, asserts that
"the earliest recorded ventures into the Western Ocean were ... made
from Ireland",[2] then goes on to elaborate and document this assertion
with careful scholarship. Now, juxtapose that early pioneering
achievement with what another marine historian cites as a serious
contemporary deficit: John de Courcy Ireland complains that the Irish
Free State "absolutely turned its collective back on the sea ... our

---

[1]   This essay is part of a book I am currently writing on Ireland and the sea in
contemporary Irish fiction.

[2]   G. J. Marcus, *The Conquest of the North Atlantic*, New York, 1981, xiv.

leaders concentrated their minds largely on the countryside and forgot our coast and the waters washing it",[3] neglecting even to this day to establish an office for the making and updating of nautical charts for local waters. And, of course, there is much popular comment on both sides of this issue: the Irish touted as the earliest discoverers of America; the Irish taunted as insular.

Medieval accounts of early Irish mariners describe them as voyaging over the sea with delight,[4] an observation in marked contrast to Maura's cry in Synge's *Riders to the Sea* that there is nothing else the sea can do to her. After a dozen or so centuries one would, of course, expect some differences. What I will explore here is a tiny fraction of the issue: not the actual nature of those differences between ancient and modern attitudes toward the sea, nor their causes. Early voyage narratives have been widely studied, stories of St Brendan, Bran, Mael Dúin, and the O'Corra. But what of the mass of literature produced now: how does the fact that Ireland is surrounded by water manifest itself in stories today? Or does it? What do we find in contemporary Irish fiction when we "row around" in it?

Most noticeable is the fact that there are virtually no writers of modern voyage narratives – no Irish Joseph Conrads, no Irish Herman Melvilles – and very few novels or short stories in which sea-going moments figure importantly. Emily Lawless, of course, reckoned with a fateful and dangerous passage in her 1892 novel *Grania*; Erskine Childers wrote with stunning accuracy of espionage and navigation in *The Riddle of the Sands*; Peadar O'Donnell favourably juxtaposed the adventurous marine experience of island folk to the conservatism of mountainy people in *The Big Windows*. There are these and other exceptions, such as the novels of James Hanley and the recent thriller, *Undertow*, by Tom Foote, but not enough to offset the observation that seagoing, actual voyaging, does not figure prominently in the literature of twentieth-century Ireland.[5] And yet, the sea is still there.

---

[3] *Ireland's Maritime Heritage*, ed. John de Courcy Ireland, Dublin, 1992, 44; see also his remark in John de Courcy Ireland, "The Contribution of Seamen of Irish Birth or Descent to Hydrography", in *Atlantic Visions*, ed. John de Courcy Ireland, Dublin, 1989: "... the separate Irish state, set up in 1922 has not been inspired by the achievements of the great Irish hydrographers of the past or by concerns for its own interests to set up its own hydrographic service" (189).

[4] Gildas quoted in Marcus, *Conquest of the North Atlantic*, 16.

[5] Throughout recent Irish fiction, the sea (which makes the very concept of "mainland" possible) itself remains a puzzling presence, an even more puzzling absence. Invoked sometimes as folk motif and archetype (as in the stories of

If actual voyaging does not provide subject or venue, are there other ways in which the sea figures in contemporary fiction? Often, it seems to me, the sea serves as indispensable witness or catalyst. In dozens of novels and stories published in recent decades, characters stop by the sea for some important conversation; they may simply sit in their cars and look out at the water, or they may actually walk along the beach, but that location, not a field, not a meadow, not a mountain side, often serves as the place of realization or confrontation. For example, in Mary Dorcey's novel *Biography of Desire*, one character suggests to another that they walk along the shore: "I need to think [she says]. And I always see things more clearly when I walk by the sea."[6] In a variety of subtle ways this explicitly stated phenomenon permeates both the plot and the texture of imagery throughout that novel. So, too, with Neil Jordan's *Sunrise with Sea Monster*, Colm Tóibín's *The Heather Blazing*, Angela Bourke's *By Salt Water*, to name but a few.

Any of these books would serve to illustrate my point that the sea now serves as witness and catalyst, a psychological rather than a physical route somewhere. But Bernard MacLaverty's new novel, *Grace Notes*,[7] provides a particularly apt example. The pivotal scene in the narrative occurs on a beach situated at the top of the triangle marking out the main character's odyssey: Catherine has moved from County Derry to Glasgow by way of Islay, that Hebridean island lying north of both her childhood home and her adulthood city. Straight across the Moyle (the North Channel) is the direct route, from one mainland to another; but she needed this island detour in order to make a more important psychological and moral transition.

A large number of personal and social issues inform this complex novel: sectarian differences, prejudices, and violence in Northern Ireland; religious faith either as a matter of dogma or a matter of individually chosen values and images; music as an art combining formal properties and deep passions; rhythm as an essential component not only of music but of life itself, nature itself; the

---

Angela Bourke), rendered sometimes as essential scenery (as in the work of William Trevor), and sometimes, though less frequently, personified as implacable foe or erotic analogue (as in the work of Liam O'Flaherty), for the most part Irish writers of the twentieth-century keep their toes out of the sea even when they walk along its edge; very few venture on to it.

6   Mary Dorcey, *Biography of Desire*, Dublin, 1997, 201.
7   Bernard MacLaverty, *Grace Notes*, New York, 1997.

difficulty of realizing personal talents and fostering interpersonal
relationships; and, especially for women, the difficult balance of
motherhood and genius. All these summarized generalizations are
actually presented with great subtlety in the novel as written.
MacLaverty presents Catherine's life in a voice centred on her own
consciousness, while she remembers a childhood in Derry both loving
and stifling, her pursuit of her musical talents, encouraged by kind
parents who are, however, unwilling to let her follow her own route;
her need to break with them by simply not returning to Northern
Ireland after her studies; her liaison in Islay with a man whose charm
turns cruel with drink; her flight from him, taking their infant daughter
Anna with her as she settles permanently in Glasgow; her triumph
there as a composer. Most of the novel is told in retrospect, beginning
in the present with Catherine's brief return to Northern Ireland for her
father's funeral and ending with the moment of her brilliant concert in
Glasgow a few months earlier. Between these two events, Catherine's
odyssey occurs and her sense of "mainland" develops.

MacLaverty abundantly laces the narrative with two sets of images
and references. First, sounds of all kinds: long before the reader
knows Catherine is a musician, the novel presents her acute awareness
of sounds (a man whistling, an engine note going up an octave, the
physical mechanics of a baby's cry); this inclusion of sounds
continues throughout the narrative, climaxing in the concert.

Equally important is the second set of images and references, to
islands and to the sea. The two sets are frequently brought together as
Catherine likens the rhythms of music to the rhythms of the sea (145),
with the same shifting variety: tides, waves, ripples (129); she even
hears the "music" of the recitation of the rosary at her father's wake to
be "as ceaseless as the pounding of the sea" (57).

These references to sounds and to the sea occur very frequently, on
almost every page, but subtly, integral to the narrative and to the
texture of the sentences that convey it. There are some passages,
however, that demand explicit attention to these sound and sea
references, one of the most important being that pivotal scene I
referred to earlier. On the morning after Catherine has been badly
punched in the face by her drunken lover, she goes for a long walk on
a deserted beach far from her cottage: "To her left-hand side, the
West, was the open ocean – to her right the beach, backed by tall sand
dunes with grey grass hissing in the dry wind, nothing else". Truly a
liminal space, the margin between earth and water. And yet she is not

completely cut off from her past, as the third element conspires to remind her: "The air was so clear that Ireland looked close, like a further headland rather than a different island. The Land of Saints and Scholars and Murderers" she thinks (204). As she walks with Anna on her back, she gradually sheds her sandals, her clothes, and finally mother and daughter bathe naked together in the sea, lie in the sun together by the sea.

For the first time in the year since Anna's birth, Catherine's postpartum depression lifts, she begins to feel good again, and the rhythms and notes of what will become her masterpiece begin to present themselves. The day marks a turning point in Catherine's emotions about her role as mother, her creative life as composer, her right to refuse punishment, her faith in herself.

This day by the sea, washed in the sea, gives Catherine the confidence to leave the abusive Dave, to accept and to unite her daughter and her music (the composition will be dedicated to Anna), and to choose for herself the city where her life will flourish: not Derry, not Belfast, but Glasgow will be her "mainland".

Lest it be thought that references to the sea and to the rhythms of the waves form such an obvious set of metaphors to describe music that it has no particular significance in itself, let me just point out that there is another section of the novel in which similar usage might have occurred and didn't. MacLaverty allots eight full pages to Anna's birth (156-64), describing Catherine's experience in detail, without once likening the pain, the contractions to waves. This is, in fact, almost the only extensive section of the novel in which there are no marine images.

Most of Catherine's various crossings of the waters around Northern Ireland and Scotland have been by plane: she flies from Glasgow to her father's funeral and back; she flies in special ambulance plane from Islay to Glasgow, for Anna's birth. The only actual crossing by boat mentioned (though not described) is Catherine's departure from Islay as she abandons Dave; then, with her boxes of books, records, household items, she uses the conventional mode of island transport, the ferry. Waiting to see if the weather will allow sailing, Catherine reflects on something she has learned on Islay because it is an island:

> At home in Northern Ireland [the weather] had meant nothing to her, it was either windy or not but since coming here she had learned the

> nuances, the difference between Force Ten and Eleven, between
> Gale and Storm, what to expect if the wind was from the north-east
> or the west. From such things you knew whether or not you would
> have fresh bread the next day. (234)

This simple fact of bread or no bread is reality, unlike the advice of
the relaxation tape she had used to try to cope with her depression:
"Imagine yourself on an island" (201) it drones in useless idealization.
But the real island, Islay, with its unavoidable sea, has taught
Catherine an effective lesson.

This detour, this time out on Islay has given Catherine a sense of
reality, a sense of wholeness. The sea has been witness and catalyst
for that transition. And, even more than that, its rhythms are at the
center of what she is, what her music is, "synchronized with the sea"
(274). The climax of the novel and of her life thus far comes in the last
few pages where her triumphant concert is described; along with other
instruments Catherine has included Lambeg drums, not as a political
statement, but as terrific producers of pure sound:

> The Lambegs have been stripped of their bigotry .... On this
> accumulating wave the drumming has a fierce joy about it – Passion
> and pattern ... the effect is as she had hoped for. Her baby. *Deo
> Gratias*. Anna's song. (276)

Catherine has found her own voice, her own music, her own faith –
in a composition esoterically titled "Vernicle", meaning pilgrim's
badge, a proof of endurance, accomplishment, survival. But her
working title had been much more straightforward; the simple phrase
"By the Sea" acknowledged not only her source of inspiration but also
something deep within herself, as she embraces her chosen mainland
in Scotland, her chosen way of life.

I want to contrast this sophisticated novel, *Grace Notes*, with a
much more typical piece of writing about islands and mainlands,
Jerome Kiely's *Isle of the Blest*.[8] This book reads like a popular
memoir and certainly may be highly autobiographical, since the author
is a priest who had been posted to a western isle writing about a priest
posted to a western isle. But much about it suggests a loosely
structured novel, made up of a series of stories from the local oral
tradition. Although Kiely names his island Inish Capaill (horse

---

[8]   Jerome Kiely, *Isle of the Blest*, Cork, 1993.

island), its location, geography, historical monuments and local tales are those of Inishbofin, the "cow" of Inishbofin becoming the "horse" of Inish Capaill. Both the real island and Kiely's fictionalized one are located opposite or near Clew Bay; both have the ruins of one of Cromwell's castles at the harbour entrance; both have a covered blowhole, a place in which priests were said to have been imprisoned in the seventeenth century; both have ruins of an ancient monastery of St Colman, with tales about dissension between his Saxon and Celtic followers; both have tales of a chain across the harbour associated with Grainne O'Malley and Don Bosco; both have a story about St Festin; and a story about Michael Hayes, betrayed by a woman's gossip. (Oddly enough, right after reading Kiely's *Isle of the Blest* I picked up a book compiled by the Inishbofin Heritage Project and was struck by the great similarity between the two volumes, in the actual information supplied, though not in the style or organization.)

But Kiely's book, whatever the source, is clearly a novel, the plot shaped at beginning and end by the narrator's arrival and then his departure seven years later. In between he recounts a series of experiences, touching anecdotes of simple faith and peasant customs, involving vivid characters, types colourfully detailed. Fresh from Maynooth, the young priest thinks of his new post as a sort of Hy Brasil (7) – and, indeed, in his years there finds it an "isle of the blest".

For my purposes in thinking about mainlands, what is striking about the book is the pervading sense that Inish Capaill is a place different from Ireland, not really the same country. At one point, the narrator refers to Inish Capaill as Ireland's "little neighbour" (22), and one of the local tales refers to St Festin and his five companions washing the sand of Ireland off their feet before rowing out there to live a life of hardship (37).

You find this sort of attitude expressed in many island narratives, most notably in those from the Blaskets and from the Aran islands, a sense that people who have to contend daily with the sea are essentially different from those who remain on land. This difference is well expressed in Kiely's narrator's remarks about Jamsey Prendeville, in a long chapter titled "God's Good Skipper", full of anecdotes about this pious and excellent sailor from his youth to old age:

> One advantage the sailor's son has over the farmer's son is that the
> sailor hands over the boat while the son is still a young man: the
> driving seas hustle him into making his decision. But the land is an
> old man's ally and it doesn't rise up in strength like the wind to tell
> him that a young man would fight it better. So at an age when
> farmers' sons couldn't set fire to a furze bush without being told,
> Jamesy was standing at the tiller of his own boat, masterful in eye
> and hand. (113)

This ability to thrive in hardship is part of what island folk see as their
distinguishing feature, they in the twentieth century and St Colman's
monks in the seventh all seeing in the "roar of the waters and the
breakers of the sea" the power of God enabling them to heroic deeds
both of body and of spirit (62). In this regard *Isle of the Blest*, though
not a voyage narrative, is a bit like accounts of St Brendan and Mael
Dúin, full of wonders. For example, an anecdote recounted by the
narrator concerns a priest in 1653 imprisoned by Cromwell's troops in
that infamous blowhole I mentioned earlier; though nearly starved to
death, he supposedly dives into the rocky sea from a great height and
swims out to a French cutter sailing along the coast, is rescued, and
gains his freedom (71). Such a feat for someone in good form is
virtually impossible; for a starving man, the stuff of sagas.

Another even more wonderful story involves a pregnant woman,
stranded on a bleak rock in the sea in a gale for eight days, giving
birth huddled against the crumbled walls of an ancient monastery, she
and her child not only surviving the ordeal but actually rescued later
by her husband who had innocently deposited her there while he
fished. The boy was christened Festin (for the saint of that monastery)
but actually called "Mananán after the Celtic god of the sea" (48). The
unaccountable robe with which he was covered when his mother
awoke alone in the storm after his birth was treated as a relic by the
islanders, and the boy himself became a miraculous fisherman, able to
talk to the fish "in their native tongue and coax them on to his hooks"
in vast numbers (47). No, not a medieval legend, but an event
supposedly within living memory of Kiely's narrator's parishioners.

Not all the tales in *Isle of the Blest* are hagiographic or heroic,
however. The chapter titled "Men Put Asunder" is about a very nasty
old woman, Agnes Lynch, who ruins her adult children's lives in
various ways and drives her daughter's husband to suicide over the
cliff, into the water. This tale, like the rest in the volume, is full of sea
references, for example, the depression Agnes generates is likened to

"being driven by a fierce gale" (103). This dark story, one of the longer sections of the book, gives point to the anxieties of the narrator's fellow seminarians, cited before his appointment: "An island was all very well, they felt, in the days of saints" (8) but now it seems an "Alcatraz" (9).

Ireland is an island; and it has its own subsidiary islands. Where, then, is the mainland? The matter is all relative, of course. For the characters in Emily Lawless's late nineteenth-century novel *Grania*, those living on the Aran island of Inishman call Inishmore the mainland, and they see people from Galway as "Foreigners" and "Black Strangers".[9] The folk on Inish Capaill a century later use the actual word "mainland" for the coast of Ireland immediately opposite, but in fact the main bit of land for them physically and psychologically is the island they live on, Ireland itself being seen as a separate country: yet even so, their situation is complex, their island being both prison and place of blessing. For Bernard MacLaverty's central character, the small island of Islay provides necessary respite from the effects of the larger island which shaped her, but "the mainland" is something to be chosen, personally, not something decided by geography or by cultural, political or even family relationships; thus in *Grace Notes* the word "mainland" is never used for Northern Ireland, only for Scotland, and only after Catherine has chosen to live there.

Thus what was once experienced and celebrated in Irish literature as a physical reality seems to have become a metaphor, with "mainland" now a matter not simply of geography but, in many cases, of psychology. Yet the issue may be even more complex. Raphael Samuel's description of plans for volume two in his trilogy, *Theatres of Memory*, is suggestive. *Island Stories* "is about the wildly different versions of the national past on offer at any given point in time, depending on whether the optic is that of town or country; centre or periphery; the state or civil society".[10] An appropriate addition here

---

[9] Emily Lawless, *Grania: The Story of an Island*, I, New York, 1979, 40. Throughout this novel Lawless, who sailed often in this area and knew it well, refers to Inishmore as "Aranmore". This seems to have been a usage not uncommon in the late nineteenth and early twentieth centuries; see *The Book of Aran*, eds John Waddell *et al.*, Newtownlynch, Kinvara, Co. Galway, 1994, 8, 274.

[10] Raphael Samuel, *Island Stories: Unravelling Britain. Theatres of Memory, II*, London, 1998, ix. This volume, left unfinished at Samuel's death, was edited by Alison Light *et al.*

might be "island or mainland". Just as Samuel's work was intended to end with an extended essay, "The difficulties of being English",[11] so too might further study of Ireland's islands lead perhaps to insights regarding "the difficulties of being Irish".

---

[11]   *Ibid.*, ix.

IRISH WRITING AND TRANSLATION

THE COLLOQUY OF THE OLD MEN:
SHAPE AND SUBSTANCE

MAURICE HARMON

Acallam na Senórach (*The Colloquy of the Old Men*) has been shaped with such intelligence and care and with such a profound understanding of Irish tradition that it is easy to agree with Gerard Murphy that it had a single author. "Some unknown Irishman of genius", he said, "steeped in the ancient lore of Ireland, but inspired also by the innovating tendencies of his time, got the idea of combining all the modes and spirits of various branches of Irish tradition in one vast literary compilation ...".[1]

The *Colloquy* contains a great variety of stories: wonder tales, romances, mythological tales, tales of monsters and magical sea journeys, revenge motifs, transmogrifications, and attacks by forces from outside Ireland and from the Otherworld. Flocks of birds lay waste areas of Munster; a woman from the Island of Women seeks protection from the Fian, but is killed before their eyes by a man from the Island of Men. Three strange men from the Otherworld kingdom of Iruath, each with a particular gift, and their dog protect the Fian but insist on sleeping in their own camp with a wall of fire about them: they do not want anyone to see them at night because every third night one of them is dead and their dog shrinks; that same dog vomits treasure on demand, wine comes from his mouth, his breath turns men's bodies to ashes and he protects Finn mac Cumaill by walking about him three times a day.[2] The Tuatha Dé Danann in one fairymound are attacked by the Tuatha Dé Danann from another and are saved only by the help of the Fian. There is also a great variety of

---

[1] Gerald Murphy, "*Acallam na Senórach*", in *Irish Sagas*, ed. Myles Dillon, Cork, 1968, 125.

[2] See Joseph Falaki Nagy, *The Wisdom of the Outlaw*, Berkeley, 1985, for a discussion of their significance.

poems: poems of praise, love poems, nature poems, elegies,
genealogical poems, catalogue poems, commemorations, eulogies,
prophecies. The *Colloquy*, in short, is a rich compendium of
imaginative literature. Instead of seeing it as a compilation of
individual tales, we may see it as a collection of contrasting tales
whose diversity and resemblances, both of substance and tone, make
for a lively imaginative experience.

The contrast between paganism and Christianity is a major
element. The author is clearly Christian and pagan Caílte willingly
accepts baptism.   Patrick journeys as a missionary bringing
Christianity to each of the provinces.[3] Caílte travels to places
associated with the Fian. While he laments the disappearance of
former comrades and all that they stood for, that seductive theme is
countered by Patrick, who maintains that Caílte is fortunate to have
survived long enough to have become a Christian. "You should not
feel sad", Patrick tells him. "Your condition and your hope are better
than all the others, since I have come to you and because the reward of
the true God, faith, holiness and prayer with the arms crossed have
come to you and not to any others of the Fian."[4]

Pagan and Christian virtues exist side by side.[5] If there are
examples of heroic deeds by the Fian in battle, of their marvellous
adventures with the Otherworld, or of their magical feats, there are
also examples of Patrick's miraculous achievements, such as raising
the dead, striking water from a rock, healing the sick and wounded,
promising salvation, and cursing evil-doers so effectively that the
ground swallows them. While Patrick's God is not judgemental, the
unmerited destruction of princes at Tara, long before the coming of
Christianity, is sufficent proof of His existence to make Finn mac
Cumaill believe in Him. Patrick is clearly successful in what he does:
kings and nobles accept baptism and readily submit to his spiritual
authority. Caílte, too, gains stature by being the narrator of and the

---

[3]   Patrick's circuit resembles that of Diarmait mac Cerbaill, High King of Ireland:
      by the right hand from Tara to Leinster, on to Munster, into Connacht, across
      Ulster and returning to Tara at the end of the year in time for the Feast of
      Samhain and to meet with the men of Ireland.
[4]   All translations are by the author: *Acallam na Senorách*, Beltresda, 2001. All
      citations are given in the text.
[5]   See Harry H. Roe, "*Acallamh na Senórach*: The Confluence of Lay and Clerical
      Oral Traditions", in *Celtic Languages and Celtic Peoples: Proceedings of the
      Second North American Congress of Celtic Studies*, ed. Cyril Byrne, Halifax,
      Nova Scotia, 1992, 331-46.

protagonist in many of the secondary stories. He bears witness to a former era and his sense of loss for the glory that has passed is often movingly expressed, as in this lament for Finn:

> The noble people do not live, princely Finn does not live,
> the spear-troops do not live nor the Fian-chief, the overlord.
>
> All of Finn's Fian are dead who roamed from glen to glen,
> it is bad to live after Finn, after Diarmaid and Conán.

(88)

The contrast between what Patrick and Caílte represent runs through the entire work but the potential for conflict has been removed. Caílte may lament what has passed but never challenges what has ensued. What he values and represents is subordinated to the Christianity he accepts. If he laments the destruction of places where the Fian used to assemble, some of those places are transformed into centres of Christian gathering and worship and that alteration is celebrated as in this poem about Clonmacnoise:

> Woe to the Fian who heard the news when we got to Snámh dá
>   Én,
> the death of Conán Mael from Moy, the death of Ferdoman.
> Druim diamar its name before the time of the Fian,
> Druim énaig since then from the fowling of Fionn and the Fian.
> A famous child will be born there by the will of the Lord of the
>   great clans,
> the worthy son of Heaven's King whom angels are waiting for.
>
> That will be holy Ciarán, he will be born in the royal rath,
> he will seize half of Ireland, the mason's son from Muirthemne.

(53)

There are confirming prophecies that validate the coming of saints to various sites, such as Ferns and Glendalough. Finn himself in his role as seer has foreseen and welcomed the coming of Christianity. The assumption throughout is that the audience is Christian.

The values of the pagan Fian that are explicitly lauded include generosity, bravery, skill in battle, desire for personal honour, fame. A poem of advice given by Finn mac Cumaill to a young man called Mac Lugach urges him, amongst other things, to respect the elderly, to

be gentle to women and children, to reward artists, to shun sexual
deviancy, to avoid gossip, to be generous:

> Do not speak in big words
> or say you will not do what is right.
> It is shameful to speak fiercely,
> if you cannot match deeds with words.
> Do not abandon your lord
> while you live in this yellow world.
> Nor for any wealth or gold
> go back on your support.
>
> (25)

The tribute most frequently made about people is that they are
hospitable. Generosity is always praised, as in this little poem about
Finn:

> Were but the brown leaf gold
> that the wood sheds,
> were but the white wave silver
> Finn had given all away.
>
> (13)

Meanness is always condemned. So, too, are deadly sins that the
Church exorts clerics to purge through the observance of the canonical
hours, Prime, Tierce, Nones, Vespers, and so on:

> Prime against the gullet's craving,
> Tierce 'gainst anger's wilful raving,
> Midday's light 'gainst lustful phases,
> Nones 'gainst greed throughout the ages.
>
> (78)

When he hears about them Caílte, the enthusiastic new convert,
immediately wants to practise them.

Early on in the work Patrick asks Caílte, "What values did you live
by?" and Caílte makes the famous reply: "Truth in our hearts, strength
in our hands, and fulfilment in our tongues." In a listing of Fian
leaders, Caílte associates each with specific qualities such as nobility,
knowledge, wisdom. They were combative, tough, fierce, strong,
loyal. Finn is the ideal: "gift-giver to noble hosts, our many-talented

wise man. / Our chief, leader, seer, judge, magician and druid." That Caílte, Finn and others shed tears is not thought to be unmanly.

The process by which pagan values are replaced by or subordinated to Christian values permeates the entire work, part of a revisionist agenda by which what the Fian represent, the pagan world of the third century, is replaced by the arrival of Christianity. Patrick is a powerful and civilized exponent of Christianity. He drives legions of demons from Caílte and Oisín when he first meets them, does the same at Cashel when he ascends the Rock and in the end will reduce the glorious Tuatha Dé Danann, the gods and goddesses of the Otherworld, to dwellers on hills and mountains who will only return occasionally to the earth in the form of spirits.

The *Colloquy* is coherent and orderly. Patrick's journeys to each province and the stories told there provide one form of organization. So does the passing of time. At its carefully orchestrated but incon-clusive conclusion all the main participants, Caílte, Oisín, Patrick, the High King, the provincial kings, significant minor figures, assemble for the Feast of Tara, where important narrative strands are brought to conclusion. Told and controlled by a single author the stories mesh, although the seamless texture, derived in part from its consistency of tone and its formulaic manner, is occasionally marred by poor transition between one story and another, by poems which do not fit well into the narrative context, or by poems which are archaic; sometimes the material is too slight to be of interest and towards the end the artistic control weakens.[6]

But these imperfections do not detract from the orderly shape of the *Colloquy* as a whole. The formulaic patterns that help to bind the tales together include the manner in which stories are introduced, the language of personal address, and the words Patrick uses to thank Caílte for his stories. Stories are invariably introduced by questions about the origin of place-names, as, for example, "Why is this rath called the Little Rath of Wonders?" or "Why is this rath called the Rath of the Dog's Head and this mound the Mound of Women?". In response Caílte tells a story that gives the explanation required. At the

---

[6] The *Colloquy* is not only a series of conversations between Patrick and Caílte. When Patrick is not present, Caílte and sometimes Oisín continue to give explanations for place names; see Joseph Falaky Nagy, "Compositional Concerns in the *Acallam na Senórach*", in *Sages, Saints and Storytellers: Celtic Studies in Honour of Professor James Carney*, eds Donncha Ó Corráin *et al.*, Maynooth, 1989, 181-99.

end of the telling Patrick compliments Caílte with the words, "Victory and blessing be yours, Caílte, this is entertainment of mind and spirit for us", or some similar form of words. When the artistic control weakens, the pattern of question and answer is handled abruptly and the formula becomes automatic.

More generally, the atmosphere of medieval romance casts an attractive ambiance over the entire work so that accounts of battles, beheadings, fights against monsters, or against the Tuatha Dé Danann all fit into a pleasure-giving style. In addition the narrative skills of the author include not only the formulaic patterns, but a sophisticated handling of a complex narrative world. This encompasses the story of the journeys made by Patrick, Caílte and Oisín, the establishment of a geographical context for them, as well as various kinds of stories within the frame story, and sometimes a story within one of them. The author is also able to sustain a narrative across several stories by introducing characters, leaving them aside, introducing other stories, and then returning to the original characters.

The entire work has an imaginative splendour. We are persuaded, without questioning the practicalities involved, that vast numbers of people, kings, nobles and followers, Christians and pagans, travel with Patrick and Caílte from place to place. Even the journeys that seem to be along verifiable routes go through places that are more imaginary than real. At the same time the author gives substance to the past through the identification of place, the formal naming of mainly fictionalized kings and their particular territories, and emphasizing directions north, south, east or west from where the teller stands. In the course of this complex work a particular cast of Fian characters and of Tuatha Dé Danann figures emerges through their recurrent appearances. The same is true of a specific number of places, in particular royal sites and homes of the Tuatha Dé Danann, but the literary nature of the author's imagination is indicated by the absence of descriptions of particular landscapes. The Tuatha Dé Danann are also part of a cavalcade that is romantic, atmospheric and unrealistic. The medieval imagination enjoys magnitude, crowded canvas, splendid figures, formulaic address, banquets and feasts.

The aesthetic interaction of prose narratives with poetic comment or illustration is also effective, providing a contrast with the prose and often highlighting particular events or figures. When Caílte finds a well for Patrick, he recites a poem about it:

Well of Tráig Dá Bán,
lovely your pure-topped cress,
since your verdure has been neglected,
your brooklime cannot spread.

Trout out from your banks,
wild pigs in your wilderness,
deer good to hunt on your crags,
dappled red-breasted fawns.

Mast on the tips of your trees,
fish in your river mouths,
lovely colour in your arum shoots,
green brook in the woody hollow.

(12-13)

One of the most attractive aspects of the *Colloquy* is the connection
between the visible and invisible worlds, between the landscape in
which Patrick, Caílte, Oisín and the provincial kings travel, and the
places under fairymounds or on islands where the Tuatha Dé Danann
live. To some degree the people below ground or off-shore are no
different from those who live above ground. They, too, have
elopements and battles, make alliances for purposes of marriage or
combat, and have a range of feelings. Of course, they live forever, are
forever young and beautiful, wear beautiful clothes, carry beautiful
weapons, live in crystal palaces, have magical powers, and enjoy an
abundance of food and drink. There are several accounts of where
they live, such as the description of Créde's house under the Paps
mountains in north Kerry:

A hundred feet in Créde's house
from one end to the other,
twenty measured feet the width
of its splendid doorway.

Its wattling and thatch
of bird feathers yellow and blue,
its wall railing to the east
of glass and carbuncle.

Four pillars for each bed
patterned with silver and gold,
the glass gem on each pillar
a pleasant crowning.

                                                    (33-34)

Créde may be a creature of the Otherworld but her lament for the
death of her husband Cael death at the Battle of Ventry is as moving
as any human elegy: Créde "then came and stretched herself by his
side and wailed out loud in great grief, 'Why should I not die of grief
for my husband, seeing that the restless wild creatures are dying of
grief for him?'":

The harbour cries out at the red race of Reenverc,
the wave against the shore laments the drowning of the man from
Loch Dá Chonn.

The crane cries in the marshes of Druim Dá Thrén,
but cannot guard her young when the fox comes close.

Sad is the cry the thrush makes in Drumkeen,
no less sad the blackbird's voice in Leiter Laíg.

Sad the sound the stag makes in Drumlesh,
for the dead doe of Druim Sílenn the stag roars.

It grieves me the death of the hero who used to lie with me
the son of the woman of Doire Dá Doss with a cross above his
head.

It grieves me, Cael, to have you dead by my side,
the wave-drench over your bright side maddens me.

Sad the sound the wave makes against the shore,
it drowned a handsome man, my grief Cael went near.

Sad the sound the wave makes to the north,
hammering hard rocks, lamenting Cael's death.

Sad the sound the wave makes to the south,
my time is done, as my appearance reveals.

Sad the sound made by Tulcha's dragging wave,
I have no future, since its tidings reached me.

Since Crimthann's son drowned, I will love no one,
his hand felled many, on a hard day his shield never cried out.

(35)

Within the romanticized world of the *Colloquy* known elements of Irish society exist and help to explain what goes on. A social world is created, various customs, values, and rituals are established. There is a history of the Fian, regnal lists, a layered landscape and a layered consciousness. One of those layers connects with the heroic world of Cuchulain. There is a reference to the shield of Conchobar which did not cry out in battle, a reference to Cuchulain's horses, to Baile's Strand, to Mesgedra's brain, to the flight of Suibhne Geilt after the Battle of Moira, to place-names in the *Táin Bó Cuailnge*. Plunderers are those without ties of kinship with a king or lord, agreements are guaranteed by people of importance, blood-fines are paid for murders, gifts are exchanged as specified in the *Book of Rights*.[7] There are associations with people, places and events in the wide popular tradition of the Fiannaighecht and in the accounts of Patrick's journeys.[8] Nevertheless, although the *Colloquy* appears to be grounded in actuality it is free-standing; its imagined and imaginative reality is superimposed on a sketchy real world. This dual perspective is in keeping with the world-view of early Irish tradition in which the real world and the Otherworld co-exist and intermingle.

There is a sense in which storytelling, not paganism and not Christianity, is the supreme value. The entire collection of over two hundred stories comes from the oral tradition and depends for its success on the author's ability to be an effective teller of tales. He adapts, shapes and creates. At this period a strong and productive oral Fenian tradition rooted in pre-Christian Celtic culture was a source of inspiration for a literary Fenian tradition. When Patrick questions the propriety and the value of listening to secular stories, his two guardian angels urge him to record what Caílte and Oisín say "for gatherings of people and noblemen in times to come will be delighted to listen to

---

[7] See F. J. Byrne, *Irish Kings and High Kings*, London, 1973, for a discussion of these.

[8] There are many borrowings from Patrician hagiography, the *Táin* and other sagas.

those stories". Indeed, they say, since the old men have forgotten two thirds of what they know, it is imperative to write down what they still remember. This endorsement is significant of the value placed on storytelling by the Christian author. Caílte values the military prowess he once possessed but in turn is valued because he knows so much and gives such pleasure as a storyteller. "Victory and blessing, Caílte", says Diarmaid mac Cerbaill, High-King of Ireland,

> where are the poets and storytellers? Let these matters be written in the tablets of the poets, in the records of the learned, in the words of the judges, so that all the knowledge of land and territory may be retained together with all of Caílte's and Oisín's great deeds of valour and prowess, and the place-lore of Ireland.[9]

Over and over the poet-minstrel-storyteller is generously praised and rewarded. In addition to Caílte, two of the most attractive figures in the entire work are Cnú Dereóil, the much-loved dwarf minstrel, and the mysterious Cas Corach who is appointed Poet of Ireland in the final pages.

It would, however, be a mistake to think that the *Colloquy* takes place in a vacuum and to see it merely as entertainment. Ultimately it offers a civilizing ideal at a time of political disruption. There are political and religious implications for society of the early thirteenth century that are outside the scope of this paper. Some stories have a moral force: they show how one should behave, they show what kinds of actions are deeply, even fatally, shameful. Many illustrate how princes ought to behave. Others focus on the just treatment of retainers. Over and over the supremacy of Christianity, the Christian God and the salvation He can provide are stressed. While Christianity and paganism exist side by side, no one experiences a crisis of conscience, no one rebels against the rulings of the church.

The point is made in the old story of Tuathal Techtmar's two daughters, Fithir and Dáirinne. The king of Leinster, Eochaid mac Echaid comes to ask for Fithir, but her father will not give her in marriage before her older sister, Dáirinne. Eochaid accepts Dáirinne, but it is the younger sister he loves. After a year he makes a secret house for Dáirinne in the middle of the forest and goes back to Tara

---

[9] Here the Christian narrator justifies his own interest in this pagan, secular material.

where he tells Techtmar that Dáirinne has died and that he wants to marry Fithir. Reluctantly the High-King agrees. Eochaid takes her back to Leinster but when they arrive they find Dáirinne there. At sight of her sister Fithir dies and at that Dáirinne also dies. As the poem says: "Fithir died from shame, Dáirinne died from grief."

We might regard this as a good clerical try. Early Irish society recognized multiple marriage. A man could have a principal wife (*cetmuinter*) and another partner, but the church taught otherwise as the author of the *Colloquy* makes clear in the story of Ailénn and the king of Connaught. When the woman, Ailénn Fialchorcra, falls in love with the king of Connaught, who already has a wife, Patrick firmly says that such a relationship is forbidden by God and by himself. Both the woman and the king accept this ruling. Significantly this story is told not by Caílte, but by the Christian narrator. Only when the first wife dies are they able to marry and that union is one of the threads neatly tied in the conclusion of the entire work.[10] The parable about the king of Connaught who would marry two wives may have been directed against a contemporary king of Connaught whose promiscuity caused internecine strife amongst his sons. Patrick's scornful reaction to a story of wife-swapping among the Tuatha Dé Danann clearly shows what he thinks about it.

It is clear that the author, who was probably a monk in one of the western monasteries, favours Connaught, where the last portion of the work is set. While Finn prophecies the coming of particular saints to Ferns, Rosbroc and Glendalough, his highest praise is for St Ciarán who will come to Clonmacnoise:

> To those who would wreck his church sudden red-speared death,
> hanging, pitless racking and the lowest pit of hell. (53)

The author also makes sure that Croagh Patrick is presented as a place of pilgrimage guaranteed by St Patrick. The reasons for this are both commercial and spiritual. "I have", Patrick declares,

> ensured that the place be a place of holiness and truth. Whoever
> commits evil or wrong there will experience withering of children,

---

[10] In ecclesiastical censure the Irish were said to be Christian in name, in reality pagan. Their marriage practices left much to be desired as far as the Church was concerned. Kings married early and often, divorce was easy, marriage alliances often political.

kindred and people. My blessing on him who will honour and
defend it.

In the next breath he promises that three Connaught kings will rule
Ireland and that the country will prosper under them. It is part of the
allusive nature of this text that we remember that in Irish tradition the
country prospers when the rightful king rules.The *Colloquy* connects
the present with the past, and revivifies what once was. It makes the
past more immediate through the living presence of Caílte and Oisín,
through their stories, and through the evidence they produce from
rock, hill and lake. The wealth and splendour of the past are celebrated
and confirmed both by storytelling and by Caílte's ability to produce
solid evidence in the shape of treasure, goblet, or armour: these, he
says, belonged to Finn, or Oscar, or Goll; here is where the woman
was killed; there is where the heroes were buried; that hill, that
mound, that ford, that plain, that lake is where these events took place.
In the end it is the narrative variety and richness of the work that are
most important. Its variety, scale, and artistic power make it one of the
greatest works in Irish literature, second in length only to the *Táin Bó
Cuailnge* (*The Cattleraid of Cooley*).

Thomas Furlong:
The Case for the Reassessment of a Forgotten Nineteenth-Century Poet and Journalist

Sean Mythen

The early nineteenth-century Wexford poet and journalist Thomas Furlong was born in 1794 at Scarawalsh, a tiny settlement consisting of little more than a public house and crossroads. He lived in Dublin from the age of fifteen and died there of consumption in 1827. In this essay I intend to deal primarily with Furlong's translations in James Hardiman's *Irish Minstrelsy or Bardic Remains* and to a lesser extent his other works including *The Plagues of Ireland, The Doom of Derenzie* and his shorter pieces in the *Dublin and London Magazine*. However, since Furlong remains relatively unknown it is important initially to set his work in context. I would therefore like to take a little time in examining his family and literary background.

Thomas Furlong was the youngest of a family of five, comprising two sons and three daughters. His place of birth, Scarawalsh, is in the townland of Clovass midway between Enniscorthy and Ferns in County Wexford. The poet's date of birth is no longer ascertainable and there are no known details of the Furlong family extant. Unfortunately many records were destroyed with the burning of Catholic churches in Wexford following the 1798 rising. Ferns Church records, which may have contained details of the Furlong family, were destroyed in November 1798.

In common with most of his contemporaries of a similar social and religious background, Furlong received a hedge-school education. His father was a tenant farmer and carman, earning his income on a small farm of twenty acres or so. It was as a result of his father's trading, delivering produce to Dublin that young Thomas Furlong came to the capital city at the age of fifteen, and took up the position of grocer's apprentice. There is some speculation that he was the recipient of some type of further education there but this has not been verified.

Furlong wrote in the aftermath of the 1798 rebellion and the
subsequent Act of Union and became an ardent member of the
Catholic Association. He thus represents the interesting aspect of an
early nineteenth-century Irish writer, supported in his literary
endeavours by a Protestant ascendancy family, the Jamesons, but
coming from the Catholic underclass, in the period immediately
following the Act of Union.

He joined in the emerging Catholic nationalist literary movement
and wrote for various papers and journals in furtherance of the cause
of Catholic emancipation. He derives his cultural and national identity
from the causes of the Catholic majority and in general the sentiments
expressed in his work are nationalist in as much as such a term can be
applied to a writer in the first decades of the nineteenth century. His
material is interesting not only for the light it throws on contemporary
politics, as the work of a writer treating of contemporary social and
political matters of the day, but also for the folk-tales he contributed to
the *Dublin and London Magazine* under the pseudonym of the
"Hermit in Ireland". Furlong further managed to achieve competence
as a minor poet in the idioms of the late Augustan and early Romantic
periods.

His current fame is primarily due to his translations of Irish poetry,
published by James Hardiman in *Irish Minstrelsy, or Bardic Remains*.
Of the hundred and thirty-six translations contained in it forty-two are
by Furlong, including all of "Carolan's Remains". These translations
are today regarded as competent in their kind, but somewhat lacking
in their interpretation of the Irish-language originals. In a series of
reviews in the *Dublin University Magazine*, Samuel Ferguson was
highly critical of them, as failing to adequately communicate the tenor
of the Gaelic originals. Modern-day criticism has largely upheld this
viewpoint and further assumes that Furlong lacked sufficient intimacy
with the Irish language to make the transformation to English
adequate. The tensions created on the one hand by Hardiman in laying
claim to Gaelic literature as Catholic, Jacobite and anti-English, and
on the other by Ferguson anxious to fuse Gaelic literature with that of
the Anglo-Irish in order to lend it legitimacy, is of particular interest
and will be dealt with in greater depth later.

Patrick Rafroidi in *Irish Literature in English* (1972) describes
Furlong as a passable poet who did not know Irish. The quality of
Furlong's translations has been the subject of further critical
examination by Robert Welch in *A History of Verse Translations from*

the Irish (1988). Welch's assessment is that Furlong's verses were unnecessarily ornamental and pay too little attention to the literal content of the Irish. He also appears to believe that they were based on literal translations supplied by Hardiman. This conclusion is primarily based on Hardiman's comment in the *Irish Minstrelsy*:

> When his aid was first solicited, the writer had the same difficulty with him [i.e. Carolan] as with others, to prove that any productions of value
>
> were extant in the Irish language. Acquainted only with the English words associated with our native airs he smiled incredulously at the asserted poetical excellence of the original lyrics, and even questioned their existence. It is true he admitted that he had often heard them spoken of, and sometimes praised, but that he considered as the mere boasting of national prejudice. "If", said he, "they possess any merit, I cannot conceive how they could have remained so long unknown."

On the basis of this statement it was assumed that Furlong knew no Irish. However, a re-reading of Hardiman's article, including the sentences immediately following the above, conveys a contrary impression. Hardiman's article goes on to state that:

> After several explanations, however, and *an examination of some of these neglected originals* [italics in the original], his opinions began to change. He at length confessed that he discovered beauties of which, until then, he had been wholly unconscious; and finally entered on the undertaking, with an ardour and perseverance, which continued until his death.[1]

It is doubtful if Furlong's conversion could have been so total on the basis of English literal translations. He gave expression to his regard for his Gaelic predecessors in one of his last pieces, entitled "The Spirit of Irish Song":

> Lov'd land of the Bards and Saints! To me
> There's none so dear as thy minstrelsy:
> Bright is nature in every dress,
> Rich in unborrow'd loveliness:

---

[1] James Hardiman, *Irish Minstrelsy, or Bardic Remains*, Dublin, 1831, I, lxxvii.

Winning is every shape she wears,
Winning she is in thine own sweet airs:
What to the spirit more cheering can be,
Than the lay whose ling'ring notes recall
The thoughts of the holy – the fair – the free
Belov'd in life or deplored in their fall?
Fling, fling the forms of art aside,
Dull is the ear that these forms enthral;

Let the simple songs of our sires be tried,
They go to the heart and the heart is all.
Give me the full responsive sigh,
The glowing cheek and the moisten'd eye;
Let these the minstrel's might attest,
And the vain and the idle – may share the rest.[2]

It is possible, therefore, to take Hardiman's comments either of two ways: as meaning that Furlong knew nothing of Irish culture, or alternatively that he knew the language well enough to be astonished at finding it was a literary medium as well as the native tongue of his less economically advantaged neighbours. It is my belief that the latter is the correct interpretation. It would be surprising if Furlong were not familiar with the spoken version of the Irish language from his childhood. The Irish language was still widely used in County Wexford, particularly in rural areas during the period in which Furlong grew up. James Alexander, for example, a prominent loyalist from the town of New Ross, states that most of the Wexfordmen he heard speaking during the battle of New Ross in 1798, spoke in Irish.[3] William Shaw Mason in his *Statistical Account* states that in 1814 the Protestant rector of Adamstown and Newbawn reported that during his constant residence in the area for the last ten years the Irish language was generally spoken but was rapidly getting out of use.[4] J. B. Trotter in his *Walks Through Ireland* in 1812 comments that "the

---

[2] *Ibid.*, lxxx.
[3] Following the 1798 Rebellion, James Alexander wrote a pamphlet entitled *Some Account of the first apparent symptoms of the late rebellioin in the county of Kildare .... With a succinct narrative ... of the rebellion in the county of Wexford in the vicinity of New Ross* (1800).
[4] William Shaw Mason, *Statistical Account or Parochial Survey of Ireland*, Dublin, 1814-19.

Irish language is spoken almost generally in the county of Wexford".[5] He observes that it was spoken everywhere at a fair which he attended in Bunclody, a village five miles from Furlong's birthplace. The *Walks* refers to several further instances of the use of Irish among the peasant class in Wexford. There is also evidence that Catholic sermons were preached in Irish in several parts of Wexford in the late eighteenth century. It is probably appropriate here to briefly deal with the political climate of the 1820s which formed the background to Furlong's work, since it was during the period 1822-27 that most of his literary efforts came to fruition. From the early 1820s onwards there was a resurgence of sectarian bitterness, which undoubtedly affected political interaction in Ireland. Furlong was closely associated with the emancipation movement through the Catholic Association and wrote extensively on the Act of Union. The historian Tom Dunne has noted the considerable influence, which the Act of Union had on contemporary Irish literature. He observes that:

> Irish fiction after the Union was intensely and often self-consciously colonial in its ambition to present a more favourable image of Ireland to the imperial political elite, and the extent to which it (like the rhetoric of Irish politicians) was shaped by awareness of this English audience.[6]

It is relatively easy to recognize this colonial influence on Furlong and his desire to please an English audience, but what is more interesting is his presentation of native Irish material. Unlike writers such as Maria Edgeworth, he writes with an insider's knowledge rather than as an observer of native Irish culture. These first stirrings of an autonomous sense of Irish culture in English, quite distinct from the Anglo-Irish literary interests of the ascendancy in some ways but quite similar in others, were beginning to be felt in the early decades of nineteenth century. As Joep Leerssen has written, the materials that best illustrate the formative stages of these beginnings are to be found in the decades following Catholic emancipation in 1829.[7] James Hardiman's *Irish Minstrelsy* may be taken as a front marker for this

---

[5]   J. B. Trotter, *Walks Through Ireland*, Paris, 1819, quoted in *The Past*, 10 (1973-74), 10.

[6]   Tom Dunne, "The Insecure Voice: A Catholic Novelist in Support of Emancipation", in *Culture et Pratiques Politiques en France et en Irlande*, eds L. Cullen and L. Bergeron, Paris, 1988, 216.

[7]   Joep Leerssen, *Remembrance and Imagination*, Cork, 1996, 178.

development. Leerssen describes it as the most important collection of original Irish literature since the days of Charlotte Brooke some forty years earlier, while Seamus Deane accords to it the status of a foundational text.[8] As his writings show, Furlong was involved in such a movement from the early 1820s, and it was therefore especially appropriate that he should be the principal translator of Hardiman's anthology.

As described in the *Oxford Companion*, *The Irish Minstrelsy or Bardic Remains of Ireland*:

> is an anthology of Irish poetry from all periods, the contents ranging from relics attributed to mythological figures   such as Torna Eigeas to the contemporary Gaelic poet Antoine Raiftearai, whom he [Hardiman] knew well."[9]

A full introduction to the subject, together with memoirs of both Carolan the blind bard and Thomas Furlong, then recently deceased, were included in Volume I of *The Irish Minstrelsy*.

Apart from Furlong's work, the other translations are by John D'Alton, Edward Lawson, Henry Grattan Curran and the Rev. William Hamilton Drummond DD. The objective of Hardiman's work was to attest to the antiquity of Irish poetry and demonstrate that it was equal in dignity to other great classical literatures. As Hardiman himself expressed it, "the subject and language of these insular poems afford internal evidence of an antiquity transcending that of any literary monument in the modern languages of Europe".[10] Hardiman, of course, had a very particular purpose in mind in producing the *Minstrelsy*. He blamed British policy for the destruction of much of Irish literature as "the conquerors who tried to silence the bards", and like Furlong enthusiastically embraced Catholic emancipation. Hardiman's Catholic nationalist leanings are almost immediately apparent in his Introduction as he describes the Irish bards as "invariably Catholics, patriots, and jacobites".[11] Hardiman at first intended to publish a collection of original Irish verse but later

---

[8]   Seamus Deane, *Strange County: Modernity and Nationhood in Irish Writing since 1790*, Oxford, 1997, 1.
[9]   *Oxford Companion to Irish Literature*, ed. Robert Welch, Oxford, 1996, 237.
[10] Hardiman, *Irish Minstrelsy* I, v.
[11] *Ibid.*, xxv.

decided to include translations. He invited Furlong to translate in the belief that only a poet should translate a poet.

As mentioned earlier, Samuel Ferguson was highly critical of the translations in a series of four successive articles published in the *Dublin University Magazine* in 1834. The undercurrent of hostility to Protestant ascendancy apparent in Hardiman's publication incensed Ferguson. It is of course highly ironic that Furlong, an Irish poet, was subjected to rebuke by an Anglo-Irish writer, Ferguson, who would, in turn, help to engender a more vital tradition of Irish verse translation through his own interpretation of the originals. Ferguson was part of an Anglo-Irish literary movement attempting a hybridization of Gaelic and ascendancy culture in opposition to a distinctively nationalist interpretation of Gaelic culture which was also just them emerging. In order to give legitimacy to his undertaking, Ferguson first needed to discredit Hardiman, and chose the quality of Hardiman's translations to do so. The *Dublin University Magazine*, with its strong ascendancy leaning, provided an ideal platform.

Ferguson's initial article in the magazine in April 1834 first describes how Carolan was given to eulogizing his hosts. The article included a good deal of literal translation, together with a rambling account of a number of poems in praise of various women. His second article in August of that year is likewise general in treatment but it is in his third article that Ferguson's hostility to Hardiman becomes apparent. In the previous two articles, Ferguson had virtually ignored the translations in Hardiman's collection; however, an extended footnote in this article leaves the reader in no doubt as to where the reviewer stands. Though already familiar from various critical sources, it is worth citing at this point Ferguson's damning comments at some length:

> We have hitherto so slightly alluded to the accompanying metrical versions of Mr Hardiman's collection, that the reader may not improbably suppose it, what we sincerely wish it were, a mere compilation of untranslated Irish pieces. It were fortunate for the subject had it been so; but the laudable desire of making the English reader acquainted with the style and sentiment of our native poetry, has, unfortunately, induced Mr Hardiman to attach versions so strangely unlike the originals both in sentiment and style, as to destroy alike the originality and the interest of Irish minstrelsy for those who can only appreciate it through such a medium. It is but justice to the gentlemen who furnished these translations to observe,

that their labour was gratuitous and the task peculiarly difficult. Indeed the disinterestedness (so far as it concerns pecuniary matters) which characterizes the whole undertaking, challenges the highest praise. Mr Hardiman collected and compiled, and Messrs D'Alton, Furlong, Curran, and other well-disposed and learned men versified the translations of the compiled matter, and presented the whole, without recompense of any kind, as a mark of their esteem to Mr Robins, the publisher. We regret that, while we applaud the purpose, we must unequivocally condemn the execution. All the versifiers seem to have been actuated by a morbid desire, neither healthy nor honest, to elevate the tone of the original to a pitch of refined poetic art altogether foreign from the whole genius and rationale of its composition. We are sorry to be obliged to add, that the majority of these attempts are spurious, puerile, unclassical – lamentably bad.[12]

Ferguson continues in like manner until he comes to his description of Furlong, for whom he reserves his greatest tirade:

Mr Furlong was a man of strong poetic feeling, but of slender poetic art. He had but little fancy, less imagination and we had almost said no judgement. In raciness, in naivete, in quaint characteristic expression, his versions fall immeasurably short of the original; and were not their mawkish poverty in this respect relieved by the genuine glow of sentiment with which his good feeling often redeems his bad taste, would deservedly fall under unmitigated censure. Mr Furlong is now no more and as he left behind him nothing worthy to live, so must his name also soon pass from the precincts of an obscure fame, to which it has been fondly elevated by the admiration of sanguine but incompetent admirers. It is cruel to his memory, although, doubtless, well intended, in Mr Hardiman, to make the obscure efforts of his mistaken genius the subject of a long memoir. Equally unfortunate for both is the dull detail; for, alas! if Mr Furlong was a sorry poet, Mr Hardiman is still a sorrier critic. It is, indeed, deeply to be lamented, that Mr Hardiman's devotion to a labour so pious as the rescue of our native minstrelsy, has not been accompanied by adequate good taste in his selection of the pieces, or a worthy spirit of liberality in their illustration.

One does not have to dig too deeply to uncover the background to this wholly negative assessment. Ferguson's Protestant ascendancy audience undoubtedly viewed emergent Catholic nationalism as a

---

[12]   *The Dublin University Magazine*, IV/10 (1834), 453.

threat to their existence. Hardiman's claim to an articulate and noble heritage on a par with that of ancient Greece was a far cry from the Protestant perception of a superstitious, savage and uncouth peasantry incapable of leadership. Earlier in 1833, Ferguson had contributed an article to the magazine entitled "A Dialogue Between the Head and the Heart of an Irish Protestant".[13] This piece gives an insight into the mentality, which he so harshly brings to bear on Hardiman and Furlong. To quote *The Field Day Anthology*:

> In this classic statement of divided loyalties the head cautions the heart against an ill-judged sympathy with Irish Catholics, warning that an apologetic wish to conciliate can only undermine the Protestant ascendancy on which the country must depend for moral intellectual, and economic leadership.[14]

As commonly understood, Ferguson's dialogue points to a crisis in his cultural and political sympathies. Ferguson's reviews of Hardiman were motivated by complex and passionate feelings arising from the divided loyalties of the Irish Protestant intelligentsia. In attempting to redefine their own cultural roots these Irish Protestants were prepared to embrace Irish culture, but obviously without its "Jacobite" tendencies.

Seamus Deane warns us against identifying Ferguson too closely with the sentiments expressed in "The Head and the Heart", noting that his major achievement in his articles on *Irish Minstrelsy* lies in the fact that he made Hardiman's position untenable, thus opening the door for others, including ultimately W. B. Yeats, the father of the literary revival.[15] Nevertheless, Ferguson's relatively juvenile attack on the translations in Hardiman has generally been taken as a definitive assessment. Furlong's background as an outspoken member of the Catholic Association and an ardent Catholic emancipationist obviously did not endear him to Ferguson, but ironically it is Ferguson's malicious approach that brings Furlong to the attention of readers of modern literature. Ferguson's sectarianism is even more apparent in the lines immediately following his virulent attack on Furlong:

---

[13]   *The Dublin University Magazine* II/5 (1833), 141.
[14]   W. J. McCormack, "The Intellectual Revival (1830-1850)", in *The Field Day Anthology of Irish Writing,* ed. Seamus Deane, Derry, 1991, I, 1176.
[15]   Seamus Deane, *A Short History of Irish Literature*, London, 1986, 69.

> One name of a higher grade in literary reputation, appears among
> the translators ... his ode to the Hill of Howth, and adieu of Gerald
> Nugent, come close on our idea of the happy mean, and induce us to
> part with him on better terms, so far as he has gone, than we can
> accord to any of his companions in the work. *Perhaps we may be*
> *prejudiced in Dr Drummond's favour, in consequence of the*
> *absence of anything like political hatred or sectarian malignity in*
> *his contributions.*[16]

It is interesting to note that Dr Drummond, like Ferguson, was an
Ulster Presbyterian whose affinities were certainly closer to Anglican
ascendancy than Catholic nationalism. Ferguson in his articles is at
times particularly mischievous, for example in his insistence that
"Roisin Dubh" is the love-song of a frustrated priest. Here he exhibits
the very "sectarian malignity" of which he accuses Furlong and
Hardiman:

> This says Mr Hardiman, is an allegorical political ballad – it seems
> to be the song of a priest in love, of a priest in love too who has
> broken his vow, of a priest in love who was expecting a dispensation
> for his paramour, of a priest in love who was willing to turn
> ploughman for his love's sake – nay, to practice the very calling of a
> priest to support her.
>   And why, in the name of holy nature, should the priest not be in
> love? and why, in the name of sacred humanity, should the priest not
> long to enjoy his love? and why in the name of divine reason, do the
> Roman Catholic priesthood of the present day submit to a
> prohibition so unnatural, monstrous, antiscriptural, and innovatory
> as that which gives the will of some old man seven centuries ago, as
> the only reason why he should not love?[17]

This might seem an unwarrantably spirited attack on the Catholic
priesthood in such a narrow context and certainly it reflects the over-
enthusiasm of a still young writer (Ferguson was twenty-four at the
time of publication). It is also indicative of how Ferguson
fundamentally misunderstood the allegorical nature of much Gaelic
poetry. Emerging tension between Catholic nationalism and Protestant
ascendancy is increasingly a feature of Irish periodicals from the
1820s onwards. Indeed in view of the political climate as described

---

[16]   *The Dublin University Magazine*, III/10 (1834), 455 (italics added).
[17]   *The Dublin University Magazine,* IV/8 (1834), 158.

previously it would be surprising if it were not so. Leerssen's asserts that Ferguson could hardly view Hardiman's enterprise as anything other than as a nationalist one, conjuring up for Protestant ascendancy a most threatening picture, "that of a peasantry which was vocal, politically informed and conscious, disaffected and anything but naïve, anything but satisfied with their humble lot in life".[18]

Leaving aside the *Irish Minstrelsy* and the politics of translation for the moment, I wish to briefly examine Furlong's other works. Apart from his contributions to various magazines, Furlong published only two small volumes during his lifetime, *The Misanthrope* and *The Plagues of Ireland*. *The Misanthrope* was self-published in London in the summer of 1819, when Furlong was aged twenty-five but was withdrawn due to the many printing errors which it contained.[19] A second edition printed in Dublin by W. Underwood was published in 1821. *The Field Day Anthology of Irish Writing* incorrectly states that Furlong was a recluse, an apparent misreading of the Introduction to *The Misanthrope* (since that poem was addressed by Furlong to an unknown friend in London who "dwelt secluded from all society").[20]

His subsequent volume, *The Plagues of Ireland*, published in Dublin in 1824, is a poetical satire written in the Augustan manner associated with Alexander Pope and is described on the title page as being printed for the author. It is highly critical of the administration of the day describing them as "a rank nest of idiots, and of knaves, / Of pamper'd tyrants, and of pillag'd slaves".

The poem describes social ills and inequalities as perceived by Furlong and calls to account a long list of public characters. In his Introduction he leaves us in no doubt as to its political purpose:

> The name of our country, and the story of her wrongs, have, at length, forced themselves upon the attention of the world. The people of Britain; the free inhabitants of America; and even the crowned slave owners of the continent have given, through different mediums, an indication of the growing interest which they take in all that concerns us as a nation .... To those who may have heard of our wrongs – to those who know that we have been injured – to those who are aware of our past sufferings, but who know not the nature or character of those under which we still labour – to such, in the

---

[18] Leerssen, *Remembrance and Imagination*, 178.
[19] Thomas Furlong's Introduction to the second edition of *The Misanthrope*, Dublin, 1821.
[20] *The Field Day Anthology*, II, 16.

absence of a more formal statement, I shall venture to offer the following little sketch.

Due to its anti-government bias and the strong sentiments expressed in the poem Furlong was tempted to publish the piece anonymously. This is hardly surprising in view of the treatment meted out to Watty Cox and John Magee less than a decade earlier. Magee had been imprisoned and fined heavily for daring to publish a critical review of the Duke of Richmond's administration in the *Evening Post* in 1813. Cox spent three years in Newgate prison from 1810 onwards following his criticism of the authorities in his magazine, the *Irish Magazine or Asylum of Neglected Biography*.[21]

The Doom of Derenzie is Furlong's longest work. Although the poem was in gestation for a considerable number of years, Furlong never succeeded in having it published during his lifetime. Manuscript copies of the work, which began as The *Old Man of Clone* and later became *Tale of Superstition* are among Furlong's papers in the National Library of Ireland.[22] In fact there is no evidence that Furlong ever used the published title *The Doom of Derenzie* and it is probable that this was the idea of M. J. Whitty, which may explain why he substituted his own introduction for Furlong's and provided his own notes.

Whitty, in any event, was a friend of Furlong and had earlier been editor of the *Dublin and London Magazine*. The poem features the wizard Old Wrue, based on a local character Sean Roe, and the DeRenzy family, Wexford Protestant gentry of the time, and is among other things an attempt to obtain poetic justice for an underclass for which little other redress was available. Wrue's cherished niece Margaret becomes pregnant in her twenty-first year and subsequently disappears, leaving Wrue distraught. Wrue through his arcane powers identifies Derenzie as the one who defiled and murdered his beloved niece. Derenzie is falsely accused of a Whiteboy crime, the murder of a peasant named Wilson, arrested on his wedding day and publicly hanged a week later.[23] As Furlong outlines in his original manuscript, the moral of the narrative is that:

---

[21] Cox was jailed for seditious libel following the printing of an article entitled "The Painter's Cut: A Vision", published in his *Irish Magazine*, III/6 (1810), 295.

[22] NLI, MS 8359, fols. 21, 27.

[23] In real life, this is an unlikely scenario. From the description in the poem Wilson, murdered by the Whiteboys, was most likely a Catholic. The Derenzies were

Heaven rarely suffers the innocent to perish, however contradictory or inexplicable external circumstances may appear – or to use the words of one of the characters introduced "That God who framed this world in goodness and in love still governs it in justice".

The poem has many Gothic features and it seems probable that Maturin's novel *Melmoth the Wanderer*, published in 1820 and still regarded as one of the finest examples of Irish Gothic fiction, strongly influenced Furlong's presentation of the story. Indeed there is evidence in Furlong's manuscripts to show that he maintained a friendship with Maturin.

Furlong's manuscripts include an eleven-and-a-half-page introduction, in which he sets out the background to the poem:

> The leading character in the following poem is one that may be deemed original. Lady Morgan, Miss Edgeworth and latterly Mr Maturin in his tale of Melmoth have favoured the public with sketches of characters somewhat similar – but no writer it is believed has as yet introduced into a poetical work the full drawn portrait of a Fairyman. The picture has in it nothing of exaggeration – in fact it is from real life – for the original Shane Rhue but a few years ago was known and followed and reverenced by all the peasantry of the upper part of the county of Wexford.[24]

Besides displaying an interest in Gothicism, Furlong exhibits traces of influence from the leading Romantic poets of the day, including Wordsworth, Coleridge and, to some extent, Burns. However, he never achieves the precision of expression and poignant simplicity which typify Wordsworth. Some elements of the poem, such as his descriptions of Old Wrue, are particularly reminiscent of parts of *The Corsair*, published by Byron in 1814.[25] Furlong was well acquainted with Byron's work and during his career wrote several pieces about him, including one on *The Corsair,* which was published in 1820 in the *Dublin Magazine or General Repertory of Philosophy, Belles*

Protestant Ascendancy class and would not have been suspected of a murder associated with the Whiteboys. Many of the Derenzies were also local magistrates, making the scene described even more unlikely.

[24] NLI, MS 8359, fol. 21.

[25] Lord Byron, *The Corsair: A Tale*, first published in 1814 and dedicated to Thomas Moore.

Lettres and Miscellaneous Information.[26] In it he compares the plot of
the poem to that of "Zelida or the Pirates", written many years before
by a certain H. Siddons, and implies that Byron has plagiarized this
source.

Furlong's work also at times shows a Keatsian influence;
Derenzie's dream in part three, for instance, is comparable to *The Fall
of Hyperion*, while his use of blank verse can at times be compared
with *The Excursion.*[27] Broadly speaking, his descriptions of nature,
drawn from scenes of his own youth, are in the tradition of the
Romanticism of the period.

As Whitty states in the Introduction to the poem, Furlong seemed
to feel that *The Doom of Derenzie* contained "more of his mind and
poetical feelings" than his other pieces. His manuscript notes show
that he was well aware of the literary faults of the poem:

> With regard to the metre the author feels it is unnecessary to say
> much – unlimited allowances have in their respect been made to
> poets who have age and learning and experience on their side, and
> surely the same or even greater degree of indulgence may be
> reasonably vouchsafed to one who is for almost the first time about
> to tempt "the award of Gods men and columns".[28]

The use of blank verse in places is well suited to the theme and
presentation of the poem, although it would have benefited from
sympathetic editing. It does not appear to have caused more than a
ripple in literary circles at the time of its publication other than a few
notices in periodicals.

The other main source of Furlong's work is the *Dublin and London
Magazine* published from 1824 to 1828 and edited by Furlong's friend
and fellow Wexfordman M. J. Whitty. Many of Furlong's smaller
pieces were published in this magazine and are worthy of further
examination.

---

[26] *Dublin Magazine or General Repertory of Philosophy, Belles Lettres and
Miscellaneous Information*, I/2 (1820), 59.

[27] Published in 1814 by William Wordsworth. See also Thomas Moore's letter to
Furlong recounted in "Memoir of Thomas Furlong", in James Hardiman's *Irish
Minstrelsy*. Furlong submitted some work written in blank verse to Moore for his
appraisal. Moore states: "There is nothing less popular at the present day than
blank verse; as some proof of which, I need not perhaps tell you (for your subject
and his are somewhat similar,) that the 'Excursion' of Wordsworth, one of our
finest geniuses, lies unbought and unread on his publishers shelves."

[28] NLI, MS 8359, fol. 21.

This essay has attempted to present a case for a re-reading and re-assessment of the work of Thomas Furlong, including his translations Hardiman's *Irish Minstrelsy* and Ferguson's assessment of them. There is still much to be learned from the developing interaction of politics and literature of the period in the aftermath of 1798 and the Act of Union. Indeed, in researching the period one is forcibly struck by the similarity of the rhetoric used with that still in use today. In the circumstances I would be surprised if my own prejudices do not shine through. I am still convinced however that Ferguson's assessment, coloured as it was, has been accepted rather too freely in modern critical appraisal. The difficulty in finding a suitable medium in the English language to do justice to original Irish verse is now all too well acknowledged. There is nevertheless a legitimacy to Furlong's work which to date has not been sufficiently recognized. Furlong's other works are also deserving of further examination and I have published an anthology which will at least make them more accessible.[29]

---

[29] Sean Mythen, *Thomas Furlong: The Forgotten Wexford Poet*, Wexford, 1998. I wish to acknowledge the assistance which I received in researching Thomas Furlong from the Centre for Irish Literature and Bibliography, University of Ulster, Coleraine. I am particularly indebted to Dr Bruce Stewart.

"THEIR JEALOUS ART":
TRANSLATORS, PRECURSORS AND EPIGONES
IN THE POETRY OF SEAMUS HEANEY

RUI CARVALHO HOMEM

My title opens with the closing words of "The Scribes", a poem in the "Sweeney Redivivus" section of Seamus Heaney's 1984 collection *Station Island*.[1] Ostensibly about medieval scribes in their scriptorium, it becomes a poem about writing in general, about the text and its margins, about translation – as is well known, these Sweeney poems grew out of Heaney's experience of translating *Sweeney Astray* (1983) – and also, as the poet himself acknowledged, a poem "very much about literary life".[2] In the Faber edition, it follows the much more often quoted "The Master" – a poem about poetic descent, poetic masters and disciples, precursors and followers. I will argue that these two poems, placed side by side at the centre of the poetic sequence, are also central to the designs served by "Sweeney Redivivus", and that this sequence is in turn central to the designs of a writing which has consistently become more metapoetic, more intertextual and self-referential. That centrality will allow me to use poems from this sequence as a vantage point from which to consider both earlier and later poems. But, before that, some brief notes are called for on the intertextual drive of modern Irish poetry, and of Seamus Heaney's poetry in particular.

Indeed, the extent to which the strengths of modern Irish poetry can be connected with the poets' mutual awareness, and with its consequence in the form of a close-knit intertextual design, has often

---

[1] Seamus Heaney, *Station Island*, London, 1984; henceforth referred to as *SI*, followed by page numbers.

[2] Rand Brandes, "'Inscribed in Sheets': Seamus Heaney's Scribal Matrix", in *Seamus Heaney: The Shaping Spirit*, eds Catherine Malloy and Phyllis Carey, London, 1996, 59.

deserved critical attention.³ This is matched by an even greater critical commonplace that points out the extent to which some of the weaknesses of modern Irish poetry can be linked to a persistent awareness of predecessors. That awareness helps account for the totemic value a term like "tradition" has long acquired in Irish critical discourse; and, insofar as it is often experienced as constraint, limitation, or as a source of anxiety, it has led to suggestions that a Harold Bloomian notion of influence might find its natural laboratory in a tradition so strongly marked by that play of desired and spurned parental and filial relationships organized around Yeats and Joyce as alternative father-figures.⁴ Finally, and since that awareness of others has its source in each poet's desire to stabilize a literary identity as a participant in a network of poetic relationships, it entails a highly strung self-awareness evinced in the poetry's tendency to become one of its own more constant referents.

Such anxious dealings might seem remote from a canonical poet like Seamus Heaney, but both his poetry and his critical writings have always acknowledged a vicarious element in this poet's strategies for self-definition. Besides often alluding in his poems, sometimes explicitly, to poets from different languages and traditions, Heaney has been a regular participant in that practice of dedicating poems to fellow poets that looms particularly large in modern Irish poetry, and by which elective affinities are more or less discreetly suggested. He has also entered canon-making ventures, by editing and introducing the section on Yeats in *The Field Day Anthology of Irish Writing*, or – in less conventional fashion – as the co-editor (with Ted Hughes) of two anthologies, the more idiosyncratic *The Rattle Bag,* and the more scholarly and authoritative *The School Bag.*⁵ But, above all, "the criticism of [this] practitioner" (to retrieve a phrase from Eliot which

³ See, for example, Douglas Dunn, "Mañana is Now", *Encounter*, XLV/5 (1975), 79; James Simmons, "I Have Seen Your Workroom", *Honest Ulsterman*, 77 (Winter 1984), 53; Robert Crawford, "Callaloo", *London Review of Books*, 20 April 1989, 23; Edna Longley, "Literature", in *Cultural Traditions in Northern Ireland: Varieties of Britishness*, ed. Maurna Crozier, Belfast, 1990, 26.
⁴ See *Tradition and Influence in Anglo-Irish Poetry*, eds Terence Brown and Nicholas Grene, Houndmills and London, 1989, *passim*; Edna Longley, "'It is time that I wrote my will': Anxieties of Influence and Succession", in *Yeats Annual No. 12. Special Number. That Accusing Eye: Yeats and his Irish Readers*, eds Warwick Gould and Edna Longley, Houndmills and London, 1996, *passim*.
⁵ *The Field Day Anthology of Irish Writing*, ed. Seamus Deane, Derry, 1991, II; *The Rattle Bag*, eds Seamus Heaney and Ted Hughes, London, 1982; *The School Bag*, eds Seamus Heaney and Ted Hughes, London, 1997.

Heaney is fond of quoting) has consistently been a way of charting his poetic development and his affinities – and (willingly or not) it has presented the reader with successive instances of self-reading refracted through readings of others. In Heaney's own words, "I suppose my criticism is some form of autobiography".[6]

One of the key texts of Heaney's criticism in this respect, with particular attention to the ways of poetic descent, is his 1985 essay "Envies and Identifications: Dante and the Modern Poet". It opens with Yeats quoted on Dante in "Ego Dominus Tuus", followed by a brief commentary, and by the assertion:

> I quote these lines at the outset as a reminder that when poets turn to the great masters of the past, they turn to an image of their own creation, one which is likely to be a reflection of their own imaginative needs, their own artistic inclinations and procedures.[7]

This is phrased as if it were an absolute truism, something that requires no demonstration (it is no more than "a reminder") and it follows that instance of a double-range dialogue – Heaney-reading-Yeats-reading-Dante. Its choice of words makes this assertion evocative, moreover, of Harold Bloom on the self-directed concerns of the "ephebe" *vs* the great precursor: the duality in the title ("Envies and Identifications") and the frequent use of the word "influence" throughout the essay make this reference inevitable, even if Heaney does not explicitly invoke it.

Although the essay opens with Yeats, it is Eliot who becomes the foremost object of attention, confirming an interest Heaney started to evince in the late 1970s – when a longing for "authority", and for enabling models of authority, became explicit in some of his pronouncements.[8] And it is about authority, and models that Heaney is writing in "Envies and Identifications": "Virgil comes to Dante ... as Dante comes to Eliot, a master, a guide and authority"[9] – a great lineage in which one can sense it is Heaney's ambition to participate (he would, in 1989, publish an essay called "Learning from Eliot"[10]).

---

[6] Randy Brandes, "Seamus Heaney: An Interview", *Salmagundi*, 80 (Fall 1988), 14.

[7] Seamus Heaney, "Envies and Identifications: Dante and the Modern Poet", *Irish University Review*, XV/1 (1985), 5.

[8] Frank Kinahan, "Artists on Art: An Interview with Seamus Heaney", *Critical Inquiry*, 8 (Spring 1982), 410.

[9] Heaney, "Envies and Identifications", 11.

[10] Seamus Heaney, "Learning from Eliot", *Agenda*, XXVII/1 (1989), 17-31.

He seems to waver, though, between the "peaceful" and grateful
model of literary descent which the passage just quoted seemed to
illustrate – a kind of descent Eliot himself envisaged and described[11] –
and the hint of a Bloomian *agon*: "Eliot begins to envy the coherence
and certitude ... available to his great predecessor."[12] This wavering
tries to resolve itself by, on the one hand, postulating an individual
yearning for triumph in re-creating the predecessor – whilst promptly
making clear that the ultimate aim is no more than the security of what
can be shared and held in common:

> Eliot was recreating Dante in his own image. He had always taken
> what he needed from the work and ... he needed ... a way of
> confirming himself as a poet ready to submit his intelligence and
> sensibility to a framework of beliefs which were inherited and
> communal.[13]

One might add that a similar balancing act is attempted in one of
Heaney's Richard Ellmann Lectures collected as *The Place of Writing*,
a lecture in which Heaney quotes and expands on Auden's notion of
reception as digestion and re-creation, but also comes to represent the
attitude of followers towards the canonical precursor rather in terms of
wilful distances and of the interchange of inscription and erasure:

> a dialectic is set in motion in which the new writing does not so
> much displace the old as strive to displace itself to an enabling
> distance away from it ... any writing is to some extent an unwriting
> not only of previous writings but even of itself.[14]

The latter notion will obviously find a particular resonance in
Heaney's experience of translation, and in the consequence that
experience has had in his own poetry – which brings us back to the
"Sweeney Redivivus" poems, the most manifest instance of such
links. But it should also at this stage be pointed out that, from the
beginning, continuity *vs* confrontation have characterized Heaney's
representation of the relationship to a precursor – even when, in early

---

[11] See, for example, T. S. Eliot, "What is a Classic" (1944), in T. S. Eliot, *On Poetry and Poets*, London, 1957, 57-58.
[12] Heaney, "Envies and Identifications", 11.
[13] *Ibid.*, 12.
[14] Seamus Heaney, *The Place of Writing*, Atlanta: GA, 1989, 55-56.

poems like "Digging" and "Follower",[15] the father-figure was the biological father. More recently, the poet's father would be elegiacally remembered in several poems in *Seeing Things* (1991), some of his symbols of authority – "The Ash Plant", "my father's stick"[16] – acquiring a metapoetic and meta-scribal value which a three-line poem in *The Spirit Level* (1996) would confirm:

> The dotted line my father's ashplant made
> On Sandymount Strand
> Is something else the tide won't wash away.[17]

This ghostly return of the father, and the persistence of his insignia of power and of the marks they left, could remind us that, in the late 1970s, the first of Heaney's "Glanmore Sonnets" had proposed writing as the outcome of the arrival of the poet's "ghosts",[18] an experience of otherness in the self. And "Widgeon", in Part I of *Station Island*, would offer Heaney's readers a memorable representation of the borrowed voice by having someone blow on a dead bird's voice box, thus making its cry sound again (*SI*, 48) – an episode reminiscent, in fact, of Ezra Pound's dictum on translation as a way of bringing a dead man to life.[19]

Rather obviously, then, the conception of the poetic suggested by such poems will find an emblematic realization in that assumption of the other's voice in one's own which happens when the poet takes up translation – which Heaney has regularly done.[20] Most of his translations can be argued to be closely connected with dominant concerns in

---

[15]   Seamus Heaney, *Death of a Naturalist*, London, 1966, 1-2, 12.

[16]   Seamus Heaney, *Seeing Things*, London, 1991, 19, 20 (henceforth referred to as *ST*, followed by page numbers).

[17]   Seamus Heaney, *The Spirit Level*, London, 1995, 62 (henceforth referred to as *SL*, followed by page numbers).

[18]   Seamus Heaney, *Field Work*, London, 1979, 33 (henceforth referred to as *FW*, followed by page numbers).

[19]   See Susan Bassnett, *Translation Studies*, revised edn, London, 1991, 83.

[20]   His best-known ventures as a translator being Dante's "Ugolino" episode, which closed *Field Work* (*FW*, 61-64); the middle-Irish epic published as *Sweeney Astray* (London, 1983); the version of Sophocles's *Philoctetes* published as *The Cure at Troy* (London, 1990); Brian Merriman's *The Midnight Court*, published together with extracts from Ovid as *The Midnight Verdict* (Loughcrew, 1993); the extracts from Virgil and Dante which respectively opened and closed *Seeing Things* (*ST*, 1-3, 111-13); and Jan Kochanowski's *Laments*, translated in collaboration with Stanislaw Baranczak, London, 1995.

Heaney's own (or "other") poetry at the time they were made, but this
process has never been more blatant and obvious than with *Sweeney
Astray*, since a whole sequence of twenty poems came out of it.
Furthermore, Heaney very explicitly commented on that venture and
its impact on his writing.[21]

Heaney's description of the experience of translating *Sweeney
Astray* lays a primary emphasis on the political reading of the
Sweeney text, and on the way it lent the poet a voice for a refracted,
indirect commentary on the Northern Irish situation. But in the poems
in *Station Island* which came out of that translation the metapoetic
dimension takes the foreground. Heaney himself acknowledged that,
at that stage, "I had got fed up with my own mournful bondings to the
'matter of Ulster'".[22] Thus "Sweeney Redivivus" was also "a very
definite reaction against the kind of deliberately unlyrical work I did
in the title poem of *Station Island*", a closing sequence written, then,
"from the perspective of a liberated, exorcised consciousness".[23]

Freedom is then one of the meanings which the Sweeney persona
takes on, a freedom which entails a different and enhanced consciousness of self and world, as suggested in the closing words of "In the
Beech": "My tree of knowledge. / My thick-tapped, soft-fledged, airy
listening post" (*SI*, 100). But, together with release, this translated (in
all senses of the word) persona of the mythical mad king turned into
bird also experiences estrangement, alienation – words whose
etymologies are here fully relevant. The same poem makes clear that
the tree as Sweeney's abode is both "a strangeness and a comfort",
and its opening line is: "I was a lookout posted and forgotten" (*SI*
100). Significantly, Heaney would re-employ the image of the lookout
as a poetic persona at least twice – the sense of freedom and
potentiality predominating in one case, the sense of estrangement,
limitation and abandonment in the other. In "The Watchman's War"
(the first poem of the sequence "Mycenae Lookout" in *The Spirit
Level*), the poetic subject defines himself as "the lookout / The
queen's command had posted and forgotten", "still honour-bound",

21 Seamus Heaney, "Earning a Rhyme: Notes on Translating *Buile Suibhne*", in *The
    Art of Translation: Voices from the Field*, ed. Rosanna Warren, Boston, 1989, 13-
    20.
22 Heaney, "Earning a Rhyme", 20.
23 Seamus Heaney, "The Frontier of Writing", in *Irish Writers and Their Creative
    Process*, eds Jacqueline Genet and Wynne Hellegouarc'h, Gerrards Cross, 1996,
    7.

whose "sentry work was fate, a home to go to", who "balanced between destiny and dread" (*SL*, 29-30). This comes, of course, from a poem and a sequence in which Heaney returns to that reflection on the artist's ethical and political responsibilities which had been so painfully central to some of his poetry in the 1970s and 1980s, but seemed to have been largely eclipsed by the emphasis on the marvellous and the transcendent in *Seeing Things*. Rather predictably, the other reappearance of the image of the lookout – the one in which the sense of freedom is favoured – occurs in a poem in *Seeing Things*, "The Settle Bed": "You are free as the lookout,/ That far-seeing joker posted high over the fog" (*ST*, 29). These words occur after the outrageous but liberating injunction to "Imagine a dower of settle beds tumbled from heaven", a triumph of the imponderable over the ponderous which is made possible by the dictum: "whatever is given / Can always be reimagined" (*ST*, 29).

This could be a motto for Heaney's (already quoted) understanding of "any writing" as "an unwriting not only of previous writings but even of itself", as also for that rewriting of the Sweeney figure which "Sweeney Redivivus" proposes – and this in a sequence also written, as we saw above, "from the perspective of a liberated, exorcised consciousness". The four lines of the opening poem, "The First Gloss", comprise all of these meanings:

> Take hold of the shaft of the pen.
> Subscribe to the first step taken
> from a justified line into the margin.

> (*SI*, 97)

Liberation means here also the transgression proper to a marginal writing, "glosses" (of which these four lines are just "the first"), which, in this case, are instances of a meta-writing at two removes: writing which is prompted by the experience of rewriting, in other words, poems enabled by the experience of producing translations of yet other poems. With "Sweeney Redivivus", such meta-writing takes centre stage: the derivative leaves the margins to question the whole notion of priority and originality. It may be significant of the continuing resonance which this questioning comes to have in Heaney's poetry that in *The Spirit Level*, under a title similar to "The First Gloss" – "The First Words" – a translation of a poem by Marin Sorescu will open with a denial of the pristine:

> The first words got polluted
> Like river water in the morning
> Flowing with the dirt
> Of blurbs and the front pages.
>
> (*SL*, 38)

In fact, *The Spirit Level* seems haunted by the notion of experience as ever re-livable and re-presentable. In its opening poem, "The Rain Stick", the pleasure afforded by the sound of the toylike implement, listened to again and again, prompts a denial of any exclusive associations between a potential for pleasure and beauty, and the original and once-only event:

> What happens next
>
> Is undiminished for having happened once,
> Twice, ten, a thousand times before.
>
> (*SL*, 1)

The metapoetic implications of this become much clearer towards the end of the book, when the poet explicitly claims descent from a craftsman whose art is usually no more than re-making, re-stitching – rather than producing the unique and original work:

> Then all of a sudden there appears to me
> The journeyman tailor who was my antecedent:
> Up on a table, cross-legged, ripping out
>
> A garment he must recut or resew.
>
> (*SL*, 67)

Nearly a decade before this, however, Heaney's attitude towards a notion of his art as a repetition of ever-renewable motions was not so mildly content as some of his poems of the 1990s seem to suggest. Dissatisfaction was patent and emphatic in "The Stone Grinder", a poem in *The Haw Lantern*; following an initial allusion to Penelope's work as comparably less dissatisfying, the poetic subject represents himself in words reminiscent of Heaney's critical notion of writing as "an unwriting ... of previous writings":

> Me, I ground the same stones for fifty years
> and what I undid was never the thing I had done.
> I was unrewarded as darkness at a mirror.[24]

The closing line of the poem lays an even greater emphasis on this craftsman's resentful awareness of his lack of consequence, by proposing *coitus interruptus* as an apt metaphor for his craft. But the middle tercets phrase resentment and anxiety in more explicit terms:

> I prepared my surface to survive what came over it –
> cartographers, printmakers, all that lining and inking.
> I ordained opacities and they haruspicated.
>
> For them it was a new start and a clean slate
> every time. For me, it was coming full circle
> like the ripple perfected in stillness.   (*HL*, 8)

Resentment that "they" enjoy the prerogative of the first, original stroke, of always cutting the renewed surface; anxiety that "I" always have to offer the surfaces "I" make for their successive palimpsestic inscriptions, my work being ever superseded by theirs: a true "anxiety of succession", to borrow Edna Longley's phrase.[25]

In the light they shed on Heaney's consideration of priority *vs* posterity, the lines above hark back to poems like "The Master" and "The Scribes"– which I will finally address, to argue that the two poems, self-containedly facing each other on opposite pages, can be taken to voice respectively an "anxiety of influence" and an "anxiety of succession" (to resort again to Edna Longley's phrase). The self-centred loneliness of "The Master", as well as his abode in his peculiar tower, made evident from the very first words of the poem – "He dwelt in himself / like a rook in an unroofed tower" (*SI*, 110) – make it highly tempting to assume that Yeats is the figure approached in this poem, even if Heaney himself declared it is rather Czeslaw Milosz.[26]

The attitude of the persona towards the figure of the master, together with several phrases and lexical choices in the poem, also seem deliberately to echo some of Heaney's critical pronouncements

---

[24]   Seamus Heaney, *The Haw Lantern*, London, 1987, 8 (henceforth referred to as *HL*, followed by page numbers).

[25]   Longley, "'It is time that I wrote my will'", *passim*.

[26]   Brandes, "'Inscribed in sheets'", 58.

on Yeats, which have, in fact, significantly evolved in the course of the past two decades. In some of the texts collected in Heaney's first volume of essays, *Preoccupations*, it would be difficult to miss the way admiration is mingled with dislike when Yeats' mode of composition is characterized as forceful and assertive – "masculine", "theatrical in its triumph", set in a "rhetorical cast", "the music of energy reined down, of the mastered beast stirring", "a mastery, a handling, a struggle towards maximum articulation" – or, from another standpoint, when we are reminded that "a very great poet can be a very bad influence on other poets".[27] But this coexists with the admission that "one is awed by the achieved and masterful tones of that deliberately pitched voice", and (even more significantly) with the recognition that "[Yeats] is, indeed, the ideal example for a poet approaching middle age".[28] (One should, of course, remember that Heaney started representing himself *nel mezzo del cammin* at a rather early age, for present-day standards, which was also when he started to declare his already-mentioned longing for "authority".)

Attraction to Yeats will become less qualified in Heaney's later criticism, a process also made easier by the fact that Heaney will, in characteristic fashion, start highlighting those aspects of Yeats' poetry more in tune with the emphases which will triumph with *Seeing Things*. As a consequence, words and phrases like "transcendence", "the marvellous", "our best-dreamt possibilities", "a universal sym-bollic force", will become dominant in Heaney's critical lexicon for Yeats – be it in the Introduction to the section on Yeats in *The Field Day Anthology*, or in one of the essays in *The Redress of Poetry*.[29]

This evolution of Heaney's perspective on Yeats will not be devoid of irony, though: one of the poems in the "Squarings" sequence of *Seeing Things* will raise a number of interrogations, both mystical and metapoetic, which will in the closing line be described, between brackets, as "(Set questions for the ghost of W. B.)" (*ST*, 78). The familiar use of the initials, together with the classroom associations of the phrase "set questions", can make this poem a possibly conscious, half-mocking instance of that ultimate "revisionary ratio" in Harold Bloom's theory of influence – "*Apophrades*, or the return of the

---

[27] Seamus Heaney, *Preoccupations: Selected Prose 1968–1978*, London, 1980, 73, 75, 109.

[28] *Ibid.*, 109, 110.

[29] *The Field Day Anthology*, II, 783-90; Seamus Heaney, *The Redress of Poetry*, London, 1995, 146-63.

dead"[30] – by which the relative positions of master and disciple are reversed.

Some other Bloomian "revisionary ratios" might be identified in "The Master", "almost an allegory of ... the anxiety of influence", as Neil Corcoran styled it.[31] In fact, the connection between "The Master" and the "Squarings" poem "for the ghost of W. B." also includes the question, in the later text: "Where does it [spirit] roost at last? On dungy sticks / In a jackdaw's nest up in the old stone tower[?]" (*ST*, 78). One should not forget, of course, that in the earlier poem the approach to the rook-like figure of the master is being attempted by the half-bird persona of Sweeney – which also helps conceal the hubris of such an attempt, allegorized as a difficult "climb up deserted ramparts", under the Master's dreaded "eye on the watch / from his coign of seclusion" (*SI*, 110). But contact with the mastery of the great figure, although it leads to a clear acknowledgment of the rigour, the exactness of his writing –

> Each character blocked on the parchment secure
> in its volume and measure.
> Each maxim given its space.   (*SI*, 110)

– will also entail a deflation of the sense of wonder. It is, after all, a writing governed by codes which, better or worse, all initiates will already know:

> Deliberately he would unclasp
> his book of withholding
> a page at a time and it was nothing
> arcane, just the old rules
> we all had inscribed on our slates.   (*SI*, 110)

If one were to try and demonstrate Neil Corcoran's suggestion that this poem might have been written to allegorize Harold Bloom's theory of influence, this passage, in the voice of the hybrid, alienated and translated Sweeney persona, might be read as a version of the fourth revisionary ratio, "Daemonization", which happens when

> an intermediary being, neither divine nor human, enters into the adept to aid him. The later poet opens himself to what he believes to

---

[30]   Harold Bloom, *The Anxiety of Influence: A Theory of Poetry*, Oxford, 1973, 15.
[31]   Neil Corcoran, *Seamus Heaney*, London, 1986, 174.

be a power in the parent-poem that does not belong to the parent
proper, but to a range of being just beyond that precursor ... [so] as
to generalize away the uniqueness of the earlier work.[32]

Or rather, in Sweeney's words, "nothing / arcane, just the old rules".
On the other hand, if the order of the ratios were arbitrary, or if they
could coexist at the same stage of a poet's development, the self-
deflation proper to the third ratio of the *agon* could be identified in the
final stanza:

> How flimsy I felt climbing down
> the unrailed stairs on the wall,
> hearing the purpose and venture
> in a wingflap above me.
>
>   (*SI*, 110)

Rather than bringing about a deflation of the precursor, thus
relativizing his own – as in Bloom's *kenosis*[33] – Heaney is here
proposing an ironical reading of his relation to Yeats, conscious as he
is of how often criticism has taken the "anxiety" of that relationship
for granted (beginning with Harold Bloom himself, in a famous
review of *Field Work*[34]). The irony is achieved by summoning a
probably unexpected Yeatsian intertext: behind the awe-struck tone of
the closing words of "The Master", "the purpose and venture / in a
wingflap above me" (*SI*, 110), there flap the wings of the best-known
Yeatsian bird, "the great wings beating still / Above the staggering
girl".[35] The travestying of the bird-man Sweeney as Leda, is assisted
by the "female" vulnerability admitted on climbing down (contrasting,
it should be noted, with the way a refusal of wonder had qualified the
awed experience of accessing the master's book): "How flimsy I felt
climbing down" (*SI*, 110) – "How can those terrified vague fingers
...". And the irony expands with the perception that Yeats' swan-god
descends imperiously on Leda – whereas Heaney's bird-man climbs
vulnerably up to Yeats-the-rook in his "unroofed tower", which, at
this point, not only alludes to Thoor Ballylee and its abundant

---

[32]   Bloom, *The Anxiety of Influence*, 15.
[33]   *Ibid.*,14-15.
[34]   Harold Bloom, Introduction to *Seamus Heaney: Modern Critical Views*, ed.
        Harold Bloom, New York, 1986, 1-10.
[35]   W. B. Yeats, "Leda and the Swan", in W. B. Yeats, *The Collected Poems*, 2nd ed.,
        London and Basingstoke, 1950, 241.

representation elsewhere in Yeats, as it also echoes "the burning roof and tower".

Finally, since "The Master" is ultimately about power, Heaney's ironical allusions in this poem may also imply the final question of "Leda and the Swan", as a hypothetical and equally ironical analogy to poetic impregnation by the great precursor: "Being so caught up, so mastered ... / Did she put on his knowledge with his power [?]."One might only add that the physical circumstances represented by Heaney in "The Master" – the climb, the "coign of seclusion", the birds above –have sufficient resonance in his imagination for a poem in *The Spirit Level* to include a record of:

> the sheer exaltation
> Of remembering climbing zig-zag up warm steps
> To the hermit's eyrie ....
> Crows sailing high and close ...
> ...
> Eleven in the morning. I made a note:
> "Rock-lover, loner, sky-sentry, all hail!"
> And somewhere the dove rose. And kept on rising.
>
> (*SL*, 26)

Irony may be common to "The Master" and "The Scribes" (albeit manifested in different ways), but the sense of awe which predominated in the former poem is replaced in the latter by sheer dislike for the scribes, manifested from the opening words, even if disturbed by the persona's reluctant sense of having "[his] place" among them. Their asceticism made of spite rather than emotional purification, the scribes become like the implements of their craft – "a black pearl kept gathering in them / like the old dry glut inside their quills" (*SI*, 111) – a craft whose fastidiousness harbours and conceals the "blackness" of their emotions.

Their "resentment" is also, very clearly, that of the derivative writer, the copyist who can only give vent to his frustration for his subaltern status by writing marginal glosses, thus somehow unwriting the subservience of "texts of praise", in whose margins "they scratched and clawed" (*SI*, 111). But this choice of verbs, together with the writing of glosses, effectively brings together the copyists, the bird-man Sweeney (with his "claws" or talons) and the authorial figure hiding behind the persona – the poet translator who now writes these glosses "in the margin" (so to speak) of his translations, of his

texts written in an attitude of acknowledgment to a previous writer. To
make it more complex, however, the persona also seems to speak in
the voice of the "original" author "against" whom (both in the sense of
confrontation and of a calque writing) the scribes use their craft:

> Now and again I started up
> miles away and saw in my absence
> the sloped cursive of each back and felt them
> perfect themselves against me page by page.   (*SI*, 111)

Resentment is mutual: but if the scribes experience that of the
derivative writer, the privilege of the first person gives the upper hand
to the "anxiety of succession" of the authorial persona, angry at those
who "perfect themselves against [him]". It is as if the speaking voice
were now that of a translated author, weary of all of his translators in
their ambition to approximate (or, the translator's hubris, surpass?) the
"original"; or it might be the previous poem's Master's voice, weary
of disciples who learned from him how "Each character [should be]
blocked on the parchment secure", and then, having dismissed the
mystery of his craft as "just the old rules", enviously strive to match
him; or the harassed poet, wearied by the over-attention of his critics,
often intent on producing a meta-literature by preying on his "pages";
or even the much imitated and adulated author, weary of the epigonal
trail which his work may have generated, who hears in his mind the
echo of the great predecessor's epigrammatic complaint: "But was
there ever dog that praised his fleas?"[36] However, that concise prodigy
of irony and litotes which the closing lines of the poem amount to –
"Let them remember this not inconsiderable / contribution to their
jealous art" (*SI*, 111) – will demonstrate this poet's ability to preserve
a detached self-assessment, by making clear that "this ... contribution"
(indeterminedly, this poem? or this sequence?) will not be left out of
what he has just represented as a "jealous art".

---

[36] *Ibid.*, 105.

TRANSLATION OR RETRANSLATION?
FIELD DAY AND THE REVERSAL OF CULTURAL COLONIZATIONS

JOHN HILDEBIDLE

Allow me to begin, eccentrically, with a short quiz. First, "locate" the following thematically-central quotations from substantial Irish (or at least Irish-American) texts:

a. If words can reach whatever world you may be suffering in, then listen. I have things to tell you.
b. Isn't he come in yet?
c. Where's himself?
d. Where the hell has he got to?
e. I'm glad to see you back. I thought you were gone forever.
f. I remember when I had it I was never lonely or afraid. I can't have lost it forever. I would die if I thought that.
g. His own identity was fading out into a grey impalpable world.
h. I hope you find what you're looking for.
i. I still haven't found what I'm looking for.

Second, compile a list of writers included in both the *Norton Anthology of "English" Literature*, and *The Field Day Anthology of "Irish" Writing*. And if you are feeling very scholarly, include texts between the covers of *A Cabinet of Irish Writing*.

Third (like Gaul, this exercise *in tres partes divisa est*, and like all examinations worthy of the name, it has an essay portion) in twenty-five to thirty words, and using complete sentences, define "Field Day".

That last is by way of being a culturally-defining question. Whenever I mention my interest in Field Day to Americans, they ask what it is. I have never encountered a similar question from a resident of the island of Ireland, no matter his or her political persuasion. Indeed, I have myself searched, for some years, for a good short answer to the question. Marilyn Richtarik offers a useful extended formulation in her fine book *Acting Between the Lines*[1] and a briefer definition on page 7 of her book: "[Field Day was] founded in 1980 with the intention of finding or creating a space between Unionism and nationalism and proving by example the possibility of a shared culture in Northern Ireland." But like the hero of some child's tale, I prefer to "do it myself". Field Day, I would assert, is at bottom an exercise in "translation or retranslation"[2] (to borrow a phrase from a likely source, Seamus Deane's General Introduction to *The Field Day Anthology*). If Field Day endeavours, as Professor Richtarik argues (with ample documentation) to find a "space between" nationalism and unionism, the hot controversy about its "nationalist agenda" from its first days suggests, at best, a noble failure.[3] Be that as it may, it must be said that, even as recently at least as its production of Chekhov's *Uncle Vanya* in 1995, Field Day struggled to reverse the long history of colonization by the British, and to reclaim Irish writing from its more customary English location, and in so doing to move Irish writing from the eccentric periphery of European writing to its generative centre.

To come at the matter another way, I propose that "The Song of Wandering Aengus", "The Dead", and *Waiting for Godot* are the paradigmatic texts of Irish literature in this century. The keynote is not *death*, as Joyce's title might imply, but loss or absence. Consider how many significant texts have as a kind of theme-note a search for a missing person or place or state of mind. Hence the first question on my little quiz.

To put it directly, Irish writing, at least since *The Real Charlotte*, has been dominated by a sense of loss, which is usually figured as a conjunction of a place, a person, and a speech act. Think of Michael Furey singing "The Lass of Aughrim" in the rain outside that Galway window, or Stephen's mother, in her sickroom, asking (begging, Buck

---

[1]   Marilyn Richtarik, *Acting Between the Lines: The Field Day Politics 1980-1984*, Oxford, 1994, 3-9

[2]   Seamus Deane, General Introduction to *The Field Day Anthology*, ed. Seamus Deane, Derry, 1991, I, xxv.

[3]   Perhaps the loudest and most persistent accuser of Field Day as a "nationalist" enterprise is, of course, Edna Longley. The index of her *The Living Stream* (Newcastle, 1994) strangely omits Field Day (although most of the board members are cited separately). But she devotes an extended section of her introductory chapter to elaborating the argument that "the *Field Day Anthology* ... [is] a symptomatic yoking of 'Irish literature' to Nationalism" (23).

Mulligan would surely say) him to pray. Thomas Kinsella formulates the situation as being the case of a "literature which people on these level plains helped to produce during a particularly brutal, and long-suffering past, when one the people's greatest losses was the loss of its own language".[4] It is a commonplace now (*vide* the American Public Television documentary *The Long Journey Home*) that this loss derives from the horrors of the Famine; but I leave that question to the historians.

The work of many Irish writers, especially perhaps the compilers of anthologies like *Poems of the Dispossessed*, is to recover to visibility lost utterances. This work can be surreptitious at times, as is evident in the following passage from Benedict Kiely's "The Eton Crop":

> I had an uncle once, a man of threescore years, and when my reason's dawn began, he'd take me on his knee, and often talk, whole winter nights, things that seemed strange to me. He was a man of gloomy mood and few his converse sought. But, it was said, in solitude his conscience with him wrought and there, before his mental eye, some hideous vision wrought.[5]

Kiely mentioned, at a reading I was able to attend at a *Cúirt* festival, that he has a mind that is incapable of not remembering tags of language, especially old songs; and it is worth wondering whether some of his books, most notably perhaps *Nothing Happens in Carmincross*, are not meditations on the issue of whether garrulity of a recognizably Irish sort can withstand an encounter with the violent realties of the modern world. Be that as it may, the rooting of "The Eton Crop" in old songs, actual or parodied, is part of the legitimizing both of the story and of the songs, and of the restoration to audibility of a body of what an American academic audience might style "popular culture".

One final variation on the anthologizing theme: *Ulysses*. If, as I will argue, Field Day is fighting a battle over the English language, then Joyce spends a career fighting over that "foreign" language he hears coming out of the Dean of Studies' mouth.[6] In a way that is

---

4 Thomas Kinsella, *The Dual Tradition*, Manchester, 1995, 5.
5 Benedict Kiely, *Letter from Peachtree*, Boston, 1988, 67.
6 An oddity may be worth mentioning. More than once I have heard Seamus Heaney firmly aver that he never reads prose fiction. But why then does Joyce appear as the final tutelary ghost in *Station Island*? And why, at a lecture at

oddly predictive of Field Day, Joyce's book tries at the very same
moment to lay claim to all of European literature, at least since
Homer, and to Scripture as well; and to the most blunt and undignified
of Dublin street speech. I suppose, having (so he imagined) won the
day on that score, Joyce goes on to new worlds entirely, to a new and
unique language, a sort of literary Esperanto, or universal translator,
or Joycespeak, in the *Wake*. And we might inveigle Yeats into this
system as well, in his role as a great (if eccentric) synthesizer/
anthologizer-by-example of mythologies: by Cuchulain out of
Madame Blavatsky, with more than a glance at Plato, we might say.

What of Field Day? When Seamus Deane first proposes an anthology it is as a way of mediating the rhetorics which he assigns to Joyce
and Yeats, and it is Yeats who seems to have pride of place.[7] But in
the first six pamphlets, republished conveniently in the single volume
Ireland's Field Day, the name of Beckett chimes in. Observe Tom
Paulin, from the very first of the Field Day pamphlets: "[Beckett's
language is] a form of cosmopolitan English [which] some Irish would
argue ... is the best available English."[8] Or we could follow Seamus
Deane's usual path, and make Edmund Burke as the *fons et origo* of
Irish writing, or even "the father of Irish national sentiment".[9]

The whole of the *Anthology* tries to make an odd tap-dance around
the vexed issues of translation and canon-formation, especially and
explicitly in Deane's General Introduction.[10] How odd, given the

---

Harvard in the autumn of 1998, on the announced subject of his translation of
Beowulf, did Heaney present Stephen's encounter with the Dean as the generative
moment in twentieth-century Irish writing? The analogy to the encounter between
the speaker of *Station Island* and Joyce is, of course, the encounter between Dante
and Virgil at the close of the *Purgatorio*; Heaney's encounter with Joyce deftly
captures Dante's mixture of accusation and encouragement.

[7] Presumably the proposal is Deane's – by all accounts the anthology has been,
since its inception, his project. The idea is broached in the unsigned Preface to
Ireland's Field Day, eds Seamus Deane *et al.*, South Bend: IN, 1986, with the
avowed purpose of allowing "a more generous and hospitable notion of Ireland's
cultural achievements [to] emerge" (vii).

[8] *Ireland's Field Day*, 12, 16.

[9] *The Field Day Anthology*, I, 809. Deane builds an even more extended case for
the role of Burke – and of Matthew Arnold – in *Celtic Revivals* (Winston-Salem,
1985, 17-27), where he grants Burke the role of a foundation-layer for the work of
the Gaelic League. But then I have heard Professor Deane (at a guest lecture at
what was then UCG, in the spring of 1995) endeavour to make a case for a direct
line of descent from Burke to the *Wake*.

[10] See especially on this point, *The Field Day Anthology*, I, xx-xxi, and Deane's
presentation of the notion of a "meta-narrative" on page xix of the General

controversies that have surrounded the work, to watch him try to forestall what he imagines will be the controversial aspects. The anthology first of all argues by its very size that there is something that can fairly and necessarily called "Irish", that it is, as we might say, multivalent and long-standing and polyvocal; that it is so bulky as to comprise – and still fall short of the true inclusivity it so proudly promised – three doorstop-sized volumes. There is an act of cultural pride, even presumptuousness in all that. "What once was lost is now found" – even if not under ideal conditions. That it does not include everything is predictable (in the US, a new anthology of American writing appears, it seems, about every week, each one expanding the canon in some important way).[11]

As for the translation side of things, consider how many substantial contemporary Irish writers have undertaken the work of translation from the Irish language. Glance sometime at the roster of contributors to *The Oxford Book of Irish Verse*[12] or *An Duanaire*[13] or the Macmillan *Book of Irish Verse*[14] and take the time to sort out translations from original works (the easiest way to do this, of course, is just to page through the opening third or so). It is hard not to find a substantial Irish versifier there, from Austin Clarke to John Montague. I miss only Derek Mahon along the way (but then he's been imperializing the French, hasn't he?).

I mentioned Deane's framing of the need for such an anthology in terms of a need to address – and restore the coherence and viability of political languages or rhetorical styles. And I have mentioned Paulin's pamphlet, which (by its title) might be an utterance from Douglas Hyde: "A New Look at the Language Question." But the apparent shadow of the Revival is a misperception. Hyde would surely go on to

---

Introduction; also, much more cursorily, his quick acknowledgement of a "language question" (xxiv).

[11] I had long wondered why the *Anthology*, whatever its flaws, generated so much passion – in American, new and loudly improved anthologies of American writing seem to appear almost weekly. Then, at a dinner, Greg Delanty cracked the code for me. In Ireland it had taken all those decades since *The Cabinet of Irish Writing* (see the General Introduction to *The Field Day Anthology*, I, xix) even to undertake such an enterprise, and given the cost and controversy, who can say when the next one will emerge? So to be excluded or ill-represented carries much more, and more lasting, weight.

[12] *The Oxford Book of Irish Verse*, ed. Thomas Kinsella, New York, 1986.

[13] *An Duanaire 1600–1900: Poems of the Dispossessed*, eds Sean Ó Tuama and Thomas Kinsella, Portlaoise, 1981.

[14] *The Book of Irish Verse*, ed. John Montague, New York, 1974.

discuss Irish itself; Paulin stays firmly on the ground of English, in its Hibernian variations. He ends with a poignant invocation of "enormous cultural impoverishment" deriving from "a living but fragmented speech, untold numbers of homeless words, and an uncertain or derelict prose". But again, remind yourself that he is discussing English as it is spoken on this island, not the lost language that Kinsella was mourning.

Which brings me to a question that has puzzled me, as I try to find some line of coherence in the apparently centripetal undertakings of Field Day. I learned, as I talked to members and friends of Field Day and then read *Acting Between the Lines*, that Field Day operated[15] in a very shaggy fashion, and tended to accede to the wishes of individual members of the directorate. So Friel and Rea took charge of the theatrical side of things, and the *Anthology* was, beginning to end, Deane's project. Why look for a strict line of coherence?

Still, as a theatre company devoted to Irish issues, why on earth so many Russian plays? And then too why the Greeks? The answer, I think, lies in part in language. Notice Brian Friel, speaking – to a journalist! Friel whom everyone avers never speaks to anyone – in the early days of Field Day, on the goal of his reworking of *Three Sisters*:

> I think the versions of "Three Sisters" which we see and hear in this country always seem redolent of either Edwardian English or the Bloomsbury set. Somehow the rhythms of these versions do not match with the rhythms of our own speech patterns, and I think they ought to, in some way. This is an area we still have to resolve, and that brings us back to questions of language, for this is one of the big inheritances we have received from the British .... We must make English identifiably our own language.[16]

---

[15] I hesitate to rest so firmly on the past tense. Although I have been firmly and publicly rebuked for failing to acknowledge what "everyone knows", i.e. that "Field Day is dead", the ongoing monograph series, the still-promised supplementary volume in the *Anthology* and the recent Belfast production of *Northern Star*, which bore, in part, the Field Day name, offer equivocal signs of revivification or continued life.

[16] I cannot with any certainty locate the source of this quotation, having uncovered it at the now-closed Field Day office in Derry City. Frustratingly, the voluminous clips file at the Field Day headquarters included a xerox of this piece – but without any sort of attribution or bibliographic citation whatever. Friel's remarks on *Three Sisters* are to be found in *Brian Friel in Conversation*, ed. Paul Delaney, Ann Arbor, 2000, 145-69, *passim*. A précis of those remarks, which include the point raised in the quote given here, is included in Robert C. Evans and Deborah

I am sure you can hear the unmistakable echo of Stephen Dedalus. Friel is careful, elsewhere in the interview, to speak of cadences rather than idioms or accents. Rita Ann Higgins spoke to me of the impact made on her by hearing (in Paulin's *The Riot Act*) Antigone speak in her own cadences, somehow. A sort of reclaiming not of what is Irish but of what is significantly larger. An instance of what I mean by Imperialism in reverse.

One more verification comes from Seamus Heaney, in 1991 in *The Observer*:

> The very fact of a play touring, with bills being posted, and greasepaint, has an actuality and a unique kind of force. We only do one production a year, but Field Day has the recurrent life that the old touring fit-up companies used to have when I was a child. The response throughout Ulster at parish level has been cumulative and genuine .... There is a sense of possession, the people possess this work.[17]

Or, finally, this formulation from Seamus Deane:

> Standard English, as a form of language or as a form of literature, is rescued from its exclusiveness by being compelled to incorporate into itself what had previously been regarded as a delinquent dialect. It is the Irish contribution, in literary terms, to the treasury of English verse and prose.[18]

That last is an especially finely-tuned gesture in linguistic/literary diplomacies, and one which leaves the issue of dominance subtly in question. English graciously "incorporates", if only for its own reasons. Irish contributes – but then subject peoples, and alumni of expensive colleges, are always being dunned for contributions.

If I may develop one final turn to my case: the question of place. One convenience of the place that figures loss is that it need not be immediate and actual and observable. Consider that mythical place "Hy Brazil", as recently presented by Dermot Healy:

C. Hill, "Friel on Friel", in *A Companion to Brian Friel*, eds Richard Harp and Robert C. Evans, West Cornwall: CT, 2002.

[17] Again, my source was the clips file, but again it offered limited bibliographic data.

[18] *Ireland's Field Day*, 47.

> In an ironic piece some time ago in "The Irishman's Diary" in the
> *Irish Times*, Kevin Myers wrote that out beyond where I live in
> north Sligo every few years Hy Brazil, like another Atlantis, rises.
> This was news to me. I have not seen it yet ...
>   I think of Hy Brazil as I sit in the living room with a terrible
> hangover .... If I close my eyes I think I can see Hy Brazil, a little
> beyond Inishmurray Island, not exactly land, not even someplace
> eternal, but a place imagined by people long before me that I must
> imagine in my turn. Imagination hands on a duty to those who come
> after. So it is with Hy Brazil.[19]

How odd to have imagination aligned thus with duty, and to fly in the
face of reality so firmly.

Or, alternately, this formulation by Greg Delanty, when he ponders
his own version of the Promised Land:

> Last night I combed sleep's shore for its name.
>   A familiar adze-crowned man appeared
> waving his crook's question mark, nursing a flame
>   on a hill and impatiently declaring in weird
> pidgin Irish that the fifth province is
>   not Meath or the Hy Brazil of the mind.
> It is this island where all exiles naturally land.[20]

I suggest that, if you replace "Hy Brazil" with "The Fifth Province,"
this could come from Field Day. Indeed, Delanty's poem is entitled
"The Fifth Province". Despite media accounts of the idea (it soon
became a cliché about Field Day) which usually assign the genesis of
the term to Seamus Deane or perhaps Richard Kearney, it can in fact
be traced back to an extended article in *Crane Bag*, by Proinsias Mac
Cana, "Notes on the Early Irish Concept of Unity".[21] I am told, by
Richard Kearney (but have not yet tracked down fully),[22] that the idea
reaches that point by way of Robert Graves and before that two Welsh
Celticist brothers named Davies. In any case, the idea is an almost too-
neat conjunction of my notions about language and place. The

---

[19]   Dermot Healy, *The Bend for Home*, New York, 1998, 276.
[20]   Greg Delanty, *American Wake*, Belfast, 1995, 3.
[21]   Proinseas Mac Cana, "Notes on the Early Irish Concept of Unity", in *The Crane
       Bag Book of Irish Studies*, eds Mark Patrick Hederman and Richard Kearney,
       Dublin, 1982, 205-19.
[22]   Mac Cana's essay wears an armour of citations, but they are remarkably
       uninformative on this point, as it happens.

province of course, like Hy Brazil, appears on no map, and indeed there is no room for it on any map of Ireland. But it is a linguistic artefact, since the Irish word for "province" denotes "fifth". Ulster, Munster, Leinster, Connacht, and ... Field Day?

One concluding this reclamation project is surely Samuel Beckett. Some years ago I went looking for a copy of *Endgame*, and I searched in that temple of bookish learning, the Harry Elkins Widener Memorial Library at Harvard. And tracking down the path sketched by the card catalogue, I found myself well outside familiar Anglo-American ground. In fact, in Widener (and Harvard will readily tell you, it never makes a mistake) Beckett is shelved as French literature. It is hard for me to imagine that aged eagle smiling warmly, but it seemed to me that the idea would please him.

I am not naive enough to argue that the Irishing of Beckett is entirely the work of Field Day, by any means. Enoch Brater, in an anthology of twentieth-century Irish drama, offers a brief analysis of *Krapp's Last Tape*,[23] in which on the one hand he acknowledges Beckett's blunt dismissal of the play's Dublin location (notably Dun Laoghaire and the canal), then on the other blandly proceeds to reassert it. And Brater's essay is followed by one written by John Harrington, with a calmly polemical title, "The Irish Beckett".[24]

The Field Day Anthology shows no qualms about the Irishness of Beckett, or his place in an anthology of Irish writing. Indeed, they grant him an entire section of his own in volume three, with an ample introduction by J. C. C. Mays: "The world thinks of him as an Irish writer, when it thinks in such categories, yet he himself said that the Irish public does not care a 'fart in its corduroys for any kind of art whatsoever ....'"[25] Whatever the nationalist agenda of the *Anthology*, Beckett finds much more room there than Mangan or Tom Moore – politics does not, in other words, altogether swamp aesthetic judgement.

---

23 Enoch Brater, "Why Beckett", in *Modern Irish Drama*, ed. John P. Harrington, New York 1991, 542-45.

24 *Modern Irish Drama*, 545-50. Perhaps the final test case will be Larkin. Andrew Motion admits (*Philip Larkin: A Writer's Life*, New York, 1988, 3) Larkin's distaste for any sort of genealogy, and then goes on to provide a healthy listing of Irish Larkins, omitting the most renowned, "Big Jim" himself. And who should stand as psychopomp to the border-crossings in Heaney's *Seeing Things* but ... Larkin. Then again, what of Paisley – has he yet been heard on his inclusion in a plenary anthology of "Irish Writing?"

25 *The Field Day Anthology*, III, 233.

In short, I would argue that *The Field Day Anthology*, and the Company's series of plays, including so many non-Irish works, is a part of the effort to reclaim European literature from the hated Sassenach, who imperialized it so successfully through the hegemonic act of translation. Consider, if you will, how many authors included in any edition of *The Norton Anthology of English Literature* also find their place between the covers of *The Field Day Anthology*. Even Heaney has taken a bold step, from the days of his "Open Letter" refusing the label "British", to his translation of *Beowulf*. Asked, rather impolitely, if that represented a political regression, he turned the question aside by remarking: "I've never been British, but I've spoken English from the cradle." And he went on to claim, rather astoundingly, that the linguistic pattern he could rely on to mould the lines of that British proto-epic were the speech-shapes he heard as a child in a Derry farm kitchen.

Field Day is, at bottom, an exercise in the repossession of language, fought on the terrain of English rather than Irish (and thus distinct from the battles of the Gaelic Leaguers and others), deriving its generative force from anthologizers or synthesizers such as Yeats and Joyce, who lay claim to all the world's literatures and mythologies, and feel no compunction about translating them into Irish situations, speech-patterns and locations. I use the word "translating" with full awareness of the hegemonic implications of the term, as dramatized in Friel's renowned play, which was of course Field Day's first undertaking. Field Day's more recent forms of anthologizing insist on the size, scope and energy, the sheer bulk if you will, of Irish writing and its formative impact on the purportedly dominant English language, and (by using the word "writing," rather than, say, "literature") asserting the place of what we Americanists are prone to call "popular culture", even (in a more Victorian locution) "low" culture as a creative and energizing body of work.

"AR LORG NA GAOITHE":
THE IMPOSSIBILITY OF TRANSLATING SÉAMAS MAC ANNAIDH'S
CUAIFEACH MO LONDUBH BUÍ INTO ENGLISH

Anthony McCann

Many paraphrase Robert Frost to suggest that poetry is that which is lost in translation. The question of untranslatability at its most extreme assumes translation, in the words of Ortega y Gasset, to be "a utopian operation and an impossible proposition".[1] Untranslatability as a concept is something of an absolute anti-ideal which for the most part acts as a reminder of the limits of human endeavour and the relative autonomies of text-bound and diachronically situated linguistic world-views, the result of perfectionist translators' yearnings for the essences of meaning.

The central concerns of *Cuaifeach Mo Londubh Buí* are incompatible with the textual extension that translation implies, without a total reworking of the text and the inclusion of the hyper-autobiographical interference of the translator. I intend to bypass much of the untranslatability discourse by focusing on what I believe are the key themes of *Cuaifeach Mo Londubh Buí*, remembering, in Susan Bassnett's words, that "It must be clear at the outset that the text, understood to be in a dialectical relationship with other texts and located within a specific historical context, is the prime unit".[2]

Cuaifeach Mo Londubh Buí
Cuaifeach Mo Londubh Buí was first published by Coiscéim in 1983 when Séamas Mac Annaidh, from Enniskillen, County Fermanagh, was twenty-two years old. It was widely acknowledged as a

---

[1]   José Ortega y Gasset, "The Misery and Splendor of Translation", in *Theories of Translation: An Anthology of Essays from Dryden to Derrida*, eds Rainer Schulte and John Biguenet, Chicago, 1992, 98.

[2]   Susan Bassnett, *Translation Studies*, London and New York, 1991, 117.

significant addition to the public corpus of Irish-language literature upon its publication. Literary critic Máirín Nic Eoin wrote at the time: "Is leabhar ar leith an leabhar seo, leabhar a mbeifear ag trácht air go ceann i bhfad."[3] ("This book stands out on its own. It will be talked about for a long time.") It can be easily separated for the purposes of study into four definite narrative strands.

The first follows Séamas Mac Anna (not, note, Séamas Mac Annaidh) in what is quite obviously a case of autobiographical fiction, time-checked throughout, through a day-in-the-life-of account of events in Enniskillen: for example, collecting the dole and wandering around town, all leading to a bizarre meeting between characters from a separate narrative strand and Séamas, as narrator, in the town square, a meeting scheduled for three o'clock.

The second narrative strand is based on the *Epic of Gilgamesh*, a Sumerian epic from approximately 2500 BC that tells of the quest of Gilgamesh, the King of Uruk, for the gift of immortality. At the end of his quest Gilgamesh meets the wise hermit Utnapishtim, who eventually concedes the secret of immortality, which is a plant, but on his way home down-river Gilgamesh pauses to wash himself, and a snake sneaks on board his boat and eats the plant.

The third and probably most striking narrative is the story of a mysterious doctor, Siamais Mac Greine, who arrives in Dublin from the Middle East with a bundle of ancient parchments. After a visit to Newgrange, where it seems he discovers the secret of eternal life, and following a series of unfortunate accidents, he takes the brain of an old man, Patrick Ó hUltánaigh, the body of a young boy, also Patrick Ó hUltánaigh (the old man's great-nephew), and the face of a paperboy. He puts them together and re-animates the lot to create a person that he, coincidentally, names "Gilly". This is an obvious and deliberate retelling of the Frankenstein myth. We then follow Gilly as he makes his way through school, very much in a typical rites-of-passage fashion. In the process he meets the old man's sweetheart, Sally Holme, from whom he has been separated in bitterness for many years since their idyllic childhood days on her father's estate. This narrative in many ways runs parallel to the Gilgamesh Epic, for example, the quest for immortality, the companionship and death of a close friend (Fánaí), and the confrontation with the monster Humbaba in the forest. Eventually Gilly forms a punk band, and he meets death

---

[3] Máirín Nic Eoin, "Úrscéalaíocht na Gaeilge", *Comhar*, 8 (1984), 19.

at Sally's hands during what turns out to be his first and final performance. It is an odd mixture of *Frankenstein*, schoolboy antics, *Bildungsroman*, heightened fantasy, cross-references to the previous two narratives, and a rather unconventional love-story.

The fourth narrative strand is another apparently autobiographical tale relating a summer on an unspecified island at an Irish College in the Gaeltacht where Séamas worked as a *ceannaire* (supervisor) following completion of his BA degree, concentrating in particular on his strained relationship with one particular student, Mícheál, who refuses to speak in Irish. It is presented to us primarily through the medium of unashamedly playful dialogue, incorporating slang, English, and pidgin *Bearlathas* (Irish with English linguistic structures).

One might argue there is another narrative thread, that of the interjecting narrative voice, Séamas Mac Annaidh himself speaking in the first person, in both the role of illusory intermediary between reader and text and the role of Creator. This is characterized by continual pleas for communication, extracts from songs, wordplay, punning, and an almost malicious bilingualism.

Cuaifeach Mo Londubh Buí could not, by any stretch of the imagination, be regarded as a traditional novel, and it would be tempting to assume that its almost flippant approach and its outrageous fantasy are indicative of a lack of thematic depth. We have in the *Cuaifeach* a text of startling complexity and profundity, and we are more than justified in treating it as a prolonged meditation on death, the nature of self, the nature of reality, immortality, and the Unjustified Self. As I shall show later, by considering, in Susan Bassnett's words, "the function both of the text and of the devices within the text itself",[4] the function of the text as hyper-autobiography and as quest for an Unjustified Textual Self is what ultimately militates against there ever being a translation, as such, of *Cuaifeach Mo Londubh Buí*.

Death

Heidegger has written that "Death, honestly accepted and anticipated, can become an integrating factor in an authentic existence".[5] Death is an all-pervasive and multifaceted presence in the text of *Cuaifeach Mo Londubh Buí*. By continually revisiting the experience of death in and

---

[4]   Bassnett, *Translation Studies*, 118.
[5]   John Macquarrie, *Existentialism*, New York, 1972, 198.

through the text Mac Annaidh attempts to objectify it for himself, whereby he can then examine its role in his own life and his responses to it. Establishing this is crucial to our understanding of this novel's function and my subsequent claim of untranslatability.

The *Epic of Gilgamesh*, as well as being one of the major structural components of this work, is also one of the main ways in which death is maintained as a constant concern throughout the text, both in the re-telling of the epic in translation and in the use of the parallel narrative involving Siamais MacGréine and Gilly. The tone of the epic is dominated by a profoundly pessimistic Mesopotamian world-view, and would seem to be the perfect complement to a modern meditation on death.

Whereas the Gilgamesh epic might seem to be the most obvious reminder of mortality in *Cuaifeach Mo Londubh Buí*, Mac Annaidh has managed to weave an awareness of death into the fabric of the text. One of the simplest ways in which this is done is by including reports of deaths, almost at random, throughout the novel. These are deaths of both anonymous and famous people, confirming death as the Great Leveller of history. Mac Annaidh incorporates twenty-eight deaths into the text in this fashion.

Ursula Le Guin has written that

> narrative is a strategem of mortality. It is a means, a way of living. It does not seek immortality; it does not seek to triumph over or escape from time .... It asserts, affirms, participates in directional time, time experienced, time as meaningful.[6]

In *Cuaifeach Mo Londubh Buí* Séamas Mac Annaidh reaffirms mortality by continually marking illusory real-time at irregular intervals in his day-in-the-life narrative. The passing of time, instead of being a comfort, even a deception, becomes a reminder that life is always a movement forwards, onwards, towards an inevitable conclusion.

But where we find the effect of passing time in one of the narrative strands, it is clear when we examine all of the strands together that the actual structure of the novel, the multiplaned narratives and their apparent random sequence militate against even passing time acting as a comfortable yardstick or support. The constantly changing narratives

---

[6]   Ursula Le Guin, quoted in Nancy Huston, "Novels and Navels", *Critical Inquiry* (Summer 1995), 713.

add to an overwhelming sense of panic and uneasiness. "Is cuma faoin scéal" ["The story doesn't matter"] becomes from the start one of the many mantras of the book, hinting that maybe the process is the priority, that maybe it is more important to convey unease, and ultimately to communicate something about the nature of the death experience, than to participate in the unfolding of a strictly linear and traditional narrative.

This apparently haphazard approach is also to be found in the style of the autobiographical narratives and the primary narrator's voice, a stream-of-consciousness simulation that has been greatly influenced by the writings of Peigí Rose (1991) in *An tUltach* magazine,[7] themselves often characterized implicity and explictly by unease. It is from Peigí Rose that Mac Annaidh borrowed the much used metaphor of the "Guairneán" (translated in Ó Dónaill [1981] as "whirling motion; whirl, spin; swirl, eddy ... Tossing about, restlessness, uneasiness, whirlpool"[8]) which is combined with the oft-repeated image of the "Charybdis", a ship-devouring monster of classical Greek mythology, identified with a whirlpool off the coast of Sicily, and the "Cuaifeach" or "Tempest" of the title to convey the confusion and tumult of life and the ever-present threat of death. Restlessness is constant: in the narration, in the personal sicknesses and angst-ridden lives of the characters, and in the style and structure of the novel. In the general thematic context of death this restlessness can certainly be linked to the imminence of the final hour.

Yet another way in which death pervades the text is in the extended use of the Garden of Eden analogy as played out through the love-story-that-isn't between Patrick Ó hUltánaigh, later to be Gilly, and Sally Holme. Eden is mythically the source of all sin, death, and self-consciousness, and, in Ernest Becker's words:

> The final terror of self-consciousness is the knowledge of one's own death, which is the peculiar sentence on man alone in the animal kingdom. This is the meaning of the Garden of Eden myth and the rediscovery of modern psychology: that death is man's peculiar and greatest anxiety.[9]

---

[7]   Peigí Rose (*alias* Seán Ó Gallchóir), *An Chéad Chnuasach: 1972-'79*, Dublin, 1991.

[8]   Niall Ó Dónaill, *Gearrfhoclóir Gaeilge-Béarla*, Dublin, 1981.

[9]   Ernest Becker, *The Denial of Death*, New York, 1973, 70.

We cannot ignore the importance of the work being written in the medium of Irish, a minority language often associated with the metaphor of dying, as explored recently in the unpublished work of Sarah McKibben. As McKibben says of Ó Cadhain and Ó Nualáin so we can also say of Mac Annaidh: "If by simply speaking they prove Irish is not dead, they go further, interrogating the metaphor and reversing it to prove that Irish is very much alive."[10]

Responses to death

Having outlined the ways in which death permeates the text of *Cuaifeach Mo Londubh Buí* it befits us to look at the ways in which Mac Annaidh has responded to death in the novel. At its most direct, the response is an actual restatement of Horace's "Carpe Diem", or "Seize the Day". It is in the context of "Carpe Diem" that the title *Cuaifeach Mo Londubh Buí* assumes most significance, incorporating as it does two of the major recurring metaphors in the novel: the *cuaifeach* and the *lon dubh* or "blackbird". Mac Annaidh uses the *cuaifeach* (meaning "tempest" or "squall" – a play on the birdcall sound "cuach") as an indicator of his hyperstimulated state of mind, reflected in the nature of the book. He uses the blackbird first and foremost as a symbol for instinctive spontaneity. As he states explicitly:

> Bhí an lon dubh aige mar shiombail den rud fhileata [*sic*] greannmhar a bhí istigh ann féin, an spiorad aerach sin nach raibh aon srian air (193).

> (The blackbird was for him a symbol of that poetic, funny thing, that bright, unbounded spirit that was within him.)

A second major response to death is through the use of humour. In *Cuaifeach Mo Londubh Buí* the humour is heavily dependent on witticisms and punning, what Ezra Pound has coined "Logopoeia". Much of the humour is to be found in the fulcrum narratives of the Gilgamesh Epic and the Frankenstinian story of Siamais Mac Gréine and Gilly. It is interesting to note that the *Epic of Gilgamesh* is, in its original form, a source of much humour. In the *Cuaifeach* the epic

---

[10]   Sarah Elizabeth McKibben, "Lamenting the Language: On the Metaphor of Dying Irish" (M.Phil. dissertation, University College Dublin, 1997).

initially retains its dignified and noble tone, but gradually gives way to low burlesque.

James Hall has written that "comedy is usually serious, however much some analysis may burlesque its kind of seriousness".[11] Koestler has argued that threat, aggression, or apprehension are indispensable ingredients of humour.[12] We have seen how the threat of death is almost a constant in *Cuaifeach Mo Londubh Buí*. This tension is continuously generated and discharged through humour along the contrasted planes of Nonsense and Death.

Any negative experience suffered is balanced by a desire, a need, to communicate. A problem shared is a problem halved. For those fully aware of their mortal condition communication can be an attempt to defeat the loneliness and isolation that comes from that knowledge. Mac Annaidh's desire for communication is expressed without reservation: "Déanaimis teagmháil. Cumarsáid ... please" (48). A constant plea is: "Amharc sna súile agam. Déanaimis caidreamh" (9). The act of reading is a form of interpersonal communication in which the eyes, of necessity, play an important part (leaving aside the use of braille), linking the reader to the author through the text. The reader is necessary in the author's attempt to make the act of communication complete, which places a focus on Mac Annaidh's use of inter-textuality throughout the novel, culled from an eclectic variety of texts, often texts that have formed part of Mac Annaidh's formal education throughout secondary school and university. Writers such as Máirtín Ó Direáin, Seán Ó Ríordáin, W. B. Yeats, Myles na gCopaleen, Oscar Wilde, James Joyce, Art Mac Cumhaidh, Dante, Wilfred Owen, Séamas Ó Grianna, Seosamh Mac Grianna, Séamas Dall Mac Cuarta, Pádraic Pearse and many, many more find their work quoted and paraphrased throughout the text, and an exhaustive sourcing of all the intertextual references in the *Cuaifeach* would be an almost impossible task, maybe even a pointless one; each reader brings their own literary or textual background to bear on the text as they read it, maybe even finding resonances that were totally unintended.

---

[11]   James Hall, *The Tragic Comedians: Seven Modern British Novelists*, Bloomington and London, 1966, 45.
[12]   Arthur Koestler, *The Act of Creation*, London, 1964.

The quest for immortality
It is necessary to ground our assessment of *Cuaifeach Mo Londubh Buí* in its treatment of death and its responses to death so that we might fully appreciate the way in which *Cuaifeach Mo Londubh Buí* is a lunge for immortality, and, as we shall see later, an attempt at eternal self-perpetuation, an attempt to conquer death. The very first words of the novel are "Biseach an Bháis", a statement of mission and intent. The central narrative structure, as we have seen, is the *Epic of Gilgamesh* – the quest of Gilgamesh, King of Uruk, for the ultimate prize of immortality. The second most important narrative of the novel, that of Siamais and Gilly, is based on Victor Frankenstein's archetypal quest to defeat death.

The perpetuation of a person's name in the collective memory of a people has long been seen as a form of immortality. It is made clear in direct references that *Cuaifeach Mo Londubh Buí* is the vehicle by which Mac Annaidh hopes to gain fame, and hence immortality. Needless to say, Mac Annaidh couches the claims in self-mockery, but the place of fame in the novel is consolidated by the importance of heroism in the text, heroism being one of the ways in which fame may be achieved. The adjectives *cróga* ("brave") and *caithréimeach* ("triumphant", "conquering") are ubiquitous. In the words of Shaler: "Heroism is first and foremost a reflex of the terror of death."[13]

Autobiography
Cuaifeach Mo Londubh Buí can be considered in many ways as autobiography. Mark Rose has written of the growing tendency in the mid-eighteenth century to think of writings as projections of authors' personalities: "No longer simply a mirror held up to nature, a work was also the objectification of a writer's self."[14] *Cuaifeach Mo Londubh Buí* is very much a reflection of Séamas Mac Annaidh's personality, but even more so, an attempted recreation of the author as a textual entity in an attempt to gain immortality in response to the experience of death. It is this autobiographical aspect that ultimately rails against the translation of *Cuaifeach Mo Londubh Buí*.

Firstly, we have the day-in-the-life narrative, a thinly-veiled autobiographical fiction, including details from various periods of Séamas' life up to the point of writing. The Gaeltacht narrative might

---

[13]   Quoted in Becker, *Denial of Death*, 11.
[14]   Mark Rose, *Authors and Owners: The Invention of Copyright*, Cambridge, 1993, 121.

also merit inclusion here. Secondly, we have the frequent emphasis on Mac Annaidh's sense of place, his attachment to his home town of Enniskillen, coupled with his paradoxical feeling of separation from his place and people as a result of his education. It could be argued that Mac Annaidh's vital sense of place, "Buachaill ón Éirne mé" (185), compensates for his increasing detachment by allowing much of Enniskillen's historical and geographical colour to become part and parcel of the fabric of the text, in much the same way as the town is an integral part of the fabric of his life and identity.

Thirdly, the intertextuality of the novel, as we have already seen, acts to incorporate most of Séamas Mac Annaidh's literary and cultural world up to the point of writing the novel at the age of twenty-one. It becomes a direct projection of his literary life. The intertextuality, though, serves both to underline the individual experiences of the author and to highlight the multiplicitous nature of this cultural production.

Fourthly, a more direct way in which *Cuaifeach Mo Londubh Buí* might be seen as autobiography is in the omnipresence of the name Séamas or Siamais. Among the players are: Séamas Mac Annaidh, Séamas Caoimhín Mícheál Mac Anna, Séamas Mac an Bhancaire, Siamais Mac Gréine, and Séamas a' Chaca, to which we might add Shamash the Sun God from the original Gilgamesh Epic. In the wider context of the novel it is clear that all of these characters become in one way or another Séamas Mac Annaidh, Author, all deliberate projections of an *alter ego*. In each case Mac Annaidh's attitude to character-as-self is particularly self-effacing.

In the novel it becomes clear that none of the characters, including Séamas in all his guises, can be said to possess a clear, distinct, or well-defined identity. Mac Annaidh succeeds in blurring many of the characters' identities, highlighting the arbitrariness of names as identifying labels. The names Gilly and Giolgamais are one and the same, the source of no little confusion. Mac Annaidh is explicitly aware of the reader's confusion: "Cé anois atá i gceist, Séamas, Gilly, Fánaí, Giolgamais nó an Caisideach Bán?" (174) ("Who are we talking about now? Séamas, Gilly, Fánaí, Giolgamais or the Caisideach Bán?"). By end of the novel things descend into chaos as one character blurs into the next: "Ba léir go raibh siad uilig cosúil leis ar dhóigh amháin nó ar dhóigh eile" (226) ("It was clear that they were all alike in one way or another"). As well as playing a part in the overall *Cuaifeach* or Tempest effect, this would almost seem to weaken the autobiographical impact of the text, but not if we accept that all the characters are Mac Annaidh himself, that *Cuaifeach Mo Londubh Buí* is hyper-autobiography.

Just in case we did not get the point Mac Annaidh spells it out explicitly for us:

> Séamas
> Caoimhín
> Mícheál
> Me all (208).

Or in the penultimate paragraph of the *Cuaifeach*:

> Mhúscail sé de gheit. Bhí sé ina lá. D'éirigh Séamas amach as a leaba, d'oscail Caoimhín na cúirtíní, chuir Mícheál a chuid éadaí air, nigh Anna a haghaidh agus chuaigh siad ceathrar síos an staighre, agus nuair a d'ól siad an caife gliondrach ba é an t-aon bhéal amháin a shlog é. (255)

> (He awoke with a start. It was daylight. Séamas arose from his bed, Caoimhín opened the curtains, Mícheál dressed himself, Anna washed her face, and then the four of them walked down the stairs, and when they drank the blissful coffee it was the one mouth that swallowed it.)

Mac Annaidh's personality, his community of characters and text, is composite in much the same way as Frankenstein's monster is composite. So, is *Cuaifeach Mo Londubh Buí* Mac Annaidh's quest for individuation, his attempt to objectify an identity, his attempt to distil his personality and present it to us, so maximizing the potential for communication between reader and writer?

Mac Annaidh also appears in the text in the role of the author-god, breaking metafictionally into the narrative of the text. By assuming the role of the author-god Mac Annaidh assumes the role of the Supreme Individual, the Absolute Unjustified self. This parallels Mac Annaidh's attempt to create in *Cuaifeach Mo Londubh Buí* a personal, unjustified, solipsist retreat. We see this clearly in the recurring metaphor of the island as it is used in the text. At a basic level the island acts as a metaphor for the two worlds of fiction and reality. At a deeper level the metaphor draws on the significance of allusions to both Seán Ó Ríordáin and Máirtín Ó Direáin. In the work of both these poets the image of the island figured prominently. For Ó Ríordáin the island is physically a place of refuge, of retreat, a place of escape, while the "other island", the "oileán eile", is an internal, spiritual space deep within the writer's psyche, a solipsist haven wherein the true essence of being is sought. For Ó Direáin the island was similarly a conceptual retreat, in many cases a romanticized construction. Mac Annaidh's island, his other life of the text, is loaded with these significances and is, first and foremost, a reflex of the terror of death. This novel is escapist in the most profound sense, an attempt to shed the shackles of mortality through a recreation of the self in autobiography, in fame, and as a self-contained textual world.

By participating in the text as author-god, Mac Annaidh not only sets himself up as the Supreme Unjustified Self, but also participates in the reality of the fictional characters, eventually coming face to face with his own creations. By engaging with the characters as author he underlines both their fictionality and their relative independence, their differentiation from himself as author. Also, by engaging with them in this way Mac Annaidh recreates himself as a fictional character. If Mac Annaidh achieves fictional status he has therefore achieved immortality, however doomed he eventually accepts this ambition to be.

The untranslatable *Cuaifeach Mo Londubh Buí*
Having established the basic thematic structure of the novel, thereby clarifying its functional aspirations, we are able now to state the case for the untranslatability of *Cuaifeach Mo Londubh Buí*. At first glance the novel is, at the very least, a difficult task for a translator to tackle. The *logopoeia* by its very nature is linguistically bound, relying almost exclusively on aural echoes and punning – difficult, but not impossible. The bottomless intertextuality of the novel would challenge a translator to explore thematically relevant texts in the target language with a view to incorporating the new linguistic milieu into the fabric of the translated text. To replicate the affected spontaneity of the synchronic snapshot the translator would have to imbue the new text with the environment-sponging qualities of the original. Finding a way to convey the internal bilingual dynamic, replete with the considerations of minority-language politics and power discourses, would require untold imagination. Again, difficult, but not impossible.

Dante Gabriel Rossetti wrote that "The task of the translator (and with all humility be it spoken) is one of some self denial".[15] Mac Annaidh's *Cuaifeach Mo Londubh Buí* is the complete anathema of self-denial. It is the quest for a individual hyper-autobiographical solipsist recreation of the author's self. This book is by definition a one-off. It relies on its status as an individual text, an individual work, to coalesce with Mac Annaidh's lunge for immortality.

This not only makes the translation of *Cuaifeach Mo Londubh Buí* difficult but ensures that any attempt at translation must needs provide us with a wholly different text in order to replicate the original function of the novel. The spirit of the novel requires that the creator of the work imbue the text with his hyper-autobiographical self. The agency of a translator requires the full textual participation of the translator as autobiographical individual, as secondary creator, the full intertextual participation of the target language's awareness of death, the synchronic participation of events at the time of writing, and many other amendments, by which stage you have another novel on your hands, certainly not the one you started out with. The spirit of the Tempest, the *Cuaifeach*, and the wings of the Blackbird demands that *Cuaifeach Mo Londubh Buí* is untranslatable, unless, of course, Mac Annaidh were to do it himself.

[15]   Dante Gabriel Rossetti, "Preface to *The Italian Poets*", in *Theories of Translation*, 65.

JOYCE AND IDENTITY

NATIONAL POETS AND JOYCE

PATRICK BOHAN

The question of what audience an Irish writer writes for is a complex one. An audience can both define and be defined by a writer and traditionally many Irish writers have found homes, publishers and their largest audiences outside Ireland. The Celtic Revival was, in different measures, the creation of a native Irish audience and a re-invention of Ireland in English literature. The critic Daniel Corkery wrote in the 1930s that "a national literature is written primarily for its own people … for normal and national are synonymous in literary criticism".[1] More recently, when Seamus Heaney was included in *The Penguin Book of Contemporary British Poetry*, he resisted the identification between the nationality of perhaps the biggest section of his audience and his own but conceded that such an identification is understandable:

> Yet doubts, admittedly, arise
> When somebody who publishes
> In *LRB* and *TLS*,
>   *The Listener*;
> In other words, whose audience is,
>   Via Faber,
>
> A British one, is characterized
>   As British.[2]

---

[1] Daniel Corkery, *Synge and Anglo-Irish Literature: A Study*, Cork, 1931 and Oxford, 1947, 2-3.

[2] Seamus Heaney, "An Open Letter", in *Ireland's Field Day*, ed. Seamus Deane, London, 1985, 25. It can be a difficult question not just for Irish writers but for any writer whose culture is seen to be outside the dominant European tradition. Jorge Luis Borges resists the call for Argentinian writers to be national in an essay "The Argentine Writer and Tradition", arguing that the "cult of local colour is a

Joyce had an even larger audience in mind when he wrote to Grant
Richards in 1905 about Dublin and speaks in terms of "present[ing] it
to the world".[3] He assumes that Irish reality must be explained,
presented and represented as if for the first time. That is to say, he
assumes his audience is not Irish or, at least, that the Irish do not form
a substantial section of his audience. Despite his ironization of Little
Chandler's imagined London and English audience, Joyce also
disdains a local audience: "The intelligence of an English city is not
perhaps at a very high level but at least it is higher than the mental
swamp of the Irish peasant."[4]

A self-aware Stephen in *Ulysses*, however, fears the relationship
with a foreign audience. Specifically he fears ending up a "jester at the
court of his master, indulged and disesteemed, winning a clement
master's praise".[5] Stephen also ironizes his own (that is, Joyce's)
earlier vague ideas about audience thinking in relation to the
"Epiphanies" that "someone was to read them ... after a few thousand
years, a mahamanvantara".[6]

These fears, however, were countered by the possible rewards of
presenting one's society in writing for the first time and thereby
becoming its definitive representation. It is this idea that provoked
Joyce's interest in the theme of the national poet. He touches on this
theme at least twice before *Ulysses*, a novel in which it is something
of a preoccupation. In the 1907 lecture on James Clarence Mangan
delivered in Trieste, Joyce links the fates of the writer as national poet
with that of the audience as nation:

> Mangan will be accepted by the Irish as their national poet on the
> day the conflict will be decided between my native land and the
> foreign powers – Anglo-Saxon and Roman Catholic, and a new
> civilization will arise, either indigenous or completely foreign.[7]

recent European cult which nationalists ought to reject as foreign" (*Labyrinths:
   Selected Stories and Other Writings*, London, 1970, 215).
3   James Joyce, *Letters of James Joyce*, ed. Richard Ellmann, New York, 1966, II,
   122.
4   James Joyce, *Stephen Hero*, ed. T. Spencer, London, 1991, 59.
5   James Joyce, *Ulysses*, ed. H. W. Gabler, New York and London, 1984, 2, 44-45.
6   *Ibid.*, 3, 143-44.
7   James Joyce, *Critical Writings of James Joyce*, eds Ellsworth Mason and Richard
   Ellmann, London, 1959, 179.

In *A Portrait of the Artist as a Young Man*, Stephen Dedalus walks through College Green on his way to university and passes Thomas Moore's statue which he calls the "droll statue of the national poet of Ireland".[8] In the National Library chapter of *Ulysses*, the writing of the Irish national epic is discussed and, according to most of those present, George Moore is the man to do it.[9] Stephen is teased on this issue by Eglinton.[10] Perhaps more obvious candidates might have been Yeats and Synge who, although strong textual presences in the novel, are both "physically" absent. Interestingly, Synge is pitted against perhaps the definitive national poet, Shakespeare: "The chap that writes like Synge."[11] Furthermore, Bloom identifies Shakespeare as "our national poet"[12] (although it should be noted that "Eumaeus" is the chapter of mistaken identities; the narrator appears to poke fun at Bloom's usage a little later).[13]

What, therefore, and who is a national poet? As Joyce suggests in the Mangan essay, the national poet is inextricable from the idea of tradition and canon. The national poet is the poet who defines the national circumstances in language and literature for the nation itself and for the world. Thus, the national poet is the origin of tradition, the reference point of the canon and the defining representation of the nation.

Following Bloom's lead and given his prominence throughout *Ulysses*, Shakespeare seems the most obvious place to begin to isolate some of the features of a national poet. Jane Austen and Harold Bloom discuss Shakespeare in quite similar terms:

> Shakespeare one gets acquainted with without knowing how. It is part of an Englishman's constitution. His thoughts and beauties are so spread abroad that one touches them every where, one is intimate with him by instinct ... we all talk Shakespeare, use his similies [*sic*], and describe with his descriptions;[14]

---

[8] James Joyce, *A Portrait of the Artist as a Young Man*, London, 1988, 183. Another monument to Thomas Moore at the Meeting of the Waters in Co. Wicklow makes the same claim.

[9] Joyce, *Ulysses*, 9, 309-10.

[10] *Ibid.*, 9, 18-20.

[11] *Ibid.*, 9, 510-11.

[12] *Ibid.*, 16, 782.

[13] *Ibid.*, 16, 840.

[14] Jane Austen, *Mansfield Park* (1814), London, 1996, 279.

> We have, almost all of us, thoroughly internalized the power of Shakespeare's plays, frequently without having attended them or read them.[15]

The national poet is part of the national character and the national consciousness by default. Most importantly, the national poet is seen to articulate the nation's thoughts and emotions. The national poet is seen to be representative and supra-individual in the identification which each member of the nation makes with him, to be the origin and father of the nation. Stephen describes Shakespeare as having "felt himself the father of all his race, the father of his own grandfather, the father of his unborn grandson ...".[16]

According to Jane Austen and Harold Bloom, the influence of the national poet is so pervasive that his texts need not even be read. It follows that those who do actually read the texts of the national poet cannot be said to have any ordinary relation to or position in those texts. Frank McGuinness writes of his own reading of Shakespeare and the expectation that "transubstantiation would occur between audience and author".[17] The interaction between the reader and the writing mind is guaranteed by the fact that the national poet is seen to have already defined the reader's mind by giving the values and language and articulation of its environment ("we all talk Shake-speare") which the reader possesses by default. The defining characteristic of a national poet, therefore, is the relationship such a writer has with an audience.

The national poet is usually seen as paternal and therefore male but, because the term is ill defined (possibly because the critical term "reader" has been much diminished as a result of reader-response theories), it has been applied to particular writers who appear to have the same quality of being representative of their communities. Toni Morrison, thus, may be described as "the nearest thing America has to a national novelist". Morrison herself described that same quality when she won the Nobel Prize for Literature in 1993: "I felt representative. I felt American. I felt Ohioan. I felt blacker than ever, I

---

[15]   Harold Bloom, *The Anxiety of Influence: A Theory of Poetry*, Oxford and New York, 1997, xviii.

[16]   Joyce, *Ulysses*, 9, 868-69.

[17]   In *Shakespeare and Ireland: History, Politics, Culture*, eds Mark Thornton Burnett and Ramona Wray, London and New York, 1997, xi.

felt more woman than ever."[18] Morrison had earlier described her writing in terms of being "representative *of* the tribe and *in* it":

> I have to provide the places and spaces so that the reader can participate. Because it is the affective and participatory relationship between the artist or the speaker and the audience that is of primary importance ... to have the reader *feel* the narrator without *identifying* that narrator ... and to have the reader work *with* the author in the construction of the book.[19]

Because of the writer's representative status, because the writer is speaking both to and for other people, and because the text itself is almost immaterial in that relationship, it is clear that the national poet and his or her audience interact with much greater complexity than is common in other reading/writing situations. Paradoxically, the autonomy of reader and writer are both much enhanced and much diminished by such a position: defining and being defined are identical acts.

There is a particular reason why Joyce should be interested in different relationships between writer and audience. His initial difficulty as a writer is the dislocation he experiences between reality and its articulation. Thus, his early texts are about how to articulate apprehension and not to whom that representation would or should be addressed. In *A Portrait*, when Stephen reasons his attraction to the "power of a priest of God"[20] and the sacredness of the ceremony, he specifies that he imagines an empty chapel; he has no concept of audience yet. For the same reason, the lyric was useful because its audience is structural. In *A Portrait*, the text's dynamic is entirely between the narrator and Stephen as reader. The very beginning of the novel shows Stephen as both narrator and the main character, "baby tuckoo", for example.

It is the complex relationship between reader and national poet that resolved the question of audience for Joyce, for whom he was writing and what relationship he has with that audience. The mixing and interchanging of readers and writers and reading and writing is noticeable throughout *Ulysses*: in Martha's and Bloom's correspon-

---

[18] "Voice of America", *The Irish Times*, 28 March 1998.
[19] Toni Morrison, "Rootedness: The Ancestor as Foundation", in *Literature in the Modern World*, ed. Dennis Walder, Oxford, 1990, 326, 328.
[20] Joyce, *A Portrait*, 161.

dence; in the writing and reading of advertisements, newspapers and books (Stephen rips a piece from Mr Deasy's letter in order to write some verse and both Bloom and Stephen write on the back pages of *Sweets of Sin*); and in the extensive use of quotation, citation and reference.

Each reader of the national poet revisits the text in order to review previous readings and is conscious of being in a tradition of interpretation. The national poet is not only seen to be able to accommodate all readings but is expected to have anticipated every reading in the same way that she or he anticipates every member of the community as a precursor. Joyce (writing of Mangan) refers to that quality of a national poet which sums up the consciousness of a nation:

> There are certain poets who, in addition to the virtue of revealing to us some phase of the human conscience unknown until their time, also have the more doubtful virtue of summing up in themselves the thousand contrasting tendencies of their era.[21]

Recognizing Ireland's absence from literary tradition, the readers in the National Library (specifically a group of interpreters) try to insert it by rereading and reinterpreting Shakespeare. Eglinton points this out: "the Bard's fellowcountrymen ... are rather tired perhaps of our brilliancies of theorising"[22] and jokingly refers to other appropriations of *Hamlet* by asking: "Has no-one made him out to be an Irishman? Judge Barton, I believe, is searching for some clues."[23] The essence of Shakespeare is his availability to interpretation and to appropriation by different causes. When Mulligan and Stephen return to the conversation Lyster is trailing off "in which everyone can find his own [Shakespeare]".[24]

Frank McGuinness expresses the same idea in his play *Mutabilitie* (1997). If Shakespeare can be brought to write Ireland into literature and into English national consciousness, then its existence will resolve the difficulties between the two countries: each will exist in the other's imaginative space and frame of reference. The Irish poet, File, asks Shakespeare to do just that:

---

[21] Joyce, *Critical Writings*, 175.
[22] Joyce, *Ulysses*, 9, 516-17.
[23] *Ibid.*, 9, 519-20.
[24] *Ibid.*, 9, 582.

Tell our story, our suffering to the people of England .... In this your theatre you will make our dead rise, William. You will raise our Irish dead, Englishman.[25]

The relationship of an Irish person and native speaker of English to the English national poet is one of the tensions of which Joyce is already conscious. It is a tension he feels when the words *"home, Christ, ale, master"*[26] seem irrevocably to exclude Stephen from the tradition of Ben Jonson and Ireland from articulation. If Jane Austen's Englishman is intimate with Shakespeare by instinct, can an Irishman like Stephen really have the same relationship to him?

Before *Ulysses*, Joyce seems to have felt keenly his exclusion from literary tradition: "it wounded him to think that he would never be but a shy guest at the feast of the world's culture."[27] However, when Joyce did leave Ireland for the "foreign legion of France in which he spoke of serving",[28] he must have found that exile only served to define him in relation to Ireland and that no such unified literary tradition existed in which he might find a spiritual homeland and the reality he expected. Failing to find his homeland in Europe, he fears "fad[ing] into impalpability",[29] becoming "a ghost by absence"[30] in Ireland: the only reality now available to him.

Far from being accepted into European tradition, Joyce becomes more aware that the tradition he venerated in literature was being engineered to exclude specifically those who were not representative, not normative in the imperial scheme of things. The mirror which he holds up to Ireland is cracked because it is the mirror of a servant. Its reality cannot be seen as anything but "cracked" when viewed from the point of view of her masters. Literary tradition, Joyce discovers, would be of little use to portray Ireland because its words and images have no representative power. Even Shakespeare and Hamlet had been enlisted to maintain its reality unarticulated and to aid imperialism thus. Stephen comments wryly on this point in *Ulysses*:

---

[25] Frank McGuinness, *Mutabilitie*, London and Boston, 1997, 57, 61.
[26] Joyce, *A Portrait*, 194.
[27] *Ibid.*, 183.
[28] *Ibid.*, 184.
[29] Joyce, *Ulysses*, 9, 147-48.
[30] *Ibid.*, 9, 174.

> Khaki Hamlets don't hesitate to shoot. The bloodboltered shambles
> in act five is a forecast of the [Boer War] concentration camp sung
> by Mr Swinburne.[31]

If Shakespeare could not be brought to articulate an Irish reality, then Joyce in *Ulysses* attempts to simulate the national poet's articulation and conjure Ireland into literary reality and expression. Now that literary tradition can no longer offer the unitary reality to free him from that of Dublin, Joyce becomes more interested in the process of tradition itself and particularly in its creation. What Joyce attempts in *Ulysses* is to establish the nature of the tradition the national poet establishes, which in turn establishes the national poet and reproduces the same relative positions of reader and writer.

In *Ulysses*, perspective becomes fragmentary, not dialectical as in the earlier texts, reflecting abandonment of the idea that any one objective reality exists. The possession of and access to tradition (Haines' enthusiasm for the Celtic movement and Mulligan's Hellenizing project, for instance) is an important theme and is symbolized in the use of keys. The importance of tradition, however, is explicit in Joyce's writing from at least 1899 when he writes in the essay "The Study of Languages" that the "venerable names" in the history of the language are "landmarks in the transition of a language" which keep it "inviolate".[32] He goes on to emphasize the importance of a knowledge of etymology:

> it is astonishing that Latin is like Shakespeare in everyone's mouth, without his seeming, in the least, to recognize the fact. Quotations are constantly employed ...[33]

Joyce gives the influence of Shakespeare precedence even over Latin (Latin is *"like"* Shakespeare"). In *Ulysses*, lines, words and phrases from Shakespeare infiltrate the everyday speech not just of Stephen, of course, but of Bloom also ("Music hath charms.

---

[31] *Ibid.*, 9, 133-35. "Throughout the period of the Seven Years' War and its aftermath, as Britain acquired ever greater colonial dependencies in the East and the Americas, ever larger claims were made for the national poet's art, praised more and more insistently in terms of world exploitation and conquest" (Michael Dobson, *The Making of the National Poet: Shakespeare, Adaptation and Authorship 1660–1769*, Oxford, 1992, 227).
[32] Joyce, *Critical Writings*, 28-29.
[33] *Ibid.*, 29-30.

Shakespeare said. Quotations every day in the year. To be or not to be. Wisdom while you wait"[34]) and Gerty MacDowell and her narrator/narration of the first part of Chapter Thirteen. What has happened is that the national poet has succeeded in imposing his idiolect on all subsequent speakers of the language: *parole* becomes *langue* without forfeiting the characteristics of either.

The phenomenon of the national poet's idiolect gaining currency in the wider language of the community is comparable to what Hugh Kenner calls the "Uncle Charles Principle".[35] Instead of Maria in "Clay" infecting the narration with her oversights and sometimes wilful ignorance, however, the national poet gifts the nation with the words, images and phrases to articulate the environment and the reality in which its people live: they "describe with his description".

Although it is in *Ulysses* that Joyce works through the theme of the national poet, it is in "The Dead" that his own relationship to the various communities he belongs or belonged to is first probed. The role Gabriel attempts but fails to play is to act as the representative voice of a disparate group of people expressing their gratitude and emotion to their hosts. The same complex relationship between audience and writer exists between the guests at the Little Christmas dinner party and Gabriel. He is nominally speaking on behalf of his fellow guests to show their collective appreciation of his aunts and of Mary Jane who have hosted the party. That is, he is speaking both to and on behalf of everyone present. His role is one of a community's spokesman, as its representative: his mistake is to treat his speech as personal expression.

Gabriel is disparaging of the guests' ability to appreciate his allusion to Browning, of his aunts' ability to understand anything of his speech and even plans to use his speech as an occasion to settle a score with Miss Ivors. During the course of the story, he moves from arrogance to the realization that he could not hope to speak on behalf of others. Instead, he is daunted by how little he knows of the reality of others' – even his wife's – experience. In contrast to his earlier efforts at self-assertion, he feels that "his own identity was fading out into a grey impalpable world":[36]

---

[34] Joyce, *Ulysses*, 11, 904-06.
[35] Hugh Kenner, *Joyce's Voices*, Berkeley, 1978, 17. Richard Ellmann describes the same effect as a "magnetization of style and vocabulary by the context of person, place and time" (Richard Ellmann, *James Joyce*, Oxford, 1982, 146).
[36] James Joyce, *Dubliners*, London, 1988, 255.

> The search for collectivity in anonymity is inspired by the fear of a
> much greater anonymity: not merely the loss of identity in death, but
> the loss of the meaning of death, which can only be protected and
> maintained by a cohesive society.[37]

What "The Dead" signals in Joyce is a reappraisal of the idea of community, especially the national community and how it is defined. Gabriel's sense of belonging to and understanding the community in which he lives, of being representative, is disturbed by three women during the story (Lily, Miss Ivors, and Gretta). In the same way that Gabriel re-examines his relationship to those around him before he can articulate reality, Joyce re-immerses himself in an Irish reality the better to articulate that reality with conviction.

What Gabriel arrives at is a more complex relationship to the idea of community – the married couple and also a wider community including his aunts and the other guests – and his own place in it: "It hardly pained him now to think how poor a part he, her husband, had played in her life."[38] Joyce, like Gabriel and Bloom, comes to a more intense relationship with tradition and is aware that all three's respective ambivalences are important elements of their understanding and character. This is the departure point of *Ulysses*: "What Gabriel Conroy has to learn so painfully at the end of 'The Dead', that we all – dead and living – belong to the same community, is accepted by Bloom from the start."[39] The tears that fill Gabriel's eyes are "generous" because they are meant to suggest a "collective social consciousness".[40]

It is not surprising that Joyce should have re-examined his relationship to the community in which he grew up once he had left. The theme of parallax symbolizes in *Ulysses* each individual's different interpretation, each individual's perspective of reality. The novel offers, within the idea of a national community, the possibility that a limited objective reality is experienced similarly and simultaneously. That is to say, a resolution is found in something less than universal truth but something more than subjective truth. This reality is epitomized in the national poet.

[37] Emer Nolan, *James Joyce and Nationalism*, London and New York, 1995, 36.
[38] Joyce, *Dubliners*, 254.
[39] Ellmann, *James Joyce*, 362.
[40] Vincent J. Cheng, *Joyce, Race and Empire*, Cambridge, 1995, 143.

The idea that animates the portrayal of the nation in *Ulysses* is what Jean Paul Sartre calls "national intersubjectivity".[41] The compromise the nation constitutes for Joyce is that reality may indeed be shared but that individual consciousness does nevertheless contribute to one's experience of that reality. The role of the national poet is to define such an interpretative community, to speak both to it and on its behalf, to express its collective consciousness or what Jung calls "collective unconscious":

> we also find in the unconscious qualities that are not individually acquired but are inherited, e.g. instincts as impulses to carry out actions from necessity, without conscious motivation. In this "deeper" stratum we also find ... archetypes .... The instincts and archetypes together form the *collective unconscious*. I call it "collective" because, unlike the personal unconscious, it is not made up of individual and more or less unique contents but of those which are universal and of regular occurrence.[42]

I do not wish to argue either that a writer can simply decide to become a national poet. Nor am I arguing that Joyce is or that he wished to become Ireland's national poet. Rather, I believe it is clear that the structures the position of the national poet creates within his or her texts offer Joyce the resolution to the stylistic difficulties which concern his writing from the beginning. Those stylistic difficulties relate primarily to the question of what audience Joyce's texts address. It is a difficulty W. B. Yeats also faces and addresses in a similar way: "his [Yeats'] ideal of the nation was organized in relation to a dangerous alternative form of collectivity: the spectre of the crowd both enabled and haunted Yeats' nation as theatre audience."[43]

I do believe also that seeing Yeats assume the role of national poet after the 1916 Rising did alert Joyce to the possibility of creating his own ideal audience; as Yeats put it, "created out of the tradition of

---

[41]   In Franz Fanon, *The Wretched of the Earth*, London, 1990, 9. Weldon Thornton captures the same idea in what he calls a "public subjective" (*The Antimodernism of Joyce's 'Portrait of the Artist as a Young Man'*, New York, 1994, 30) but denies that such a thing is possible.

[42]   C. G. Jung, *Memories, Dreams, Reflections*, ed. Aniela Jaffe, trans. Richard and Clara Winston, London, 1961, 420.

[43]   Marjorie Howes, *Yeats' Nations: Gender, Class, and Irishness*, Cambridge, 1996, 72.

myself".[44] What Joyce does, in fact, is to attempt to short-circuit the route by which a text becomes the shared property of the nation and the national poet by manipulating the relationships between readers, characters, narrators and writer in the novel. It is an endeavour he will approach even more vigorously in *Finnegans Wake*.

If it is accepted that the idea of the national poet is not a simple matter of elevation by tradition but a position into which poets can seek to situate themselves by consciously constructing the traditions that will value them most, then it is clear how useful such an idea would have been for Joyce, who was struggling with the very things the national poet and the tradition the national poet belongs to define.

The reclaiming of the national space was a major part of the various cultural movements in smaller nations seeking independence during this period. The Great War was the war fought for the freedom of small nations and the period that led up to 1914 was a time of great activity among the cultures of Europe's smaller nations.

This guarantee of understanding at the level of place and common experience is one of the main devices of *Ulysses*. The central tenet of this argument is that Joyce saw that a community establishes this communal reality by entering into the language or voice of one person (the national poet) who establishes one consciousness, one idiolect as, if not standard, then as a shared and common language. It is possible for a writer to define a community or, alternatively, it is possible for a community to define its sense of belonging in the person and/or texts of one figure. The role that such a figure has in the actual "fixing" or standardizing of a language may be seen most clearly in the case of Dante.

Having isolated himself from the narratives of family, nation and religion which sought to define him when in Ireland, Joyce must have found that exile defined him only in relation to Ireland. The shift in tone noted earlier in "The Dead" as the first major piece written outside Ireland is attributable to a revision in the identity that Joyce had carved for himself in opposition to his environment. No longer being understood in the terms of this opposition meant being incomprehensible.

Henceforth, community becomes the arena in which all Joyce's preoccupations are played out. The need for connection between people (which sometimes took the form of the supernatural, as is the

---

[44]   W. B. Yeats, *Autobiographies*, Dublin, 1988, 463.

case with James Stephens[45]) is the defining element of his writing from the first years of his exile from Ireland.

The use of the figure of a national poet to define a nation combines Joyce's concerns of community and language as the poet's works form (as Jung and Jane Austen agree) a shared consciousness from which individuals can or think they can share common experience and understanding. As I have suggested throughout, Joyce interests himself in the mechanics of such constructions, how it comes about and how it is made to come about.

Joyce's interest in archetypes needs no extrapolation here but it is a commonplace to seek to define a nation, state or community through its writers. Obviously, the writer in many circumstances writes for her or his community especially in times of difficulty. The rejection of Joyce in Ireland until recently and of Salman Rushdie in India, for example, may be explained in terms of the new states refusing to be defined by a voice seen to be disloyal by criticizing the nation to a foreign audience.

However uncritical, perhaps even fanciful, this notion of community and connection may be, it is and has been a powerful concept. I have mentioned how this status can be thrust upon a writer (perhaps unwillingly), but another aspect is how the writer might actively seek this status for political purposes. Joyce was, at the very least, aware of the concept and wrote to Nora in 1909 of becoming "the poet of my race".[46]

There is obviously movement in both ways; a national poet both creates himself or herself and is created by the community seeking to establish itself. I argue that Joyce became interested in this process as a natural progression of his concern about communication and knowledge, shown in his earliest introverted texts, in the inability of the characters to articulate in *Dubliners* and in the young boy's alternating immersion in and isolation from structures which would define him in *A Portrait*.

---

[45] See Ellmann, *James Joyce*, 592.
[46] James Joyce, *Selected Letters of James Joyce*, ed. Richard Ellmann, London, 1992, 169.

JAMES JOYCE'S ANXIETY OF INFLUENCE: HIS PLACE INSIDE AND OUTSIDE THE IRISH LITERARY TRADITION

MARISOL MORALES LADRÓN

In respect to the author's increasing experimentation with new styles and techniques, James Joyce's literary canon, *Dubliners*, *A Portrait of the Artist as a Young Man*, *Exiles*, *Ulysses* and *Finnegans Wake*, constitutes an inseparable entirety. His self-imposed exile from Ireland to escape from the oppressions of religion, nationality, language and from what he regarded as the limitations of being Irish, led him to a continuous search for a personal and unique voice outside the Irish literary tradition. Although Joycean aesthetics have been acknowledged as landmarks of extreme originality and innovation, his literary discourse cannot be analysed outside the context of Irish literature and history. If, according to Harold Bloom, literary tradition equates influence with imitation because one cannot write or read without making reference to prede-cessors, Joyce's anxiety of influence manifests itself in his desire to move away from his social, political, and cultural heritage. Nevertheless, Joyce's literary legacy in his pervasive references to other sources, emerges as the paradigm of intertextuality. The purpose of my discussion, therefore, is to offer a brief consideration of Joyce's position in both the Irish and the European literary tradition. My approach will be essentially twofold: to evaluate the function of Joyce's Irishness in the light of his apparent rejection; and to analyse his incorporation of European models as an alternative that would bring fewer anxieties and which has led his legacy to being recognized as the epitome of Modernism.

T. S. Eliot, in his famous essay "Tradition and the Individual Talent", claims that when analysing the work of an author, we generally tend to look for the individual essence or for aspects that share less common ground with previous writings, without considering that in many cases the peculiarities of the writer are those on which the immortality of his or her predecessors was based. Since novelty, he continues, is more welcoming than repetition, literary tradition acquires a wider meaning because it cannot be inherited and, therefore, we can only make sense of it from a historical perspective:

> This historical sense, which is a sense of the timeless and of the temporal together, is what makes a writer traditional. And it is at the same time what makes a writer most acutely conscious of his place in time, of his contemporaneity.[1]

The theoretician Ihab H. Hassan also suggests that studying tradition, experimentation, continuity and development entails adopting a broader view of history or of the dynamics of what is usually termed influence, and that these are the parameters that should guide and direct the evaluation of the relationship of writer to writer, period to writer, or period to period.[2] In the same vein, Harold Bloom in *The Western Canon* points out that, when trying to rediscover the traditions that form the bases of a given author, the literary critic is to be confronted with the questioning of whether writers choose a tradition or are chosen by it. According to Bloom, writers do not select "their primitive precursors", rather they are chosen and modified by tradition.[3] As Bloom had already argued in his previous work, *A Map of Misreadings*, there are no texts but relationships among texts and, for this reason, one cannot write, read or interpret outside the frame of a tradition:

> You cannot write or teach or think or even read without imitation, and what you imitate is what another person has done, that person's writing or teaching or thinking or reading .... Literary tradition begins when a fresh author is simultaneously cognizant not only of his own struggle against the forms and presence of a precursor, but is compelled also to a sense of the precursor's place in regard to what came before *him*.[4]

Bloom's ideas are clearly grounded on Eliot's when the latter considered that a writer should create "not merely with his own generation in his bones, but with a feeling that the whole of the literature

---

[1] T. S. Eliot, "Tradition and the Individual Talent", in T. S. Eliot, *The Sacred Wood. Essays on Poetry and Criticism*, London, 1969, 48-49.

[2] I. Hassan, "The Problem of Influence in Literary History: Notes Toward a Definition", *Journal of Aesthetics and Art Criticism*, 14 (1955), 75.

[3] Harold Bloom, *The Western Canon: The Books and School of Ages*, London, 1995, 11.

[4] Harold Bloom, *A Map of Misreadings*, New York, 1975, 32.

of Europe from Homer and within it the whole of the literature of his own country has a simultaneous existence and composes a simultaneous order" because writers cannot acquire a total meaning by themselves. Their significance is the appreciation of their relation with the writers who precede them.[5]

Within this frame of reference, my aim is to revise Joyce's commonplace originality and his position as one of the greatest innovators of literature. The concept of originality has traditionally been used as an opposed category to that of tradition confusing the traditional with the conservative. In this context, however, the term "originality" acquires a wider meaning by which I refer not only to pure innovations in form or content but also to reorganizations based on previous models. Thus I conceive tradition as the other side of originality since: "The *original* author is not necessarily the innovator or the most inventive, but rather the one who succeeds in making all his own, in subordinating what he takes from others to the new complex of his own artistic work."[6]

James Joyce, an author who from a self-imposed exile only wrote about Dublin, has been acknowledged as the greatest of all Irish writers; yet his Irishness has been questioned. Seamus Deane, in *Celtic Revivals*, contends that writers like Joyce, Yeats, Synge and O'Casey produced literary works which, although they can clearly be regarded as Irish, at the same time, cannot be defined solely by this term because:

> Irish experience, different from English and anxious to assert that difference to the ultimate extent, needed a new form of realization which would not only differentiate itself in formal terms from its English counterparts, but would also have to do so while fretting in the shadow of the colonizer's language. In accepting these challenges, formal and linguistic, in accepting the unique role of the artist in whom a minority culture, characterized by incompleteness and fracture, would achieve completeness and coherence, Joyce necessarily became a rebel in all that preceded him.[7]

Joyce's much acclaimed rebelliousness, based on the rejection of both his own country and the literary tradition which shaped it should,

---

[5]   Eliot, *The Sacred Wood*, 49.

[6]   J. T. Shaw, "Literary Indebtness and Comparative Literary Studies", in *Comparative Literature: Method and Perspective*, eds N. P. Stallknecht and H. Frenz, Carbondale, 1961, 60.

[7]   Seamus Deane, *Celtic Revivals: Essays in Modern Irish Literature 1880-1980*, London, 1985, 100.

nevertheless, be interpreted in the light of his strong desire to free himself from the oppressive forces that surrounded him. Stephen Dedalus embodies Joyce's early ideas when, in *A Portrait*, he tells his friend Davin that "When the soul of a man is born in this country there are nets flung at it to hold it back from flight. You talk to me of nationality, language, religion, I shall try to fly by those nets."[8]

Joyce's collection of essays, reviews and critical articles constitutes a significant point of reference from which to interpret his own literary interests and affinities and his position towards Ireland. In his two lectures on James Clarence Mangan,[9] he comments on the literary quality of the poet objecting to a general tendency among Irish writers who refuse to pay homage to their contemporaries. For this reason, Joyce claims:

> if he [Mangan] finally emerges into the posthumous glory to which he has a right, it will not be by the help of any of his countrymen. Mangan will be accepted by the Irish as their national poet on the day when the conflict will be decided between my native land and the foreign powers – Anglo-Saxon and Roman Catholic.[10]

In "Ireland, Island of Saints and Sages", Joyce interprets Irish history as ignoble and servile from its very beginnings, when it allowed itself to be sold to the first English adventurers, affirming that:

> It is well past time for Ireland to have done once and for all with failure. It she is truly capable of reviving, let her awake, or let her cover up her head and lie down decently in her grave forever.[11]

Contending that Ireland was a country destined by God to become the caricature of the modern world, Harry Levin suggests that Joyce would become the caricaturist maintaining the position of a "wildgoose, a cosmopolitan Irishman, keeping aloof from nationalism and seeking to Europeanize Irish culture".[12]

---

[8]   James Joyce, *A Portrait of the Artist as a Young Man*, ed. C. Anderson, New York, 1968, 203.

[9]   Although Joyce's views on Irish literature were formed at an early stage of his literary career, they remained constant during his life.

[10] James Joyce, *The Critical Writings of James Joyce*, eds Ellsworth Mason and Richard Ellmann, New York, 1958, 179.

[11] *Ibid.*, 174.

[12] Harry Levin, *Grounds for Comparison*, Cambridge, 1972, 362-63.

Joyce overtly criticized the ideas of the Irish literary revival for their provincial patriotism and their literary n arrowness. As he clearly asserted in his essay "The Day of the Rabblement":

> If an artist courts the favour of the multitude he cannot escape the contagion of its fetishism and deliberate self-deception, and if he joins in a popular movement he does so at his own risk. Therefore, the Irish Literary Theatre by its surrender to the trolls has cut itself adrift from the line of advancement. Until he has freed himself from the mean influences about him – sodden enthusiasm and clever insinuation and every flattering influence of vanity and low ambition – no man is an artist at all.[13]

Joyce's rejection of the Irish emergent nationalism, mainly concerned with the search for the roots of the Irish tradition, should be interpreted in relation to his disregard for the vision of literature as a closed unity. Accordingly, in his essay, "Ireland, Island of Saints and Sages", he adds that "the Irish nation's insistence on developing its own culture by itself is not so much the demand of a young nation that wants to make good in the European concert as the demand of a very old nation to renew under new forms the glories of a past civilization".[14]

In "Home Rule Comet", Joyce also claims that Irish history is characterized by the betrayal of its own heroes, "always in the hour of need and always without gaining recompense. She has hounded her spiritual creators into exile only to boast about them",[15] and, moreover, in "The Day of the Rabblement", he affirms: "A nation which never advanced so far as a miracle-play affords no literary model to the artist, and he must look abroad."[16] Regarding Irish cultural heritage as inferior to that of other countries, Joyce chose exile as a liberating force which would free him from the constraints of a parochial Ireland – defined in *A Portrait* as "the old sow that eats her farrow"[17] – and also from any kind of oppressions that would limit his yearning for artistic and spiritual freedom.[18] His work, however, cannot be analysed without pondering his debts to his forebears. Joyce's appropriation of both the English and the

---

[13] Joyce, *Critical Writings*, 71-72.
[14] *Ibid.*, 157.
[15] *Ibid.*, 213.
[16] *Ibid.*, 70.
[17] Joyce, *A Portrait*, 203.
[18] Once again, this is nothing more than an inheritance from the idealism of Romantic poets like Byron, Shelley, Wordsworth or Coleridge.

Irish tradition without attempting to be faithful to the original and without recognizing the primary sources is clearly noticeable. In this context, if Joyce's writings can be considered as major examples of innovation, at the same time it is also true that each of them can easily be included in one or several of the literary traditions that precede him.

Dubliners follows the naturalist tradition of Flaubert, Balzac or Zola, in a style which Joyce himself described as "scrupulous meanness", claiming that "meanness is the character and quality of Dublin life".[19] The collection of stories strives to function as mirrors of reality in the extraordinary accumulation of details which surround all descriptions blending a naturalistic procedure with the symbolic dimension of each detail. The economy of style is, in fact, one of the most significant aspects of the work characterized by the use of a deliberately limited and concentrated language (which has the purpose of reflecting the paralysis of Irish life through a minimum of action), a sparse use of dialogue and a significant number of unfinished sentences, in an attempt to represent Dubliners in their passivity and immobility. It is not surprising that Joyce had to struggle for almost nine years before he could find a publisher for a work through which he tried to reflect the moral history of his own country, since most editors considered his work immoral and irreverent. Convinced of the value of his own real depiction of the Dubliners and determined to have his work published, he warned the editor Grant Richards that he was retarding the course of civilization if he refused to allow Irish people to look at themselves in this "nicely polished looking glass", positioning himself as "one of the writers of this generation who are perhaps creating a last conscience in the soul of this wretched race".[20]

From the portrayal of the different perspectives which form the basis of *Dubliners*, in *A Portrait* Joyce limits the narration to the single angle of vision of the protagonist, adopting, once again, a European model, the *Bildungsroman*. In this novel, Joyce abandons the realistic tradition of his first work and confronts the reader with the subjective consciousness of Stephen and with his own fragmented and contradictory views of a Catholic Ireland. Its most significant aspect though is Stephen's process of growing up, which parallels his linguistic evolution and, ultimately, Joyce's own awareness of using the language of the oppressor, affirming

---

[19]   Quoted in W. Johnsen, "Joyce's Dubliners and the Futility of Modernism", in *James Joyce and Modern Literature*, eds W. J. McCormack and A. Stead, London, 1982, 7.
[20]   Quoted in Richard Ellmann, *James Joyce*, Oxford, 1983, 222, 332.

that "I am Irish by race ... but the English have condemned me to speak the language of Shakespeare".[21] Throughout the novel, Stephen is obsessed by the use of words and by the effect of their multiple associations, and one of his main preoccupations is to discern whether words are used "according to the literary tradition or according to the tradition of the marketplace". Noticing that there are words, which do not belong to him, Stephen feels strangled by language and he realizes that he will not be able to fully communicate until he overcomes the domination and oppression that language is exerting on him. This discovery takes place in the famous scene when the English dean of the school tries to show Stephen how to light a fire and Stephen fails to understand him because they do not communicate in the same language:

> – The funnel through which you pour the oil into your lamp.
> – That? said Stephen. Is that called a funnel? Is it not a tundish? [...]
> – Is that called a tundish in Ireland? asked the dean. I never heard the word in my life.
> – It is called a tundish in Lower Drumcondra, said Stephen, laughing, where they speak the best English.[22]

In *Exiles*, once again Joyce moved away from the romantic idealism of Yeats and the chauvinist nationalism of other members of the group while adopting the Norwegian dramatist Henrik Ibsen as his master; a writer whose works had been considered immoral by his Irish contemporaries. In his rejection of the postulates of the revivalists, Joyce was reacting against the cult of the heroic past, represented by the mythological hero Cuchulainn "Hound of Ulster", the paradigm of courage, strength and fierceness, which had been adopted and revived by the leaders of the Irish literary renaissance like Yeats, Lady Gregory or Patrick Pearse. For Joyce, this old heroism offered neither a real nor a fair image of Ireland and, as Kiberd notes, he opted for the ordinary as the domain of the artist, claiming that heroism and sensationalism should be left for journalists. Joyce interpreted Irish nationalism, therefore, as an imitation of the original English model rather than as a radical renewal of the consciousness of the Irish race.[23]

---

[21] Quoted by Declan Kiberd, *Inventing Ireland: The Literature of a Modern Nation*, London, 1996, 35.
[22] Joyce, *A Portrait*, 188.
[23] Declan Kiberd, Introduction to James Joyce, *Ulysses*, London, 1992, xii-xiii.

Consequently, in *Ulysses* Joyce grounds the Greek epic myth of the *Odyssey* into the reality of Dublin in 1904 and, at the same time, the novel incorporates the wider and diverse traditions of writers like Homer, Dante, Giordano Bruno, Vico, Flaubert, Shakespeare, Lewis Carroll, Swift, Freud, Dujardin, Tolstoy, Baudelaire, Mallarmé, Ibsen and Nietzsche, to mention only a few. To Joyce, the choice of a Greek myth rather than a Gaelic one offered a better example of humanity and pacifism than the warrior hero Cuchulainn and, by and large, it allowed him to extend the significance of the Dublin setting towards a more universal conception of human experience. The hero Ulysses, clearly demythologized in the character of Leopold Bloom, was regarded by Joyce as the most complete character of literature because he played the multiple roles of son, father, husband, lover and king of Ithaca, "evad[ing] military service by simulating madness"; and although he had to confront a number of trials, his wisdom and courage allowed him to overcome all of them, because he "was not a god, for he had all the defects of the ordinary man".[24] In *Ulysses*, the heroism of the myth contrasts with the representation of the most ordinary reality of human beings, including that of their physiological functions, rendered in an inhibited language which describes, for instance, Bloom's flatulence, his masturbation on the beach or Molly Bloom's sexual obsessions. Far from a pornographic purpose, Hodgart maintains that Joyce built "the creatures of his imagination as *creaturely* as possible",[25] offering a less heroic but more real understanding of the Irish country.

If in the traditional novel, Eco points out, characters could not blow their nose unless this had a function in the development of the story, Joyce, on the contrary, fills his work with trivial details in order to establish the universal basis of human behaviour. As Kiberd suggests, Joyce describes Leopold Bloom, "pissing and shitting" to show that he is a human being completely free from abstract pretensions, self-hatred and a rejection of his own body:

> Joyce saw, earlier than most, that the modern cult of the body had been made possible only by a century of coy evasion; and his close analysis of Bloom's daily actions exposed the laughable inadequacy of both attitudes. Like Lawrence, Joyce wanted to afford the body a recognition equal to that given the mind, but to a post-Victorian

---

[24]   Ellmann, *James Joyce*, 435-36.
[25]   Matthew Hodgart, *James Joyce: A Student's Guide*, London, 1983, 73.

generation which had lost this just balance, both men *appeared* to elevate the body above all else.[26]

Joyce's masterpiece *Finnegans Wake* emerges as his major endeavour to reconstruct not only the whole literature that precedes him, including a parodic rewriting of the themes and motives which had appeared in his own writings, but an overwhelming rendering of the universal history of humankind in its blending of literary references with the culture, history, philosophy and ethics of humanity. The revolutionary and sophisticated language of *Finnegans Wake* tries to represent the paradigm of multiplicity, plurality and totality. The story from which Joyce takes his myriad of references is, as in *Ulysses*, very simple. *Finnegans Wake* is the dream of a Dubliner, Humphrey Chimpden Earwicker, whose initials, HCE, also stand as "Here Comes Everybody", representing the universal man. It is also the story of his wife, Anna Livia Plurabelle, ALP, who stands as the symbol of life embodied in the river Liffey (in Irish *abhann*), which in old maps was called Anna Liffey. With life, she also incarnates death and rebirth as blurring dichotomies that successively fuse and confuse. It is also the dream of the twins Shem and Shaun – Jerry and Kevin – and of the daughter Issy; the three of them adopting different names and identities along a never-ending phantasmagoric metamorphosis.

The title of the work comes from an old Irish ballad, in which the bricklayer Tim Finnegan falls down a ladder and dies. In the wake, his friends drop some whiskey – in Irish "uisce beatha" or water of life – in his mouth and he resurrects. The legend of Finnegan becomes the story of any human being from Adam to Christ to Parnell and other archetypal figures with which Joyce tries to represent the fall, death and resurrection of the universal history of humankind. The structure of the work is thus cyclical, without beginning nor ending, rewriting itself in a continuous rebirth. The first sentence of *Finnegans Wake*, introduced *in medias res*, starts in small caps: "riverrun, past Eve and Adam's, from swere of shore to bend of bay, brings us by a commodius vicus of recirculation back to Howth Castle and Environs",[27] introducing the keys which will orient its reading. The words "vicus of recirculation", for instance, echo the theories of the Neapolitan philosopher Giambattista Vico on the circularity of history, while "Howth Castle and Environs" reinscribe in its initials, the name of the protagonist "HCE", who is also Adam, the

---

26 Kiberd, Introduction, xvi.
27 James Joyce, *Finnegans Wake*, London, 1992, 3.

first Biblical man and, with him, any human being. The last sentence repeats the first letter of the alphabet and ends without a full stop, connecting with the first one: "The keys to. Given! A way, a lone, a last, a loved, a long the." From the ending of the text, from its death, we go to the beginning and then back to the end again rewriting the cycle of dreaming and awakening, of dying and being reborn. For this reason, *Finnegans Wake* entails the most absolute of realities, nothing is what seems to be yet it is everything at the same time. Opposing extremes fuse and confuse in unique and indivisible identities that also change and modify themselves. Thus in this process of transmutation the very principle of perpetuity consecrates in an eternal continuity.[28]

The main concern of *Finnegans Wake* is to represent not only the realm of dreams but also the chaotic and fragmented oniric language, which makes it the most difficult and inaccessible of Joyce's works. At a stage when Joyce had discovered "that I can do anything with language I want", he told his friend Eugene Jolas that it was not he alone who was writing the work: "It is you, and you, and you, and that man over there, and that girl at the next table." Thanks to his extraordinary linguistic memory, Joyce could remember fragments of conversation or even syllables outside context that he would reproduce in their multiple variations in order to represent the plural language of humanity. [29]

Joyce's accomplishments as an artist are, consequently, inseparable from his recreation of old models and traditions in his own original contribution to the new conception of the genre. Joyce himself stated in *Stephen Hero* that no aesthetic theory has any value if it relies on tradition, since each culture has its own and it is almost impossible to attempt to reconcile all of them:

---

[28] J. G. Carnero, *James Joyce y la explosión de la palabra*, Sevilla, 1989, 141-42.

[29] Eugene Jolas, "My Friend James Joyce", in *James Joyce: Two Decades of Criticism*, ed. Seon Givens, New York, 1948, 13. Joyce's writings emerge as the paradigm of intertextuality and *Ulysses* and *Finnegans Wake* especially cannot be conceived without considering a myriad of writers and texts which preceded Joyce, both canonical and popular, and which are subject of the writer's own recreation and transformation. His appropriation of sources involved any popular and cultural aspect that could be significant for his work, from newspapers and magazines to romances or guides. Kershner affirms that Joyce was always fascinated by the use of words in popular culture and that most of his work was in fact serialized in popular journals before it appeared in book form, making Joyce "a contributor to the popular press as well as a consumer". (R. Kershner, *Joyce, Bakhtin and Popular Culture: Chronicles of Disorder*, Chapel Hill, 1989, 7).

No aesthetic theory, pursued Stephen relentlessly, is of any value which investigates with the aid of the lantern of tradition. What we symbolize in black the Chinaman may symbolize in yellow: each has his own tradition. Greek beauty laughs at Coptic beauty and the American Indian derides them both. It is almost impossible to reconcile all tradition whereas it is by no means impossible to find the justification of every form of beauty which has been adored on the earth by an examination into the mechanism of aesthetic apprehension whether it be dressed in red, white, yellow or black.[30]

Stephen's ideas illustrate not only Joyce's rejection of all kind of limitations, in his yearning for an artistic and spiritual freedom, but should also be interpreted as Joyce's search for a personal voice to create his own tradition. For this reason, Joyce's work should be placed at a middle point between the literary tradition that precedes him and which he incorporates in his work by means of parody, irony and satire and his own re-writing of the past into a new aesthetic solution that adapts better to the fragmentation of the modern world, breaking with rational thought in order to show the chaos of the human mind.

Joyce has been acknowledged as one of the major Modernists in his rejection of most of the values that defined the literary tradition of the past, which tried to represent a mimetic image of reality and which had turned out to be insufficient to describe the complexity of modern life. Although the term "Modernism" was first coined to give a name to a new kind of literature that implied a certain kind of modernity, it later came to designate a literary movement associated with experimentation in the arts which in the 1920s produced works such as *Ulysses*, T. S. Eliot's *The Waste Land*, Virginia Woolf's *Jacob's Room*, Sinclair Lewis's *Babbit* or Yeats' *The Tower*. Modernism as a "movement towards sophistication and mannerism, towards introversion, technical display, internal self-scepticism".[31] is the context which frames Joyce's works. If he has historically become an epitome of this literary movement, it is not so much for his bond to any of the *avant-garde* movements that shaped it but rather for the innovative techniques, stylistic devices and narrative experimentation with which he was able to create a new literary output that identifies itself with Modernist rupture. As Margot Norris suggests, "Joyce historicizes his own modernist

---

[30] James Joyce, *Stephen Hero*, ed. T. Spencer, London, 1986, 189.
[31] Malcolm Bradbury and James MacFarlane, "The Name and Nature of Modernism", in *Modernism: 1890–1930*, eds Malcolm Bradbury and James MacFarlane, London, 1976, 26.

Marisol Morales Ladrón

aestheticism by grounding it in the nineteenth-century liberal tradition's separation of art from social life".[32]

Joyce's place in literary history as a major Modernist, however, cannot be separated from his identity as both an Irish and a European writer. According to Seamus Deane, Joyce was the Irish writer who rejected the limitations of being Irish and the writer in the English language who also rejected the limitations of being an English writer, measuring his loyalty towards himself against his disloyalty towards any kind of forces that had moulded him.[33] Joyce's rejection of the ideas of the Irish revival find a proper place within the spirit of Modernism, which advocated the need to overcome the limitations of language and the search for alternative forms of aesthetic expression in its defence of the autonomy of the work of art. Joyce consequently strove to represent a language that would be above all languages, free from national or cultural limitations. As he affirmed: "I cannot express myself in English without enclosing myself in a tradition."[34] On the other hand, nationality, should be revised in the light of his own conception of a world in which geographical boundaries were nothing more than prejudiced divisions of identities. The "Cyclops" chapter of *Ulysses* is perhaps the best satirical example of Joyce's ideas about this issue, when Bloom is asked about the meaning of "nation" and he answers:

> – Persecution, says he [Bloom], all the history of the world is full of it. Perpetuating national hatred among nations.
> – But do you know what a nation means? says John Wyse ....
> – A nation? says Bloom. A nation is the same people living in the same place.
> – By God, then, says Ned, laughing, if that's so I'm a nation for I'm living in the same place for the past five years.
> So of course everyone had a laugh at Bloom and says he, trying to muck out of it.
> – Or also living in different places.[35]

As this quote suggests, the concepts of nationalism and cosmopolitanism in Joyce's work dissolve in such a way, that the most Irish features of his

---

[32]   Margot Norris, *Joyce's Web: The Social Unravelling of Modernism*, Austin: TX, 1992, 7.
[33]   Deane, *Celtic Revivals*, 100.
[34]   Ellmann, *James Joyce*, 410.
[35]   James Joyce, *Ulysses*, London, 1986, 271-72.

work cannot be separated from the cosmopolitan atmosphere – although generally restricted to Europe – which surround it.

As I have tried to show, the apparently opposing polarities of the Irish and the European Joyce both complement and modify each other. There is no other writer who can exemplify better the conflict between the self and the other, between the unity of the personal and the plurality of the otherness. Joyce's identity as an Irish writer is inseparable from his very desire to move away from the oppressions of a culture that he wished to enlarge by opening it out to a continental Europe. Rather than adopting the views of his contemporaries, who were concerned with the revitalization of a heroic past and the revival of the Irish language, Irish myths and Irish traditions, Joyce widened his scope in an ultimate attempt to free Ireland from the oppressions of its own past, of its own "nightmare of history", which so pervasively haunts most characters in *Ulysses*. Irish experience, culture and motives, nevertheless, are the main subjects of all his writings – with the exception of *Giacomo Joyce*, set in Trieste – locating Dublin and, by extension, Ireland at the centre of the universal creation. It is in this context that one can affirm that Joyce succeeded in revitalizing the Irish literary tradition by transforming the whole conception of literature not only in the European context but at a universal level. As Kiberd has affirmed, Joyce

> did not become modern to the extent that he ceased to be Irish; rather he began from the premise that to be Irish was to be modern anyway. Yet he saw his art as a patriotic contribution to "the moral history of my country"; and he believed that he had done more than any politician to liberate Irish consciousness into a profound freedom of form. In this, as in so much else, he was accurate. It was the politicians who, in cleaving to tired, inherited forms, failed to be modern and so ceased being Irish in any meaningful way.[36]

His large literary legacy illustrate the concerns of an exiled writer who could only write about Dublin in a language which, however difficult and disruptive, should be read as his decolonizing response to his own country. As he affirmed:

> In spite of everything Ireland remains the brain of the United Kingdom. The English, judiciously practical and ponderous, furnish

---

[36] Kiberd, *Inventing Ireland*, 266-67.

the over-stuffed stomach of humanity with a perfect gadget – the water closet. The Irish, condemned to express themselves in a language not their own, have stamped on it the mark of their own genius and compete for glory with the civilized nations. The result is then called English literature.[37]

Joyce's work has not only produced followers in the fictional world but also a large material for literary critics who have used his writings to explain the development and evolution of contemporary narrative. One can only end by pointing out that Joyce never questioned his gifted qualities as an artist. In a letter to his brother Stanislaus, he declared: "My mind is of a type superior to and more civilized than any I have met up to the present", and in a letter to his wife, he said: "I hope that the day may come when I shall be able to give you the fame of being beside me when I have entered into my Kingdom." In addition, he prepared for his own immortality by thinking of his centenary when on Bloomsday 1924 he wrote in his diary: "Today 16 of June 20 years after. Will anybody remember this date?"[38]

---

[37] *Ibid.*, 35.
[38] Richard Ellmann, *Four Dubliners: Oscar Wilde, William Butler Yeats, James Joyce and Samuel Beckett*, London, 1987, 53, 54.

"IDENTITIES IN THE WRITER COMPLEXUS":
JOYCE, EUROPE AND IRISH IDENTITIES

EUGENE O'BRIEN

The point at issue in the concluding sections of *A Portrait of the Artist as a Young Man* is the conflict between different notions of Irish identity. In lines that have become a *credo* of Joyce's own exile from Ireland, he puts into the mouth of Stephen Dedalus this astute summary of the effect of essentialist notions of Irishness on an individual consciousness. Here, speaking of the soul, Stephen makes the point that:

> The soul is born, he said vaguely, first in those moments I told you of. It has a slow and dark birth, more mysterious than the birth of the body. When the soul of a man is born in this country there are nets flung at it to hold it back from flight. You talk to me of nationality, language, religion. I shall try to fly by those nets.[1]

This can be seen as a programmatic statement of what I will term a negative sense of identity. It is very different in theme and in style from the preceding stories of *Dubliners*, where the style was covert and implicit, as narrative voice tended to blend with that of different characters in free indirect discourse, with little personal input from any central narrative presence. Here, the narrative voice expressed in the personal pronoun first person singular, is actively embracing the outward heteroglossic movement towards Europe which will be seen as creative of a new form of cosmopolitan and complex Irish identities.

I will examine these forms of "identities in the writer complexus"[2] in terms of two intersecting verbal axes: Joyce's own term, "gnomon"

---

[1]   James Joyce, *A Portrait of the Artist as a Young Man*, ed. R. B. Kershner, Boston, 1993, 177.
[2]   James Joyce, *Finnegans Wake*, London 1975 [first published 1939], 114, 33.

and Jacques Derrida's term "hauntology". The word "gnomon" appears in the opening story of *Dubliners*, entitled "The Sisters".[3] The term derives from Euclid's *Elements*, Book II, in which a "gnomon" is defined as what is left of a parallelogram when a similar parallelogram containing one of its corners is removed. However, it can also refer to a pointer on a sundial which, by its shadow, indicates the time of day.[4]

I would suggest that both meanings of the word, that of a geometrical figure and that of a pointer on a sundial, provide symbols of the Joycean concepts of negative identity. The figure of a parallelogram, with a smaller parallelogram removed, suggests a desire for closure and completion that can never be achieved, for, if the parallelogram in the corner is filled in, then the shape will cease to be a gnomon and instead will revert to being a parallelogram. To this extent, the gnomon defines a process which tends towards closure, but never quite achieves it, always seeming to have a phantom dotted line haunting its ontology, and always tending to be what it is not. It is a diagrammatic and conceptual signifier which stresses that identities and definitions are always processes of becoming, as opposed to positions of fixity. It is also an indication that identity as a self-present essentialism is not what Joyce has in mind; for the gnomonic view of identity, what I term "identities in the writer complexus", self is always defined in terms of the other. In ethical and political terms, such a position is the very antithesis of the fundamentalism that has been seen, world-wide, in the Drumcree standoff in recent years in Northern Ireland, where self and other were in violent opposition. I think this example is an eloquent synecdoche of the dangers that fixed and simplistic definitions of identity can bring into being. Indeed, I would argue that it is such fundamentalist identificatory attitudes and ideologies that have been the *terminus a quo* from which much of the violence in Northern Ireland over the past thirty years has originated.

In *Specters of Marx*, Jacques Derrida discusses what he terms *hauntology*. In this book, he explores the spectrality of many areas of meaning, seeing ghostly hauntings as traces of other possible meanings. Derrida's spectrality involves acknowledging that the other that haunts the self; it involves acknowledging the possibility that the "h" in "hauntology" is a hovering presence over the certainties of ontology (in French phonology the words sound remarkably similar

---

[3]   James Joyce, *Dubliners*, London, 1994, 1, Introduction by Anthony Burgess.
[4]   Don Gifford, *Joyce Annotated: Notes for "Dubliners" and "A Portrait of the Artist as a Young Man"*, Berkeley, 1982, 29.

when spoken).[5] In practical terms, this means that Joyce's Irishness is always inhabited by spectral presences of other languages, other cultures and other mindsets.

To be a gnomon is to have a "hauntological" relationship with a parallelogram, and yet never to become that parallelogram; it is to have an independent ontology of "self" which is, at the same time, imbricated in terms of the "other". It is to be defined, negatively, by an other which, while not a part of the self, is nevertheless "hauntologically" present in relation to that self. It suggests a metaphor of identity that is open to other identities, other ideologies and to notions of plurality – hence the plural form of the noun "identity" in this discussion. In Joyce's case, Ireland is defined gnomonically and "hauntologically" by Europe, and European language and culture. This definition complicates and deepens any simplistic desire for an *echt* Irishness which is simply Gaelic, Catholic and nationalist.

The desire of Joyce, and of Stephen, to seek out such new dimensions and new modes of identity should not, however, be seen as a flight from his own country or his own sense of Irishness. Rather is it an attempt to create a new sense of Irishness which acknowledges alterity. This contradictory position, of being part of a culture while at the same time attempting to offer a critique of the ideology of that culture, is discussed by Theodor Adorno, in his essay "Cultural Criticism and Society". The two subject positions from which criticism may be offered are seen by Adorno as being either immanence or transcendence, and both positions are fraught with difficulty. The immanent critic participates in the culture: he or she is shot through with the ideologies and attitudes of that culture and hence has little chance of making any real objective statements about this position of "total immanence"[6] and therefore is doomed to repeat the errors of the culture. The transcendent critic, on the other hand, "aims at a totality" and assumes an "Archimedean position above culture and the blindness of society". However, such a position "outside the sway of existing society", is "fictitious",[7] and ultimately as monological as that

5 Jacques Derrida, *Specters of Marx*: *The State of the Debt, the Work of Mourning and the New International*, trans. Peggy Kamuf, Introduction by Bernd Magnus and Stephen Cullenberg, London, 1994, 10.
6 Theodor Adorno, *Prisms*, trans. Samuel and Shierry Weber, Cambridge: MA, 1981, 26.
7 Adorno, *Prisms*, 31.

of the immanent position within ideology. Adorno's answer to this dilemma is the notion of "negative dialectical criticism", which takes up a position in culture and yet not in culture at the same time. In this sense, the position of transcendence is achieved dialectically by looking at a microcosmic part of a totality, and by then relating that to the cultural macrocosm. The knowledge achieved is negative and it is in search of such a negative sense of Irishness that Joyce, and fictionally Stephen, leave Ireland. It is in the cause of some redefinition of Irishness that he feels he must achieve a quasi-transcendent position, and move to Europe; here he will attempt to redefine a sense of Irishness within a European context.

What Joyce, through Stephen, is attempting to do is to create a negative portrait of Irish identity. To create this, he must have some regulative point from where he can begin to dialectically juxtapose the immanent and the transcendent so as to create these more complex forms of identity. Two tropes allow him to achieve this, Stephen's unusual name and the trope of emigration, as both combine to offer a transcendental perspective on Ireland, and both imbricate Irishness gnomonically with Europe.

Stephen's name is a signifier of otherness from the very beginning of the book. Nasty Roche, on first hearing it asks, "What kind of a name is that?",[8] while later in the opening chapter, Athy says, "you have a queer name, Dedalus".[9] This strangeness of name, allied to Stephen's early preoccupation with words, names, and stories, marks him out as different from the other boys. It places him within a Greek frame of reference, alluding to another artist and artificer who combined immanence and transcendence (through flight) on his own culture, namely Daedalus.

From the earliest stage, Stephen situates himself in terms of a society and a *Lebenswelt* that reaches out beyond Ireland, and nomenclature is a seminal trope of this situation. His friend, Fleming, inscribed the following doggerel on his geography book:

> *Stephen Dedalus is my name,*
> *Ireland is my nation.*
> *Clongowes is my dwellingplace*
> *And heaven my expectation.* [Italics in the original.]

---

[8]   Joyce, *Portrait*, 21.
[9]   *Ibid.*, 34.

In Fleming's placement, Stephen has been slotted into an expected range of definitional identificatory parameters: he is Irish and Catholic, and his future path is predetermined. Here, there is an anticipation of Davin, who tells him that his country must come first. The identificatory epistemology is foundational in that there is no room in this narrow prescriptive paradigm for alterity of any sort; again one is put in mind of the essentialism of Drumcree and the Garvaghy Road, where self is defined in contradistinction to the other.

However, on the flyleaf of his geography book, Stephen inscribes his own name, but in a manner which redefines himself within a far wider set of parameters than the above, and which anticipates his later flight to Europe in the closing chapter:

> *Stephen Dedalus*
> *Class of Elements*
> *Clongowes Wood College*
> *Sallins*
> *County Kildare*
> *Ireland*
> *Europe*
> *The World*
> *The Universe.*

Here, Stephen is locating himself within a far broader spatial span that that allotted him by Fleming. Here, the self is defined very much in terms of an otherness that is part of the defining constituents of that self. For Joyce, the "hauntological gnomonic" definition of an identity "complexus" will always see the present Ireland defined dialectically against the hovering alterity of Europe, and the world.

The proper name, as synecdoche of identity itself, is central to any epistemology of identity; one's name is that which locates one as part of a language and a culture. Just as the signifier "Dedalus" conjures up mythic images of a spectral father who will provide his foster-son with a means to fly above the maze, and also above the nets of nationality, so the name of God, itself a potent signifier of Catholic essentialism, is invoked in the opening chapter of *A Portrait of the Artist as a Young Man*, but the evocation is through the ironic eye of Joyce, telling us from a transcendental perspective, about the young Stephen's immanent participation in essentialist modes of thinking:

God was God's name just as his name was Stephen. Dieu was the French for God and that was God's name too; and when anyone prayed to God and said Dieu then God knew at once that it was a French person that was praying. But, though there were different names for God in all the different languages in the world and God understood what all the people who prayed said in their different languages, still God remained always the same God and God's real name was God.[10]

Through Joyce's ironic eye, an eye which will, in *Finnegans Wake*, speak of a "thousandfirst" name,[11] the essentialism of seeing the name for God in one language as somehow better, as somehow more authentic, than others is expressed through the simplistic thought processes of a small child. Indeed, such dogmatism is ironically amusing, until we extrapolate from such essentialist ideas of religion the mindset that allowed people to petrol-bomb a house in Ballymoney, in the summer of 1999 and murder three young boys who happened to adhere to a different view of "God's real name" from that of the petrol-bombers, or of the ten Protestant workers lined up and shot by the IRA at Kingsmills, in 1976, merely because they were Protestants. Through the ironic positioning of the narrative voice, Joyce the author achieves a transcendent perspective on Stephen the character, and as such can achieve something very like Adorno's notion of negative dialectical criticism.

Joyce as author will make a space and a time for alterity, a point that is abundantly clear in the "hauntological" evocation and transformation of the opening lines of *A Portrait* in a later passage from *Finnegans Wake*:

> Once upon a time and a very good time it was there was a moocow coming down along the road and this moocow that was coming down along the road met a nicens little boy named baby tuckoo ....[12]

> Eins within a space and a wearywide space it wast ere wohned a Mookse. The onesomeness wast alltolonely, archunsitslike, broady oval, and a Mookse he would a walking go ....[13]

---

[10]   *Ibid.*, 27.
[11]   Joyce, *Finnegans Wake*, 254, 19.
[12]   Joyce, *Portrait*, 19.
[13]   Joyce, *Finnegans Wake*, 152, 18-20

It is clear that the childish narrative certainties are "hauntologically" redefined in the analogous piece from *Finnegans Wake*, which in Bakhtinian terms is "heteroglossic" in that different voices and different languages are allowed to confront each other and achieve some kind of dynamic interaction, or dialogization.[14] In the quotation from *A Portrait of the Artist as a Young Man*, there is an experiential familiarity evident throughout the piece. The opening, borrowing from the *topos* of the fairy- or folk-tale, is comforting and recognizable, as is the baby-talk which is the frame of reference of the story. There is *one* time, *one* road, *one* cow and *one* "nicens little boy". There is no problem with complexity of identification here; temporally and spatially the reader is in familiar territory. One could see such a simplistic narrative as analogous to the already created conscience of Joyce's race, where as Davin puts it, to be Irish is to be nationalist, Catholic and Gaelic. To again advert to Mikhail Bakhtin's terminology, this notion of narrative is monologic as opposed to dialogic. By "monologic", he means the denial that, outside one particular opinion or reading, there exists "another consciousness, with the same rights, and capable of responding on an equal footing".[15]

However, the granting of an equality of rights, as seen in Northern Ireland in recent years, is an extremely difficult and complex exercise in reality – both sides often seem to be speaking in different languages. Perhaps the *Finnegans Wake* quotation articulates this by subjecting the opening lines of *A Portrait* to a destabilizing linguistic polyglossia. In the case of the German words "eins" and "wohned" (the latter also deriving from Old and Middle English sources), there is an opening up to alterity voiced in the language of Europe and in the language of difference. The *Finnegans Wake* quotation, then, offers a negative critique of the epistemological assumptions regarding narrative, teleology, and language that are inherent in the *Portrait* quotation, as the "hauntological" presence of languages and stories destabilizes the seeming singularity of *one* story and *one* language. Thus, different languages provide a perspective from whence to mount an immanent critique of one's culture. However, there is another perspective from where a parallel critique may be offered, and that is through a sense of Irishness which is spatially

---

[14] Mikhail Bakhtin, *The Dialogic Imagination: Four Essays*, trans. Caryl Emerson and Michael Holquist, Austin: TX, 1981, 263.
[15] Tzvetan Todorov, *Mikhail Bakhtin: The Dialogical Principle*, Minneapolis, 1984, 107.

negative, namely, an Irishness which is not, of necessity, located in Ireland.

Near the end of *A Portrait*, Stephen is recalling a conversation with Davin, the young Fenian, and a symbol of a narrow vision of Irishness. Davin sees himself as "an Irish nationalist first and foremost", and he asks Stephen if he is "Irish at all?", before enunciating his own green nationalist view of Irishness: "be one of us .... Why don't you learn Irish?"[16] Stephen retorts, on being asked why he is going to emigrate that he told Davin that "the shortest way to Tara was *via* Holyhead",[17] and this aphorism, I would argue, gestures towards the epistemological position of emigration as a trope for the creation of a more complex form of Irishness which does not become subject to closure or totalization.

Tara was the traditional seat of the high-kings of Ireland. It is a place-name commonly featured in the Celtic, heroic tales of the revival, and associated with the coming of Christianity to Ireland through stories of St Patrick. Symbolically, Tara would be the epicentre of an ur-Ireland, a place of pre-invasion purity, where Irish language and culture were the norm. Holyhead is that port in Wales where Irish emigrants traditionally alight in Britain, before moving on to mainland Europe. The core point here is that Stephen is not leaving Ireland because he is in some way renouncing Irishness; he is leaving so that he can discover a new form of Irishness, and express it, as he famously puts it at the end of the novel:

> Mother is putting my new secondhand clothes in order. She prays now, she says, that I may learn in my own life and away from home and friends what the heart is and what it feels. Amen. So be it. Welcome, O life! I go to encounter for the millionth time the reality of experience and to forge in the smithy of my soul the uncreated conscience of my race.[18]

Here, Stephen is espousing emigration as an epistemological perspective through which a more complex sense of Irish identity can be created. By adopting a perspective that is outside the culture, he hopes to achieve a twofold aim: to distance himself from the "nets" of "nationality, language, religion", and to give a voice to those of his

---

[16]   Joyce, *Portrait*, 176.

[17]   *Ibid.*, 216.

[18]   *Ibid.*, 218.

"race" who are physically outside Ireland. Interestingly, he equates the "nets" with being born in Ireland: "When the soul of a man is *born in this country ...*",[19] and would seem to be attempting to transform the fixed categories of identity through the experience of European culture, an experience which is enunciated through the trope of emigration. Stephen, in attempting to define some sense of Irish identity, feels that he can only achieve this by moving away from the fixed centrality of the Irishness of the revival, and instead attempting to create a "hauntological", plural view of Irishness and of complex identities, which contrasts sharply with that of Davin. He is attempting to define the culture of Irishness in a way which is "to be not identical to itself" but rather to be "different *with itself*";[20] in short, he is attempting to define Irishness otherwise.

In this context, and in the context of Adorno's dialectical criticism, the verbal construction of the *credo* "I will fly by those nets" is ambiguous. "By" can mean around or past, indicating a desire for the avoidance of the entrapping nets. However, "by" can also mean "by means of" or "using as an aid", and in this sense, the term implies a dependence on, or an attachment to, such notions almost as a mode of articulation. I would suggest that the dialectical interaction of these two meanings acts as a further metaphor for the Joycean concept of identity "complexus". Bypassing the nets still involves taking them into consideration, just as the moving shadow of the sundial is still dependent upon the static pointer of the gnomon. Similarly, making use of the nets to achieve something beyond them also involves a dialectical progression. So, in both cases, the nets can never be totally destroyed or done away with; their function is to provide some limits in terms of self-identity, but also to allow for the opening to alterity that is so necessary to the Joycean project. To be inside these nets is to be delimited by past concepts of nationality, language, and religion. To bypass them, or to use them to move on, is to be open to a future that will, while taking on board some of the baggage of the past, travel to new destinations, redefining itself in the process.

His attitude to history is different to that of Davin, he sees not a glorious Gaelic past, but the reality of linguistic metamorphosis which in turn led to cultural metamorphosis: "My ancestors threw off their language and took on another .... They allowed a handful of foreigners

---

[19] *Ibid.*, 177 (italics added).
[20] Jacques Derrida, *The Other Heading: Reflections on Today's Europe*, trans. Pascale-Anne Brault and Michael Naas, Bloomington: IN, 1992, 9-10.

to subject them."[21] Between these personal pronouns – "my" and "they" – is the interstitial position, what Bhabha terms a "liminal" space,[22] which the trope of emigration offers Joyce. In this "in-between" is the Derridean notion of an identity which, in the case of culture, person, nation, or language, is "a self-differentiating identity, an identity different from itself, having an opening or gap within itself".[23] In his later books, especially *Finnegans Wake*, this gap is symbolized by Joyce in terms of a self-differentiating language, wherein meaning is never self-identical.

Finnegans Wake's multilingual spectralization of the beginning of *A Portrait of the Artist as a Young Man*, further underlines this transformation. English is no longer seen as the property of the colonizer; instead it is defined gnomonically in terms of its negative relationship with the many other languages and discourses in *Finnegans Wake* (over fifty at the last count). As Joyce puts it in the above quotation, the "onesomeness wast alltolonely";[24] this "one-someness" is precisely that monological strain that has given rise to the ideological ossification that is defined, in Northern Ireland, as Unionist and Nationalist, or as Orange and Green. Such "onesome-ness" is, of course, practically impossible in terms of the modern world, a point which is mimetically demonstrated in *Finnegans Wake*, where an indigenous Irish person has no readier insight into the range of meanings codified in the text than has a person of any other nationality.

In this sense, the text itself functions as a critique of all essentialist epistemological positions. Earlier in the same text, Joyce pointedly refers to the tale of Shem a "blind blighter"[25] who is also a "fain shinner",[26] and the blindness of immanent simplistic nationalism, be it political, linguistic, or cultural, is clearly the source of such parodistic reference, especially given an address that comes slightly later in the same section: "Gentes and laitymen, fullstoppers and semicolonials, hybrids / and lubberds!"[27] Here, Joyce is addressing his "nation" and the address could be seen as an echoing answer to the question of

21 Joyce, *Portrait*, 177.
22 Homi K. Bhabha, *The Location of Culture*, London, 1994, 4.
23 Jacques Derrida, *Deconstruction in a Nutshell: A Conversation with Jacques Derrida*, ed. John D. Caputo, New York, 1997, 14.
24 Joyce, *Finnegans Wake*, 152, 19.
25 *Ibid.*, 149, 2.
26 *Ibid.*, 149, 7.
27 *Ibid.*, 152, 16-17.

Irishness – "Hush! Caution! Echoland!"[28] – with which our discussion
opened, but here the Irishness in question is an example of "identities
in the writer complexus."

For Joyce, his nation is a transactional blurring of the binarisms of
essential identity. "Gentes and laitymen" can refer to people, deriving
from the Latin noun *gens*, or to ladies and gentlemen, or to the people
sharing descent along the male line, or to class distinction between
some form of aristocracy and those who are ordinary, or to clergy (in
the sense of patriarchal power in the church), and the laity. The words
"fullstoppers and semicolonials" can refer to the rules of grammar,
which make meaning and nationhood possible by delimiting the play
of language, or to the ongoing dialectic of colonialism and
colonization, or to the ambiguous position of Ireland in terms of its
status as a post-colonial country. The final phrase, "hybreds and
lubbberds", conflates land and sea with differences of identity in a
pairing that is very much at odds with the "onesomeness" noted
earlier. Here, hybridity, complexity and above all plurality, are seen as
natural conditions of modern identities, a perspective which
completely contradicts Stephen's earlier comments regarding God and
Dieu.

In short, each word is signifying "otherwise" inasmuch as there is a
constant openness to alterity of all sorts. The language of *Finnegans
Wake* offers a gnomonic epistemology of Irishness in that it allows for
the voice of the other to fill the gap in the gnomon, while never
allowing any form of closure. The "writer complexus" creates
"hauntological" Irish "identities complexus" through the achievement
of a position outside Ireland, and through the creation of an "English"
language (and never were inverted commas more deserved) which is
shot through with traces of European languages. In the face of the
essentialism that we have all seen in evidence at Drumcree in recent
years, perhaps there is something to be said for what Joyce (the writer
complexus *par excellence*) is attempting, namely the avoidance of
what he calls "life's high carnage of semperidentity by subsisting
peasemeal upon variables".[29] "Semperidentity", an identity that is
always the same, is by definition unchanging. The memory of the
most recent "high carnage" brought about in Northern Ireland in the
name of such "semperidentity" is still fresh in all of our minds. Such a

---

[28] *Ibid.*, 13, 5.
[29] Joyce, *Finnegans Wake*, 582, 15-16.

simplistic and fixed identity is necessarily temporally focused on the past. Its sense of definition derives from the past, and its whole *raison d'être* is predicated on conserving the trans-temporal nature of its own identificatory characteristics. Change, in such a *Weltanschauung*, is to be blocked at all costs, including those of "high carnage", in order to preserve this simplistic form of selfhood. Arguing for a more complex form of Irishness, as created through literature, Joyce suggests an avoidance of such simplicity and instead argues that the "variables" of alterity should be embraced as they occur, "peasemeal", in order to constantly redefine our notions of selfhood.

I would finish this essay with a quotation from *Ulysses*. Leopold Bloom, a Hungarian Jew, symbolic of the European influence on Irishness, enunciates the complex form of Irishness that is the subject of this paper, and I would argue one of the aims of Joyce's project:

> What is your nation if I may ask? says the citizen
> Ireland, says Bloom. I was born here. Ireland.[30]

What is at stake here is that very sense of gnomonic and "hauntological" identity that we have been discussing, with Bloom, like Stephen before him, functioning as Joyce's *raisonneur*. The point at issue is that, for Joyce, Ireland, or to be more correct notions of Irish identity, must be sufficiently complex and plural to include those, like Leopold Bloom, who are not Irish in any essentialist sense. Writing at the time of the Gaelic, Celtic and Irish revivals, Joyce was making a point which was unlikely to be popular given the notions of post-colonial self-fashioning that were taking place in an Ireland about to go through the throes of decolonization. These notions were simplistic in the extreme, with members of political and cultural groups mining a narrow seam of Irishness for the essential qualities of nationalism, Catholicism, Gaelicism and a strong sense of anti-Britishness. Looking back on this period, another writer who enunciated a similar complex sense of identity, John McGahern, gave the following account of a simplistic form of Irishness:

> It was a young, insecure state without any traditions, without any manners, and there was this notion that to be Irish was good. Nobody actually took any time to understand what to be Irish was.

---

[30] James Joyce, *Ulysses*, eds Hans Walter Gabler, Wolfhard Steppe and Claus Melchior, London, 1989, 272.

> There was this slogan and fanaticism and a lot of emotion, but there
> wasn't any clear idea except what you were against: you were
> against sexuality; you were against the English.[31]

It is against such simplistic definitions of Irishness that Joyce sets up
his own complex sense of Irishness, an Irishness which defines itself
negatively in terms of European culture.

The drive towards unity, fuelled by literature about Celtic heroes
and *prosopopeic* female embodiments of Irishness (Erin, Kathleen Ni
Houlihan, Banba, Mother Ireland, the Shan Van Vocht), tended to
make Irishness monological and essentialist, and as such, part of a
politics of the *unum*, of a notion of "oneness", which, as Derrida
notes, can be "a terrible catastrophe" in a state or a country.[32]
However, as Mikhail Bakhtin has perceptively observed, language,
especially in its literary incarnation, is a powerful tool in the
deconstruction of such centralizing drives, as the "uninterrupted
processes of decentralization and disunification go forward" alongside
the language of "verbal-ideological centralization and unification".[33] It
is these processes, I would suggest that underpin the Joycean notion of
"hauntological" and gnomonic identities that have been the subject of
this essay.

Like Derrida, Joyce is unwilling to see an identificatory politics
predicated on the simplistic notions of "semperidentity", of an *unum*
which brooks no other notion of selfhood. If we take the cultural
context of Joyce's work into account, the dangers of such notions of
semperidentity would have been all too clear to him. Much of the
writing of the Gaelic and Irish Literary revivals would have been
attempting to validate a Celtic self-fashioning by foregrounding core
values in terms of a politico-cultural version of Irishness. Elsewhere, I
have made the point that such a simplistic notion of Irish identity

> seeks to ground itself vertically in terms of historical development
> along a single ethnic and identificatory wavelength; the past has
> defined Irishness, and the contemporary function of literature is to
> conserve and preserve this handed-down heritage; its spatial
> dimension is narrow in the extreme, encompassing the verities of the

---

[31] Julia Carlson, *Banned in Ireland: Censorship and the Irish Writer*, ed. Julia
Carlson, London, 1990, 63.
[32] Derrida, *Deconstruction in a Nutshell*, 15.
[33] Bakhtin, *Dialogic Imagination*, 272.

transcendental signifiers of Irishness, Catholicism, Celtism, republicanism, nationalism, and language.[34]

For Joyce, however, the role of the writer is very different. Rather than seeing writing as validating the socio-cultural *status quo*, he sees his role as offering new paradigms of identity, identities complexus, for his own culture. It is no accident that, at the end of *A Portrait of the Artist as a Young Man*, he sets out his artistic credo as the forging in the smithy of his soul of the *uncreated* conscience of his race. It will be his role to create that conscience by opening up the seeming certainties of identity to an ongoing critique which will allow for a definition of Irishness that will be "not identical to itself" but rather "different *with itself*";[35] in short, he is attempting to define Irishness *otherwise*, and this, I conclude is the Joycean definition of the role of the artist. It is the creation of "identities in the writer complexus", with the stress on the plural form of the noun. If selfhood is to be defined in terms of alterity in an ongoing process which will encompass the "variables" of both, then simplistic identity, as enunciated in the opening of *A Portrait of the Artist as a Young Man*, must be transformed into the linguistic and cultural polysemy of *Finnegans Wake* if the pluralization and complication of "Ireland untranscended"[36] is to be achieved.

---

[34]   Eugene O'Brien, *The Question of Irish Identity in the Writings of William Butler Yeats and James Joyce*, Lampeter: Wales, 1998, 33.
[35]   Derrida, *The Other Heading*, 9-10 (italics added).
[36]   Joyce, *Finnegans Wake*, 429, 17-18.

COUNTERVOICES IN IRISH WRITING

YEATS' REPRESENTATION OF ROMANTIC IRELAND:
HIS OBSESSION WITH PROPER OR SINGULAR NOUNS

HIROYUKI YAMASAKI

Benedict Anderson, the Anglo-Irish political scientist, writes in *Imagined Communities*:

> In fact, all communities larger than primordial villages of face-to-face contact (and perhaps even these) are imagined. Communities are to be distinguished, not by their falsity /genuineness, but by the style in which they are imagined.[1]

Following Anderson's suggestion, I will analyse the style in which Yeats has imagined Ireland in his writings, comparing Yeats' conception of Ireland with Anderson's views of nation-states as imagined communities. They have something in common, though they are quite different in several respects. I hope this comparison will clarify not only the unique nature of Yeats' conception of Ireland, but also the reason why he obsessively uses proper or singular pronouns to represent his imagined Ireland.

Anderson's major concern in *Imagined Communities* is to explain the attachment that people feel for the nation, the invention of their imagination, and why they are ready to die for this invention. In order to explain this, Anderson tries to describe the processes by which the nation came to be imagined, and once imagined, modelled, adapted and transformed. According to Anderson, such pre-modern, sacred communities as Christendom and kingdoms disappeared, and such secular imagined communities as modern nation-states came into being, under the impact of economic change, social and scientific discoveries, and the development of communications. Anderson

---

[1]   Benedict Anderson, *Imagined Communities: Reflections on the Origin and Spread of Nationalism*, London and New York, 1983, 6.

emphasizes that the rapid development of capitalism, particularly what he calls print-capitalism, was largely instrumental in bringing about this change.[2]

Anderson's model of imagined communities is based on the modern anonymous readers of novels and newspapers mass-produced by print-capitalism, who are imagined as sharing a sense of simultaneity by reading novels and newspapers steeped in homogeneous, empty time as contrasted with Messianic time. According to him, Messianic time is something seen through the eyes of God. In a Messianic system of time, the present is no longer a mere link in an earthly chain of events; it is simultaneously something which has always been, and will be fulfilled in the future. In short, Messianic time is a simultaneity of past and future in an instantaneous present, which is characteristic of old imagined communities like Christendom and kingdoms.[3]

In this connection, it is very significant to notice that Yeats' imagined Ireland is usually associated with either singular or proper nouns. Yeats does not like to express his Ireland in abstract terms. On some occasions he attempts to personify it, and on others, he associates it with a particular, concrete individual, whether mythical or historical. In other words, Yeats habitually imagines his Romantic Ireland to have a human face or heart or mind. Typical examples can be seen in "September 1913" ("Romantic Ireland's dead and gone, / It's with O'Leary in the grave"), "To Ireland in the Coming Times" ("After the red-rose-bordered hem"), "The Statues" ("The lineaments of a plummet-measured face"), "Red Hanrahan's Song about Ireland" ("Of Cathleen, the daughter of Houlihan"), "The Fisherman" ("A man who is but a dream"), "The Municipal Gallery Revisited" ("An Abbot or Archbishop with an upraised hand"), "Parnell's Funeral" ("Had Cosgrave eaten Parnell's   heart"), and "Under Ben Bulben" ("Horseman, pass by").

How should we make sense of this habit? Benedict Anderson's theory of imagined communities may partly account for it. According to Anderson, "Christendom as a sacred imagined community, defined by a Messianic system of time, assumed its universal form through a myriad of specificities and particularities: this relief, that window, this sermon, that tale, this morality play, that relic". Anderson suggests that these mundane particulars helped the illiterate masses to imagine

---

[2]   *Ibid.*, 37-46.
[3]   *Ibid.*, 24.

the cosmic-universal of Christendom.[4] This theory suggests that Yeats' habitual association of his imagined Ireland with particular individuals aims to help common people to imagine and share an ideal Ireland easily. But it accounts only partially, for Yeats' practice. It cannot sufficiently explain why Yeats was so interested in linking his imagined Ireland to particular individuals, though. I suggest this tendency has something to do with his theory of symbolism. Yeats writes about symbolism:

> There is symbolism in every work of art. A work of art moves us because it expresses or symbolizes something in ourselves or in the general life of men.[5]

Symbols, as Yeats understands them, express something not only in particular individuals themselves, but in the life of men in general. Yeats suggests here that symbols have both private and public meanings. Yeats as a senator expressed a strong dislike of the abstract idea of the nation to which, for example, Japanese or American children in those days, were totally sacrificed. The reason was not only that the Japanese or American idea of the nation, as he understood it, was merely abstract, but also that their nations, as he understood them, did not admit the eternity of the individual soul, but the eternity of the racial family.[6] In Yeats' imagined Ireland, both must be equally respected. Here, I must point out that as a senator Yeats often praised the Italian philosopher Gentile, because Gentile studied even religion not in the abstract but in the minds and lives of Italian saints and thinkers.[7] I think that like Gentile Yeats studied imagined Ireland not in the abstract but in the minds and lives of many different eminent individuals. In other words, the meanings of these national symbols are both individual and public.

There are several pieces of evidence showing that Yeats seems to have intended these national symbols to be not only public, but also private and individual. For example, we know that Yeats believed that Parnell and O'Leary possessed something of the beauty of the

---

[4] *Ibid.*, 23.
[5] A. Norman Jeffares and A. S. Knowland, *A Commentary on the Collected Plays of W. B. Yeats*, London, 1975, 275.
[6] Donald R. Pearce, *The Senate Speeches of W. B. Yeats*, Bloomington, 1960, 111-12.
[7] William Butler Yeats, *Explorations*, New York, 1962, 337.

individual soul.[8] We must pay attention to the fact that they are all singular and proper nouns. It should be noted that a proper noun belongs characteristically to one individual or species only. It distinguishes a person, a thing or a place from all others of the same class. It cannot, however, be invented or imagined by that individual or species, but must be bestowed by others. So the use of a proper noun is supposed to be socially appropriate and in accord with established traditions. Hence it enables an individual or species to be at once singular or personal, and public or shared by other people. In this sense, a proper noun is similar in function to a human face, which has the dual role of representing both an individual personality and a social or public mask. A proper noun and a singular noun are two sides of the same coin. Yeats' obsession with singular or proper nouns seems to imply that his romantic Ireland is intended to symbolize something not only in Yeats as the last Romantic poet, but in the general life of other people both within and outside Ireland.

Here let me hasten to add that Yeats used singular and proper nouns as the very symbols of his imagined Ireland defined by a Messianic system of time. He said in a senate speech of 1924 that a system of culture which would represent the whole of Ireland and which would draw the imagination of the young towards it must be created, so that what he calls "the two Irelands" might be united.[9] Though Yeats did not elaborate on what this future system of culture of his imagined Ireland should be like, I think there is a key to this in "Pages from a Diary in 1930", in which Yeats refers to the three convictions needed for his imagined Ireland. What Yeats calls the three convictions are the three things in which all the people of his imagined Ireland must believe: Freedom of the soul, God, and Immortality.

Freedom of the soul, God, and Immortality are originally the elements upon which Yeats desires his idealized literature to be founded. He complains that the fading of these three elements "before Bacon, Newton, Locke" made literature decadent. Yeats asserts that since these convictions are gone, tragedies are gone and literary realism has appeared instead.[10] He defines the scientific thought of Bacon, Newton, and Locke as mechanical philosophy and attributes it

---

[8]   *Ibid.*, 336.
[9]   Pearce, *Senate Speeches of W. B. Yeats*, 87.
[10] Yeats, *Explorations*, 332-33.

to modern Britain.[11] Now it is clear that these three convictions reflect his strong antipathy to secular time-oriented capitalism and modern natural science. Yeats' assertion is accurately parallel to Benedict Anderson's theory that since sacred imagined communities are gone, Messianic time is gone and nation-states as secular imagined communities have appeared, accompanied by homogeneous, empty time. In one of his later poems "I am of Ireland", Yeats describes a woman who has come out of the Holy Land of Ireland, asks a man for a dance and cries, "Time runs on". The man cocks a malicious and ironical eye and declines her request by saying "time runs on", too. I suggest that what the woman means by the phrase "time runs on" is intended to be quite different from what the man means by the same phrase. The woman's remark means the passage of Messianic time, whereas the man refers to the passage of secular time. What we see in this poem is Yeats' awareness of the conflict between his desire and the actual reality concerning the concept of time.

Exactly the same kind of awareness of the conflict can be seen in "Sailing to Byzantium", where Yeats contrasts those dying generations singing all summer long "whatever is begotten, born and dies", with a golden bird singing "what is past, or passing, or to come". Several critics have identified the phrase "Whatever is begotten, born, and dies" with the phrase "what is past, or passing, or to come". But I think that these two phrases are quite different from each other. In fact, "what is past, or passing, or to come" is not the same as "what is past, passing, and to come". The repeated use of the word "or" in the former phrase clearly suggests the identity of the past with the present and the future. So the phrase "what is past, or passing, or to come" implies Messianic time, while the phrase "whatever is begotten, born, and dies" implies secular time. In this poem, Yeats, dissatisfied with the real Ireland, tries to imagine Byzantium as a substitute for his ideal Ireland.

Yeats' dissatisfaction with the real Ireland dominated by a secular system of time and his desire for the imagined Ireland dominated by a Messianic one can be found in several other poems. For example, in one of his later poems "The Statues" (1938), we can see another variant of Yeats' conflict between his desire for a Messianic system of time, symbolized by the singular noun "a plummet-measured face" of Greek origin and his dissatisfaction with a secular system of time,

---

[11] *Ibid.*, 172 .

symbolized by the plural "the many-headed foam" of Asian origin. In
another later poem "Under Ben Bulben", he calls on Irish poets to
"scorn" the "unremembering hearts and minds" of their contemporaries and to "cast their mind on other days" so that "we in coming
days may be still the indomitable Irishry". It seems that Yeats, in his
extreme old age, still yearns for a future Ireland defined by Messianic
time in face of the present Ireland defined by secular time.

In this connection, Yeats is very satirical about realistic literature
and newspapers. He refers to realistic literature as "pot-house
literature"[12] or "mirror dawdling down a lane,"[13] and denounces newspapers as a sort of stimulant, which has excited the English mind and
turned it into a "bed-hot harlot".[14] Yeats is very critical of capitalism,
too. For example, he criticizes Britain as a capitalist nation.[15]
Anderson is also critical of imagined communities, which have been
brought about by print-capitalism. According to him, imagined
communities and their fraternity have made it possible for so many
millions of people not so much to kill as willingly to die for such
imaginary things in various wars over the past two centuries. He
thinks, therefore, that nothing can be usefully done to limit such wars
unless we do our best to learn the real and imagined experience of the
past fanatical nationalism.[16]

However, on the matter of the sovereign rights of the nation-states,
Yeats differs enormously from Anderson. Yeats believes that it is one
of the fundamentals of his imagined Ireland that it should be given the
sovereign right to demand the sacrifice of its citizens' lives. He
strongly argues for the sovereign right of his imagined Ireland to take
life in order to breed instinctive patriotism as the stronghold of its own
security against enemies.[17] But his argument for the right of Ireland to
take life must not be mistaken for an appeal to blind Fascism or
jingoism which demands the sacrifice of every citizen's life including
children's. They are very alike in appearance, but quite different in
nature. For one thing, his argument for the right of imagined Ireland to
take life was perhaps made within the framework of modern

---

[12]   Yeats, *Explorations,* 336.
[13]   *Ibid.,* 333.
[14]   *Ibid.,* 443.
[15]   *Ibid.,* 334.
[16]   Anderson, *Imagined Communities,* 161.
[17]   Yeats, *Explorations,* 338, 441.

international laws, which permit each nation-state the right to demand the sacrifice of its citizens' lives.

Besides, Yeats' model of his imagined Ireland was neither a fascist nation like Italy and Germany, nor a communist nation like the Soviet Union, nor a capitalist nation like Britain, but a nation ruled by a belief in the three convictions, God, Freedom of the soul, and Immortality. Yeats calls this belief "Free Power". He writes:

> When I speak of the three convictions and of the idea of the State I do not mean any metaphysical or economic theory. That belief which I call free power is free because we cannot distinguish between the things believed in and the belief; it is something forced upon us bit by bit.[18]

This remark suggests his imagined Ireland is not a military power-based nation of totalitarianism, but a moral power-based nation of individualism.

As Yeats indicated in his extreme old age, the reason why he chose patriots like O'Leary and Parnell as symbols of his imagined Ireland was that these patriots had what he called beauty.[19] In this case "beauty" means something displayed by an individual's freedom of the soul. Yeats' imagined Ireland never demands the total surrender of the individual free soul to itself. It is based on the conflict between the nationalism of the race and the freedom of the soul. Yeats was well aware how anachronistic his imagined Ireland was in the modern secular world of capitalism. He writes: "But today the man who finds belief in God, in the soul, in Immortality, growing and clarifying, is blasphemous and paradoxical."[20] Here, Yeats is satirical of the fact that capitalism defined by a system of homogeneous, empty time has established itself as a substitute religion. This definitely indicates that he was well aware of the imaginariness of his Romantic Ireland. In fact, there is ample evidence to show Yeats' awareness of its imaginary status. While it is true that Yeats imagined an Ireland defined by a Messianic system of time, he never wanted to go back to the Middle Ages, for example, because he realized no Irishman wanted to return to the fourteenth century.[21] Yeats told the Senate:

---

[18] *Ibid.*, 335.
[19] Yeats, *Explorations,* 336.
[20] *Ibid.*, 334.
[21] Pearce, *Senate Speeches of W. B. Yeats,* 179-80.

> Our imaginative movement has its energy from just that
> combination of new and old, of old stories, old poetry, old belief in
> God and the soul, and a modern technique.[22]

Yeats was never a Luddite-like nationalist. He was a realistic conservative.

Finally let me say a little as to whether the system of culture in Yeats' imagined Ireland is unitary or hybrid. It is quite doubtful that Yeats wished his imagined Ireland to be ruled only by, for example, the culture of Protestant Ascendancy, or the Celtic culture of ancient Ireland.[23] In this connection, it is significant that proper nouns associated with Yeats' imagined Ireland are quite different in racial or national origin. For example, Parnell is Protestant whereas O'Leary is Catholic. "A plummet-measured face" is modelled on ancient Greek statues. A fisherman, a horseman and Kathleen are from the Celtic tradition. An abbot or archbishop is presumably Catholic. Besides, as we have already seen, Yeats sings in "Under Ben Bulben":

> Cast your mind on other days
> That we in coming days may be
> Still the indomitable Irishry.

These lines suggest that Yeats imagined future Ireland's culture system to be hybrid, rather than unitary. What Yeats meant by "other days" is crucial here. In the drafts of "Under Ben Bulben", as well as in its final version, Yeats refers to other days in various countries from which Irish poets should learn what he called "wisdom":[24] other days not only in Ireland, but also in countries like Japan, India, China, Egypt, Greece, Italy, and even England, when people were able to believe in God, the Freedom of the soul and Immortality, namely in a Messianic system of time. In "Pages from a Diary in 1930", Yeats writes: "Every nation is the whole world in a mirror."[25] I believe that

---

[22] *Ibid.*, 179-80.

[23] Cf. W. J. McCormack, *Ascendancy and Tradition in Anglo-Irish Literary History from 1789 to 1939*, London, 1985, 8-12; Seamus Deane, *Celtic Revivals: Essays in Modern Irish Literature 1880-1980*. London, 1985, 28, 38; Edna Longley, *The Living Stream: Literature and Revisionism in Ireland*, Newcastle, 1994, 10, 24-25, 46; and Declan Kiberd, *Inventing Ireland*, London, 1995, 2, 7, 162-65.

[24] W. B. Yeats, *Last Poems: Manuscript Materials*, ed. James Pethica, London, 1997, 13, 15–16.

[25] Yeats, *Explorations,* 337.

Yeats' imagined Ireland is, as it were, the whole hybrid world in the mirror of his literary and political mind.

SEAMUS HEANEY'S *VERSUS*, OR POETRY AS STILL REVOLUTION

JOANNY MOULIN

In a lecture Seamus Heaney gave in May 1998 in Rennes (France), he announced that the title of his new book of selected poems would be *Opened Ground*. That was also the title of his lecture, and, of course, it looked back to a now well-known metaphor of his, according to which poetry is more or less of the same order and nature as tillage. The first poem in the reading was, rather expectedly, "Digging":

> But I've no spade to follow men like them.
>
> Between my finger and my thumb
> The squat pen rests.
> I'll dig with it.[1]

Then he pushed the simile to include a Greek word, *boustrophedon*, which is made of *bous*, "the ox" and *strophe*, "the turning", or literally "the revolution". *Boustrophedon* is a form of writing used in ancient Greek manuscripts, which consists of writing from left to right then from right to left, and so on, just in the same way as a team of oxen pulls the plough in a field, coming and going from one sillion to the next.

This is an old image with Heaney, and already in *Preoccupations* he compared the poet to a ploughman, noting that "'Verse' comes from the Latin *versus* which could mean a line of poetry but could also mean the turn that a ploughman made at the head of a field as he finished the furrow and faced back into another".[2] And again in *Field Work*, poetry is seen as "Vowels ploughed into other, opened ground, /

---

[1]   Seamus Heaney, *Death of a Naturalist*, London, 1966, 1-2.
[2]   Seamus Heaney, *Preoccupations: Selected Prose 1968-1978*, London, 1980, 65.

Each verse returning like the plough turned round".[3] Heaney never seems to be tired of dwelling on this homely agricultural grounding of literature, as in "Alphabets", where the scholar learns to write, and "He is the scribe / Who drove a team of quills on his white field".[4]

Now, looking at any kind of *boustrophedon* long enough, one may come to think that it is also reminiscent of the winding pipes of a still, where vapours go a long way while really covering little ground, but finally to come out as something different from what they were when they went in. One reason why this apparently simple-minded metaphor is so often reiterated is that it tells something rather essential about one of the things poetry means for Heaney. I have a notion that this is what Helen Vendler calls "Heaney's historical revisionism",[5] his turning over of the plough or the quill, and that this "turning time up and over" is a patient commitment to the ideological field of our time, with a mind to change it in the long run, or at least to cultivate it and render it more habitable and tame.

I want to look at a few poems from that angle, and examine how they operate, if at all, from an ideological point of view. For, generally speaking, Heaney is not at first perceived as a very strongly committed poet, and some people like Anthony Easthope consider him at best what in the 1930s would have been called an "escapist" poet, and at worst someone whose pastoralism is reactionary, at least in terms of aesthetics. This is perhaps equally true of collections like *Death of a Naturalist* or *Field Work*. Yet, in between, the poems of *Wintering Out* have the roughly-hewn political bias one could rightly expect from an Ulster poet in the 1970s, with a vision of a world clearly split up into two apparently irreconcilable camps; witness poems like "A Constable Calls", "The Other Side", or "Servant Boy", although a text like "No Man's Land" sounds like an early realization of some inadequacy in that particular use of poetry:

> Why do I unceasingly
> arrive too late to condone
> infected sutures
> and ill-knit bone?[6]

3   *Ibid.*, 34.
4   Seamus Heaney, *The Haw Lantern*, London, 1987, 2.
5   Helen Vendler, *The Breaking of Style: Hopkins, Heaney, Graham*, Cambridge: MA, 1995, 66.
6   Seamus Heaney, *Wintering Out*, London, 1972, 40.

It is nothing much, but merely the honest voicing of restless misgivings about the comfortable adoption of an axiology, in which *we* are right and *they* are wrong, and which seems to have been what his Northern-Catholic community more or less explicitly expected from him in those days.

What I am driving at, trying to show and explain, happens first quite clearly in *North*. The collection, and especially its title poem, is an effort to forge the uncreated conscience of the race, and to graft contemporary history to a distant past and half-forgotten mythology. This is no longer or not yet poetry as ploughing and tillage, but rather as haulage and the excavating of obscure subconscious motivations and blueprints, of "memory incubating the spilled blood". The poet presents himself as a seer, or rather hearer, of those "ocean-deafened voices", "buoyant with hindsight".[7] It is a highly seductive kind of discourse, yet one that has been greeted with birchwood and raisings of critical shields since the book came out. Ciaran Carson ("Escaped from the Massacre?")[8] or Edna Longley ("*North*: 'Inner Emigré' or 'Artful Voyeur?'")[9] have been among the most articulate to wage disparaging questioning of Heaney's ideological attitude in *North*. And in a sense, Seamus Heaney has backed out of that position in the poetry that he has written afterwards.

Yet I would like to argue that perhaps there was something that both the poet and his critics have overlooked at the time, and that is closely related to the *versus*, *boustrophedon* and poetical revisionism. In "Trial Pieces", for instance, there is a fascination with the calligraphic toil of a child's engraving on a piece of bone, where

> like an eel swallowed
> in a basket of eels,
> the line amazes itself.[10]

And this triggers off the day-dream of a quasi-Joycean invocation of the barbarity of the Vikings:

---

[7] Seamus Heaney, *North*, London, 1975, 19-20.
[8] Ciaran Carson, "Escaped from the Massacre?", *Honest Ulsterman*, 50 (Winter 1975).
[9] Edna Longley, "*North*: 'Inner Emigré' or 'Artful Voyeur?'", in *The Art of Seamus Heaney*, ed. Tony Curtis, Bridgend, 1982.
[10] Heaney, *North*, 21.

> Old fathers, be with us.
> Old cunning assessors
> of feuds and or sites
> for ambush or town.[11]

This kind of claim for violent instincts is far from being politically correct. But, remarkably, what is happening here is that the poem is, as it were, overturning its ideological position, from culture to barbarity, from the innocence of a child to the apologia for murder, from building to destroying. In a case of literary *enantiodromia*, the poem is a soaring reverie that is pushed to the limit and topples into its nightmarish opposite.

The full title of this poem is "Viking Dublin: Trial Pieces", and its four parts are successive attempts by the poet to try his voice at that kind of cathartic reversal, which willy-nilly succeeds in bringing readers and critics to pass judgement on some apparently innocuous fantasies. The same effect of axiological reversal is paramount in *North*, and that is how I read these much debated stanzas of "Punishment", a poem about the preserved body of a young woman fallen victim to ritual murder in Jutland:

> I almost love you
> but would have cast, I know,
> the stones of silence.
> I am the artful voyeur.
> ....
> who would connive
> in civilized outrage
> yet understand the exact
> and tribal, intimate revenge.[12]

For this is a recognition of barbarity, that is to say foreign abjection, as an intimate truth about oneself.

One remark to prove my point, which may be seen as particularly apposite, is that some Protestant critics came up saying substantially, see, there is Catholic ritualism for you. But more seriously, this is an application of what Geoffrey Hill calls "Poetry as 'Menace' and

---

[11]   *Ibid.*, 24.
[12]   *Ibid.*, 38.

'Atonement'" which he also writes "at-one-ment",[13] considering poetry as a dangerous but necessary flirting with suppressed ideological positions, with a view to purging their emotional potential, or defusing their societal charge. This radical change which was silently taking place in *North* is graphically expressed in the translation from "Antaeus" to "Hercules and Antaeus".

In the classical legend of Antaeus, the titan regained his strength by contact with his mother Gaia every time he touched ground, and Hercules vanquished him by holding him up in the air. Heaney says it is a post-colonial poem: "the more you push them down the more they rear up their heads, so the best way to quiet them down is to educate them."[14] But here again, we have an instance of poetry as still revolution in the form of a paradox, for as Antaeus says:

> He may well throw me and renew my birth
> But let him not plan lifting me off the earth,
> My elevation, my fall.[15]

The still revolution of poetry may be a way out of a deadlock fight, and a movement towards something other than a perpetual battle between two camps, a future for which those sleeping giants are discarded as "pap for the dispossessed".[16]

What I have been trying to describe here is something that Heaney has considered from a theoretical point of view in *The Redress of Poetry*, as for instance when he compares his own poem "Squarings" with Zbigniew Herbert's "The Pulley", saying that "[b]oth poems are about the way consciousness can be alive to two different and contradictory dimensions of reality and still find a way of negotiating between them".[17] Of course, this brings water to the mill of a definition of the poet as a go-between, which is Helen Vendler's position in *The Breaking of Style*, where she says he is "a Mr Facing-Both-Ways". But I would like to give a slight inflexion to this interpretation of Heaney's poetry, via a detour by the theory of

[13] Geoffrey Hill, *The Lords of Limit: Essays on Literature and Ideas*, London, 1984, 1-19.
[14] Seamus Heaney, "Address", Monaco, March, 1998.
[15] Heaney, *North*, 12.
[16] *Ibid.*, 53.
[17] Seamus Heaney, *The Redress of Poetry: Oxford Lectures*, London, 1995, xiii.

Mikhail Bakhtin and the notion of *double-voicedness*. In "Discourse in the Novel", Bakhtin wrote:

> The double-voiced prose word has a double meaning. But the poetic word in the narrow sense also has a double, even a multiple, meaning. It is this that basically distinguishes it from the word as concept, or the word as term. The poetic word is a trope, requiring a precise feeling for the two meanings contained in it.[18]

"Double-voicedness", which leads to "double-languagedness", is a form of "dialogization" that in Heaney's poetry is the early stage of a development that was to reach the stage of "polyglossia" in *Station Island*, where more than two discursive voices are at work. Very famously, now, it is what is exemplified in the very title of *The Redress of Poetry*, which means both how poetry can be *redressed*, and how it can *redress* things. This is an instance of Heaney's forked tongue, or how his discourse can be diffracted and say two things at the same time. Being simultaneously both active and passive, this is a case of what Greek grammar called "middle voice", as Heaney calls it in *The Government of the Tongue*, with the example of W. H. Auden's poem "The Watershed",[19] identifying this writing technique as "a sleight of semantic hand which unnerves and suspends the reader above a valley of uncertainty".

The point is not so much for the poet to intercede between two or more constructions of meaning, but to exalt his poetic speech on to a plane situated above discourse and any too easily constructed vision or reality, or any form of too ready-made doxa. The title of *The Redress of Poetry* is a minimalist exemplum of a poetic voice that revolves around its own semantic axis, much as Roland Barthes said that myth operates like a "sort of constantly moving turnstile".[20] It is an

---

[18] Mikhail Bakhtin, *The Dialogic Imagination: Four Essays by M. M. Bakhtin*, ed. Michael Holquist, Austin: TX, 1981, 327.

[19] Seamus Heaney, *The Government of the Tongue: The 1986 T. S. Eliot Memorial Lectures and Other Critical Writings*, London, 1988, 123: "Similarly, the grammatical peace of the present participle is disturbed by lurking middle voice: the grass is chafing, active, but in so far as the only thing being chafed is itself, it is passive. Then, too, the participle occupies a middle state between being transitive and intransitive, and altogether functions like a pass made swiftly, a sleight of semantic hand which unnerves and suspends the reader above a valley of uncertainty."

[20] Roland Barthes, *Mythologies*, London, 1993, 123: "To keep a spatial metaphor, the approximative character of which I have already stressed, I shall say that the

exemplum of *versus*, a language which is travailed, like kneaded dough or ploughed earth, and which therefore is no longer rigid, but opened to new becomings. To borrow an idea from yet another French philosopher of the 1960s, it may be worth noting that Althusser used to say that ideology, like philosophy for Hegel, is a still revolution, a motionless movement, which means that ideology does change, while remaining in the same place and keeping the same form.[21] In that sense, Heaney's poetry is fighting ideology with its own weapons and on its own ground, as if taking an active part in its necessary change. And this particular use of language was theorized first in *The Government of the Tongue*, yet another book with an iconic title. For, it has often been noted too, the government of the tongue is both the effort to govern the tongue or to exert control over one's words, and the expected consequence of this, that is, to place the tongue in a governing position, which is the peculiar power of poets.

In a review of *Field Work* (the collection that came immediately after *North*), Terry Eagleton wrote that Seamus Heaney is an "end-of-ideologies" writer,[22] which in fact amounts to the same thing as that which I am trying to demonstrate at much greater length. For the main thesis that both *The Redress of Poetry*, and *The Government of the Tongue* before that are striving to maintain, in a de facto *ars poetica* of Heaney's, is that poetry is a mode of literature which uplifts itself to operate above discourse as the ideologically constructed order of language. In the theory of Jean-François Lyotard, this would indeed make him a post-modern poet, if the post-modern condition is agreed to be posterior to all constructed narratives.[23] In a sense, this would

---

signification of the myth is constituted by a sort of constantly moving turnstile which presents alternately the meaning of the signifier and its form, language object and a metalanguage a purely signifying and a purely imagining consciousness."

[21]   Louis Althusser, *Lire le Capital*, Paris, 1975, 182: "L'idéologie change donc, mais insensiblement, en conservant sa forme d'idéologie; elle se meut, mais d'un mouvement immmobile, qui la maintient *sur place*, en son lieu et son rôle d'idéologie."

[22]   Terry Eagleton, "Review of *Field Work*", *Stand*, XXI/3 (1980), 77-78: "Heaney, whatever evidence of global imperialist crisis he may find on his doorstep, handles that evidence in the style of an 'end-of-ideologies' writer."

[23]   Jean-François Lyotard, *La Condition Postmoderne*, Paris, 1979, 63: "Dans la société et la culture contemporaine, société postindustrinelle, culture postmoderne, la question de la légitimation du savoir se pose en d'autres termes. Le grand récit a perdu sa crédibilité, quel que soit le mode d'unification qui lui est assigné: récit spéculatif, récit de l'émancipation."

tend to qualify the kind of radical judgement that someone like
Anthony Easthope has passed on Heaney in his article "How Good is
Seamus Heaney?", which still rests on the assumption that "what
makes poetry poetry is what makes poetry ideological".[24] For
Heaney's poetry is demonstrably using narratives and discourses as
raw material or fuel to soar with its readers to another order of
language and another mode of thinking.

To try and end up more than half-facetiously, in a poem in *The
Spirit Level* (which has got something to do with both spirituality and
bricklaying), there is a double poem entitled "Two Lorries",[25] where
the "engine-revs" of the diesel engine are the objective correlative of
the factor that sets going the performative action of writing. Heaney's
poetry is a mode of revisionist writing, and it revises discourses both
from the outside and from the inside. The Derridaean notions of
iterability and *trace* would be more apposite tools for a further
evaluation of these poems, as, for instance, the very deconstructionist
conviction that concepts are not to be trusted in the absolute, but may
be used provisionally as necessary props of writing, and therefore of
thinking, but bound from the start to be revised later on. In
"Heaneyspeak", as Philip Hobsbaum would have it, this is called
"mud pies".[26] Constructed narratives and ideological positions are
poetically processed or used as temporary scaffoldings towards future
horizons.

[24]   Anthony Easthope, *Poetry as Discourse*, London, 1983, 22.
[25]   Seamus Heaney, *The Spirit Level*, London, 1983, 13-14.
[26]   Philip Hobsbaum, "Craft and Technique in *Wintering Out*", in *The Art of Seamus
       Heaney,* ed. Tony Curtis, 3rd edn, Swansea, 1994.

BRENDAN KENNELLY'S *POETRY MY ARSE* (1995):
AN ALTERNATIVE *ARS(E) POETICA*

ÅKE PERSSON

It would be fair to argue that Brendan Kennelly's two radical and controversial works, *Cromwell* (1983) and *The Book of Judas* (1991), aspire to undermine fixed socio-cultural attitudes and values. Both volumes do so through what could be termed assaults on the Irish reader's comfort and expectations as to what the art of poetry should contain, what rules it should follow and what it should deal with and reflect. Indeed, the last section of *The Book of Judas* allows the main figure, Judas, to comment on the nature of poetry and its limitations.

Kennelly's subsequent sequence, *Poetry My Arse* (1995), takes this provocation even further. Where the two earlier works focus on two characters, Cromwell and Judas, who have shaped – some would say damaged – the Irish psyche, the central figure in *Poetry My Arse* is another mythologized figure in Ireland, and possibly equally crucial to the Irish identity, namely the Poet. It is interesting to note that in the same month, October 1995, as Seamus Heaney was celebrated by the Swedish Academy and most of the literary world for the "lyrical beauty" of his poetry, Kennelly published a work that radically challenges that notion of poetry. As I will show, there is a direct and highly significant reference to the Nobel Prize winner in the sequence.

As the ambiguous title, *Poetry My Arse*, strongly indicates, the art of poetry is its principal concern. The "arse" in the title plays on and draws attention to the Latin for art – *ars* – as well as to the colloquial term for one's behind. Thus, the title simultaneously reflects a respectful and a dismissive attitude to poetry. Therefore, the sequence can be read as a tongue-in-cheek but thought-provoking intervention in the literary debate as to what constitutes poetry and what "good poetry" is, opening up the important question of what literature is and what is worthy of praise. By focusing on the nature and function of poetry, *Poetry My Arse* brings to the fore such issues as the values of established literary institutions as well as cultural and artistic elitism. What will paradoxically emerge in my discussion is that *Poetry My Arse* is Kennelly's most literary work, while, at the same time, it is in significant ways his most explicitly non-literary work. It challenges, as part of what I see as his social and artistic protest, the refined tastes of poetry readers and the idea of art as a commodity. This challenge will be seen in the wider perspectives of orality as a strategy to contaminate lyrical poetry and to challenge dominant tastes. It will emerge that I read as an alternative *Ars Poetica*.

That literary and artistic politics and literary value are in fact major concerns is indicated by the names of the poet and the dog in the sequence. The poet is mischievously named Ace de Horner, pronounced just as the Irish Aosdána, the body founded by the former Taoiseach, Charles Haughey, to financially support Irish writers and artists. The members of this organization are implicitly upholding the artistic standards in Ireland and expected to continue producing high-quality work in their art form. Ace de Horner, therefore, is an ironic name, as the poet does not correspond to the high ideals implicitly underlying Aosdána. Because Kennelly has chosen to name his poet thus, Ace becomes a persona through which various attitudes towards the art of poetry can be voiced. Although sympathetic with Ace's personal and artistic struggles, Kennelly's attitude to Ace is by no means uncritical, and it would appear that Ace utters views that Kennelly promotes as well as detests.

If Ace de Horner's name is important, the name of the poet's canine companion and support, the pitbull terrier Kanooce, is equally so. It is Irish and literally means a pile of money, that is, financial reward or support. As will be shown, the use of a dangerous and ferocious pitbull terrier as the poet's support in life and in the creative process is also highly ironic, since Kanooce represents a kind of poetry radically different from the established kind that is usually praised.

The first three poems, "The Song of Ace de Horner", "First words" and "Adam's apple", set up what is principally at stake in this sequence: attitudes to and function of poetry and the poet's position as an artist. The fact that the first poem is entitled "The Song of Ace de Horner" makes it possible to read it as the poet's manifesto, ideals and aspirations. The poem, chant-like in its repetitive nature, firmly implies that real poetry, as perceived by Kennelly, permeates everything in life. It is able to reflect all aspects and facets of existence:

> I am the wind on the Liffey
>
> I am the youngster fleeing the policeman on O'Connell Bridge
>
> I am the Warrington Daycare Centre
>
> I am the fire plan, the smoke alarm, the smoke that kills in seconds
>
> I am the woman up from the country rambling among bargains, fingering
>
> I am the paperback written to lighten the journey
>
> . . . .
>
> I am a terrified whisper on the phone
>
> I am the scream that wakes me in the darkness ...[1]

"The Song of Ace de Horner" suggests that nothing can escape the searching and probing eye of poetry and that this is the responsibility poetry should ideally shoulder. However, the third poem, "Adam's apple", from which the sequence gets its title, questions this artistic position and instead suggests that poetry, often seen as the most refined and genuine expression of human existence, is an inadequate and limited medium through which to reflect and express fundamental human experience such as deep suffering and pain. It is suggested that there is a vast gap, even an abyss, between real experiences gone through by real people and this poet's eager attempts to shape these experiences into art:

> "I was raped," she said
> "by two youths who lay
> on each other first on
> the kitchen floor, then upped
> and attacked me."

---

[1]   Brendan Kennelly, *Poetry My Arse*, Newcastle upon Tyne, 1995, 22-23.

"That's horrible," he murmured
touching his Fellini shirt
at a point below his Adam's apple.

"It was hell," she said.

"I know that," he said, "I know that.
I think I'd like to write
a poem about it,
a vivid poem that would be widely read."

She looked at his finger
operating near his Adam's apple.

"Poetry my arse," she said.[2]

The notion that good literature should be imitation is emphatically refuted here, as the experience retold by the woman cannot possibly be captured adequately in a poem. By wishing to make the woman's experience into poetry, that is, by aestheticizing it, the poet in this poem is accused of trivializing her horrors and pain. If they are made into a poem, "a vivid poem that would be widely read", it means that everything can be made into a product, a commodity, to be consumed by many. This would do severe injustice to her experiences and violate them, just as she has been violated physically. Thus, this kind of poet is presumably seen by Kennelly as a parasite, exploiting other people's pain for his own needs and showing no real understanding of the woman's feelings.

Furthermore, the references to the "Fellini shirt" and the poet's gesture of touching his Adam's apple give an impression of a carefully studied and artificial pose as a response to the rape victim's account, hence dishonest. In view of this, the woman's response, "Poetry my arse", seems an understandable one to the dishonesty, pretentiousness, pomposity and lack of compassion of this poet.

If the poet feels trapped between the aspiration to express the fullness of life and the impossibility adequately and honestly to reflect all facets of life, what is the alternative? Is there an alternative to the "vivid poem that would be widely read", the poem encapsulating experiences, feelings and emotions in a tight, balanced, well-made

---

[2]   *Ibid.*, 24.

work of art appealing to everybody? The whole sequence becomes a search for this alternative and arguably results in a refutation of conventional notions of poetry.

Much of Ace's search takes place on the streets of Dublin. The fact that Ace is aimlessly moving around Dublin is central to the new kind of poetry seemingly advocated by Kennelly as a kind of counter-poetry to much existing poetry, for it is partly the streets that give the sequence its energy, annoying and controversial though that energy may seem. It is the streets that provide Ace with his material. However, it is material and experiences that reject the notion that poetry should consist of experiences "recollected in tranquillity", emotions shaped into a lyric of careful balance and thoughtful contemplation, which is what Wordsworth advised and which has been so influential since then, not least in Seamus Heaney's poetry, for example. Instead, the reader is confronted with chance meetings, snippets of conversation, jokes, toilet humour, graffiti-like wisdoms and aphorisms, banalities, trivia, gossip, overheard street talk. Indeed, as early as the fifth poem, "Overheard streetballad", the irreverent attitude to poetry, and to its reader, is introduced and the dismantling of the high art of poetry is in full swing:

> The streets of Dublin
> are my Parnassus,
> I love to walk 'em
> night and day.
> If you don't like me
> you can kiss my assus
> and go rob your cousins
> in Amerikay.[3]

Parnassus, the epitome of poetic excellence and the home of poetic inspiration, is replaced by "The streets of Dublin", and the intimate relationship between writer and reader, on which most lyrical poetry relies, is replaced by a confrontational and disrespectful one in a direct address, presumably also including critics. Ace will not write poetry, he defiantly declares, to please readers and critics. The linking, through rhyming, of the high and sublime, "Parnassus", to the low and physical, his "assus", establishes the tension between a refined and arguably elitist attitude to poetry and an unpolished and popular

---

[3]   *Ibid.*, 25.

attitude. The fact that the poet chooses to entitle the poem a ballad, a traditionally popular genre, further emphasizes his position.

On his walks in the Dublin streets, Ace meets or is stopped by people who offer him insights into their lives by revealing details about their situation, or they tell him crude jokes and anecdotes, or, indeed, tell him in no uncertain terms what they think of him and his poetry. Street life consists of hustle and bustle, disorder and coincidental encounters. The sequence attempts to capture that somewhat chaotic atmosphere. In a big city, there is a constant flow with very few fixed points of reference, except for the physical streets and buildings. Ace becomes part of that flow with no beginning and no end, or as he states in "Fable", "the perfect no-ending to a story / forever incomplete".[4] The result is a scattering of fragments of lives, a fragmented existence, a flux, far removed from the unity and sense of completion usually sought in poetry. There is, it is suggested, no easily defined wholeness nor any fixity.

Furthermore, it means that the high and sophisticated art of poetry must give way to the low, the popular, the vulgar and the unpoetic, as in "A consequence of good fortune":

> A Dublin woman won the Lotto,
> Ever after, in the pub,
> she'd order two drinks,
> sip one herself
> and pour the other down her knickers.
> When asked by a fascinated bystander
> what in God's name
> she'd do a thing like that for
> she replied
> "It's a mean, mean world, brother.
> There's only one cunt
> I'll buy a drink for!"[5]

Or more Dublin lingo, as in "Counter attack":

> "Has the pride of Irish whiskey come to this?
> I'd be better off drinkin' Parnell's piss!"[6]

---

4   *Ibid.*, 134.
5   *Ibid.*, 105.
6   *Ibid.*, 117.

Often we are allowed to listen in on gossip, which is a most important part of Dublin life. More importantly, it can be instrumental in the perception and construction of a reputation, as in "On or off it's knock or scoff":

> "He's off the drink."

> "Christ! What a bore!"
> "He's back on the drink."

> "Dangerous fucker!"[7]

The list could be made far longer, but the examples just quoted, and numerous others like them, permeate the sequence and leave the reader perplexed as to what is going on. They take the reader by surprise and just as Ace cannot predict what or whom he will meet in the street, so the reader does not know what to expect.

In addition to this, the frequent references to the male and female sexual organs, as well as the many explicit references to excrement and to other bodily functions, often make the tone aggressively irreverent. In a society dominated by the Catholic Church's views of sex, physicality and bodily pleasures as sins, the many references to the sexual may be provocative to an Irish reader. Therefore, if the reader seeks verbal music, balance, formal perfection and thoughts lending themselves to quiet meditation, his or her expectations will be crushed. Instead, the crudeness, bordering on the tasteless, and the unpredictability make the sequence highly uncomfortable to sensibilities educated at viewing poetry as an expression of the sublime.

Consequently, the poems just quoted and numerous others like them amount to an assault on conventional poetry. Readers may even be justified in asking whether what they are reading is poetry at all, at least if traditional criteria are applied. Since there is often a strong feeling that the reader is toyed with or even made fun of, it could even be argued that the strategies usually exploited when approaching and exploring poetry are frequently fruitless and inadequate, which frustrates and annoys readers but which constantly forces them to review their attitudes to the art of poetry.

---

[7]   *Ibid.*, 229.

After winning a dog Lotto Ace gets a companion, namely the ugly and ferocious pitbull terrier Kanooce. We soon realize that Kanooce is admired by Ace, so much so that the dog becomes a kindred spirit, a kind of alter ego. In fact, in "Strength" it is implied that they have become so much part of each other that they are one, since Kanooce is physically carved on Ace's body as a tattoo:

> Ace de Horner has a tattoo of Kanooce
> on the bicep of his right arm.
> "When I look at it," he mutters to himself
> in the Bluebell pad, "I know I'll never come to harm.
>
> I know I've earned a spot in his pitbull heart
> as he is engraved on my skin.
> I'm part of him, he of me.
> Thank God for the beast within ..."[8]

Kanooce is also envied by Ace because the dog poses the kind of threat to society that Ace wishes to be and because it does what Ace wants to do: bite people who are seen as representatives of middle-class values, wealth, hypocrisy, including politicians, businessmen, literary critics and pompous writers. In "On Dalkey Hill" money speculators are torn to pieces by Kanooce, who is "feasting on buttocks, on calves / of legs, on bits of belly too".[9] Dalkey, largely populated by middle-class and upper middle-class businessmen and entrepreneurs, is a suburb south of Dublin and one of the wealthiest areas in Ireland, and the poem is most fruitfully read as an attack on a society obsessed with easy money and creating a small financial elite interested only in accumulating wealth.

If in "On Dalkey Hill" representatives of economic, and political, power are mutilated, in "Real balls" Ace's attitudes to professional critics, powerful cultural gatekeepers, is revealed. Significantly, the poem takes place in Merrion Square in central Dublin. It is a square in one of the old office districts, but more importantly in this context it is here that the office of the Irish Arts Council and that of Aosdána are located. It is implied that the party referred to has been organized by them, suggesting that established literature is more about going to the right parties than about, for example, challenging existing values. It

---

8   *Ibid.*, 342.
9   *Ibid.*, 81.

further highlights the notion that harsh evaluations are perhaps too easily made, coldly with a drink in hand at a cocktail party, a seemingly important part of Irish literary politics:

> At a party in Merrion Square
> > or somewhere near there
> Ace de Horner met a critic with real balls
> > who'd shat upon his verses
>
> in public. This was the sort of
> > excremental response
> that made Ace forget his dreams of skill
> > and feel a dunce.
>
> What the critic did not know was that
> > Ace kept Kanooce in the Gents.
> The critic drank, pronounced, revealed. Convinced
> > he'd left de Horner feeling small
>
> our critic chortled out to relieve himself.
> > He met Kanooce in the loo.
> Kanooce ate him, balls an' all.[10]

It is suggested that a poet's success and respect have as much to do with social appearance as with the intrinsic literary merit of his or her works. If you want to be included and allowed into the higher realms of literature, it is hinted, it is essential to obey the codes, social and otherwise, set up by the cultural elite, but also to backstab your competitors when the opportunity is given.

Ace's dream, we come to understand, is for his poetry to become as radically and dangerously biting and savage as Kanooce's actions in order to expose dishonest behaviour and hypocrisy. Kanooce thus becomes a kind of alternative muse to Ace, as the dog is not hindered by strictures and social conventions, whereas Ace seems trapped in and frustrated by them. In "A new metre" Kanooce becomes a "metre-chewing monster", tearing traditional poetic forms apart in a "creative crime", an act which, it is hoped, will open up new creative possibilities and affect future poetry:

---

[10]   *Ibid.*, 46.

sonnets epigrams villanelles
   chunks of epics
     lyrics pure as bells

   disappear

into that devouring maw
   that knows no law
   but its own
....
a new metre is born
in the chewing music of Kanooce's jaws,
   a metre stranger
than the harmony of the spheres
which it renders rather tame.

   This new
   ecstatic
callous barbaric
   metre

is Ace's music for a moment

   and if he can
through skill and right devotion
   word-incarnate
that creative crime

it may be yours
     and mine

   in time.[11]

That Ace and Kanooce have a deep affinity with each other is made clear in "Ifology", in which there is a kind of telepathic understanding between the two. One look at Kanooce liberates Ace, as if the dog knows what Ace needs:

his eyes say ...
jump into the sea, be a criminal of rhyme,
write like I bark, write like I bite,
mix my fangjuice with your timid ink.

---

[11] *Ibid.*, 74.

Ace listens ...
Ah, yes, this is the way to think.[12]

Thus, Kanooce, the uninhibited and uncontrollable force, becomes the solution to, and way out of, the creative stalemate Ace is in and the necessary alternative to the timid, nice and pleasant but ultimately harmless kind of poetry Ace thinks dominates the poetic scene and which only regurgitates the same old styles and concerns. Therefore, it is not a coincidence that Ace views himself as a terrorist, wearing on his wanderings around Dublin an IRA trenchcoat, a most treasured possession.

Kanooce becomes, then, a muse to Ace from whom the poet seeks inspiration, a muse radically different from the traditional one usually associated with poetry. His woman partner, Janey Mary, can be read as another. If the street gives the sequence much of its energy, the intimate talk between Ace and Janey Mary provides another kind of energy. If the fragments and coincidental meetings in the street generate the kind of poems discussed, challenging and undermining the reader's expectations of what constitutes poetry, the exchanges between the poet and his partner also produce a kind of poetry that continuously forces the readers to renegotiate their views on what poetry is or what it should be.

Many of these exchanges take place in bed and could best be described as raw pillow talk, or sexual banter, often just before, during or just after sexual activities, far removed from the public arena but recording everyday and intimate conversations between the two. The sequence seems to ask, is pillow talk, snippets of silly and unpoetic conversation, frequently full of sexually explicit language, "proper" material for poetry? As in "Facing faces":

> "You're a tripper in bed," sighed Ace,
> "Zipping through me like a silken fairy.
> You've the face of an angel," he moaned.
>
> "And you've a face like a slapped arse," said Janey Mary.[13]

Or "Two sides":

---

[12]   *Ibid.*, 259.
[13]   *Ibid.*, 217.

"I'm impotent tonight," said Ace,
"an erection is what I dream of
        and cannot get."

"Surprisingly," said Janey Mary,
"my nipples are erect for you,
        my clit is hot and wet."

"O would," said Ace "it were not so."

"Right now, for you, you fluke, my juices flow."

"O no!"[14]

To many readers, particularly perhaps those with a strong Catholic background in which sexual matters are to be kept behind closed doors, the examples just quoted, and many similar ones, would be offensive, provocative and unsettling. The openness with which this sexual banter is conducted may conventionally be found in popular softporn rather than in love poetry. Nevertheless, these poems reflect a reality rarely so explicitly expressed in poetry. The underlying idea seems to be that conventional love poetry written in the lyrical mode has left out an important dimension of human relationships, presumably because it has been deemed inappropriate and in bad taste.

The rawness and intimacy between the two lovers permeate the sequence and are part of the subversive qualities of *Poetry My Arse*. So is Janey Mary's frankness towards Ace. Rather than being the conventionally supporting woman behind the angst-ridden artist, Janey Mary is Ace's severest critic, as she tells him truths about himself and reveals his self-centred nature. She constantly deflates his big ego, thus suggesting that poets in general are annoyingly and pathetically self-absorbed and need to be told that life is more than trying to write a few lines of profundities that very few will read. In "The art of pinning", Janey Mary airs her views of Ace's aphoristic wisdom "the horror of separation / outweighs the crime of being together":

"Aren't you the philosophical ould bollocks," she replied,
pinning the poet against the bedroom wall.

---

[14]   *Ibid.*, 309.

"Sleeping with you is an experiment in absurdity.
Why do I bother my arse with you at all?
If I release you now, rag doll, will you fall?"[15]

The image of the poet as a threat to society is eroded and dismantled. Indeed, in "Bubbles, or Janey Mary's *Defense [sic] of Poetry*", Janey Mary physically and metaphorically dismembers, or deconstructs, the poet by cutting off his male organ after Ace's amorous adventure with an inflatable doll. His member is saved and successfully reattached, but the event changes Ace and forces him to look at himself and Janey Mary in a different light. "What is a poet without his prick?",[16] it is asked. The poem implies that a radical change is possible only if the self-absorbed, navel-gazing male poet is castrated, forcing him to confront that uncomfortable question but also to get off his high horses and open up to more everyday and pressing concerns.

Janey Mary, then, undermines the image of the Poet, an image so cherished among the Irish, and his ambitious aims. Perhaps even more importantly, however, in what I read as one of the most central poems of the sequence, "By the ears", like a stern teacher reprimanding an unruly pupil, she also offers advice on what kind of poetry she would want Ace to write and implicitly tells him what short-comings his writing presently has:

Janey Mary grabbed him by the ears and said
"Sweep the caution out of your heart, stand up and sing,
what use to man or God if you're clever and tame-blooded?
Whatever you say, say something
wake-the-dead true, my unopen man.
           If God had made me a poet
                    I'd thank Him
                         I'd praise Him
                              I'd thank Him again
                                   and then

I'd fling all the damned shit in the fan!"[17]

This poem seems directly addressed to those poets and critics who favour the traditional, slim and carefully crafted volume of poetry and

[15] *Ibid.*, 230.
[16] *Ibid.*, 344.
[17] *Ibid.*, 337.

who would dismiss Kennelly's poetry as "slapdash". The solution to the fear of creative inadequacy and staleness proposed by Kennelly through Janey Mary can be read as a comment to those who advocate the lyrical beauty pointed to in Seamus Heaney's poetry, whose often quoted phrase "Whatever you say say nothing"[18] could be read as reflecting, fairly or unfairly, a poetry of reticence, caution and lack of commitment in times when leaders of moral stature and integrity are few and far between. It is interesting to note that critics praising Heaney's achievement acknowledge his reluctance to take sides in political and social issues, and imply that it is the appropriate position to take in poetry. For example, in his *The Achievement of Seamus Heaney*, significantly published shortly after the announcement of the Nobel Prize in 1995, John Wilson Foster writes:

> Unlike John Montague and Thomas Kinsella, two other fine poets, Heaney did not speak out directly against British policy in Northern Ireland .... But if he did not speak out, he spoke in, which is what a poet in his truest office does. Events are absorbed and internalized, re-issued, and sometimes recognizable in their translation only by our disciplined reading.

Later on we read: "It is as if Poetry has been Heaney's conscience, preventing blatant partisanship or propaganda, keeping him in the political no-man's land as fidelity to Poetry dictates."[19] Poetry, if it is good, it is implied here, should not speak out, and belongs to those experts who are able to decipher the various layers of meaning in a "disciplined reading". To be true to Poetry (capital P) the poet should stay away from politics and explicit comments. It would certainly seem as if this position of reticence and caution is elevated to a very special poetic quality indeed.

Kennelly here moves in the opposite direction, and in what I read as a direct reference, and possibly a mild rebuke, to the Nobel Laureate, he recommends through Janey Mary "Whatever you say, say something" and "fling all the damned shit in the fan". It is suggested that dialogue and open (oral) communication are always preferable to silence and caution if locked positions on artistic and

---

[18]   Seamus Heaney, "Whatever You Say, Say Nothing", in Seamus Heaney, *North*, London, 1975, 57-60.

[19]   John Wilson Foster, *The Achievement of Seamus Heaney*, Dublin, 1995, 3, 4.

political levels are to be unlocked and if an alternative to an exclusive and elitist poetry scene is to be made possible.

Given the importance of oral communication in *Poetry My Arse*, we may briefly pause to speculate about the challenge that orality poses to conventional views of literature and poetry. In his innovative book *Orality and Literacy*, Walter J. Ong examines the differences between oral and written work and also what mentalities the two kinds represent. Oral work, he claims, is "close to the human life-world".[20] This means, among other things, that the emphasis is on human interaction, which in turn results in oral work frequently being antagonistic, situational and non-permanent. A common feature, Ong argues, is what he terms "verbal and intellectual combat", a version of which is the phenomenon of "reciprocal name-calling" and "tongue-lashings". In other words, because oral work relies on "direct word of mouth", it is part of a "give-and-take dynamics"[21] of the "here and now."[22] Thus, it is a communal, socially-oriented and immediate activity.

On the other hand, written work, and its modern printed version, can be seen as distancing people from each other. When the shift from oral to print culture had taken place, it was, Ong holds, "a major factor in the development of the sense of personal privacy that marks modern society"[23] as it "created a new sense of the private ownership of words".[24] What Ong terms "the orality-literacy shift"[25] has far-reaching consequences for the way in which humans act in and perceive the world in that print, generally speaking, closes down rather than opens up. Ong makes a highly interesting, albeit controversial point: "A correlative of the sense of closure fostered by print was the fixed point of view, which ... came into being with print."[26] What Ong seems to suggest, and what is pertinent to my discussion of Kennelly's provocative strategies in *Poetry My Arse*, is that orality, and features of orality, constitute a communal act in which human interaction is essential and which encourages exchange

---

[20]   Walter J. Ong, *Orality and Literacy: The Technologizing of the Word* (1982), London and New York, 1997, 42.
[21]   *Ibid.*, 44.
[22]   *Ibid.*, 47.
[23]   *Ibid.*, 130.
[24]   *Ibid.*, 131.
[25]   *Ibid.*, 145.
[26]   *Ibid.*, 135.

and confrontation, whereas written and printed work discourages direct human contact and is therefore anti-social. Viewed in this light, orality potentially poses more of a threat to dominant forces.

In his *Oral Poetry*, Paul Zumthor seems to agree with Ong but stresses the subversive nature of much of that kind of poetic activity. "The oral text", he holds, "for the most part, is multiple, cumulative, many-colored, sometimes diverse to the point of being contradictory",[27] thus upsetting our notions of unity. Zumthor insists that oral poetry forms an important part of the resistance – he goes as far as to use the term "sabotage" – against the increasingly oppressive and static lifestyle of the modern world, in which technology and written texts are crucial elements:

> Writing stays put and stagnates; voice flourishes .... By voice we remain part of the antique and powerful race of nomads. Something in me refuses the city, the house, the security of order.[28]

One more aspect brought up by Zumthor in relation to oral poetry is highly relevant to my reading of *Poetry My Arse*, namely the tradition of blind poets, since Ace de Horner is slowly going blind. As Zumthor points out, the figure of the blind poet is believed to have qualities and gifts, an "awesome power", denied others. Significantly, however, the fascination with blind poets goes deeper. The modern world is dominated by a value system in which observation and scientific and empirical data are cherished, but blind poets are linked to another system. Because of this, they pose a potential threat to our world view: "Cut off from the symbolic and moral values attached to the eye, the blind man is the old King Lear of the Celtic legend, mad and cruel – or else, sombre translucidity, the Seer beyond the body, the man *forever free of writing*."[29]

It seems to me that *Poetry My Arse* can fruitfully be read in the light of the above arguments on orality presented by Ong and Zumthor. I suggest that Kennelly's insistent exploitation of oral elements, together with his explicit recommendation "whatever you say, say something", constitutes a consciously radical, indeed political,

---

[27]   Paul Zumthor, *Oral Poetry: An Introduction* (1983), Minneapolis; MN, 1990, 103.

[28]   *Ibid.*, 227-28.

[29]   *Ibid.*, 177 (italics added).

move to resist dominant views of poetry, a move that goes beyond the stylistic and formal.

It cannot be ignored, of course, that the sequence is written and not spoken. Nevertheless, just as oral qualities and elements from primarily oral cultures demand an opening up to wider definitions of the category of literature, so oral features – what Ong terms "oral residue"[30] – of *Poetry My Arse*, for example in the form of gossip, jokes, sexual banter, name-calling, confrontational exchanges, situational encounters and overheard street talk, insist on a possible redefinition of poetry. They encourage an application of evaluative yardsticks radically different from those in which formal aspects dominate, for example, social commitment or social protest. The result is an opening up to a wider range of experiences than is usually allowed for in discussions about poetry. Because the strategy of the sequence insists on inclusiveness and openness to alternative experiences, the issue is ultimately one of democracy and freedom versus oppression and control. *Poetry My Arse* emphatically chooses democracy.

A moving away from conventional poetry includes a moving away from conventional channels of distribution of that poetry, that is, publishing. It means refusing to accept poetry as a commodity, a product to be consumed by connoisseurs and experts. Therefore, it is not a coincidence that Ace seeks other outlets for his art in an attempt to free himself from established means of spreading his insights. At the end he finds a radical alternative to conventional publishing. In "Published at last!", the penultimate poem of the sequence, Ace publishes his poems by dropping them into the river Liffey, freeing himself from past experiences and old ways of looking at life:

> Ace stood on O'Connell Bridge, dropped
> his poems into the Liffey. One by one
> they floated down the air, fell
> into the scummy water. One by one
> by one they went from him as they had
> come to him,
> > down the foul air
> > into the foul river –
>
> > all he knew of love

---

[30]   Ong, *Orality and Literacy*, 37.

killers he'd met in public
his education in hate
stories sharp as
Janey Mary's words
dreams nightmares readings
wisps of hope and horror
bits and pieces of the city
that raged and slept in him
like hell and heaven and the little
he knew of earth

fell-floated
    down the air
   into the Liffey
    and drifted
      out to sea
        slowly
          calmly
like happy ghosts ...[31]

The poem implies not a death but a rebirth, a new beginning that includes viewing life and poetry from a fresh perspective. Although it does not imply that he will be "forever free of writing", this way of publishing his work nevertheless suggests he has broken out of the strictures of conventional writing and conventional pressures of publishing. It may even be speculated that by publishing them in the river, he is free from the forces making artistic demands on him in the shape of publishers, editors, critics and readers, that is, arbiters of taste and value.

Admittedly, it can be read as an act of failure, in that he gives up the written medium through which he may be able to influence people and to reform society. Yet, as the last poem, "Laugh", implies, he will not be inactive in the future. It is just that his involvement will take another form: laughter, arguably the most subversive activity there is. It emphasizes not only that orality is fundamental to his new outlook on life and art, but also the ludic and irreverent qualities of *Poetry My Arse* as a whole. And even if we cannot be completely sure that the laughter is Ace's, the implication is that Ace's almost defiant laughter pervades Dublin, emphasized by the omission of a final full stop,

---

[31] Kennelly, *Poetry My Arse*, 349-50.

resisting a sense of closure and leaving the sequence open-ended, incomplete and in a flux:

>   ... down on the town
>   and all around
>   comes the sound
>   of laughter
>
>   laughter untrammelled
>   laughter of nowhere
>
>   abundant
>   dancing
>
>   exorcist
>   laughter [32]

Ultimately, then, as I have shown, *Poetry My Arse* challenges poetic taste and value as well as the concept of art as a commodity and is, therefore, a contribution to the Irish literary debate. At this stage, it seems, not only in Kennelly's writing but also in Irish poetry in general, a recharging is deemed necessary in order to incorporate language and experiences that usually fall outside what one poet and critic terms the "normal poem".[33] The sequence insists on asking questions such as: What is good poetry and bad poetry? What function should poetry have? For whom is it written? What kind of experiences should it express and reflect? What language is appropriate and proper? Some of Kennelly's answers, I would suggest, lie in the oral qualities of the street talk, pillow talk, sexual banter and confrontational meetings permeating the sequence. They are unsophisticated, unrefined, raw, crude and provocatively frank, sometimes arguably annoyingly so. Therefore, they can be read as an attempt to remove poetry from the artistic pedestal and to dismantle and resist the elitist attitude often linked to this art form. Thus, in an act of revolt, *Poetry My Arse* tries to retrieve poetry from the exclusive literary institutions and bring it back to the people and their varied experiences. Consequently, it is highly important in Kennelly's social and artistic protest and constitutes, in ways that I have tried to present, an alternative *Ars Poetica* or, dare I state it, *Arse Poetica.*

---

[32]   *Ibid.*, 350.
[33]   Pat Boran, "From the Fragile to the Wild" (review of *Poetry My Arse*), *Sunday Tribune Magazine*, 1 October 1995, 20.

INTERTEXTUAL RELATIONS IN MEDBH MCGUCKIAN'S POETRY

SHANE MURPHY

In Medbh McGuckian's early poetic manifesto "The Seed Picture",[1] the analogy between "seed-work" and creative writing appears to reinforce a conception of her method as simply dual in nature. The importance of intuition and her willingness to allow unconscious or submerged elements to take the lead is suggested when the poet states that:

> The seeds dictate their own vocabulary,
> Their dusty colours capture
> More than we can plan.

The secondary activity, then, is one of arrangement: "I only guide them not by guesswork / In their necessary numbers." Although this reads very much like Seamus Heaney's well-known distinction between craft and technique, what has not been recognized is that her process of writing actually entails three stages, the neglected one being the primary activity of gathering seeds (vocabulary). While this poem only states the theme that words "capture / More than we can plan", most of McGuckian's work enacts this process because the words are taken from a variety of memoirs, biographies, critical essays, etc. and are arranged by the writer who attaches them "by the spine to a perfect bedding" (that is, her book of poems).

The arrangement within a single poetic text of McGuckian's carefully selected quotations can be described as a "patchwork", the function of which is akin to, but significantly different from that

---

[1] Medbh McGuckian, "The Seed-Picture", in Medbh McGuckian, *The Flower Master*, Oxford, 1981, 23.

described in the second verse of Michael Longley's poem of the same name:

> I pull over us old clothes, remnants,
> Stitching together shirts and nightshirts
>
> Into such a dazzle as will burn away
> Newspapers, letters, previous templates ...[2]

The idea of creating poetry by re-cycling other people's images and phrases is not all that artistically purposeful in itself; however, if the "previous templates" are not burned away but held together and made self-regarding, meta-textual, ironic or parodic, the writer can make use of the dialogic potential of a precursor's own words. One example of McGuckian's emphasis on the relational aspects of quotation is "Little House, Big House",[3] a poem that uses unacknowledged borrowings from a biography to set up a parallel between herself and another writer.

It must be admitted that precise knowledge of the particular biography or memoir the poet is using would save the critic from making unwarranted assumptions like those contained in Patricia Boyle Haberstroh's recent assessment of McGuckian's poetry. Analysing "Little House, Big House", Haberstroh contextualizes the poem within the literary/socio-political paradigm of the Anglo-Irish Big House tradition: "Alluding to the big houses inhabited by English settlers and the small homes of the Irish cottagers, the speaker imagines a different kind of house ...."[4] Since the poem is bereft of footnotes, dates, or historical personae, this is a curious reflex on Haberstroh's part; indeed, the text does not invite such an interpretation, hinging solely on the poem's title. It is noteworthy that she overlooks the poem's only cited place name, Tarusa – a town whose Eastern European location weakens the plausibility of her narrowly focused argument:

[2]   Michael Longley, "Patchwork", in Michael Longley, *Poems 1963-1983*, London, 1991, 188.
[3]   Medbh McGuckian, "Little House, Big House", in Medbh McGuckian, *On Ballycastle Beach*, Oxford, 1988, 33.
[4]   Patricia Boyle Haberstroh, *Women Creating Women: Contemporary Irish Women Poets*, New York, 1996, 145.

> Since our blood
> Is always older than we will ever be,
> I should like to lie in Tarusa under matted winter grass,
> Where the strawberries are redder than anywhere else.[5]

Knowing that Tarusa was the town in which Marina Tsvetaeva's family had their summer residence, Meva Maron was able to take the reference as evidence of a possible intertext: "But Tarusa and all the strawberries at the end of 'Little House, Big House', which caught my eye because I used the same quote in a more satirical poem presumably about the same time ... does more than let you say, 'Aha, Tsvetaeva! I've solved the crossword ...'".[6] However, her letter to the *Honest Ulsterman* is yet another example of unintentional misdirection since McGuckian's reference is far more indirect than Maron suspects. Although "Tarusa" and the "strawberries" are mentioned in Tsvetaeva's *A Captive Spirit: Selected Prose* and although the strawberries are mentioned again in her poem "Much like Me" ("It's true that graveyard strawberries / Are the biggest and sweetest of all"), McGuckian in fact appropriates her final lines from Olga Ivinskaya's reminiscences concerning her life with Boris Pasternak. Describing the tragic fate of Tsvetaeva (who committed suicide on 31 August 1941), she laments the fact that the poet was buried in an unmarked grave in Yelabuga, contrary to her wishes:

> In May 1934, while she was still in Paris, Marina had written: "*I should like to lie* in the khlyst [Russian religious sect. Tsvetaeva's family spent their summers in Tarusa before the Revolution] cemetery at *Tarusa*, under an elder bush, in one of those graves with a silver dove on it, *where the wild strawberries are* larger and *redder than anywhere else in those parts*."[7]

In this respect, the poem is a meditation upon Tsvetaeva's suicide ("So different from an ordinary going-away"). That McGuckian is not simply quoting Tsvetaeva, but Ivinskaya's account of her death, is confirmed by further unattributed quotations within the poem. In the

---

[5]   McGuckian, "Little House, Big House", 33.

[6]   Meva Maron, "The Stamps Had Squirrels on Them", *Honest Ulsterman*, 88 (1989), 33.

[7]   Olga Ivinskaya, *A Captive of Time. My Years with Pasternak: The Memoirs of Olga Ivinskaya*, trans. Max Hayward, London, 1979, 191 (italics added).

final line of the second stanza, McGuckian states that she deepens shadows with her "autumn brown raincoat".

The connotations of death and decay are confirmed when we learn that, during her final days, Tsvetaeva was "dressed very badly – in a long dark dress, an old brown autumn raincoat, and a beret of a dirty-blue colour she had knitted herself".[8] Similarly, in the previous lines, McGuckian asks the question: "Why should I take / My apron off for a wineless dinner?" The growing apathy and despair to which these lines allude are made all the more poignant when we realize that before her death, Tsvetaeva "did not even take off the apron with the large pocket in which she had been doing her housework that morning ...".[9]

That McGuckian regarded Tsvetaeva's suicide with compassion (and even respect) is confirmed by a personal interview in which she contrasts Tsvetaeva's conduct with that of Mayakovsky:

> I suppose hers [suicide] was more understandable, hers was more choreographic. He had written one poem against it, and then he did it, I found it disappointing – whereas I felt that her reasons were not cowardice but real despair, and that I could admire her.[10]

Her ability to identify with the poet is not belied by their different social or political circumstances, as shown by her comments in a review of Tsvetaeva's prose:

> But I understand something of her obsessive maternal instinct towards both husband and son, a reaction of sorts to those bereavements; her absolute need for the emotional involvement in her subject matter; her abject loyalties; and the social, psychic break between her prolonged adolescence with its security and material comfort, its privileged education, and the nightmare of her maturity, its wars, deprivation, and exile: "caught up in the middle of her life by a brutal era" (to quote Joseph Brodsky).[11]

---

[8]   *Ibid.*, 188-89. This account was given by Tsvetaeva's neighbours, a couple called Bredelshchikov (Lily Feiler also quotes them in her biography, *Marina Tsvetaeva: The Double Beat of Heaven and Hell*, Durham, 1994, 259, but she translates the reference as "an old fall coat").

[9]   *Ibid.*, 190.

[10] Medbh McGuckian, personal interview at the Marine Hotel, Ballycastle, 19 August 1996.

[11] Medbh McGuckian, "How Precious Are Thy Thoughts Unto Me", *Common Knowledge*, II/1 (Spring 1993), 135.

"Little House, Big House" the poem's title, which Haberstroh so decisively misreads, points towards another reading as it contains a veiled reference to the love affair between Boris Pasternak and Olga Ivinskaya. She describes how he kept a country house (dacha) at Peredelkino, a village situated twenty kilometres from Moscow, and how he lived there with his second wife, Zinaida Nikolayevna, in what is called "the big house" as opposed to Ivinskaya's "little house" nearby:

> I think Zinaida Nikolayevna understood very well that by making a good home for BL, she strengthened her position as his legal wife and the mistress of *the "big"* house – which made it easier for her to reconcile herself to the open existence of *the "little"* house (that is, mine), and she knew that any ill-considered attempt to put pressure on BL would have meant disaster for her.
>
> But it was not quite as simple as that. In his last years, the study with his favourite books and his desk had its due place in his heart, but he often said to me: "I am going off to work. I have to be worthy of you. My place of work is over there."[12]

Several narratives are conjoined, the thematics of which differ according to our own identification of the speaker and addressee. For instance, when, in the fourth stanza, McGuckian says "And the house like me / Was tangled with the emotion of cut flowers", the emotion in question alternates between despair (Tsvetaeva) and frustration (Ivinskaya), depending on which historical figure she is empathizing with at the time. It is also important to note the implicit link between Pasternak and Tsvetaeva which the poem makes. Ivinskaya reports in her memoirs that "During my years with BL I heard him speak over and over again about his sense of responsibility for Marina's return to Russia, for her feeling that she was utterly abandoned, and for her death. Till the end of his life he never ceased to mourn her."[13] This guilt was occasioned by his reluctance to allow Tsvetaeva to stay at the "big house" when she turned to him for help towards the end of her life, a refusal which he later deemed a contributing factor to her decision to commit suicide: "Years later BL told me that he had not invited Marina to stay – the thing he would really have liked to do –

---

[12]   Ivinskaya, *Captive of Time*, 187 (italics added).
[13]   *Ibid.*, 171.

partly because of his own indecisiveness and partly because of the domestic situation at the Peredelkino house."[14]

Medbh McGuckian's use of dovetailed quotations is not limited to establishing an empathy with precursor female poets. Other people's words are often brought to bear upon a situation when the author herself, due to some traumatic event, is unable to speak in her own words. One such occasion was the death of her father. In "The Finder Has Become the Seeker",[15] the poet addresses her deceased father using a combination of her own images and those culled from Osip Mandelstam's prose.[16] McGuckian's verses strive to become "resurrective" and, in her struggle to celebrate her father, she turns to an existing wordhoard. Contrary to Jehan Ramazani's contention that the modern elegy is anti-consolatory, McGuckian's elegies attempt to resurrect the father-figure – biological and literary – using Mandelstam's words to do so: "I think in my loss of a father I took on M. as a poetic ancestor."

It is somewhat appropriate that she should turn to Mandelstam since he himself contended that "poetic speech may be compared to a piece of amber in which a fly still buzzes, having long ago been buried under layers of resin, the living foreign body continuing to live even when fossilized". Such an image describes the immortality which she wishes to establish for her father through her own words:

> Sleep easy, supposed fatherhood,
> resembling a flowerbed.
> Though I extract you here and now
> from the soil, open somehow
> your newly opened leaves:
> I like to breathe what ought to be.

The poet implicitly compares "fatherhood" to poetic composition by describing each activity using related organic metaphors: while fatherhood is said to resemble a "flowerbed", the poet's focus on the present time of writing ("here and now") implies that the picking of a flower is an analogy for the writing process. This can also be seen in

---

[14] *Ibid.*, 180.

[15] Medbh McGuckian, "The Finder Has Become the Seeker", in Medbh McGuckian, *Captain Lavender*, Oldcastle: Co. Meath, 1994, 41.

[16] Osip Mandelstam, *The Collected Prose and Letters*, trans. Jane Grey Harris and Constance Link Harris, London, 1991. McGuckian borrows primarily from "Journey to Armenia" (344-78) and "Conversation about Dante" (397-442).

the ambiguous order to open "your newly opened leaves" since the "leaves" can refer to both a flower and a book of poems. Paradoxically, death becomes life-giving: although the father has departed from his earthly existence, he is urged to flourish on a new spiritual/textual level. Yet the poem is hesitant in its optimism: "somehow" and "ought" may well be imperative, but they are also optative in mood, more hopeful than assured. Matters are made even more complicated by her questioning the essential maleness and ultimate source of "fatherhood". The poet extends the concept beyond a narrow biological definition by giving it a literary slant *vis-à-vis* poetic ancestry. Indeed, using the same organic metaphor, she has stated that "I have always believed that the lives of people who lived before us were the rightful soil in which poetry grows".

> You desire to exist through me;
> I want to disappear exhausted in you.
> We are things squeezed out, like lips,
> not that which serves as coverings –
>
> give me the strength to distinguish myself
> from you, such ill-matched wings.

In this second stanza, the poet puts forward two seemingly antithetical wishes: "to disappear exhausted in you" and "to distinguish myself / from you". On one level, McGuckian is expressing filial love and seeking the fatherly protection which, in the physical world, she has lost, but she does not wish to lose her identity in the process; on another level, by adopting a palimpsestic form, she is fulfilling her need to use another writer's words to express her emotions while still maintaining her own inimitable style. Asked why she borrows so heavily from Mandelstam in the elegies, McGuckian replied that "in the initial stages of loss and grief one is less in control of one's consciousness than usual and therefore for me to hand my consciousness over to another poet's full keeping was necessary".[17]

One such borrowing has to do with poetic form itself. In "Conversation about Dante", Mandelstam writes that

> There is not just one form in Dante, but a multitude of forms. One is
> squeezed out of another and only by convention can one be inserted

---

[17]   Medbh McGuckian, personal correspondence, 16 January 1997.

into another .... "I would squeeze the juice out of my idea, out of my conception" – that is, he considers form as *the thing which is squeezed out, not as that which serves as a covering.*[18]

McGuckian's form, like Dante's, both creates and depends on its content, and it is this symbiosis she wants to establish with her biological and her literary father. By using Mandelstam's words in a new context, her texts become dialogic and polyphonic in the manner of much mainstream contemporary British and Irish poetry.[19] Her words become ambivalent, taking on new meanings while retaining the old; in particular, her words adopt what Julia Kristeva calls a "hidden interior polemic", characterized by "the active (modifying) influence of another's word on the writer's word. It is the writer who 'speaks', but a foreign discourse is constantly present in the speech that it distorts."[20] Such a strategy allows her text to retain its "nomadicity":[21] incorporating Mandelstam into her work, she is all the while being free from his overweening authority.

She self-reflexively comments on this process in the third stanza:

> Night furs you, winter clothes you,
> Homerically studded in your different planting.
> You jangle the keys of language
> you are not using, your understanding
> of sunlight is more language than that,
> your outcast sounds scatter their fluid carpet.

The second line is ironic as the words "Homerically studded" are themselves newly planted from a different context: in "Journey to Armenia", Mandelstam states that the entire island of Sevan "is Homerically studded with yellow bones, leavings from the pious picnics of the local populace".[22] The reference bears little trace of its original meaning, the name of "Homer" suggesting an alternative literary provenance.

[18] Mandelstam, *The Collected Prose*, 408 (italics added).
[19] See Ian Gregson, *Contemporary Poetry and Postmodernism: Dialogue and Estrangement*, London, 1996, 5-11.
[20] Julia Kristeva, *Desire in Language: A Semiotic Approach to Literature and Art*, ed. Leon S. Roudiez, trans. Thomas Gora, Alice Jardine and Leon S. Roudiez, Oxford, 1987, 73.
[21] See Thomas Docherty, *Alterities: Criticism, History, Representation*, Oxford, 1996, 76.
[22] Mandelstam, *The Collected Prose*, 345.

She follows this with a quotation from the same essay describing the Armenians' use of language:

> As a result of my incorrect subjective orientation, I acquired the habit of looking upon every Armenian as a philologist .... However, this is partly correct, for these people *jangle the keys of their language* even when they are not unlocking any treasures.[23]

This discordant music, in its new "planting", refers to the effect which is produced by McGuckian's layering and sampling of pieces of text. However, not only do the quotations produce readings which are non-synchronous, but they also allow McGuckian to communicate with two distinct people at the same time. Asked in an interview why she uses the Russian poet as a literary source, she commented that "now that I was left without my father I would have to adapt to a new way of being communicated with and I would have to refine all my senses in a spiritual way, which would be painful, but it was up to me to turn more sophisticated now, to keep in touch with the dead person who was gone – so I would be able to differentiate between them".[24] The "outcast sounds" that "scatter their fluid carpet" ensure that such polyphony occurs. Indeed, this metaphor is itself taken from a passage where Mandelstam describes poetic discourse in terms which have much in common with dialogism:

> Poetic discourse is a carpet fabric containing a plethora of textile warps differing from one another only in the process of coloration, only in the partitura of the perpetually changing commands of the instrumental signalling system. It is an extremely durable carpet, woven out of fluid: a carpet in which the currents of the Ganges, taken as a fabric theme, do not mix with the samples of the Nile or the Euphrates, but remain multicolored ....[25]

McGuckian's poetic texts are not only intertextual in the sense of using literary sources, but also in the more specialized Kristevan sense of transposition which "specifies that the passage from one signifying system to another demands a new articulation of the thetic – of enunciative and denotative positionality". McGuckian's use of quotations translated from the Russian produces "a semiotic

---

[23]   *Ibid.*, 349 (italics added).
[24]   Medbh McGuckian, personal interview at Ballycastle.
[25]   Mandelstam, *The Collected Prose*, 398.

polyvalence"[26] which works against the grammatical rationale of the English language. Analysing the final stanza, one could interpret it solely in terms of her borrowings from Mandelstam,[27] yet this would neglect the discordance that results from her estrangement from the language.

Writing in terms reminiscent of Thomas Kinsella's "divided mind" thesis,[28] McGuckian has described her own feelings of linguistic dislocation and her need to use her literary precursors to effect a rebellion against what she considers to be a colonized language:

> How can your so self-righteous tutors in Cambridge lay down the laws about pilfering – when they and their race have destroyed *our* tongue, all my heritage, hand and limb. Fair exchange is no robbery and every word I take *back* from *their* shelves and *their* books and their imposed culture into *my* mouth and hand is to feed all those who died (but not spiritually) in the Famine and elsewhere. And if I'm schizophrenic, who divided the country and the soul? And everything they stole I will take back before I die, every word over and over because it's all *they gave us* in return.[29]

She asserts her status as a female Irish writer by rejecting the "supposed fatherhood" of her inherited language, by working against its socio-symbolic order and by tapping into what Kristeva calls the semiotic: "Indifferent to language, enigmatic and feminine, this space underlying the written is rhythmic, unfettered, irreducible to its intelligible verbal translation; it is musical, anterior to judgement, but restrained by a single guarantee: syntax."[30] While "acoustic earth", "travelling eye" and "layered with air" are written in English, they still carry traces of their context in Mandelstam's Russian text, and it is the disjunction between the two contexts which evokes the semiotic, that which "remains itself immaterial and simply ghosts like a faint echo the text's articulated symbolic order".[31] Since her own "language and

---

[26] See Julia Kristeva, *Revolution in Poetic Language*, trans. Margaret Waller, New York, 1984, 60.

[27] See Mandelstam, *The Collected Prose*, 364-65.

[28] See Thomas Kinsella, "The Irish Writer", in *Davis, Mangan, Ferguson?: Tradition and the Irish Writer*, ed. Thomas Kinsella, Dublin, 1970, 57-66 and "The Divided Mind", in *Irish Poets in English*, ed. Seán Lucy, Cork 1973, 208-18.

[29] Medbh McGuckian, personal correspondence, 22 January 1997.

[30] Kristeva, *Revolution*, 29.

[31] Thomas Docherty, *After Theory*, Edinburgh, 1996, 35.

grammar is so doubly foreign", she uses quotations from other writers to create a montage effect, writing in the form of non-English.

McGuckian's resistance to the English language and her desire to articulate the inexpressible are best described in "Elegy for an Irish Speaker",[32] an elegy whose five stanzas comprise of forty quotations taken from twenty-one essays by Osip Mandelstam.[33] The tortured syntax and uncertain referents of the opening stanza are an example of the semiotic emerging through the symbolic order:

> Numbered day,
> night only just beginning,
> be born very slowly, stay
> with me, impossible to name.

It is difficult to tell when the "Numbered day" ends and the "night" begins. By juxtaposing the two, McGuckian again links birth with death, but reverses the usual chronology by having the former follow on from the latter. The male persona, (a fusion between her own father and Mandelstam), is said to "fertilize" death and make a new level of communication possible. This partly explains the ambivalence surrounding the phrase "impossible to name". While it seems to signify McGuckian's inability to name death through the medium of language, the original context suggests that this is far from negative:

> How dreadful that man (the eternal philologist) has found a word for this: "death". Is it really possible to name it? Does it warrant a name? A name is a definition, a "something we already know". So Rozanov defined the essence of his nominalism in a most personal manner: the eternal cognitive movement, the eternal cracking of the nut which comes to nothing because there is no way to gnaw through it.[34]

McGuckian's use of language is neither static nor monological, but metamorphic and dialogical, and it facilitates her assumption of a priest-like role:

---

[32] Medbh McGuckian, "Elegy for an Irish Speaker", in McGuckian, *Captain Lavender*, 42-43.
[33] McGuckian again borrows from Mandelstam's *Collected Prose and Letters*.
[34] Mandelstam, *The Collected Prose*, 124.

Today a kind of speaking in tongues is taking place. In sacred frenzy poets speak the language of all times, all cultures. Nothing is impossible. As *the room of a dying man is open to everyone*, so the door of the old world is flung wide open before the crowd. Suddenly everything becomes public property. Come and take your pick. Everything is accessible: all labyrinths, all secret recesses, all forbidden paths. The word has become not a seven-stop but a thousand-stop flute, brought to life all at once by the breathing of ages. The most striking thing about speaking in tongues is that the speaker does not know the language he is speaking [emphasis added].[35]

The passage from which McGuckian takes her quotation emphasizes the inspired and unconscious manner in which a poet writes. Here she is reiterating the earlier thematics of "Harem Trousers" which contrasted the conscious use of language with what she called the "involuntary window". It is on this level that communication can take place with her father/Mandelstam:

He breaks away from your womb
to talk to me,
he speaks so with my consciousness
and not with words, he's in danger
of becoming a poetess.

The father/Mandelstam are said to be reborn when celebrated in McGuckian's poetry, and a fusion occurs between all three. The fact that the dead do not use "words" confirms the unconscious nature of the exchange. McGuckian deliberately reads Mandelstam's text against the grain and uses her quotation to modify the poles of his word/consciousness binary opposition:

But too often we fail to see that the poet raises a phenomenon to its tenth power, and the modest exterior of a work of art often deceives us with regard to the monstrously condensed reality contained within. In poetry this reality is the word as such. Right now, for instance, in expressing my thoughts as precisely as possible, but certainly not in a poetic manner, *I am essentially speaking with my consciousness, not with the word.*[36]

---

[35]   *Ibid.*, 116.
[36]   *Ibid.*, 61 (italics added).

For Mandelstam, speaking with one's "consciousness" is not poetic and contrasts with the inspired use of "the word", the religious overtones of which re-emphasize the poet's "speaking in tongues". McGuckian subtly alters the quotation by pluralizing "the word" (thereby secularizing it) and by emphasizing the spiritual nature of her communication with the dead. Whereas Mandelstam uses "poetess" as a term of abuse for Mayakovsky,[37] McGuckian's use is wholly positive:

> Most foreign and cherished reader,
> I cannot live without
> your trans-sense language,
> the living furrow of your spoken words
> that plough up time.

Two of her quotations are from passages which she has already referred to in earlier poems. In "Constable's 'Haywain'",[38] McGuckian describes the father's coffin as if it were a funerary ship and she repeats the image here: "How can one equip this ship for its distant voyage, without furnishing it with all the necessities for *so foreign and cherished a reader?*".[39] In "The Dream Language of Fergus",[40] the poet uses a religious register of language when distinguishing the poetic from the non-poetic use of language:

> Not the rudiment
> Of half a vanquished sound,
> The excommunicated shadow of a name ..."

Repeating the reference, she reaffirms her commitment to what is poetic:

> *I cannot live without language,* I cannot survive excommunication from the word. Such, approximately, was Rozanov's spiritual state.

---

[37] *Ibid.*, 147.
[38] Medbh McGuckian, "Constable's *Haywain*", in McGuckian, *Captain Lavender*, 36.
[39] Mandelstam, *The Collected Prose*, 132 (italics added).
[40] Medbh McGuckian, "The Dream Language of Fergus", in McGuckian, *On Ballycastle Beach*, 57.

> The anarchistic, nihilistic spirit recognized only one authority: the
> magic of language, the power of the word ....[41]

While it is obvious from the context that the audience to whom her
poetry is addressed is her father/Mandelstam, the poem's title offers
an alternative reading of what she might mean by "foreign".
McGuckian extends the meaning of "trans-sense language" to include
not only "those transitional forms which succeeded in not being
covered by the semantic crust created by the properly and correctly
developing language",[42] but also the unconscious/uncolonized traces
of the Irish language which reside in McGuckian's father (and,
implicitly, in McGuckian since the two have become one). This is
emphasized by the connection she establishes between land and
language: while not quite "racy of the soil", the "trans-sense
language" is a form of earth writing, creating "the living furrow of
your spoken words / that plough up time". She has need of this
language for a deeper understanding of the past. When she states that:

> Instead of the real past
> with its deep roots,
> I have yesterday

she is quoting Mandelstam's belief that one should study the literature
of *both* the past and the present in order to get a fuller understanding
of both:

> whoever fails to comprehend the new has no sense of the old, while
> whoever understands the old is bound to understand the new.
> Nevertheless, it is our great misfortune when, instead of *the real
> past with its deep roots*, we understand the past merely as
> "yesterday".[43]

Medbh McGuckian's use of quotation does not present the reader
with a collage of decontextualized phrases; rather, she imposes her
own vision upon the array of intertextual references, each of which is
used to achieve a particular effect. In the poems discussed in this
article, her use of Ivinskaya, Tsvetaeva and Mandelstam allows her to
critically examine the ideas of each writer while at the same time

---

[41]   Mandelstam, *The Collected Prose*, 123 (italics added).
[42]   *Ibid.*, 168.
[43]   *Ibid.*, 176.

discussing her own poetic practice. Although such allusive writing tends toward obliquity and produces disjointed, fragmentary texts, the apparent irrationalism is precisely the effect McGuckian strives for, subverting as it does the traditional masculinist preference for linearity and logic. In conclusion, one should begin to celebrate the vast intelligence and intricate beauty of her work, despite (or in spite of) those who persist in writing her poems off as mere "surreal obliquities".

"THAT IS A LIE":
VERBAL DECEIT IN BRIAN FRIEL'S *THE COMMUNICATION CORD*

GIOVANNA TALLONE

"It's a lie, Crystal, all a lie ... I made it all up."[1] In Brian Friel's *Crystal and Fox* (1968) lies have a destructive and a creative power. In his attempt to restore the dream of his past, Fox loses even the deception of his travelling show. Friel's plays are full of liars and their fabrications. They loom largely in the political satire *The Mundy Scheme* and their voices dominate in *The Freedom of the City*. In *Aristocrats* Casimir's impossible tales of family lore are nothing but "phoney fiction".[2] In *Faith Healer*, Frank Hardy is a great fabulist, "whose lies are not to be believed".[3] In *Translations* the unseen presence of Anna na mBréag – Anna of the Lies – is a background to the act of translation that is also an act of violence.[4]

"The language of lies may be innate with the theatrical phenomenon";[5] actions, says Martin Esslin, are "makebelieve", "play is a simulation of reality".[6] The fiction of drama makes "identity ... a construct of performance, the stage an arena of illusion".[7] Everything plays at being.[8] Therefore lies draw attention to the fiction of drama and so become pivotal in structure.

---

[1] Brian Friel, *Crystal and Fox*, London, 1970, 73.
[2] Brian Friel, *Aristocrats* in *Selected Plays of Brian Friel*, intro. Seamus Deane, London, 1984, 278.
[3] Anthony Roche, *Contemporary Irish Drama: From Beckett to McGuinness*, Dublin, 1994, 108.
[4] Brian Friel, *Translations*, London, 1981 (also in *Selected Plays*).
[5] Guido Almansi, "Harold Pinter's Idiom of Lies", in *Contemporary English Drama*, ed. C. W. E. Bigsby, London, 1981, 87.
[6] Martin Esslin, *An Anatomy of Drama*, London, 1976, 19.
[7] John Orr, *Tragicomedy and Contemporary Culture: Plays and Performance from Beckett to Shepard*, London, 1991, 10.
[8] Mary C. King, *The Drama of J. M. Synge*. London, 1985, 106.

Brian Friel's *The Communication Cord* is based on the power of
lies. As in Synge's *Playboy of the Western World*, word becomes
deed, an *Ersatz* to the real thing. *The Communication Cord* is a play of
verbal deceit, in which multiple identities are created and the cultural
construct embedded in "the fiction of romantic Ireland"[9] is displayed
and destroyed, so that the "romantic ideal we call Kathleen"[10] is
turned upside down. That the fiction of romantic Ireland is a fiction is
not new in Brian Friel's plays. In *The Gentle Island* (1971) Peter falls
in love with the western island of Inishkeen, which to him represents
"heaven".[11] Likewise, in *Translations*, another conscious outsider, the
English soldier Yolland, describes his stepping into Ballybeg as "a
momentary sense of discovery".[12] The East-West dichotomy[13] is
reworded in *The Communication Cord* by Senator Donovan as
"restorative power".[14]

Yet, in the three plays place turns out to be a sort of self-sown
myth. Inishkeen is a setting for exile, deceit and violence. Ballybeg is
identified with its dying hedge-school. In *The Communication Cord*
Friel "sees the danger of false romanticizing and an ossification in
self-contemplation".[15] Ballybeg is now a holiday resort visited by
"part time subscribers" to the West of Ireland.[16] Brian Friel has been
authoritative, as he wanted the play to be seen "in tandem with
Translations".[17] So *The Communication Cord* is a sort of translation
of *Translations*,[18] a conscious rewriting of the former play:[19]

9   Elmer Andrews, *The Art of Brian Friel*, London, 1995, 118.
10   Brian Friel, "Plays Peasant and Unpeasant", *Times Literary Supplement*, 17
     March 1972, 306.
11   Brian Friel, *The Gentle Island*, London, 1973 [also Oldcastle, 1993], 25.
12   Friel, *Selected Plays*, 416.
13   Ulf Dantanus, *Brian Friel: A Study*, London, 1988, 14.
14   Brian Friel, *The Communication Cord*, London, 1983 [also Oldcastle, 1989], 38.
15   Jochen Achilles, "Intercultural Relations in Brian Friel's Works", in *The
     Internationalism of Irish Literature and Culture*, ed. Joseph McMinn, Gerrards
     Cross, 1992, 3.
16   Dantanus, *Brian Friel*, 203.
17   Fintan O'Toole, "The Man from God Knows Where", *In Dublin*, 28 October
     1982, 23.
18   Neil Corcoran, "The Penalties of Retrospect: Continuities in Brian Friel", in *The
     Achievement of Brian Friel*, ed. Alan Peacock, Gerrards Cross, 1991, 14.
19   It may have been a coincidence that when *The Communication Cord* was
     premièred by Field Day in Derry in September 1982, on the other side of the
     Atlantic *Translations* was being staged in Ontario, thus enhancing the quality of
     the plays as "companion pieces" (see George O'Brien, *Brian Friel: A Reference*

"*Translations* ... was offered pieties that I didn't intend for it .... And this was one of the reasons I wanted to attempt a farce."[20]

The medium of farce imposes certain expectations, such as improbable coincidences, frenetic activity, untimely entries, embarrassing props disclosed at the wrong time,[21] "objects acquire a life of their own".[22] In fact, in *The Communication Cord* the smoke from the fireplace attacks the protagonist and gusts of wind assail the house, thus adding a subtext of violence to the play. Yet, the perception of farce as some sort of "inferior status"[23] may be responsible for the reception of *The Communication Cord* as an "uproarious departure" for Brian Friel from his "more serious style".[24]

Whatever Friel's intentions in *The Communication Cord*,[25] the play remains problematic in terms of its position within the Friel canon and in terms of reception. It has been read as a language play together with *Faith Healer* and *Translations*[26] or as "a satire of false culture"[27] along with *The Mundy Scheme*, *The Gentle Island* and *The London Vertigo*, whose "manic Anglophilia" matches "the equally manic Hibernophilia" in *The Communication Cord*.[28] When the play was premièred by Field Day in Derry, it was described as the work of a "student who knows the rules of farce but never sees the funny side of it".[29] Alternatively, the consensus on the play was that it was "a major comic performance"[30] in spite of being "a slight work".[31] If it is "not

---

Guide 1962-1992, New York, 1995. The expression "companion pieces" is used by Neil Corcoran, "The Penalties of Retrospect", 17.

[20]   O'Toole, "The Man from God Knows Where", 21.
[21]   See Leslie Smith, *Modern British Farce*, London, 1989, 1-2.
[22]   *Ibid.*, 11.
[23]   *Ibid.*, 5.
[24]   Claudia W. Harris, "The Martyr Wish in Contemporary Irish Dramatic Literature", in *Cultural Contexts and Literary Idioms in Contemporary Irish Literature*, ed. Michael Kenneally, Gerrards Cross, 1988, 266.
[25]   "Friel's attempt in *The Communication Cord* to undermine the 'national classic' status of *Translations* only added to the popular sense of the latter play's significance" (O'Brien, *Brian Friel*, 7). The reference is to the review by Irving Wardle in *The Times*, 9 May 1983, 13.
[26]   Richard Kearney, "Language Play: Brian Friel and Ireland's Verbal Theatre", *Studies*, 72 (Spring 1983), 20-56.
[27]   Andrews, *Art of Brian Friel*, 51.
[28]   *Ibid.*, 234.
[29]   Wardle, in *The Times*, 9 May 1983, 13.
[30]   David Nowlan, "New Friel Fare at Derry Guildhall", *The Irish Times*, 14 September 1982, 8.

one of Friel's most interesting experiments",[32] nevertheless it is seen as "interesting in the questions it provokes".[33] The questions are of various kinds and invest cultural and ideological phenomena as well as theoretical approaches, namely linguistic and theatrical.

As in *Translations*, the setting is the Donegal village of Ballybeg, where the "disused barn"[34] has been replaced by a "'traditional' Irish cottage".[35] The stage directions focus on the self-conscious fictionality of the place. This piece of fake authenticity belongs to Jack McNeilis, a young lawyer, who lends it for a few hours to his friend Tim Gallagher. Tim, a junior lecturer in linguistics, wants to impress his fiancée's father, Senator Doctor Donovan, by pretending to own the place and to cherish it as the "true centre" of Irishness. By doing so, Tim hopes to secure both the girl, Susan, and tenure for himself. A series of mistaken identities, misunderstandings, mistimings and misplacings occur at quite a rapid pace, and end in the collapse of the cottage.

The extremely detailed stage directions in both *Translations* and *The Communication Cord* point out similar props: a double door, a stairway leading upstairs, a churn, even a "battle of hay" which will give rise to a linguistic diversion in *The Communication Cord*. "The remains of five or six stalls"[36] are a priority in the stage directions of *Translations* as they are in the later play.[37] The posts and chains are functional to the farce since at the end of Act One Senator Donovan will chain himself to the wall in an attempt to reproduce the idyllic lifestyle of the Ireland of his mind.

Manus "the lame scholar"[38] in *Translations* is recast as "myopic" Tim;[39] as a lecturer in linguistics, he is also the counterpart of Hugh.[40]

---

[31]   See Fintan O'Toole, "Barriers", *In Dublin*, 28 October 1982), 52, and Dantanus, *Brian Friel*, 206.

[32]   Brian McAvera, "Brian Friel: Attuned to the Catholic Experience", *Fortnight*, 3 March 1985, 20.

[33]   Emelie Fitzgibbon, "All Change: Contemporary Fashions in the Irish Theatre", in *Irish Writers and the Theatre*, ed. Masaru Sekine, Gerrards Cross, 1986, 39.

[34]   Friel, *Selected Plays*, 383.

[35]   Friel, *Communication Cord* (1989), 11.

[36]   *Ibid.*, 60.

[37]   "On the wall left there are three wooden posts complete with chains where cows were chained during milking. (A hundred years ago this was the area of the house where animals were bedded at night.)" Friel, *The Communication Cord*, 11.

[38]   Friel, *Selected Plays*, 432.

[39]   *Ibid.*, 21.

[40]   Andrews, *Art of Brian Friel*, 192.

Owen has turned into Jack: the go-between in *Translations* is now a manipulator in other people's lives. Maire is split between Susan, "a sly, devious and calculating little puss",[41] and Claire, whose unplanned presence in the McNeilis cottage is the motor of the farce. The intensity of the love triangle involving Manus, Maire and Yolland is transformed into "one-night stands and seductions".[42] And if *Translations* is resonant with Greek, Latin and Irish, EU languages and imitated accents fill the space of Ballybeg in *The Communication Cord*.[43] A rich German who wants to buy the cottage and the French girl Evette Giroux are imitated and evoked by other characters in turn before appearing on stage. The cast is completed by a local woman, Nora Dan, who also appears as one of the former pupils in *Translations*.[44]

The Communication Cord is similar to *Translations* in that both can be seen as a treatise on language.[45] Friel reminds us that *Translations* "has to do with language and only language".[46] Likewise, *The Communication Cord* is the exemplification of a linguistic theory, which is verbalized by Tim early in Act One:

> All social behaviour, the entire social order, depends on our communicational structures, on words mutually agreed on and mutually understood. Without that agreement, without that shared code, you have chaos.[47]

And chaos is generated by language twisted into the direction of "pastiche",[48] and for its part it generates farce.

To focus on the farce, however, is to divert attention from the metatheatrical dimension of the play, which is endowed with a variation of the play-within-a-play technique. If Friel's most obvious exploitation of this strategy appears in *Living Quarters*, role play is a

---

41 Friel, *Communication Cord*, 16.
42 Michael Etherton, *Contemporary Irish Dramatists*, London, 1989, 207.
43 Dantanus, *Brian Friel, 203*.
44 "Nora Dan can write her name – Nora Dan's education is complete" (Friel, *Selected Plays*, 398).
45 Deborah Cottreau, "Friel and Beckett: The Politics of Language", in *Literary Interrelations: Ireland, Egypt, and the Far East*, ed. Mary Massoud, Gerrards Cross, 1996, 163.
46 Brian Friel, "Extracts from a Sporadic Diary", in *Ireland and the Arts*, ed. T. P. Coogan, special issue of *Literary Review*, 1983, 58.
47 Friel, *Communication Cord*, 19.
48 George O'Brien, *Brian Friel*, Dublin, 1989, 109.

leitmotif already in *Philadelphia, Here I Come!*, in which Gar O'Donnell performs – he is a music director, a football player, and other personae in turn. In *The Communication Cord* role-playing is magnified and the unity of space is nothing but a void to be filled with roles. The fiction of drama itself is highlighted, so that the play is very much a post-modern concern, preoccupied with its own making. That is the reason why it deserves attention of its own, no matter how significant its correspondences to *Translations* may be.

    Living Quarters revolves around a rehearsal, directed by Sir, who is entrusted with the only copy of the script. In *The Communication Cord*, Jack takes up the role of Sir as authority and director. Sir has a ledger, Jack has his plan, for which he has set a timetable. Early in Act One, when both the audience in the theatre and the audience in the play (Tim) must become acquainted with it, the word "plan" is repeated several times, and is not disjointed from Jack's obsession with timing. When he appears on stage, his first words concern time: "Two and a half hours exactly from the city centre to the bottom of the lane."[49] And time underlies the construction of his plan:

> It's three o'clock exactly ... he [Donovan]'ll have to leave at four thirty at the latest .... You'll have from three thirty until four thirty – one full hour ... I'll disappear for that hour ... and the moment I see them leave I'll return and drive you down to the bus.[50]

    In Friel's "comedy of errors" an echo of Shakespeare's *Comedy of Errors* seeps through, in which the obsessive presence of time – the reference to dinner at five o'clock in particular – is a leitmotif. However, by fixing his plan in words, Jack turns into the author of an unwritten script, he is the director of the make-believe which is about to be staged. In this dramatic metarole, his self-assurance is the confidence of the stage manager, ready to put his plan into practice. Tim's uncertainty is the lack of confidence of the actor who has not learnt his part yet. A polarity is enacted between Jack's timing and Tim, who has forgotten to wind his watch. The opening scene revolves around miscommunication, yet it also strikes a metadramatic note. The cottage door is open, yet Jack gives Tim directions on how to turn the key. The fast interlacing of brief sentences is punctuated by Tim's inconsequential repetition of "Yes":

---

[49]   Friel, *Communication Cord*, 13.
[50]   *Ibid.*, 15-16.

Jack – You're turning the key the wrong way.
Tim – Am I?
Jack – Turn it clockwise – OK?
Tim – Yes.
Jack – Got it now?
Tim – Yes.
Jack – Good.[51]

By obeying fake orders, or by pretending to obey what Jack says, Tim is lying, he is role-playing for him. The gesture of taking the motor-bike helmets off is also significant: dressing and undressing anticipate the assumption of roles on which the play is based. The presence of clothes on stage purposefully exposed and replaced (a nightdress, a waist slip, a bathing suit, a pair of tights) belongs to farce, but is also the metadramatic stage business of changing costumes. Likewise, a settle bed "concealed behind curtains" is nothing but a microcosm of the stage itself, provided with curtain. The "substantial beam of wood" which "supports the floor of [...] [the] loft"[52] is a theatrical device destined to collapse, like the deception which supports the play. Tim also suggests that language is nothing but a form of dressing and undressing, of performing different roles: "Perhaps we are both playing roles here, not only for one another but for ourselves."[53]

Strong features of the Pirandellian issue of masks are present, of the individual being at the same time one, nobody and one hundred thousand. Tim's comments on Jack's expletive "God" actually provides one of the keys to the play: "Maybe – because we're both playing roles, if we're both playing roles – maybe your 'God' is a PRETENCE at surprise, at interest, at boredom."[54]

In Tim's tentative interpretation role-playing is suggested and negated at the same time ("*if* we are playing roles"). Light is shed on pretence, on the fiction which fills the empty space of the cottage. The latter too is cast into a role according to an unwritten script, it is a "traditional cottage", "a love nest", "a miniature museum".[55]

Only an outline of the make-believe exists, however, similar to the guidelines of *Commedia dell'Arte*, in which actors improvise the plot. The text is changed, reduced and magnified. Jack's description of the

---

[51] *Ibid.*, 12.
[52] *Ibid.*, 11.
[53] *Ibid.*, 19.
[54] *Ibid.*, 20.
[55] *Ibid.*, 11, 30, 20.

house repeats the stage directions, the catalogue of objects which Tim
(the actor) cannot repeat before Jack (the director) is repeated before
Senator Donovan (the spectator):

> One double bed ... Fireplace. Usual accoutrements. Tongs. Crook.
> Pot – iron. Kettle – black. Hob. Recess for clay pipes. Stool. Settle
> bed. Curtains for same. Table. Chairs.[56]

This list draws attention to the props as fiction on both the dramatic
and theatrical axis, and is the first of a series of summaries necessary
to highlight the simulation of the script:

> for two furtive hours on a sunny October afternoon *I'm to pretend*
> I'm the owner of a-a-a-a miniature museum just because Susan
> thinks that would impress her pompous father who fancies himself
> as an amateur antiquarian.[57]

The emphasis on pretence enhances the lie that is going to be staged
for the benefit of the spectators on stage. Claire, who is supposed *not*
to be in the script, is cast into the double role of spectator and
participant. "I'm going to enjoy this",[58] she says. Jack McNeilis is also
a spectator; he has no part in his script ("I'll disappear for that hour"),
he watches ("the moment I see them leave") but still supervises in his
authority ("That should be adequate").[59]

   The conscious play-within-a-play goes hand in hand with a
distortion of the "caerimonia nominationis" in *Translations*. The
"intimate genealogy" implicit in the names of Maire Chatach, Sarah
Johnny Sally, Jimmy Jack Cassie[60] is reduced to "the queer way we
have of naming people about here"[61] and replaced by nicknames –
Tim the Thesis, Jack the Cod, Barney the Banks. Names and
renamings proliferate as roles multiply. Tim the Thesis (whom Jack
keeps calling "Professor") is to become Jack as the owner of the
cottage. Jack is cast into the role of Jack the Cod, a local fisherman
and the village idiot, and he enlarges his own script by pretending to
be the German millionaire:

[56]   *Ibid.*, 34; see also 17.
[57]   *Ibid.*, 20 (italics added).
[58]   *Ibid.*, 30.
[59]   *Ibid.*, 16.
[60]   Andrews, *Art of Brian Friel*, 192.
[61]   Friel, *Communication Cord*, 22.

What about this, professor? When Susan and Daddy Senator are here I'll appear *disguised as Barney the Banks* and offer you a fortune for the place.[62]

In this masquerade of self-performances Barney the Banks is a victim. His name is not Willie Hausenbach any more[63] but Barney Munich, then Barney the Banks, so his identity is distorted and reinvented as the violent husband of "Evette"/Claire.[64] Barney assumes that Susan is Evette too. When the real Evette appears on stage halfway through Act Two, the triple split of identity leads to utmost confusion. Nora Dan chooses the role of "a country woman who likes to present herself as a peasant".[65] "She is a stage Irishwoman who has perfected her stagecraft",[66] but is then cast into the role of Nora the Scrambler – "she scrambles on the sand dunes".[67] Senator Doctor Donovan (his titles are already a role) is nicknamed Dr Bollocks, and from the end of Act One to the end of the play he takes up the role of a cow by chaining himself to the wall. Role play as a mimetic art is shed light on three times:

> Nora – He was imitating a cow for us – weren't you? And he did it very well too.[68]

By adding "for us" Nora enhances the pretence of imitation for the sake of an audience. Later on, it is Jack's turn to explain the Senator's condition to Evette Giroux, mixing identity ("That's Susan's father") with role play ("I think he's imitating a cow".[69] A bit earlier, imitation was highlighted as a form of savagery, nearly a violent possession of another identity, and therefore a sin: "Nora [to Jack] – God forgive you imitating poor Barney the Banks like that."[70]

The "echoic character"[71] of the dialogue belongs to the imitative quality of the play. Speeches and words are borrowed or stolen.

---

[62] *Ibid.*, 24 (italics added).
[63] *Ibid.*, 67.
[64] *Ibid.*, 57.
[65] *Ibid.*, 22.
[66] Kearney, "Language Play", 50.
[67] Friel, *Communication Cord,* 47.
[68] *Ibid.*, 68.
[69] *Ibid.*, 78.
[70] *Ibid.*, 67.
[71] Andrews, *Art of Brian Friel*, 195.

Descriptions and stories are repeated nearly verbatim by different characters to different characters. Jack tries to convince Susan to leave the house using the words of another love affair ("Part of me died"[72]). Senator Donovan says "Words are superfluous" to the fake and the real Evette Giroux.[73] Language loses its creative power and is reduced to clichés: for Tim the house is "nice", for Susan it is "unbelievable". Even the rhetoric surrounding the house is as inauthentic as the "traditional" cottage, so that Jack uses the syntax of religion as another set of borrowed words: "This is where we all come from. This is our first cathedral. This shaped our souls. This determined our first pieties."[74]

Jack's honesty[75] in his attitude towards a past he does not believe in is contrasted by Tim in a sort of play-within-a-play-within-a-play. Tim talks to Barney taking him for Jack; his speech revolves on a double axis, it is "true" communication (to the wrong persona) in a low voice, but at the same time his recital of Jack's "religion" for an audience (Susan and Donovan) is marked by speaking aloud:

> Gulder man! You're supposed to gulder. (Loudly) This is our first cathedral, isn't it? The question is: are we worthy of it? (Softly) D'you know what she wants me to do? Take her scrambling! On Nora Dan's motorbike![76]

Nora Dan's exchanges with other characters are characterized by the continuous repetition of the last word or phrase of her interlocutor, e.g.:

> Donovan – Back to the true centre.
> Nora – The true centre, surely.[77]

This binary rhythm sheds light on dramatic antagonism. By doing so Nora seems to be pursuing him, trying to take possession of the other as she would like to take possession of the place. This kind of sing-song may have the effect of comic relief, yet it suggests a form of violence that is embedded in the text.

---

[72]   Friel, *Communication Cord*, 25, 73.
[73]   *Ibid.*, 36, 79.
[74]   *Ibid.*, 15.
[75]   Dantanus, *Brian Friel*, 203.
[76]   Friel, *Communication Cord*, 52.
[77]   *Ibid.*, 46.

Likewise, questions run after each other and parts of the dialogues are a continuous follow up of question marks, with semantic blanks. In the Tim-Jack exchange early in Act One, both questions and question-tags make each sentence end with a question mark:

> Jack – You took her out a few times yourself, didn't you?
> Tim – Claire?
> Jack – We all thought that was terminal at the time. What happened between you?
> Tim – Between Claire and me?
> Jack – That's who we're talking about, isn't it?[78]

This is accompanied by a reiteration of hesitations and pauses, graphically rendered by dots and dashes, on the part of Tim: "Yes ... oh that was years ago ... a student thing ... she–she–she– there was nothing much to –."[79] The hesitations in Tim's fragmented and faltering answer match with the pressing of questions just before that. Besides expressing restraint at exposing feelings and taking time, delaying the reply, they also contribute to build up a defensive mask with question marks, the search for the most appropriate role for the moment.

An expansion of the litany of repetition occurs in the comic interlude in which Tim is questioned by Senator Donovan about the cottage he is assumed to possess:

> Donovan – What did you thatch with?
> Tim – Thatch.
> Donovan – Straw or bent?
> Tim – Straw.
> Donovan – It's warmer than bent but not as enduring. Do you find that?
> Tim – It's not as enduring but it's warmer.
> Donovan – Right. What sort of scollops?
> Tim – Oh, the usual.
> Donovan – Hazel or sally?
> Tim – Hazel.

---

[78] *Ibid.*, 14.
[79] *Ibid.*, 15.

> Donovan – Not as resilient but they last longer. Is that your
> experience?
> Tim – They last longer but they're not as resilient.[80]

The double chiasmus magnifies the device of borrowed words; it is a
variation of Nora Dan's catch-up phrase, but it is also a comic
variation of the Maire–Yolland love scene, in which the chiasmus of
incomprehension is more revealing than words:

> Maire – The grass must be wet. My feet are soaking.
> Yolland – Your feet must be wet. The grass is soaking.[81]

The verbal smokescreen[82] makes *The Communication Cord* a tale
of total deceit. In it every character is both deceiver and deceived,
actor/protagonist in the production of lies and victim of these
fabrications. The double axis is expressed by Tim, too, in terms of
linguistic and communicational devices: "We can hardly explain the
individual as being simultaneously creator and creation of his own
communicational possibilities."[83] The script itself is both creator and
creation; by being unwritten it is fluid and flexible. Roles are created,
destroyed and reinvented, expanded and diluted. Tim's thesis itself on
response cries is fluid, as at the end of the play Tim admits he will
have to rewrite/recreate most of it.

And in the final part of the play there is an intensification of
deception. The repeated words "lie", "lies", expressions like "skilled
liar" and "lying bastard"[84] are by themselves a form of conscious and
potential aggression, in that each character in turn is a victim of the
script, which is a lie. The two sentences Claire/Evette is supposed to
master – "That is a lie" and "I understand perfectly" – are defined by
Donovan as "a précis of life".[85] As a matter of fact they are also a
précis of the play and work on the metanarrative/metadramatic
dimension drawing attention to the construction. The same sentence

---

[80]   *Ibid.*, 33.
[81]   Friel, *Selected Plays*, 426.
[82]   Ginette Verstraete, "Brian Friel's Drama and the Limits of Language", in *History
       and Violence in Anglo-Irish Literature*, eds Joris Duytschaever and Geert Lernout,
       Amsterdam, 1988, 86.
[83]   Friel, *Communication Cord*, 36.
[84]   *Ibid.*, 71-72.
[85]   *Ibid.*, 35-36.

"That is a lie" is reiterated in Act Two by Jack who, by denying inviting Evette to Ballybeg, denies also his own script.[86]

An innuendo of violence takes over in the scene at the end of Act One in which Donovan tied to the wall becomes the victim of unexpected verbal and physical violence on the part of Nora: "Stand still, you brute you, or I'll hop the stick off you!"[87] The comic facet of this disquieting episode is revealing of the way in which the world of *The Communication Cord* – the plan and the make-believe – has turned upside down. As it is gradually disclosed as a fabrication in Act Two, the script crumbles down, as the cottage collapses at the end of the play.

"What a bloody day! A total disaster in every respect",[88] exclaims Jack, planner, schemer, director, author, rejecting the lies he has performed in his own playhouse in Ballybeg. As the actors retreat, words also retreat. "Maybe", says Tim, "silence is the perfect discourse".[89]

---

[86] *Ibid.*, 81.
[87] *Ibid.*, 63.
[88] *Ibid.*, 90.
[89] *Ibid.*, 92.

ANOTHER HISTORY OF IRISH LITERATURE:
CREATING SPACES FOR THE HOMOSEXUAL IN IRISH PROSE

KLAUS-GUNNAR SCHNEIDER

The men of Easter 1916 – and particularly Patrick Pearse – were much inclined to envisage the Irish nation they fought for in quite outspokenly masculine terms:

> I hold that before we can do any work, any *men's* work, we must first realize ourselves as men. Whatever comes to Ireland she needs men.[1]

In the very text of the Proclamation of the Irish Republic on Easter Monday 1916 the assertion of Irish independence thus becomes an assertion of the manhood of the Irish nation, producing a rather ironic clash with the pronouns used to denote Ireland: "Having organized and trained *her manhood ... she* strikes in full confidence of victory."[2]

When the young London actor Alfred Willmore in the years running up to the Irish revolution decided to take classes in the Irish language, to change his name into the Irish Micheál MacLiammóir, and finally, in March 1917, to travel to Dublin in order to join a London theatre company on their tour through the West of Ireland, I am sure he was quite unaware of the finer points in the gender politics of the nationalist Irish revolution. Yet regarding utterances such as Pearse's, which are very much in tune with the common stereotype of Ireland's rather problematic relation to issues of gender and sexual identity, it comes as a surprise that Alfred Willmore not only decided to make Ireland, namely Dublin, his permanent home together with his lifelong partner Hilton Edwards, but also to re-invent himself

---

[1] Patrick Pearse, "The Coming Revolution", in *The Field Day Anthology of Irish Writing*, ed. Seamus Deane, Derry, 1991, II, 557 (italics added).

[2] Text of the proclamation taken from R. F. Foster, *Modern Ireland, 1600-1972*, Harmondsworth, 1989, 597-98.

exclusively as Irish, changing not only his name, but also his birth-place from London to Cork.

As Éibhear Walshe has argued in detail, part and parcel of MacLiammóir's interest in this role-playing was his homosexuality and his conflict with prevailing social norms of gender and sexuality resulting from this:

> Michael MacLiammoir [*sic*], Cork-born Irish actor and writer never actually existed. It was a name and personal history conjured up by London-born actor Alfred Willmore, when he left England for Ireland in 1917. Alfred Willmore, born in Kensal Green in London in 1899, had no Irish connection whatsoever .... More acutely, he was ... seeking, in the aftermath of the Wilde trials, an acceptable persona within which to be both homosexual and, at the same time, visible.[3]

The consciously employed mechanisms of MacLiammóir's identity re-invention inform much of his dramatic work as writer, director and actor and find expression most clearly in his one-man show *The Importance of Being Oscar* and his play *Prelude in Kazbeck Street*.

The significance of MacLiammóir's story at the beginning of this essay is that in re-enacting himself as Irish in order to give voice to his homosexual identity, he consciously employs Ireland as a place of and Irishness as a metaphor of homosexuality. Micheál MacLiammóir, like his model Oscar Wilde a few decades before,[4] was obviously, and quite successfully, able to see and make a connection between these two allegedly wildly different things – of being Irish and being homosexual. Comparing Pearse and MacLiammóir, it is the question of the apparently highly ambivalent relation between these two sets of identities, Irishness and homosexuality, which prompts my investigation into representations of the homosexual in Irish prose writing in the twentieth century.

The homosexual, as the publication of Éibhear Walshe's collection *Sex, Nation and Dissent in Irish Writing* in 1997 signifies, has not played any significant part so far in the writing of Irish literary history. Taking the ambivalence in the relation between Irishness and

---

3   Éibhear Walshe, "Sodom and Begorrah, or Game to the Last: Inventing Michael MacLiammoir", in *Sex, Nation and Dissent in Irish Writing*, ed. Éibhear Walshe, Cork, 1997, 151.
4   Cf. David Alderson, "Momentary Pleasures: Wilde and English Virtue", in *Sex, Nation and Dissent*, 43-59.

homosexuality I have just outlined as a starting point, I will argue that an engagement with concepts of identity in gay and lesbian Irish writings allows a radical deconstruction of those fundamental concepts of identity that presently form the basis of received understandings of Irish literature. By focusing on the significance of semantic organization of space and place in five paradigmatically chosen texts I will in the first part of the essay show in what sense it is possible to speak of a homosexual tradition in Irish writing. My central thesis is that the homosexually identifiable subject is an end product of this tradition, depending on its discursive forms of representation, rather than its transcendental point of origin. The second part will, again in a paradigmatic analysis of semantic spaces in a fictional text, discuss how recent homosexual writing has developed an awareness of the historic constructedness of gay and lesbian identities. On this basis I will finally draw the conclusion indicated in the title of my essay of how homosexual Irish writing may constitute an Other history of Irish literature.

"Productive perversions" – James Joyce's "An Encounter"

James Joyce's short story "An Encounter" in *Dubliners* tells the story of two young boys setting out on their first adventurous excursion into the Dublin beyond their immediate neighbourhood. On their otherwise rather unexciting tour they encounter an old man, "a queer old josser", as they call him, who first engages them in a surprisingly liberal conversation about girl-friends and a rather less liberal talk about chastising rough and unruly boys and then leaves them to masturbate in their sight at "the near end of the field":

> After a long while his monologue paused. He stood up slowly, saying that he had to leave us for a minute or so, a few minutes, and, without changing the direction of my gaze, I saw him walking slowly away from us towards the near end of the field. We remained silent when he had gone. After a silence of a few minutes I heard Mahoney exclaim:
> – I say! look what he's doing![5]

What is significant in this extract is the combination of narrative focalization and the semantic structuring of space. Using a first-person

---

[5]   James Joyce, *Dubliners* (1914), in *The Essential James Joyce*, ed. Harry Levin, London, 1997, 34.

narrator to portray the action, Joyce firmly establishes a sense of centre in the text. The gaze of the first-person narrator sets the fictional world into perspective for the reader. Thus, the homoerotic act is explicitly projected on to the margin of this world and appears only in a mediated form through the consciousness of this narrator, effectively distancing the reader from it. Linguistically, this projection of the homosexual on to the margin is reflected in the silence the narrator keeps over the actual happenings. In the decisive moment of the narration the narrator retreats – or should I say, hides – behind his characters and leaves a blank space in the narrative, sufficiently encoded to make sense, in order to escape actually having to name the action. Therefore the text thus makes use of the homosexual as something "other" than Irish society, a threat to the symbolic order of Irish culture which nevertheless initially fascinates the narrator. The protagonist's failure in this story, which in the context of *Dubliners* stands as an example of the general paralysis diagnosed in Irish society, is his breakdown faced with this threat and his subsequent retreat into the clear-cut gender roles of the symbolic order personified in the protagonist's friend Mahoney, whom he calls for help.[6]

Though Joyce's story does not at all draw simplistic conclusions and is far more complex in relation to gender roles than can be indicated here, it still serves well as an example of the potential of the homosexual to function as a literary code of Otherness. In George Moore's *A Drama in Muslin*, a similar potential can be identified in the fate of his lesbian character Cecilia Cullen and this kind of homosexual Otherness informs texts throughout the twentieth century by many Irish authors, such as Maurice Leitch, Dermot Bolger, Danny Morrison, William Trevor or Jennifer Johnston, to name just a few.

The birth of the homosexual subject
"Internal exiles" in Forrest Reid's Uncle Stephen

If such texts project the homosexual as an Other on to the margins of Irish society, Forrest Reid's novel *Uncle Stephen*, published in 1931,[7] searches for a position of his focal character exactly within such a fictional space situated on the margins of the social world. The novel

---

[6] For a detailed analysis of these aspects of the story, see Garry M. Leonard, "The Detective and the Cowboy: Desire, Gender, and Perversion in 'An Encounter'", in *Reading Dubliners Again: A Lacanian Perspective*, ed. Garry M. Leonard, Syracuse: NY, 1993, 56-72.

[7] Forrest Reid, *Uncle Stephen*, Leyburn: North Yorkshire, 1931.

tells the story of Tom Barber's boyhood. At age fifteen, following his father's death, he runs away from his home with his stepmother's family, prompted by a yet uncertain sense of his difference. He seeks out his Uncle Stephen and in his relation to him finally asserts his homoerotic sensibility. In the course of the story his difference gains a name: "I love Uncle Stephen", Tom tells his step-family towards the end of the novel just before he and Stephen embark upon a trip to the Mediterranean in search of the ancient Greek way of living.

The world of Uncle Stephen, his manor house in the country with its extensive grounds surrounding it, to which Tom retreats from the restrictive social world of his stepmother's house in the city, is a distinct other-world, clearly set apart as a place of Tom's homosexual self. This he comes to realize in the act of consciously crossing "the boundary-line between two worlds":

> Then [Tom] turned round and through the gate looked into the green avenue from which he had just emerged. Within *there*, was something not so simple. While he lingered there deepened in him a strange impression that he was on the boundary-line between two worlds ... one world ... stretched all round these stone walls, but within them was the other, and as soon as he passed through that gate he would become a part of the other. Here he was free to choose, but if he took a step further all would be different. What he should enter seemed to him now a kind of dream-world, but once inside, he knew it would become real .... He took a little run forward, tugged at the bar, pushed: and the latch dropped back into place as the gate clanged behind him.[8]

The world of Tom's awakening to his homosexuality is as much positioned on the margins of society as was the "queer old josser" in Joyce's "An Encounter". What is different here is that the narrative focus in *Uncle Stephen* directs the reader right into this other world, thereby emancipating the edge of the field in Joyce's story into a full-blown, distinct world of its own. Using a strongly focalized third-person narrator, Reid makes the reader follow Tom when he metaphorically probes deeper and deeper into the jungle-like woods on Stephen's manor ground. And slowly, what was a threatening wilderness becomes a lively place of self, accessible by an ever widening path:

---

[8]   *Ibid.*, 83.

> The track through the wood had become a path .... He kept it clear, not only by tramping it daily, but also by vigorously swinging a stick; and gradually it was widening".[9]

"External exiles" in Kate O'Brien's Mary Lavelle

If Forrest Reid's hero Tom Barber in search of an understanding of his self chooses to retreat into this world of an internal exile in Ireland and thus creates a rather introverted and self-absorbed kind of literature, Kate O'Brien's fiction engages much more directly and openly with issues of sexual politics by sending all her homosexual characters into exile from Ireland. For them exile is the only way of negotiating a place for themselves in between desire and cultural origin.

In Kate O'Brien's *Mary Lavelle* Spain, which provides the setting of the story, is identified as a place where Mary intends to spend just a year as "a tiny hiatus between her life's two accepted phases. To cease being a daughter without immediately being a wife." Spain is from the very outset of the novel constructed as a foreign place of difference and the "Other" which is at the same time also strangely familiar. On arrival in Spain, Mary writes to her fiancé:

> I wish I knew how to describe this place so as to make it real to you – but I never could. You see, it's entirely unlike everything you and I know, but it's not a bit like my idea of Spain – or yours, I imagine. And if I say that already after twenty-four hours I feel familiar with it, you'll say I'm mad.[10]

This strangely familiar foreign place has become the home of Agatha Conlon, like Mary herself one of the Irish Misses working for wealthy Spanish families. The masculine violence of the bullfight is the novel's central metaphor for Agatha's homosexuality, which is thus depicted in close relation to the contemporary sexological theory of inversion. The character of Stephen Gordon in Radclyff Hall's famous novel *The Well of Loneliness* (1928) provided the foil for the conception of Agatha's character. Inviting Mary to accompany her to one of these bullfights is Agatha's declaration of her love for Mary: a love however that remains unrequited. Instead of Agatha, Mary falls in love with Juanito, the oldest and married son of the family Mary works for.

---

[9]   *Ibid.*, 172.
[10] Kate O'Brien, *Mary Lavelle*, London, 1936, 6.

It is exactly this complication of matters that makes Kate O'Brien's novel a significant point on the map of the homosexual in Irish literature. Sending her characters into Spanish exile is not just a means of metaphorically creating possibilities of writing a homosexual love story. It is not in the homosexual nature of Agatha's feelings of love for Mary that O'Brien finds her central theme. Rather, the homosexuality of Agatha is turned into a given fact of the story. It is in the comparison and parallelization of Agatha's form of loving with Mary's involvement with Juanito that O'Brien makes "not a special plea for lesbians, but ... for sexual self-determination", as Emma Donoghue has argued.[11]

Therefore the Otherness within herself Mary discovers in Spain consists of nothing but those other possibilities of realizing one's emotional relationships that the accepted order of the centre by implication of its own definition projects on to the horizon of cultural discourse. For Mary Lavelle this discovery will forever thwart the possibility of returning to the ordered world of her home town and marrying her fiancé. Like Agatha, though in a very different way, Mary, at the end of her time in Spain, has become a wanderer in between the world of fixed orders, forever seeking out places of her own. Talking about *Mary Lavelle*, Emma Donnoghue has wonderfully paraphrased this basic idea in O'Brien's writing: "The longings [of her characters] do not form a sewer, a pit, a cage – merely a tangle, because people rarely long for each other in neat couples."[12]

"Gay Realism" in-between psychiatric wards and cruising areas
Re-membering the past in John Broderick's The Waking of Willy Ryan

The next turn in the "the way in which sex is 'put into discourse'", as Foucault phrased it, are attempts to make such marginal voices as those created by Forrest Reid or Kate O'Brien heard in the centre. And again, a shift in the aesthetics of representing the homosexual goes along with it. If the homosexual is symbolic of Otherness in Joyce and metaphorically utopian in Reid and O'Brien, I am inclined to term this next step the "realist turn" in Irish homoerotic fiction.

This turn to realism brings the central character's exile from society that constituted the basic background situation of Reid's and

[11] Emma Donoghue, "'Out of Order': Kate O'Brien's Lesbian Fictions", in *Ordinary People Dancing: Essays on Kate O'Brien*, ed. Éibhear Walshe, Cork, 1993, 39.
[12] *Ibid.*, 46.

O'Brien's novels to an end, as in John Broderick's *The Waking of Willy Ryan*, published 1965.[13] Willie Ryan's enforced exile in the mental home, to which he had been committed by his family with the friendly support of the local priest twenty years earlier, ends at the beginning of the novel. Willie's return to his home town disrupts the official story of his madness, told by his home town and family, by means of another version of the events, thus telling a bleak and tragic story of the impossibility of homosexual life in Ireland, reminiscent in many ways of the social realism of nineteenth-century English literature. For his family and the community of his home town, Willie Ryan's escape from the mental home is the return of the repressed, the return of what had been projected as the Other beyond the borders of society.

If I suggest that this step should be termed a "realist turn" in the history of gay Irish writing, this is meant in a specific sense in relation to the earlier texts I have discussed. In these gay realist texts the homosexual is neither a mere symbolic means, a literary device for commenting on some other topic, as it was the case in the Joyce text, nor is the homosexual to be sought out in the subtext of these fictions, camouflaged behind a curtain of metaphors and thus suggesting a utopian potential of sexual self-determination, as was the case with Reid and O'Brien. Instead, in texts like Broderick's *The Waking of Willy Ryan* the homosexual becomes the explicit, unambiguous denotative meaning of the surface structure. Broderick's text suggests that it breaks the veil of symbolic and metaphoric significations of the homosexual and suggests itself as realist in this sense.

Re-presenting the present in Keith Ridgway's "Graffiti"
This realist construction of a homosexual collective past of oppression and suffering in Broderick is, almost necessarily I am tempted to say, followed by a turn towards the present. In fact, the "Project of Modernity", to use Habermas' term, at this point in history requires and morally sanctions a depiction of the homosexual in as much detail as possible. Thus the strategy of constructing complex fictional spaces of the homosexual becomes obsolete. Such a literature will rather seek to throw open the door of the gay closet and show in detail all the places of gay life as it – supposedly – happens *in* Ireland. An extract

---

[13] John Broderick, *The Waking of Willy Ryan*, London, 1965.

from the beginning of Keith Ridgway's "Graffiti" will, I believe, suffice to clarify my point of breaking the secrecy of the gay closet:

> "Hi."
> "Hi."
> "What are you into?"
> "I love to be sucked."
> "So do I."
> The man with the bottle green-jeans moved up against him and rubbed his crotch gently, finding his hard-on and gripping it through his trousers. They opened each other's belts and buttons and zips and caressed each other's cocks and balls. The man in the bottle-green jeans pushed his hand through the other man's legs to find his hole and to rub his buttocks. To do this he had to crouch slightly. Then he went down on his knees and took the man's cock into his mouth, sucking it gently at first and then moving his head back and forth. (32)

The explicit and detailed portrayal of gay sex, which flies in the face of traditional morality, in a text that is in the context of its publication explicitly marked as literature distinctly expressive of gay Irish identity rather than a text catering for baser instincts is, so to speak, the climax of what I termed "gay realism". Its underlying socio-political rather than literary idea is to liberate the homosexual from the prison of a marginal social existence and establish him/her centre stage.

Gay identity as an act of narration

So far then, this culmination of the history of the homosexual in Irish writing, which began with the symbolic euphemism of the Joyce text answered by the metaphoric marginal landscapes of Reid and O'Brien, coincides significantly in the realism of place and action in Broderick and Ridgway with Michel Foucault's summary of present conceptions of the homosexual in Western culture under the heading of the "repressive hypothesis" in his *History of Sexuality*. The narrative history of homosexuality, which Foucault finds generally accepted, is that of oppression and, more importantly, identification with this history of oppression. Foucault then poses the question of how to evaluate this view of the repressed homosexual:

> The question I would like to pose is not, Why are we repressed? but rather, Why do we say, with so much passion and so much resentment against our most recent past, against our present, and

against ourselves, that we are repressed? .... What led us to show, ostentatiously, that sex is something we hide, to say it is something we silence? And we do all this by formulating the matter in the most explicit terms, by trying to reveal it in its most naked reality.[14]

This last sentence in particular seems to relate directly to the Irish literary history of the homosexual I have outlined so far. Quite literally, texts like Ridgway's reveal gay sexuality in its most naked terms. The problem Foucault raises for a discussion of my topic is in what sense it is legitimate to unify the texts I have discussed in one tradition under the term "homosexual"; in what sense is it viable to speak of a homosexual tradition in Irish writing?

Aware of recent theoretical problems with such unifying terms as "tradition", Éibhear Walshe, in the Introduction to his collection *Sex, Nation and Dissent in Irish Writing*, was careful to make it quite clear that his book does not claim that gay and lesbian writing "constitutes a coherent tradition".[15] Yet despite this disclaimer of the idea of a homosexual tradition, he quotes Elaine Showalter to legitimize his subject: "When women are studied as a group, their history and experience reveal patterns which are almost impossible to perceive if they are studied only in relation to male writers."[16] In other words, Walshe wants to study homosexual writers as a group. Therefore, Walshe substitutes the concept of "tradition", which he finds problematic, with the concept of the "homosexual writer", which is in no respect less problematic. In Walshe's perspective, the homosexual author as a member of the group of homosexuals – and, additionally, the critic's knowledge about this homosexuality – becomes an unidentified prerequisite to the study of the homosexual in a literary text. Thus without any doubts, the homosexual is presumed as existent and identifiable, knowable. The homosexual is projected as the only authority to speak authentically about homosexuality.

My inclusion of Joyce and Broderick into the "homosexual tradition" in Irish writing – presuming that their difficulties in qualifying for Walshe's league of homosexual writers are easily settled – tries to make a different point. What has emerged from my

---

[14] Michel Foucault, *The History of Sexuality, I: An Introduction*, Harmondsworth, 1990, 8-9.
[15] Éibhear Walshe, "Introduction: Sex, Nation and Dissent", in *Sex, Nation and Dissent*, 1.
[16] Quoted in Walshe, "Introduction", 2.

analysis is that these texts, in dealing with same sex desire or relations, do not share any essential feature or characteristic that could be used to define a concept of a homosexual aesthetic, and thereby validating in turn the idea of an essential homosexuality. Instead, moving from narrative modes of ellipsis and euphemism via metaphor and comparison to realism, this tradition of narrative techniques brings the homosexual into being by constructing its knowability in the forms of signification – and it is exactly on these forms that approaches like Walshe's depend. The homosexual as an identified subject emerges only at the end of this tradition, not at its beginning. The homosexual as a meaningful way of making definite sense of an experience appears as the result of a tradition of ruptures and shifts in the forms of thinking about same sex desires and acts, rather than as a recognition of some inherent essential quality in a unitary and coherent tradition of writings based on such a quality.

What strikes me as significant from a cultural studies point of view is that the seminal texts of this tradition – in the case of my presentation here James Joyce's "An Encounter" – appear not as authentic self-assertions of homosexual voices or even authors, but rather as projections of homosexual Otherness when talking about Irish culture and conceptions of Irishness. Seen from this perspective, the realism of texts like Ridgway's "Graffiti" appear less as truthful and genuinely authentic expressions of a formerly suppressed essence of gayness than as revelations of identities carefully constructed in terms of dominant discourse formations and even more carefully hidden away in the process of defining the centre of Irish culture. The shifting forms of the representation of the homosexual in literature bear witness to the historic process of constructing and bringing into being gay and lesbian identity; they are – in the Foucauldian sense – monuments, not documents, of the history of the making of homosexual identity.[17]

---

[17] In this sense the history of the homosexual in Irish culture does not of course vary greatly from that in Western culture in general. It is, to stay in Foucauldian terminology, connected to the same epistematic shift from the classic to the modern age which Foucault describes in *The Order of Things: An Archaeology of the Human Sciences*, New York, 1970.

"Gay metafiction" – Deconstructing gay identity in Padraig Rooney's "Tabernacles"

Padraig Rooney's short story "Tabernacles", which was included in David Marcus's anthology *Alternative Loves* published in the wake of the law reforms in 1994, seems to me to be a text that is devised in awareness of this history of the homosexual as a form of thought, a discursive organization of human experience. Such awareness, I would argue, constitutes a recent fundamental revision in the thinking of the homosexual that manifests itself in the form of what I call homosexual metafiction. Again, this shift is recognizable in the structuring of semantic space in Rooney's story. "Tabernacles" is a story of homosexual initiation. It tells of the first attraction of the unnamed first-person narrator to a fellow boy in the local church choir acted out weekly at Sunday mass. His initiation takes place in the interior space of the spire of the church's clock tower:

> I imagined ourselves as having been chased to the spire. I imagined, point blank. *This* point, the here and now. And all the rest a kind of panlogism which the spire was the centre of, I its inhabiting spirit, a *deus in machina*, endlessly inverting myself into existence.

Beyond the walls of this interior space lies an outside world which in its very orderliness has the church tower as its centre:

> The shadow of the spire was thrown across the white-lined parking spaces in front of the episcopal palace by the bright morning sunshine, like an ink-stain, or a long, slim pen on dark paper. It seemed such a nice peaceful world outside in the exterior air. Already the people were going to their cars. And the cars would go to the newspaper shops.[18]

So the birth of the narrator's homosexual self happens as an inversion of the ordered world; not as a projection beyond the borders of the norm, but in a space right within the centre of control – a space necessarily created when the church tower had been designed as the centre overlooking its surroundings. The homosexual subject comes into itself as an imagination of "having been chased" to the spire, thus becoming the "inhabiting spirit" of the space within the centre; the homosexual is "a *deus in machina*".

[18]   Padraig Rooney, "Tabernacles", in *Alternative Loves*, ed. David Marcus, Dublin, 1994, 103.

In this structuring of its semantic spaces, "Tabernacles" dramatizes what Foucault theoretically formulated as the indistinguishable dependency of discourse and counter-discourse:

> To be more precise, we must not imagine a world of discourse divided between accepted discourse and excluded discourse, or between the dominant discourse and the dominated one; but as a multiplicity of discursive elements that come into play in various strategies .... Discourses are not once and for all subservient to power or raised up against it .... Discourse transmits and produces power; it reinforces it, but also undermines and exposes it, renders it fragile and makes it possible to thwart it ... it also makes possible the formation of a reverse discourse: homosexuality began to speak in its own behalf, to demand that its legitimacy or "naturality" be acknowledged, often in the same vocabulary, using the same categories by which it was medically disqualified.[19]

Therefore Rooney's short story comes to stand paradigmatically for a position in the history of gay writing which confidently narrates its homosexuality as a given fact of a present discursive reality, while at the same time being aware of the historic cultural constructedness of homosexual identity and the problematic relation between homosexual experience and homosexual identity that results from this constructedness. By being designed in relation to the concept of heterosexuality, any presumably assured sense of homosexual identity as a collective quality threatens the open-ended realm of individual sexual experience by its potential to operate, like heterosexuality, as a definition of "normal" human behaviour.

Because of his homosexuality, the homosexual has to act as a homosexual. Additionally, only the homosexual is allowed to do so, which is why the moment of the Coming Out presently remains the most significant turning point in the narrative of one's own homosexual identity.[20] As a result, the homosexual subject may find himself locked away in what turns out to be the prison-house of his homosexuality and the potentially disruptive force of homosexual experience in a heterocentric culture is neatly contained. Rather than merely liberating the homosexual, allowing and accepting homo-

---

[19] Foucault, *History of Sexuality I*, 100-101.
[20] The relevance of the Coming Out in gay and lesbian identity politics finds an equivalent in the importance of the Coming Out novel in the history and constitution of gay and lesbian literature. A current Irish example of this genre is Colm Tóibín, *The Story of the Night*.

sexuality in an abstract concept of the homosexual is also recognizable as an effective means of keeping the distance between the heterosexual centre and its homosexual margin and is in fact often employed to strengthen that centre.

A cracked looking-glass to the nation: the importance of Gay Irish Studies

Kieran Rose's account of the Gay and Lesbian Movement in Ireland up to that historic moment in the summer of 1993 serves as an example of such processes of containing subversive potential; and this brings me back to the issue of how Irishness and homosexuality relate to each other as two different concepts of identity. In discussing Rose's "idea that these changes [in the legal situation of gays and lesbians] stem from positive traditional Irish values arising from the anti-colonial struggle"[21] as a conclusion to my essay I am going to point out in what sense I see a possibility of using an engagement with the homosexual in Irish literature as a productive deconstruction of received perceptions of Irish literature and the relation of these perceptions to cultural identity politics in Ireland. An engagement with the Irish literary history of the homosexual may indeed result in an Other history of Irish literature.

Rose's conviction about the "positive traditional Irish values" rubs problematically against David Norris' often quoted phrase from the early years of the Gay and Lesbian Movement in Ireland: "There remained in the minds of many people until recently a doubt as to whether the terms 'Irish' and 'Homosexual' were not mutually exclusive."[22] Obviously, what has happened here between 1981 and 1993 is a radical transformation in perceiving the relation between Irish nationalist and homosexual ideology. Rather than disrupting a simplistically positive perception of Irishness, as David Norris' statement did, Kieran Rose's thesis achieves the direct opposite, endorsing the notion of a wrongly suppressed traditional Irishness. And a look at Éibhear Walshe's collection *Sex, Nation and Dissent in Irish Writing* seems to suggest that this transformation may be a current trend in perceiving the relation between Irish nationalism and the homosexual.

---

[21]   Kieran Rose, *Diverse Communities: The Evolution of Lesbian and Gay Politics in Ireland*, Cork, 1994, 3.

[22]   David Norris, "Homosexual People and the Christian Churches in Ireland", *The Crane Bag*, 2 (1981), 31.

Walshe wholeheartedly endorses Kieran Rose's thesis when he argues that "Ireland provides a striking example of ... post-colonial censorship".[23] Ultimately, he suggests, it is the English influence that prompted the suppression of the homoerotic within Irish nationalist discourse. Consequently Walshe is eager to locate the homoerotic "quite close to the source of national pride and identity" and even asserts that "Irish lesbian and gay writing, in common with most other Irish writing, evinces a connection and a preoccupation with politicized Irish nationalism".[24] An endorsement of the Irish homosexual obviously has developed into a viable strategy of reinforcing nationalist thinking which had fallen into disrepute in the light of debates about the implications of post-structuralist and post-modernist ideas for perceptions of history.

Looking through the material presented in Walshe's book, however, might also suggest that this connection he makes between political nationalism and gay and lesbian identity politics is a tenuous one. To give just one example: in his pioneering study of W. B. Yeats' early work Forrest Reid, one of the authors discussed in Walshe's collection, concluded that "Whether Ireland is to have a literature or not depends upon whether she can evolve an artistic conscience – at present she has only a political one".[25] Such scepticism about the artistic usefulness of a "connection and preoccupation with politicized Irish nationalism" hardly suggests a natural affiliation between homosexual and national experiences in twentieth-century Ireland.

Instead, what I have tried to argue in my analysis of the first five texts by Joyce, Reid, O'Brien, Broderick and Ridgway is how a tradition developed in Irish writing which might be termed "homosexual" on the basis that it formed part of a discursive construction of the idea of the homosexual subject. Within this historic process the homosexual came into existence as a negative foil in the attempt to positively re-define Irishness. Recently, however, within this homosexual tradition there developed a sense of this historic cultural constructedness that allowed it to reflect on essentialist understandings of one's own identity. Not least in the light of Michel Foucault's work, there has been a growing awareness within gay subculture of the basis on which homosexual self-

---

[23]   Walshe, "Introduction", 6.
[24]   *Ibid.*, 3.
[25]   Forrest Reid, *W. B. Yeats: A Critical Study*, London, 1915, quoted in Russell Burlingham, *Forrest Reid: A Portrait and a Study*, London, 1953, 18.

identification has become possible. Reflecting on this awareness, literary texts like Padraig Rooney's short story make one aware of the limitations of one's own identifications which result from their necessary fixation on particular versions of one's own position within a presumably collective past. Such stories allow and encourage us to deconstruct ourselves time and again in order to overcome the disabling threats which too fixated identities pose to the realm of future self-experience.

Rather than seeing any need for negotiating or re-negotiating the relation between sex and nation, I would argue that a consideration of gay and lesbian Irish writing, particularly of the deconstructionist strand within this tradition, may allow us to recognize that those omnipresent narratives of Irish nationalist and unionist identities are not at all such monolithic blocs as they often appear. In fact, stories of homosexual experience in Ireland or in relation to Irish culture may serve to show that there are many different – and maybe more important – ways of identifying besides identifying as Irish. Rather than being absorbed into dominant discourses of nationalism, I would hope that gay and lesbian writing in Ireland, as for gay and lesbian subculture in general, will realize its potential to help open up those traditional fixations in Irish culture, contribute to the deconstruction of traditional identities and perhaps substitute for the limited idea of identity and unity an open-ended idea of *différence* in the sense of a post-modern ethics of a pluralism of narratives. Such an engagement with the homosexual in Irish culture could further the process of opening up fixations in ways of thinking of Irish identity.

The text of the Multi-Party-Agreement signed in Stormont Castle on Good Friday 1998 for the first time officially recognizes as a fact of contemporary Northern Irish culture "the birthright of all the people of Northern Ireland to identify themselves and be accepted as Irish or British, or both, as they may choose".[26] Identity is conceived of here as a matter of choice, something that develops and may change, rather than something that is essentially determined. From a homosexual perspective, as I have suggested in this essay, this development might still be pushed further. My approach suggests the need to recognize

---

[26] *The Belfast Agreement: An Agreement Reached at the Multi-Party Negotiations*, Cmd 3883, April 1998, 28.

the right to identify as Irish or British, or both, or none of these, but as something completely different.

IRELAND AND THE WIDER WORLD

SHADOWS OF AN IRISH GRACE ON THE ELIZABETHAN STAGE:
A PRELUDE TO FURTHER READINGS OF SHAKESPEARE

B. R. SIEGFRIED

Christopher Highley's recent book, *Shakespeare, Spenser, and the Crisis in Ireland*, has done much to shift scholarly interest from the ways in which England influenced the development of an early modern Irish theatre towards the means by which Ireland contributed to the Elizabethan stage. I concur with Highley that in Shakespeare's London, the "growing fascination with England's troubles in Ireland was satisfied less by printed materials than by the public stage".[1] This discussion is meant to encourage continued consideration of the ways in which sixteenth-century Ireland influenced the imaginative work of English playwrights such as Shakespeare. This prelude to further readings of English drama will, first, gesture toward what I call the perception of proximity that paradoxically fuels English preoccupations with Irish alterity, and second, chart the probable influence of a particular Irish woman on the development of Shakespeare's comic heroines. In short, this study is a sketch of possibilities, a preliminary mapping of a realm of literary terrain (the influence of Irish culture, politics, and individuals on Elizabethan drama) that has yet to be fully appreciated by scholars.

While the Elizabethan government tended to consider Ireland a significant but lesser concern on the political agenda, Ireland's symbolic valence within English culture was, in fact, unexpectedly powerful. Indeed, popular texts of the period characterized the Irish bards as seditious and as wielding a kind of perilous wordplay that politically emasculated the English military's swordplay. Irish women, like the bards, were also seen as fomenting resistence, if not

---

[1] Christopher Highley, *Shakespeare, Spenser, and the Crisis in Ireland*, Cambridge, 1997, 2.

outright rebellion, and were commonly assumed to be consummate spies who traded in valuable and politically sensitive information detrimental to the English colonial cause. Not surprisingly, the Irish figured large in the emergent discourses of race and ethnicity, in which Ireland was construed as an exotic place whose inhabitants were inferior to the English in social, religious and political development. Perhaps the most striking convergence of all three caricatures is found in the familiar *True Exemplary, and Remarkable History of the Earle of Tirone* (London, 1619). Thomas Gainsford writes that the Irish bards are

> [the] very bane and confusion of Ireland, living in such obscenity and filthinesse, that no Gentlewoman thinketh herselfe happy without them, and supposeth it no disgrace even to bee prostituted unto them .... So that (in my conscience) the most of the rebells and strumpets amongst them, are the bastards of these rogues and vagabonds: and all the treasons, which have turmoiled our Nation, have received life and orignall from their imposturing and perswasions.

Rebels, then, are the result of a union between Ireland's women and Ireland's poets, an hysterical portrait of gender and discourse run wild.

Given that in this decade the Irish bards were as likely to work for English officials as they were for Irish lords, and considering the extent to which the colonizing English settlers and soldiers frequently married Irish women and were swiftly assimilated into Irish culture, Gainsford's rhetorical and hyperbolic insistence on Irish filthiness appears to be an extension of broader political concerns – the sword of conquest cut both ways, with English military persuasion being consistently countered by Irish profferings of better things to desire: Irish women and Irish stories. In short, the Irish question was, for Elizabeth's government and for Shakespeare's London, a matter of preserving English subjectivity in the face of the enticing proximity of the Irish other.

The English bard of the London theatre was certainly aware of the interesting social and political complexities revolving around England's colonial policy in Ireland. Indeed, recent critics have suggested that *Henry IV* "can be seen as reconfiguring the coalition of factions and families ranged against the English in Ireland".[2] This is not surprising given that many of the families affiliated with literary and

---

[2] *Ibid.*, 89.

theatrical patronage had their fortunes bound up with Ireland in one way or another. Such contingencies serve to remind us that, in addition to the explicit allusions to Ireland and Irishness in English plays, playwrights were bound to draw upon larger socio-cultural concerns that, though obviously Irish in origin, could be reconstituted to reflect upon English identity.

Consider, for instance, what the popular literature of the period illustrates, and what Shakespeare would have had great difficulty missing – the extent to which England's domestic poor and Ireland's resistant "rebels" were often conflated.[3] Indeed, what might have remained metaphorically relevant but conveniently distant in the popular imagination (particular colonial campaigns on the neighbour isle) instead became an issue of wrenching and fearful proximity. Any English beggar (but more particularly those categorized in opposition to the "deserving poor" by English law) could be construed as cousin to the Irish enemy: both were a threat to social and political stability and both, therefore, had to be controlled.

With this point in mind, we can push further than the editors of *Representing Ireland: Literature and the Origins of Conflict, 1534–1660* who write that

> Englishness and English nationality have been historically defined against non-Englishness. So that one of the most important ways in which Ireland was read in this period was as a series of negative images of Englishness. Ireland, in this respect, as well as being a text, is a negative photograph of English identity which never comes into view; we have only the negative, not the original print. The development of "Englishness" depended on the negation of "Irishness".[4]

---

3   Such conflations are well documented by historians; see, for example, Christopher Hill, *A Nation of Change and Novelty: Radical Politics, Religion and Literature in Seventeenth-century England*, New York, 1990; A. L. Beier, *The Problem of the Poor in Tudor and Early Stuart England*, New York, 1983 and *Masterless Men: The Vagrancy Problem in England, 1560-1640*, New York, 1985; Paul Slack, *The English Poor Law, 1531-1782*, London, 1990; John Pound, *Poverty and Vagrancy in Tudor England*, London, 1986; *Aspects of Poverty in Early Modern Europe*, ed. Thomas Riis, Stuttgart, 1981; Robert Jütte, *Poverty and Deviance in Early Modern Europe*, Cambridge, 1994; and *Poverty, Inequality and Class Structure*, ed. Dorothy Wedderburn, Cambridge, 1974.

4   *Representing Ireland: Literature and the Origins of Conflict, 1534-1660*, eds Brendan Bradshaw, Andrew Hadfield and Willy Maley, Cambridge, 1993, 7.

Consider, however, that although at one level Englishness may function as a simple negation of Irishness, on another level something more complicated is taking place, for it is the perception of proximity that fuels English preoccupations with Irish alterity. Difference, after all, is contingent – a matter of degree, angle of perception, cultural memory, imagination and socio-political context. Bear in mind that the negation of Native American cultures on the American continents, of Jewish culture within England and Europe, of island cultures in the Carribean, and of Muslim cultures in Africa were also part of the development of sixteenth- and seventeenth-century "Englishness". While there is an overarching similarity in how these negations functioned to promote English identity – there are, for instance, rhetorically identical passages in Thomas Harriot's *Brief and True Report of the New Found Land of Virginia* (1590) and Walter Ralegh's *Discovery* (1596) – there are also crucial distinctions to be made. In order to illustrate this point, I turn to English representations of a particular Irish woman – representations that emphasize her otherness, but quickly dissolve into what is clearly a marked concern with her iconographically devastating *proximity*.

The map of Ireland drawn for Elizabeth Tudor by Baptista Boazio (1599) includes topographical details, landmarks, and the names of rulers inscribed over their respective demesnes. In large letters clearly marking a peninsula between Clew Bay and Galway Bay is the name "Grany O Male", notably the only woman's name in the realm (other than Elizabeth Tudor's) marking the territory of a woman's reign. Strangely, although she is famous in the tradition of Irish folklore, O'Malley has not been the object of much scholarly attention – a noticeable lacuna in the growing body of literature dealing with late sixteenth- and early seventeenth-century Ireland.[5]

As an Irish ruler on the west coast of Ireland in the late sixteenth century, O'Malley enjoyed considerable success in running a network of ports and castles in the service of piracy by sea and cattle raids by land (what she would refer to euphemistically, in a letter to the

---

[5]   In fact, O'Malley is barely given even glancing attention by prominent scholars of Irish history such as Ciaran Brady and Brendan Bradshaw. The only substantially researched historical account of O'Malley's life is Anne Chambers' *Granuaile: The Life and Times of Grace O'Malley, c. 1530-1603*, Dublin, 1988, a work notable for its sound sorting of fact from fable. Further scholarly examinations of O'Malley's life and influence are certainly in order.

English queen, as her "maintenance by land and by sea"). Local economic and military dominance made her extremely influential among those who were resisting the English colonial project while attempting to use the politics of the same to further their own local political interests. This is especially significant since the English were initiating a conquer and regrant strategy by which Ireland was to be circumscribed by English rule; O'Malley and other Irish leaders could feign a limited allegiance to the English crown, benefit from temporary alliances with English governors, yet ignore policies that stood in the way of local Irish leadership, culture, and tradition. However, in 1584, Richard Bingham was given the English governorship of Connaught and immediately began a fierce attempt at suppressing all who had until then resisted English rule, even those who occasionally donned the guise of friend. O'Malley and her fleet proved to be especially irksome to Bingham, and she became the focus of several unsuccessful campaigns to smother political resistance on the west coast.

Because Elizabeth I on various occasions expressed displeasure with colonial policies that were too harsh and that provoked the native Irish to further resistance, local colonial officials often had to make use of carefully engineered rhetorical ploys in their correspondence with the English policy-makers of London in order to mask their divergent agendas. A brief consideration of two of the many descriptions of O'Malley in the *State Papers of Ireland* illustrates the ways in which the English colonials had to construc her as monstrous in order to vindicate an imperial policy of escalating violence. Perhaps more interesting (as it is certainly paradoxical), this representation of the Irish leader also demonstrates how the very act of marginalizing O'Malley as monstrously gendered unexpectedly evokes an iconographic alliance with Queen Elizabeth – a woman whose own rhetorical manipulation of gender expectations was both politically astute and socially disturbing. Before continuing, it is helpful to consider a point made by Karlyn Campbell and Walter Fisher who suggest that

> rhetorical experience is more usefully viewed ontologically than epistemologically. Put another way: rhetorical experience is most

fundamentally a symbolic transaction in and about social reality. In
this experience "knowledge" may or may not loom large.[6]

In noting that persuasive strategies more often hinge on what a
person or group of persons intends to be rather than on a claim to
know, we can more easily understand why a figure such as O'Malley
would loom so large in the minds of English politicians when, in fact,
the Irish political situation was not of primary importance in the
broader scheme of England's international political agenda. In other
words, we might say that epistemologically, the Elizabethan
government tended to consider Ireland a significant but lesser concern
on the political map. Yet ontologically, O'Malley's position on that
same map was unexpectedly threatening. To put it another way, the
knowledge of minor rebellions in relation to English power was not
overly worrisome. However, the threat to English (and in this case,
male) identity posed by the accounts of a "pirate" queen sailing the
waters off the coast of Connaught was another matter altogether.
Ruled by a woman monarch who kept a tight reign on her colonial
officials in Ireland, and threatened by a woman rebel who undid many
of their best laid plans, these men found themselves constructing a
narrative that would allow them to cast O'Malley as a shadow version
of Elizabeth, the bad queen whose authority could be openly made
monstrous and then literally contained in jail at Limerick.

By 1577, O'Malley had become such a prize that the earl of
Desmond, who was eager to prove his loyalty to the English crown,
captured O'Malley and turned her over to Lord Justice Drury. Drury's
rhetoric is representative of much of what was written about Grainne
by the colonial government:

> Grany O'Mayle, a woman that hath impudently passed the part of
> womanhood and been a great spoiler, and chief commander and
> director of thieves and murderers at sea to spoille this province,
> having been apprehended by the Earle of Desmond this last year, his
> Lordship hath now sent her to Limrick where she remains in safe
> keeping.

In another letter to Dublin, he describes her in similar terms, and it
becomes clear that correspondence between members of the local
colonial government tends to highlight O'Malley's otherness in terms

---

[6]   Walter R. Fisher, *Human Communication as Narration: Toward a Philosophy of
Reason, Value, and Action*, Columbia: SC, 1987, 17.

of what we might call a "foreign" gender: O'Malley's femininity is not English.

In stark contrast to such local exchanges, colonial correspondence with the London government granted a more respectful depiction of the Irish captain-queen. In 1578, Drury reports to Walsingham that Desmond had

> sent in also unto me Granny Nye Male one of power and forces which he took prisoner, which demonstracions of so loyall partes of dealing, argueth in myne opynyon a steadfast hope of his stayed fidelytie.[7]

By November of that same year, Drury would write to the Privy Council that at Leighlin:

> was brought unto me Granie ny Maille, a woman of the province of Connaught, governing a country of the O'Flaherty's, famous for her stoutness of courage and person, and for sundry exploits done by her by sea. She was taken by the Earl of Desmond a year and a half ago, and has remained ever since with him and partly in her Majesty's gaol of Limerick, and was sent for now by me to come to Dublin, where she is yet remaining.[8]

Curiously, the Irish woman's incarceration and the subsequent celebration of her capture did little to mitigate the disturbing power of O'Malley's "narrative" presence. In fact, Drury's two letters are notable for their abrupt change in tone, a change, I want to suggest, that is rhetorically aware of the difference in audience. The first letter, which lingers on O'Malley's impudence in transgressing gender norms and the resulting despoilment of the region, is addressed to the Irish colonial government in Dublin. The second two are reporting to Elizabeth's councillors and would enter the discursive bounds of the London government. No surprise that from one to the next, these letters move from outrage at the fact that O'Malley had "passed the part of womanhood" to an account in which the Irish queen is described as "one of force and power" who is famous for "her stoutness of courage and person".

In fact, for Henry Sidney, the memory of O'Malley would remain similarly ambiguous when several years later, in another letter to Walsingham, he recalled a meeting he had had with O'Malley:

---

[7]   *State Papers of Ireland*, 63/19, nos. 56, 186.
[8]   *History of the County Mayo*, ed. Hubert Knox, Dublin, 1982, 188.

> There came to me also a most famous feminine sea captain called
> Grany Imallye, and offered her services unto me, wheresoever I
> would command her, with three galleys and 200 fighting men, either
> in Scotland or Ireland; she brought with her her husband for she was
> as well by sea as by land well more than Mrs. Mate with him ....
> This was a notorious woman in all the coasts of Ireland. This
> woman did Sir Phillip Sydney see and speak withal, he can more at
> large inform you of her.[9]

Sidney's tone is indulgently humorous, though his stress on her
notoriety suggests a lingering discomfort with her position as a leader
in relation both to her husband and the land of which she was queen.

That the rhetoric of otherness is audience-specific suggests an
acute awareness on the part of these male governors that O'Malley
was sailing along the same horizon of meaning and possibility that
their own queen inhabited. Not coincidentally, the state papers of
Ireland manifest an abbreviated fantasy of female government tamed
and chastened. For these writers, O'Malley becomes an emblematic
referent, a hermaphrodite that functions (more generally) as a
synecdoche for Irish politics on the one hand, and (more specifically)
as a shadowy reflection of Elizabeth's rule on the other. Her iconographic proximity, in this sense, becomes as seductive to these writers
as sporting her otherness had been earlier. To put it another way, Irish
resistance to English colonial expansion and female rejection of
patriarchal gender assignments are both collapsed into the symbolic
figure of the pirate queen, a figure that was to become far more
slippery than the local English governors could have anticipated.

While the English correspondence concerning O'Malley is
revealing of the ways in which her Irish otherness was very much a
matter of rhetorical expediency (to be inflated or deflated depending
on the pressures of the particular political moment) her growing fame
influenced more than local epistolary exercises in rationalization.
Within the broader context of London's popular culture, O'Malley
offered Shakespeare and other Elizabethan writers a fount of symbolic
significance. Indeed, O'Malley could do iconographic work –
especially playing off of her gendered position as Irish other – that
even the monumental Elizabeth I simply could not do. For in addition
to being, for the English, the epitome of the Irish rogue woman,
O'Malley's famous sea exploits and successful "maintenance by land

---

9   Quoted in Chambers, *Granuaile*, 85.

& by sea"[10] off the west coast of Ireland also made her the object of fear and admiration for an England gambling much of its economic well being on sea trade, exploration, and sanctioned piracy.

Even so, there is no simple parallel between Ireland's sea-queen and Shakespeare's independent heroines. Rather, we should see O'Malley's presence as opening up figurative possibilities for Shakespeare that the larger political context and social imaginary could and did reinforce, allowing the playwright, and other dramatists as well, to layer theatrical fiction with various nuances of immediate relevance for the play-going audience. To this extent, we do well to explore the ways in which the popular entertainment of London participated in the continuation and steady refashioning of Anglo-Irish politics.

Although O'Malley does not stride into any of Shakespeare's plays in the way that the historical Mary Frith later would bound onto the boards as the fictionalized Moll Cutpurse in Thomas Middleton's *The Roaring Girl*, Shakespeare's plays nevertheless might be seen as bearing the imprint of O'Malley's influence. After all, Ireland's famous female queen and pirate neatly encapsulate England's colonial preoccupations with subjectivity in the face of Irish otherness (she is the Irish female other to the English masculine subject). In fact, she is the rogue woman writ large upon the page of Tudor sea trade and imperialism; she is the antinomial figure to Elizabeth's careful symmetry between national monument and English government institution. An example of this might be seen in *The Merchant of Venice* (1598), written ten years after the crisis with the Spanish Armada in which Ireland played a crucial role, and within two years of O'Malley's famous visit to Elizabeth Tudor's court. The play demonstrates the degree to which the drama of international policy flickered shadow-like behind the drama on a London stage.

The play begins with a conversation between Antonio, Salerio, and Solanio during which the mental state of the Merchant is explicitly linked to venture for profit on the sea:

> Your mind is tossing on the ocean,
> There where your argosies with portly sail,
> Like signors and rich burghers on the flood –
> Or, as it were the pageants of the sea.[11]

---

[10]   *State Papers of Ireland*, 63/170, no. 0204.

(I.1, 8-11)

The invocation of pageants at sea invites us to consider the socio-political drama of England's colonial ventures in the same way we might approach any theatrical production: attuned to the success or failure of proposed roles in relation to imminent action.

Salerio goes on to enumerate and foreshadow the dangers to which Antonio's investments are prone; rocks, shallows, poor navigation, etc., are invoked with teasing relish. Later, after Antonio and Bassanio make their proposition to Shylock, the lender adds to the list of dangers. Shylock says:

> ships are but boards, sailors but men. There be land rats and water rats, water thieves and land thieves – I mean pirates. (I.3,18-23)

Shylock's quick assurance that by water thieves and land thieves he means pirates suggests a comical and sly elision between mercantile/colonial investments in sea-faring venture-for-profit and common robbery. Thus, momentarily at least, the alliance of merchant and aristocrat in the friendship of Antonio and Bassanio is implicated in an immoral project – yet in danger of failure from precisely their ethically proximate Other, the pirates. That this implied critique is advanced by an ethnic and racial other, Shylock the Jew, only enhances the play's insistence on making English colonial subjectivity a theme that is central to the play's subsequent plot.

Further, when Portia disguises herself as a man and impersonates a clerk of law, two counts of felonious behavior that bracket her entrance in terms of undeniable roguery, she mirrors precisely the ontological concerns exhibited by the English in the narrative discourse surrounding Grace O'Malley. Portia's manipulation of gender expectations and resistance to simple notions of male governance, her challenge to the epistemologically inflexible institution of the Venetian law by appealing to the ontological status of the merciful (a stance that urges an identification with the other and that moves us to render up precisely what we most desire for ourselves), and her paradoxical position as other-in-proximity all reflect the same set of preoccupations exhibited by the English colonial government in Ireland with regard to O'Malley. Portia may thus be seen as a theatrical transposition; the social and political

---

[11]   William Shakespeare, *The Complete Works*, eds Stanley Wells and Gary Taylor, Oxford, 1998, 425-51. All citations refer to this edition.

concerns amplified by O'Malley's international influence are from the shores of Connaught carried over to a London stage, then distilled into a female character that the play-going English audience is invited to admire and embrace.

Although we have neither space nor time to give this dramatic moment its interpretative due, these points at the very least suggest an active reflexivity in the conduct of dramatic language and social life. The enticing proximity of Ireland generally, as well as the narrative influence of O'Malley specifically, provided English playwrights with a wealth of discursive possibilities. Indeed, by exploring the possibility of an Irish Grace on the Elizabethan stage, we may begin to appreciate the various subtleties of inter-cultural influences that are yet to be recovered, considered, and knowledgeably wound into our literary histories.

LADY MORGAN'S *ITALY*:
TRAVEL BOOK OR POLITICAL TRACT?

DONATELLA ABBATE BADIN

What would an Irish reader expect when a nineteenth-century Irish author writes about a country "betrayed and hopeless", whose "rich soil bathed in the blood of her sons, vainly shed in her defence" and which, "like some splendid but pensive queen of tragic story, presenting herself at the bar of the royal tribunal" demands its parliament?[1] Naturally, that the subject of the discourse is Ireland. These, instead, are Lady Morgan's words about Italy.

Lady Morgan and her husband, Sir Charles, travelled throughout Italy between 1819 and 1821, visiting the kingdom of Sardinia, the Habsburg-ruled Lombardy and Veneto, the Vatican states, the Grand Duchy of Tuscany, the Kingdom of the Two Sicilies, and staying for extended periods in Milan, Como, Rome, Naples and Venice. *Italy*, which appeared simultaneously in English and French in June 1821, is a successful travel book and a political work inspired by radical ideas, hovering on the borderline between description and interpretation, guidebook and personal diary, journalism and history. Lady Morgan affirmed that, in writing her book, she espoused the "jargon of liberty and of rights"[2] of the first Italian supporters of the French Revolution, a jargon, we should add, that, while sharing stereotypes of all nationalist discourse, suspiciously sounds also very Irish in its insistence on blood sacrifice, slavery and chains, while the oppressed country is cast in a feminized and victimized role and the oppressor as a parasite or vampire.

---

[1] Lady Morgan (Sydney Owenson), *Italy*, London, 1821, I, 10, 154. For Lady Morgan's views of Italy, see also *Passages from My Autobiography*, London, 1859 and *Lady Morgan's Memoirs: Autobiography, Diaries and Correspondence*, ed. W. Hepworth Dixon, London, 1842, both miscellanies of diary extracts and letters.

[2] Morgan, *Italy*, I, 142.

On the basis of the rhetoric used, and even more so, of the strong attacks against despotism, of the dialectics of oppressor race and oppressed race and of the evocation of a lost dignity soon to be conquered, *Italy* not only aims at "aiding the great cause, the regeneration of Italy",[3] as she writes to her sister, but is often a pretext for disguising a nationalist message about Ireland. Between the lines regarding the political and social conditions of the various states of the Italian peninsula, there lurks a tacit comparison of the plight of Italy[4] with the situation in Ireland.[5] *Italy* at times can also be read, paradoxically, as a patriotic tract, as Lady Morgan herself acknowledges, even if the term refers (as the *OED* reminds us) to "love of or zealous devotion to one's own country" and not to a foreign country as Italy was.

Recent criticism of Lady Morgan's novels has highlighted her role in introducing a new discourse on the relationship between individuals and community and in raising the problems of national identity through the dynamics of a sentimental plot.[6] In the dozen texts in which Lady Morgan makes Ireland her subject, she takes radical positions which may even appear in contrast with those of the Ascendancy to which, with her title and her Protestant faith, she

---

[3] Morgan, *Passages*, 339.
[4] At this point, some very brief remarks on the history of Italy are in place. Italy, like Ireland, is a young country: its political unity and independence only go back to 1861 although, as in Ireland, the sense of a national identity existed long before that date. In Lady Morgan's days neither country was free. There were, however, great differences between the two: Ireland was a single, undivided country enjoying a parliamentary representation of sorts and, at least formally, an equal partnership in the United Kingdom, while Italy was divided into a mosaic of small states, some of them under foreign rule, and agitated, in the years Morgan visited them, by a ferment of constitutional requests. On the other hand, Italy was often conquered, but not colonized; foreign rule in Italy (as in the case of Austrian-controlled Lombardo-Veneto), had not led to the erosion and final destruction of the indigenous culture and language. There was no occasion, therefore, for that kind of cultural nationalism that characterized Irish Romanticism.
[5] The same could be said about *France*; see Mary Campbell, *Lady Morgan: The Life and Times of Sydney Owenson*, London, 1988, 155: "Her travels in France had led her to make comparisons with her own country that were highly critical of the state of things as they were in Ireland."
[6] In her "national tales", such as *The Wild Irish Girl* (1806), *Florence McCarthy* (1818), *The O'Briens and the O'Flaherties* (1827), Lady Morgan makes what Nicola Watson defines as "an attempt to nationalize the sentimental heroine" (Nicola Watson, *Revolution and the Form of the British Novel*, Oxford, 1994, 111).

would be expected to conform.[7] However, what has been little noted is that her Irish concerns determine also the kind of attention she lends to the other countries she deals with: Belgium in *The Princess; or, the Beguine* (1835), Greece in *Ida of Athens* (1809) and, more particularly, France and Italy, the subjects of her two widely successful travelogues which constitute no exception to the intensely political colouring of her other writings as, indeed, of Irish Romantic literature in general.

Italy was written upon the insistence of her publisher, Colburn, who, pleased with the success of *France* (1817), had offered her £2,000 for a similar book about Italy. Being one of the first accounts of a Grand Tour after the Napoleonic era during which British travellers had been excluded from Italy, it promised success. Not only would it bring fresh information to the British public, affected by an incurable Italomania and avid for travel accounts about Italy;[8] it was also authored by a writer who, through *France* and her other works, had shown on which side she stood in an age when, as Jack Lynch remarks, Italy had become "a ... *locus amoenus* of radical utopian escapism".[9]

The book confirmed Colburn's rosiest expectations and "produced a greater sensation than even the work on France",[10] drawing the attention of both admirers and detractors for its polemical content rather than for its information and descriptions. Byron and other radical writers admired it[11] while it was fiercely attacked at home by the *Quarterly Review* and in Italy where, in addition to receiving irate

---

[7]   Contrary to appearances, Lady Morgan, née Sydney Owenson, did not belong to the Ascendancy. She was the daughter of an improvident Irish actor, Robert MacOwen (who changed his name to Owenson) who, though a Catholic, had her baptized into the Church of England. Her husband, Charles Morgan, a doctor, was knighted just before their marriage for services rendered to their common patrons, Lord and Lady Abercorn.

[8]   See Andrew Brayley, "The Phenomenon of *Italomania* in the Nineteenth Century", *Journal of Anglo-Italian Studies*, 4 (1995), 29.

[9]   Jack Lynch, "'Observation, with Extensive View?': English-Italian Travel Narratives, 1700-1820", *Journal of Anglo-Italian Studies*, 4 (1995), 11.

[10]   Morgan, *Memoirs*, 144.

[11]   Byron wrote to Tom Moore, "her work is fearless and excellent on the subject of Italy". But he could also jibe at her: "I suppose I know a thing or two of Italy – more than Lady Morgan has picked up in her posting" (Lord Byron, *Letters and Journals*, ed. L. A. Marchand, London, 1973-82, VII, 170).

reviews, it was banned in several states.[12] Lady Morgan, shrewdly
conscious of the propaganda value of even adverse criticism, declares
she is indifferent to it:

> It is in vain that reviewers calumniate! and journals denounce! That
> *Quarterlys* and *Quotodiennes* fulminate bulls, and utter anathemas.
> Their briefs of condemnation (like other briefs) are now but waste
> paper; while days and nights passed in the societies of Geneva,
> Milan, Florence, Bologna and Naples, are entered in the records of
> the heart, and are at once the reward and stimulus of exertions,
> which, however inadequate, have never been made, but in the full
> conviction that they tended to forward the cause of truth and of
> virtue.[13]

To forward such a cause by commenting on "the condition of the
country" and doing "good by telling truth according to our
impressions"[14] was the declared "business" of Lady Morgan's work
which, however, answers several other criteria as well, the first being
that of doing good to the author herself. Lady Morgan makes no
bones about it; with characteristic self-deflation, she comments:

> Alas! that money should have so much influence over our noble
> intentions! Knowledge, power? not a bit of it! Money is power; it
> subsidizes all powers.[15]

Hers is the work of a professional writer who must make a living. As
such it must be useful and sellable by providing the readers with what
they need.

Travel writing, as Chloe Chard points out in *Pleasure and Guilt on
the Grand Tour*, must "provide information about a particular
topography of the foreign" and "is concerned with the ordering of

---

12 Among Italian reactions against her views on Italy, see the anonymous *Le
    Morganiche, ossia, lettere scritte da un Italiano a Miledi Morgan*, Edinburgh,
    1824 and Ginevra Canonici Fachini, *Prospetto biografico delle donne italiane
    rinomate in letteratura dal secolo decimoquarto fino a' giorninostri .... Con una
    risposta a Lady Morgan risguardante alcune accuse da lei date alle donne
    italiane nella sua opera l'Italie*, Venezia, 1824.
13 Morgan, *Italy*, II, 398.
14 *Ibid.*, II, 124.
15 Morgan, *Passages*, 8.

knowledge of the world".[16] Lady Morgan's travelogue, like other works of the kind, selects and comments on the sights – both artistic and natural – to view along the standard Grand Tour itinerary and offers methodical and pedantic information about them as well as about the history and the social characteristics of the place. The informative material is embedded in a first-person narration deploying an array of standard rhetorical strategies and predictable reactions on one hand but also of idiosyncratic observations on the other. In spite of her proffered declaration that she will not attempt "to describe indescribable things"[17] and of the litotes underpinning her frequent pretence of being unable to describe, describe she did and in great detail and with a wealth of literary and classical references and footnotes[18] according to the fashion of the travel accounts of her times, from which she freely quotes and adapts.

Italy is a very rich Baedeker *ante litteram*: the representation of the picturesque and the sublime, the search of which was the goal of every self-respecting Romantic traveller, is not foreign to Lady Morgan. It is a prerogative of travel writing, to borrow Chard's analysis, to "impose on the foreign a demand that it should in some way proclaim itself as different from the familiar":[19] Lady Morgan's writings too convey the thrill of the encounter with the foreign and the unfamiliar and she employs all the rhetorical tropes and *topoi* which Chard in her study indicates as playing an important role in travel writing for "representing the foreign as dramatically different":[20] the hyperbole, the invocation of the category of the sublime, the talk of wonders, the intense emotional responsiveness, the sprinkling of the text with foreign phrases and so forth.

But the foreign becomes also, especially in the digressions and divagations which characterize Lady Morgan's style, a privileged space on which to project the desires, aspirations, and the affective

---

[16] Chloe Chard, *Pleasure and Guilt on the Grand Tour: Travel Writing and Imaginative Geography, 1600–1830*, Manchester, 1999, 9.

[17] Morgan, *Italy*, I, 124.

[18] For the significance of Lady Morgan's excessive use of footnotes, see Jeanne Moskal, "Gender, Nationality, and Textual Authority in Lady Morgan's Travel Books", in *Romantic Women Writers: Voices and Countervoices*, eds P. R. Feldman and T. M. Kelley, Hanover: NH, 1995, 171-93.

[19] Chard, *Pleasure and Guilt on the Grand Tour*, 3.

[20] *Ibid.*, 4.

and cultural memories of the subject.[21] It is in these interstices of the useful and conventional discourse of travel that the political subtext surfaces and that the rhetoric of diversity is juxtaposed to the rhetoric of sameness.

Lady Morgan's firsthand though biased account of the social and political situation in the various states of Italy is pervaded by a strong spirit of Jacobinism. Italy, in her eyes, is not a mere "geographic expression", as Metternich had affirmed at the Congress of Vienna, but an ideal community in which a sense of nation was just beginning to affirm itself. By writing about Italy she can explore the meaning of national identity as she was doing for Ireland in her fictional production. *Italy* is also a thorough indictment of all forms of despotism (be it Austrian or Bourbon tyranny or papal misrule) and an evocation of the benefits of the liberal and progressive rule Italy had experienced under Napoleon during both the Republic and the Empire. What Lady Morgan laments about Italy in the pre- and post-Napoleonic era is not, as in the case of Ireland, the loss of language and culture, but the loss of its dignity as a united and independent state, a condition it had enjoyed in a few privileged moments of its history (for example in the days of the Lombard League) and most notably under the "intelligent sway" of Napoleon during what to Lady Morgan was "one of those great epochs in the history of humanity which return at remote intervals like astronomic phenomena".[22]

Napoleon is exculpated from being a foreign invader of Italy and a looter of its artistic treasures and even admired for his "splendid," his "giant despotism";[23] in comparison with him, the sovereigns of the restoration of the *ancien régime* are "pigmy successors".[24] Her Francophilia and her defence of England's arch-rival, considered as a champion of the fight against the enemies of liberty, is tantamount to an indirect attack against England, numbered among the tyrants and oppressors of the world. Morgan's Italian enthusiasm for France, "that nation which dared to redress the wrongs, and stem the abuses of a thraldom of ages",[25] is coloured by the strong feelings her countrymen

---

[21] See Christian Jacob's comments about the fascination of maps in *L'empire des cartes*, Paris, 1992.

[22] Morgan, *Italy*, I, 16.

[23] *Ibid.*, I, 135; 159.

[24] *Ibid.*, I, 59.

[25] *Ibid.*, I, 28.

had for what was considered a land of refuge of the exiled and the repository of Irish hopes.

Resentment against England can often be perceived in her writings and in her choice of what to highlight. With a sensibility exacerbated by her own country's situation, for instance, she dwells with participation on various moments of the history of Naples which must have struck her for their affinity with Ireland. Charles V and his heirs, she writes, "successively governed this beautiful and unhappy country, by that refinement upon all bad government, *the delegated power of foreign despotism*".[26] "As the English did in Ireland", we read between the lines. Those who governed Naples did not have "any legitimate right to reign over a distant land of whose language they were ... ignorant".[27] "As the English did in Ireland", again we read between the lines. "Their imposts upon the abundant produce of that teeming soil, on which Nature has lavished all her bounty, continually reduced the people to famine, perpetuated their poverty, and drove them into ... insurrection"[28] – and again we could add, as in Ireland.

Morgan is more explicit in her attacks against England as a betrayer of Italian hopes. She underlines England's repeated treacherousness in promising Italy constitutional rights, only to disappoint it hypocritically: "When England signed the contract of emancipation, Italy, in spite of the recollection of Austrian tyranny, believed, confided – and was betrayed!"[29] Count Confalonieri, pleading with Lord Castlereagh for a constitution like that of England, is imaged as a feminized Italy raising "her suppliant looks to the representative of the English cabinet" who "smiled blandly on her sorrow" and coolly hinted "that her Constitution was not the best thing that England had to boast".[30] The icon of the male Sasannach and of the female Ireland is here adapted to an Italian situation as in several other circumstances in the work.

England's role in consigning the proud ancient maritime republics of Genoa and Venice into foreign hands reveals something the Irish people were familiar with, England's "disregard of national rights":

---

26 Morgan, *Italy*, II, 361.
27 *Ibid.*, II, 362.
28 *Ibid.*, II, 361.
29 Morgan, *Italy*, I, 152.
30 *Ibid.*, I, 153.

> It is humiliating thus to find England upon all occasions the political
> scavenger of Europe, performing all the dirty work with which more
> crafty cabinets contrive not to sully their character; but far beyond
> the folly and wickedness of such acts, is the hypocrisy with which
> they are accompanied.[31]

In spite of her pretence of feeling humiliated as a British citizen,
Morgan is here speaking as an Irish patriot openly denouncing
England's actions in Italy and tacitly at home.

As in the example above, Morgan, however, tries to tone down the
transgressive impact of her work by using repeatedly the subterfuge of
presenting herself as a sentimental and naive woman: "Politics can
never be a woman's science; but patriotism must naturally be a
woman's sentiment",[32] she writes, and also "in a woman's work, sex
may plead its privilege; and ... if the heart will occasionally make
itself a party in the concern, its intrusions may be pardoned".[33] The
patriotism and partisanship of her support of Italy, with its implicit
extension to her home country, thus, are both acknowledged and
exonerated as irresponsible. By adopting a female point of view and
by transferring feelings regarding Ireland to an Italian context, the
author finds a way to write a patriotic and progressive tract without
running too many risks.

We must not forget, in fact, that Lady Morgan was a British citizen
and that she wrote for a British publisher and British readers. Her
success was due to Anglo-Irish and English patronage. Like Tom
Moore and other successful contemporaries, she had to mask her
resentment. In her *Letter to the Reviewers of Italy* she emphasizes that
her intention had been to compare Italian degradation with the model
of excellence offered by a constitutional and Protestant Great Britain:

> As for *Italy, I* attempted to expose the evils of despotic
> governments, in opposition to the blessings and benefits of a
> representative government; – to display the fatal effects of a
> powerful and intolerant superstition, as opposed to the enlightened
> doctrines of rational and revealed religion.[34]

---

[31] *Ibid.*, I, 48.
[32] *Ibid.*, I, xii.
[33] *Ibid.*, I, 71.
[34] Morgan, *Italy*, II (reprinted in some later editions as an Appendix to *Italy*), *New Monthly Magazine* (October 1821).

Being aware of the "blessings" of democracy, Morgan resented bitterly the loss of the Irish parliament and the arrogant British disrespect for Irish identity which turned people into vassals shorn of their rights. She was, for instance, a staunch supporter of Catholic emancipation. So whenever in her travels, as for instance in Italy, she encountered "privilege against the rights of nations",[35] and "ignorance, degradation, and passive obedience in the vassal people",[36] Lady Morgan reacted with a passion that owed some of its vehemence to the bitterness she felt about Ireland. Conversely, the resilience and love of liberty in spite of the oppression, which survived in the many Italian states she had observed, calls for the same admiration she voices for her country in *Patriotic Sketches*: "That mind indeed must be endued with great native strength ... which can breathe the spirit of liberty beneath the lash of despotism."[37] There are innumerable similar expressions of admiration for the Italians.

Although she did not aspire to Irish independence and looked rather for a mutual recognition and understanding of the two countries (as is apparent in the closure of many of her national tales where a sentimental liaison signals political reconciliation), she reacted strongly whenever she was faced with arrogance of power, disregard of a country's claims and divisiveness. Commenting about Lombardy, she condemns the Habsburg form of government "that insulates the inhabitants of each petty state" and "The illiberal and narrow policy of the present day which knows no means of governing but to divide, and no method of tranquillizing but to degrade".[38] This is the more angrily felt because it matches the situation she describes in *Florence Macarthy*, that is, in her husband's words, "the execrable system of 'divide and govern', the demoralization and insecurity which the system inflicts upon the agents no less than on the victims of oppression".[39]

The disaster of 1798 had killed her great Irish hopes that the benefits of the French Revolution would reach the country. For this reason she is deeply moved by the movement leading to the creation of the Jacobin republic of 1799 in Naples and to its bloody repression.

---

[35]   Morgan, *Italy*, I, 28.
[36]   *Ibid.*, I, 49.
[37]   Lady Morgan, *Patriotic Sketches*, 2 vols, London, 1807, 48.
[38]   Morgan, *Italy*, I, 110.
[39]   Charles Morgan, Introduction to Lady Morgan, *Florence McCarthy, an Irish Tale*, 4 vols, London, 1818; quoted in Campbell, 157.

The Neapolitan revolution had been as ephemeral as the 1798 Rising, but, like the latter, had heralded a new conscience and new aspirations.

The cast of characters of her long account of the Neapolitan events is similar to that of *The O'Briens and the O'Flaherties* (1827), her novel set in the days of the Rising and of the Act of Union. The representatives of the ruling class, who are responsible for the suffering of the country, are pictured in both works as selfish, cruel and corrupt and the masses are poor, degraded and oppressed. Her fictional heroes and the patriots figuring in the novel – Theobald Wolfe Tone, Edward Fitzgerald, Robert Emmet – belong, as do the Neapolitans who gave their lives to the cause, to "a large body of ... revolutionists ... whose education fitted them to see into the abuses of the government; and whose spirit, patriotism, talents, and consideration, rendered them formidable at a moment when the French revolution was striking terror into the feudal despots of Europe".[40]

Lady Morgan underlines the generous and romantic idealism of the Neapolitan heroes who, inspired by the principles of the Enlightenment, like their Jacobin Irish brothers, had started by asking for reforms and, having become part of a republican and revolutionary organization, ended up on the scaffold. Lady Morgan tries to make the dying words of the Neapolitan patriots as immortal as those of William Orr or Robert Emmet. Emmanuele di Deo is remembered for his heroical refusal to betray his associates: "As he ascended the scaffold an offer of life was made if he discovered the rest of his associates in treason: his bold answer was that he preferred death to infamy, and that he had nothing to reveal."[41] A long footnote supplements the narration, celebrating the noble words and gestures of those who were arrested and condemned after the victory of Cardinal Ruffo and Nelson's betrayal of the cause: Cerillo, Vitagliani, Nicolò Palomba, Carlomagna, Granali, Velasco, Eleonora Pimentel, Vincenzo Rosso, and admiral Caracciolo are part of the tearful list. Through their stories, Lady Morgan, with her knowledge of the sentimental power of this type of anecdote, tries to awaken in the hearts of her English readers a revulsion from despotism, a condemnation of the anti-liberal policies of the government and sympathy for the 1821 rising in Naples. She comments ironically: "let those who rejoice in the defeat of the Neapolitan patriots of 1821,

---

[40]	Morgan, *Italy*, II, 371-73.
[41]	*Ibid.*, II, 309.

remember the fate of those who were exposed to the royal clemency of Ferdinand the Fourth in 1799."[42] In her long, detailed and painful account of the Neapolitan revolution we can also read a reflection of her disappointment and preoccupations about Ireland.

Such is Lady Morgan's political passion that she reads signs of Italian oppression or conversely of the patriots' love of liberty in the most unexpected everyday events. This peculiarity of her style makes her a semiotician *ante-litteram*, akin, say, to a Roland Barthes in his attention to the "everdayness" of social and political life. There are many examples of her interpreting anodyne details as spies to the political history of the country. Even Italian ballet, admired at La Scala, "borrows its perfection from causes which may be said to be not only physical, but political":

> a habit of distrust, impressed upon the people by the fearful system of espionage, impels them to trust their thoughts rather to a look or an action, than to a word or a phrase. It is not easy to denounce a smile, or to betray a beck; and communications are thus made, over which the police holds no control.[43]

This last remark could well apply to her own method. It would have been difficult to call her to task for something she had written about a foreign country. Her readers, however, were not dupes, nor were the critics who attacked her. It was all too obvious that Morgan in her travel book had found a way to enact her Irish nationalist and progressive agenda by displacing it to the Italian context. "Instances of the Other", writes Michel de Certeau, "are often the best way for knowing oneself".

---

[42] *Ibid.*, I, 377.
[43] Morgan, *Italy*, I, 98.

MARKING TIME:
SOME CONSIDERATIONS ON DANTE'S PRESENCE IN *STATION ISLAND*

GIOVANNI PILLONCA

The relevance of the example of Dante for the work of Seamus Heaney has been emphasized not only by critics but by the poet himself on more than one occasion. Nowhere is the presence of the Florentine more evident than in Heaney's "ghostly colloquies" on Lough Derg as depicted in *Station Island*. The aim of this essay is to consider some of the implications of the choice Heaney made by apparently privileging Dante's *Purgatorio* over the *Inferno*, and therefore taking a stance over something he had not been so convinced about in *Field Work*. *Field Work*, although containing Heaney's first direct allusion to Dante's *Purgatorio*, does indeed close, as it were, on an infernal note, namely with the poet's rendering of the Ugolino episode in Cantos XXXII-XXXIII. In *Station Island* – both the title-poem and the entire collection – the purgatorial allusion is the dominant one although references to the *Inferno* are far from absent.

Recently, Maria Cristina Fumagalli, a critic who has worked extensively on assessing Heaney's translations of Dante, went so far as to argue that

> the direct point of reference of "Station Island" is more frequently Dante's *Inferno* than his *Purgatorio* and, most importantly ... Heaney's poem is in fact a sort of miniature of *The Divina Commedia*.[1]

By heeding Fumagalli's suggestion to the full, one finishes, as she does, by having Joyce at the close of the title sequence as a modern

---

[1] Maria Cristina Fumagalli, "Station Island: Seamus Heaney's *Divine Comedy*", *Irish University Review*, XXVI/1 (1996), 127.

version of Cacciaguida, the ancestor Dante meets in the *Paradiso*.[2]
Such an interpretation, besides appearing far-fetched, may also have
the paradoxical effect of overshadowing the very function that Dante's
work, especially the *Purgatorio*, performs at a more profound level. In
connection with Joyce's presence in the poem, some have, in fact,
suggested Brunetto Latini's figure – one already used by Eliot in *Little
Gidding* – as being a more convincing reference, so drawing us back
to the *Inferno*, albeit to one of the least infernal shades of the *Cantica*.

I would argue that the *Purgatorio* rather than the *Inferno*, let alone
the *Commedia* as a whole, provides the poet not only with a range of
allusions but with an ideal frame of reference for the composition of
Station Island. The *Purgatorio* not only offers a structural model but
also allows the poet to draw on a more productive vein tapping deep-
rooted cultural paradigms, images and symbols consistently referring
the reader back to the Irish experience. When I employ the term
"paradigm", what I have in mind, among other things, is the insight
provided by Jacques Le Goff in his book, *The Birth of Purgatory*.
According to Le Goff, the creation of purgatory at the end of the
twelfth century replaced the former binary system consisting of
heaven and hell with a tripartite system that envisaged purgatory as a
middle ground. Le Goff goes on to argue that this change brought
about "a shift from blunt opposition, bilateral confrontation, to the
more complex interplay of three elements".[3]

Such a pattern, whose relevance to Heaney's particular
predicament can hardly be overstated, would not be sufficient in itself
to grant poetic viability to any work of art. What gives it a necessity of
its own, in Heaney's case, is its fitting perfectly within the perimeter
and range of the poet's profoundest motivations. Heaney's
progression within the Dantean canon is to be regarded as the natural
step forward in the process – to use the words Heaney uses to define
Kavanagh's achievement – aimed at raising "the inherited energies of
a subculture to the power of a cultural resource".[4] Far from being a
passing whim, the reference to Dante's *Purgatorio* does indeed find

[2]   Carla de Petris has also pointed out the Cacciaguida connection in two interesting
      contributions: "Heaney and Dante", in *Critical Essays on Seamus Heaney*, ed. R.
      F. Garrett, New York, 1995, 161-71 and "Heaney's Use of Dante against Joyce",
      in *Fin de Siècle and Italy*, ed. F. Ruggieri, Rome, 1998, 79-90.
[3]   Jacques Le Goff, *The Birth of Purgatory*, Chicago, 1981, 225.
[4]   Seamus Heaney, "From Monaghan to the Grand Canal: The Poetry of Patrick
      Kavanagh", in Seamus Heaney, *Preoccupations: Selected Prose 1968-1978*,
      London, 1980, 116.

its motivation within the culture where the poet's inspiration finds its sources and roots.

As a Catholic, Heaney's horizon of expectations was moulded by the set of beliefs behind, and in turn shaped by, the invention of purgatory. Furthermore, at about the same time, an Irish purgatory, the same providing the setting and title for Heaney's book, had been established. St Patrick's Purgatory features significantly both in Ireland's popular culture and in its modern literature in English and this allows Heaney to continue his conversation both with the culture he was born into and with the literary tradition of his own country. The purgatory, in fact, allows a range of references that any poet might envy, while at same time it stands as a comprehensive and effective metaphor for life and for the poetic act itself.

With hindsight, Heaney's drawing on Dante's work seems also perfectly justified and entirely consistent not only with his development but also with his preoccupations at this particular stage of his career. The five-year period between the publication of *Field Work* (1979) and the appearance of *Station Island* (1984) was marked, in Northern Ireland, by the build-up of the level of confrontation between the Protestant and Catholic communities, and especially between the nationalist activists and the RUC. The period saw, to name only some of the most conspicuous events, the killing of Lord Mountbatten in 1979; the cancellation of the Pope's visit to the province; the death of eighteen British soldiers at Warrenpoint, and the hunger strike which started in 1980 and lasted through part of 1981, leading to the death of Bobby Sands and nine more prisoners after him.

Heaney's "journey with conversations" was composed against this tragic backdrop and heavily conditioned by the responsibility the poet felt towards his community as well as by a feeling of impotence in the face of the brutality of history. The same can be said of *Field Work*, the prevalent elegiaic tone of which is largely determined by tragic current events. In spite of the dark note on which the book closes, *Field Work* already contains the intimation that Dante's second *Cantica* might offer the poet a more beneficial paradigm of balance and redemption than could be provided by the harsh images and unrequited and restless shades of the *Inferno*. The first attempt at tuning in with the *Purgatorio* is represented in *Field Work* by "The Strand at Lough Beg". This is the well-known elegy in memory of Colum McCartney, the poet's second cousin shot by loyalist paramilitaries in 1976. The poem constitutes also the first tentative move in the singling out of the *Purgatorio* as a new point of reference in the poet's search for enabling images in the presence of highly intractable material.

The elegy is introduced by a quotation from *Purgatory*, in Dorothy L. Sayers' translation:

> All round this island, on the strand
> Far down below there, where the breakers strive,
> Grow the tall rushes from the oozy sand.[5]

(I, 100-102)

The quote is significant as it is part of Cato's directions to Virgil. The poet is supposed to perform the ritual of cleaning the dirt of Hell from Dante's face, and of girding him with rushes symbolizing humility, before actually starting the ascent of the mountain of purgatory. The call for *humilitas* contained in Cato's advice carries in its wake a plea for forgiveness echoed and reworded by Heaney in other poems in the same collection. I have in mind, in particular, the second and third sections of "Triptych" which precede and serve to introduce Colum's elegy. In the second piece, entitled "Sibyl", the Sibyl's answer to the question "What will become of us?" is, in this respect, eloquent:

> I think our very form is bound to change.
> Dog's in a siege. Saurian relapses. Pismires.
> Unless forgiveness finds its nerve and voice,
> Unless the helmeted and bleeding tree
> Can green and open buds like infants' fists
> And the fouled magma incubate
>
> Bright nymphs [6]

Such a plea is the first answer the poet can provide to the imperative he must have felt at this particular time, to confront, to use Seamus Deane's phrase, "the ineffable, unspeakable thing for which violence is our inadequate word".[7]

---

[5] Dante Alighieri, *The Divine Comedy*, trans. Dorothy L. Sayers, Harmondsworth, 1979. All translations, unless otherwise stated, are from her version of the *Comedy*.

[6] Seamus Heaney, *Field Work*, London, 1979, 13.

[7] Seamus Deane, *Celtic Revivals*, London, 1985, 186.

While Dante seems at this point to provide adequate images, the poet is uncertain as to which of Dante's realms to refer to in order to deal with a particularly unbearable predicament in the here and now. Does the *Inferno* provide a suitable framework, as the "Ugolino" translation closing the book seems to indicate, or is the *Purgatorio* a more appropriate imaginative domain? *Field Work* stretches between these two extremes: it opens with references to *Purgatorio* and closes with Heaney's rendering of the Ugolino passage in *Inferno*, one of the most atrocious among the recounted deeds of medieval violence. This is less an element of indecision than of tension on the part of the poet, justified by the fact that *Field Work* has, as regards this particular issue, the characteristics of an experiment. New territory is being explored and this reflects the search for that new style and altogether new voice to be found in *Station Island*. In *Station Island*, it is definitely Dante's second *Cantica* that is Heaney's point of reference, not only as a structural and poetic model but as one of its generative principles.

In an essay the poet wrote soon after the publication of *Station Island*, he acknowledges his debt to Dante. Dante's achievement, Heaney writes:

> encouraged my attempt at a sequence of poems which could explore the typical strains which the consciousness labours under in this country. The main tension is between two often contradictory commands: to be faithful to the collective historical experience and to be true to the recognition of the emerging self. [8]

Dante does indeed come to Heaney as an important guide-figure at a crucial moment in his development. Seamus Deane has suggested that Dante's example is paramount in Heaney's attempt to manoeuvre atrocity and poetry "into a relationship which could be sustained without breaking the poet down into timorousness, the state in which the two things limply coil". [9]

The task of relating atrocity and poetry has always been very problematic. In a century of devastating wars and violence, this applies to poets and writers all over the world who have had to confront terror and horror up to the present day. Even if we limit our

---

[8]   Seamus Heaney, "Envies and Identification: Dante and the Modern Poet", *Irish University Review*, 15 (1985), 5.
[9]   Deane, *Celtic Revivals*, 186.

review to the background of Heaney's work we have to acknowledge
that the 1960s and 1970s not only saw the eruption of the Troubles in
Northern Ireland, but also the Vietnam War, the suppression of
democracy in Greece and then in Chile, the ferocious rule of dictators
almost everywhere in Central and South America, post-colonial
turmoil in several countries, a blood-bath in Cambodia, the ongoing
wars between some Arab countries and Israel, apartheid and white
oppression in South Africa and in the southern states in the USA,
terrorism in Italy and Germany, and so on. Having yet to come to
terms with the violence of the Second World War, the Western world
hardly needed such terrible reminders of the everlasting recurrence of
evil and dread.

Let us now turn to the way Heaney faces up to the task in *Station
Island*. In a poem contained in the first section of the collection –
"Sandstone Keepsake" – we are provided with a significant example
both of the poet's brooding on atrocity and violence and the
equilibrium, the momentary stay, which the poet's "full look at the
worst" gains in a poetry which draws on Dante's work:

> Sandstone Keepsake
>
> It is a kind of chalky russet
> solidified gourd, sedimentary
> and so reliably dense and bricky
> I often clasp it and throw it from hand to hand.
>
> It was ruddier, with an underwater
> hint of contusion, when I lifted it,
> wading a shingle beach on Inishowen.
> Across the estuary light after light
>
> came on silently round the perimeter
> of the camp. A stone from Phlegethon,
> bloodied on the bed of hell's hot river?
> Evening frost and the salt water
> made my hand smoke, as if I had plucked the heart
> that damned Guy de Montfort to the boiling flood-
> but not really, though I remembered
> his victim's heart in its casket, long venerated.
>
> Anyhow, there I was with the wet red stone
> in my hand, staring across at the watch-towers

from my free state of image and allusion,
swooped on, then dropped by trained binoculars:

a silhouette not worth bothering about,
out for the evening in scarf and waders
and not about to set times wrong or right,
stooping along, one of the venerators.[10]

The poem is aimed at rendering the complexity of feelings triggered
by the act of confronting one of the most direct consequences and
effective reminders of violence unleashed in society. It could be taken
as specular to the poem that precedes it, "Chekhov on Sakhalin",
based on Chekhov's own visit to the convicts in Siberia. The
uneasiness provoked by the presence of the Magilligan internment
camp facing the persona in the poem across the river Foyle is worked
out by evoking a shade from Dante's *Inferno*, Guy de Montfort. It is
the colour of the stone – described first as russet, then ruddy, and
finally red – which carries the mind from the shingle beach to Phlege-
thon and this metamorphoses the stone into "the heart that damned
Guy to the boiling flood".

Guy de Montfort is a personage who, although eliciting a mere three
lines in Canto XII, remains a memorable figure in the gallery of the
damned. He is among the violent against their neighbours who are
immersed in the river of boiling blood. The Centaur who accompanies
the faring poets shows them a shade that remains unnamed:

Mostrocci un'ombra da l'un canto sola,
dicendo: "Colui fesse in grembo a Dio
lo cor che 'n su Tamisi ancor si cola."

He showed one shade set by itself apart,
Saying: "There stands the man who dared to smite,
Even in the very bosom of God, the heart
They venerate still on Thames."[11]

One of the reasons why Dante may have chosen to dispose of the
character in such a brief space is probably the fact that he did not need
to remind his contemporaries of the atrocity committed by Guy, the
murder having made such a sensation according to Villani. In 1272,

[10] Seamus Heaney, *Station Island*, London, 1984, 20.
[11] Dante, *Inferno*, XII, 118-20.

during Mass in a church in Viterbo, Guy de Montfort killed Prince Henry, nephew of Henry III of England, whom Guy held responsible for the death of his father, Simon, at the battle of Evesham. In the notes to her translation of the *Purgatorio*, Dorothy L. Sayers reports the legend according to which "a statue of Henry with the casket containing his heart was placed on London Bridge".[12]

Summoning a shade from *Inferno* seems at first entirely justified as a poetic device in this particular context. Guy's sin, violence against one's neighbours, could in a way be consistent with the reality of the internment camp. Both the inmates and the prison guards have been or are violent against their neighbours. What they stand for is indeed based upon or sustained by that sin. The persona in the poem, however, refrains from pursuing the matter further:

> as if I had plucked the heart
> that damned Guy de Montfort to the boiling-flood
> *but not really*. [Italics added.]

Weighed up against the reliability and solidity of the stone, the allusion to Dante appears unwarranted and is consequently dropped. The fact that the persona has second thoughts, while serving as an anti-aggrandizing check, has also the effect of giving credibility to what follows: "though I remembered / his victim's heart in its casket, long venerated."

I would argue that it is in the middle of the fourth stanza that a symbolic watershed takes place at various levels. The violence and brutality represented by the camp do not elicit a call for retribution but bring about an attitude of humility that in turn engenders veneration. "Veneration" alludes to the fact that traditionally the only means to deal with violence was represented by religion, the sacred being the first barrier man was able to devise against the recurring threat of reciprocal violence. This was far from effective, as Henry's murder in a church and during Mass testifies. In the case of Dante and Heaney, art intervenes where religion fails and, in fact, in creating its own rituals, it seems to replace religion as a way to deal imaginatively with violence in a secularized society.

According to some of the most perceptive among Heaney's critics, the bent image of the "venerator" "out in scarf and waders", amounts

---

[12]   Dante, *Divine Comedy*, 148.

to an "admission of inadequacy",[13] on the poet's part, when he comes to confront Ireland's "Troubles". This may well be so, but I like to believe instead that the image, while consistent with Heaney's position throughout his work, also offers an alternative view, in the long term, to the one provided by the strategy of sectarian strife. I am referring to a principle asserted not only by Heaney on more than one occasion, but by most of the Northern poets, one which has been effectively summarized by Michael Longley: "In the context of political violence the deployment of words at their most precise and suggestive remains one of the few antidotes to death-dealing dishonesty."[14]

Moreover, although this is not the last reference to Dante's *Inferno* in the book, I would argue that Heaney at this point discards the *Inferno* as a symbol or allegory of suffering. The use of the *Inferno* as a metaphor for an unbearable predicament has been in the course of this century associated with many cases of extreme pain and destitution. The Holocaust is a case in point, as is the abomination of Stalin's regime. The latter was very much in Heaney's mind at the time due to the growing importance of the figure and lesson of Osip Mandelstam, both to his reflection on current events and his poetic development. As concerns the Holocaust, the use made by Primo Levi of Dante's *Inferno* in *Se questo è un uomo* is instructive. Far from being evoked to render the dire atrocity of the writer's predicament at Auschwitz, Dante's poetry – the canto where Ulysses speaks – is recalled in order to provide comfort, as a powerful instance of light in the darkness, the only available form of assuagement against terror and abjection. The same applies to Mandelstam who, according to his wife, carried the *Commedia* with him when he was deported to the labour camp where he was to meet his death.

The only other reference to the *Inferno* in *Station Island*, is in "The Loaning", but there it possesses an urgency of its own, referring and giving voice to the suffering of known and unknown victims of dictatorhips all over the world. The "bleeding wood" of suicides [15] is

---

[13]   Cf. Michael Parker, *Seamus Heaney: The Making of the Poet*, Houndmills, 1993, 187 and Thomas C. Foster, *Seamus Heaney*, Boston, 1989, 115.

[14]   Michael Longley, *Tupenny Stung*, Belfast, 1995, 74. The view has been recently reaffirmed by the poet: "Observing the Sons of Ulster" (Michael Longley interviewed by Eileen Battersby), *The Irish Times*, 9 March 2000, 13.

[15]   Dante, *Inferno*, XIII.

associated with secret jails where "At the click of a cell lock somewhere now / the interrogator steels his *introibo*".[16]

In "Sandstone Keepsake", there is not only a question of discretion or self-deflation on the part of the poet when his persona performs that shift in the poem signalled by the phrase "but not really". The poet's decision originates in a set of principles and imaginative needs operating at a deeper and more consistent level. One gets a glimpse of the complexity of the process in the choice the poet makes when it comes to translating the verb which Dante uses in the line quoted above: "lo cor che 'n su Tamisi ancor si cola". *Cola* has been the crux of contrasting interpretations among Dante's scholars: the ancient commentators took it to mean "venerate", while some scholars nowadays would rather have it signify "still dripping blood", and, therefore, still exacting vengeance. This is the interpretation chosen by both Charles Singleton and John Sinclair. Here is the latter's rendering:

> And he pointed out to us a shade on one side alone
> and said: "That one clove in God's bosom
> the heart which still drips on the Thames."[17]

Dorothy L. Sayers translates *cola* as venerate. Heaney, maybe unaware of the dispute, follows suit. One could safely state that had he known about the discussion, his propensity would have led him to privilege Sayers' reading. However the decision was made, it marks, in my opinion, a turning point in his poetry. The memory of violence is not put aside; victims have to be remembered. This is the duty of the poet who has to give them a voice and that voice is not meant to claim revenge but justice tinged, as it is, with that special attitude which the ancients called *pietas*. It is appropriate that the poem ushers in the section dedicated to objects which, according to Heaney, have a "ghost life" and can become "temples of the spirit". These objects "suggest obligations to the generations who have been silenced, drawing us into some covenant with them".[18]

---

[16] Heaney, *Station Island*, 52.

[17] Dante Alighieri, *The Divine Comedy*, with translation and comment by John D. Sinclair, New York, 1961.

[18] Seamus Heaney, "Place, Pastness, Poems: A Triptych", *Salmagundi*, 68-69 (Fall/Winter 1985-86), 30-31.

This same principles are found at work in "Station Island", of which I can only present a few instances. Let us take Colum's case. His shade makes a brief appearance again to reproach the poet for the way he dealt with his murder in *Field Work*:

> You confused evasion and artistic tact.
> The Protestant who shot me through the head
> I accuse directly, but indirectly, you
> dew who now atone perhaps upon this bed
> for the way you whitewashed ugliness and drew
> the lovely blinds of the *Purgatorio*
> and saccharined my death with morning. [19]

In this indirect palinode, it is as if the poet regrets having too hastily referred to Dante's work in his plea for forgiveness, as if he acknowledges that the way out of violence exacts a much longer engagement and a much deeper reflection. Moreover, what Colum is saying is that using the *Purgatorio* – besides being, in that particular instance, a sentimental and inadequate way to deal with violence – was not entirely justified from a poetic and an aesthetic point of view either.

The problem is not with the choice of the *Purgatorio*. The revenant's reappearance is again within a purgatorial setting. The problem is with the attitude of the poet who, in *Field Work*, had not yet fully accepted all the implications of the purgatorial choice which does not amount to just going "barefoot, foetal and penitential", as is said in "At the Water's Edge". The choice includes also the duty for the poet to "have a full look at the worst", while the adjective "foetal" there, a telling one, seems to point to a regressive pulsion rather than to the search of an active involvement. This I believe is implied in Colum's accusation. Colum's confrontation with the pilgrim comes after a memorable encounter with yet another victim of violence who is, at the same time, a friend of the poet.

In section VII, William Strathearn enters, a shopkeeper who was shot in cold blood by two off-duty policemen. Here the very traces of violence are described. There is no question of the poet cleansing the revenant's face as if to efface all signs of brutality. Furthermore, the example of the *Purgatorio* works at a less discernible level and therefore much more effectively than in *Field Work*:

---

[19]   Heaney, *Station Island*, 83.

> I turned to meet his face and the shock
> is still in me at what I saw. His brow
> was blown open above the eye and blood
> had dried on his neck and cheek. "Easy now,"
>
> he said, "it's only me. You've seen men as raw
> after a football match ..."[20]

A reader acquainted with the *Comedy* is reminded of another figure in Dante's *Purgatorio*. The character in question is Manfred, the son of Frederick II, whom Dante meets in the third canto among the souls of the excommunicated who managed to repent at the last moment:

> And one of them began: "Whoever you are turn your face as you
> thus go: consider if ever you saw me yonder." I turned to him and
> looked at him fixedly; blond he was, and handsome, and of noble
> mien, but a blow had cloven one of his eyebrows.[21]

The similarities do not end in the image of the cloven eyebrow. It is rather the same attitude of detachment, a complete lack of animosity, let alone any spirit of vengeance, that distinguishes both characters. Here is Strathearn as described by Heaney:

> Big-limbed, decent, open-faced, he stood
> forgetful of everything now except
> whatever was welling up in his spoiled head,
>
> beginning to smile.[22]

It is the poet, rather surprisingly, who asks for forgiveness:

> "Forgive the way I have lived indifferent –
> forgive my timid circumspect involvement,"
>
> I surprised myself by saying. "Forgive
> my eye," he said, "all that's above my head."
> And then a stun of pain seemed to go through him
>
> and he trembled like a heatwave and faded.[23]

---

[20]   *Ibid.*, 77.
[21]   Dante, *Purgatorio*, III, 108.
[22]   Heaney, *Station Island*, 79.

Like Louis O'Neill, the casualty in the poem of the same name in
Field Work, William Strathearn has a touch of the artist about him:

> Through life and death he had hardly aged.
> There always was an athlete cleanliness
> shining off him and except for the ravaged
>
> forehead and the blood, he was still the same
> rangy midfielder in a blue jersey
> and starched pants, the one stylist on the team,
>
> the perfect, clean, unthinkable victim.

This, among other things, confirms the general allusion to the
Purgatorio. In the *Purgatorio*, Dante meets a number of friends as
well as poets and artists. Poetry is given back its full potential in a
relationship between peers.

In the first cantos of the *Purgatorio* violence bows down to poetry,
atrocity is distanced and transformed not just by the poet but by the
very victims who retell their gruesome deaths. This applies in
particular to those shades that Dante meets in the ante-purgatory. The
feeling the reader gets is precisely the one pointed out by Heaney in a
conversation with John Haffenden, just after the completion of *Field
Work*. In reply to a question about the word "assuaging" which
Haffenden sees as being a favourite of Heaney's, he has this to say
about his view of the *Purgatorio*:

> It's the opposite of exacerbate. There is a kind of writing that sets
> out to exacerbate. But I believe that what poetry does to me is
> comforting ... if I read the *Divine Comedy*, the *Purgatorio*, it's in the
> highest, widest, deepest sense, *comforting*. Great art is comforting,
> in some odd way. I think that art does appease, assuage.[24]

To read *The Divine Comedy*, Heaney has said, recurring to yet
another purgatorial image, "is to go through a refining element, to be
steadied and reminded of the possible dimensions of life".[25] This does
not mean that the possibility of redress is forfeited – on the contrary.

---

[23]   *Ibid.*, 80.
[24]   John Haffenden, *Poets in Conversation with John Haffenden*, London, 1981, 68.
[25]   Quoted in Blake Morrison, *Seamus Heaney*, London, 1982, 82.

What is in fact noteworthy in Le Goff's paradigm, something relevant also to Heaney, is the observation that the emergence of the concept of purgatory was inspired:

> more by a need for justice than by a yearning for salvation .... The other world was supposed to correct the inequalities and injustices of this one.[26]

This too is a feature that cannot fail to appeal strongly to a poet like Heaney who is so interested in the question of political/poetical redress, as is shown by the title and content of his latest book of prose, *The Redress of Poetry*.

The third section of *Station Island*, "Sweeney Redivivus", appears consistent with the purgatorial paradigm I have been illustrating so far. Sweeney's estrangement from the world of men, far from being a release from purgatory, as Corcoran believes,[27] is the confirmation of a view of our existence as a purgatory of sorts. "Sweeney redivivus" does indeed provide not only a redescription of life as a condition of spiritual purging and purification but also a synopsis of some of the structural oppositions of Heaney's poetry. The contrast between Sweeney and Ronan parallels the one between Oisin and Patrick, between oral and learned, between the *pagus* and *urbs*, between mythology and history and religion, barbaric and classic, the instinctual and the rational, Antaeus and Hercules. What is imperative for the poet is to find, among these opposing claims, the "space where all contrarieties can be held and harmonized, composed in momentary poise".[28]

Through the purgatorial pattern provided by Dante and existing in the culture to which he belongs, Heaney manages to find that space where poetry is enabled to relate to atrocity. That ideal space, that middle ground, created in a poetical world, suggests a way out of confrontation, away from reciprocal violence. Poetry offers, to use Robert Frost's phrase which Heaney is fond of quoting, "a stay against confusion", or according to Heaney's own rephrasing in "The Government of the Tongue", a means for "marking time". The latter expression is used to illustrate the mysterious working of poetry. The figure chosen is Christ in St John's Gospel confronting a mob, which

---

[26]   Le Goff, *The Birth of Purgatory*, 210.
[27]   Neil Corcoran, *Seamus Heaney*, London, 1986, 154.
[28]   Elmer Andrews, *The Poetry of Seamus Heaney*, London, 1988, 194.

intends to stone the adulteress. Instead of directly answering the questions posed by the Pharisees, Jesus writes on the ground. Poetry, Heaney says:

> is like the writing in the sand in the face of which accusers and accused are left speechless and renewed. The drawing of those characters is, like poetry, a break with the usual life but not an absconding from it. Poetry, like the writing, is arbitrary and marks time in every possible sense of that phrase. [29]

Marking time is, in fact, what souls in purgatory and people in life do. It is what poetry does when it finds its equilibrium. Far from being an escape from one's responsibilities or an "absconding" from life, the marking of time envisaged by Heaney is one of the most effective ways for poets to deal with past and contemporary atrocities, remaining at the same time "faithful to the collective historical experience" and "true to the recognition of the emerging self".

---

[29]   Seamus Heaney, *The Government of the Tongue*, London 1988, 108.

THE POETICS OF VIOLENCE:
THE PARALLEL CASES OF SEAMUS HEANEY
AND MONGANE WALLY SEROTE

NICHOLAS MEIHUIZEN

> We can forgive a man for making a useful
> thing as long as he does not admire it. The
> only excuse for making a useless thing is
> that one admires it intensely. All art is quite
> useless.[1]

In addressing the work of Irish poet Seamus Heaney and South African poet Mongane Wally Serote under a single umbrella, I hope to reconcile to an extent my natural interest in my motherland with my interest in Irish letters. From one perspective the task is not that difficult, for as political entities South Africa and Ireland have both been subjected to histories of violence based on colonial ethnic discrimination and its variations, including the binaries inherent in colonialism: Master and Slave, First World and Third World, Settler and Indigene. What are the responses of Heaney and Serote to this violence? Leading from this initial broad-based question is another more specific and more contentious one (though certainly not a new one), which has to do with the social reverberations of art.

Can Serote's and Heaney's poetic responses to violence have any value for the individual who is continually subject to the brutality of the times? This is the question I need to consider as a person living in one of the most violent countries in the world today, who nevertheless devotes all his time to the study of literature rather than, say, the abolition of hand guns. I suppose I am especially sensitive to the unqualified certainty of Oscar Wilde's "All art is quite useless" because of the growing admiration in South African educational

---

[1]   Oscar Wilde, *The Picture of Dorian Gray*, New York, 1931, 10.

institutions merely for what are considered useful skills, at the expense of art, music and literature. Educational bureaucrats are not particularly receptive to Wildean irony.

Mongane Wally Serote will need some introduction for most international readers. He was born in Sophiatown near Johannesburg in 1944, four years before the assumption of power by the Nationalist Party. Because he is always conscious of himself in relation to his society, his life and writing afford a chronicle of and commentary on the apartheid era. His writing also provides a means for moving beyond the apartheid mind-set, and so is socially constructive in orientation (though never blandly didactic).

An avid reader from childhood, Serote became aware of the Great Tradition of English Literature at an early age, consuming the works of writers such as Shakespeare, Dickens, Lawrence, Hardy, Wordsworth and Keats. But while imbibing it, he also reacted against this exotic tradition, and, at the age of fourteen, started writing his own work in response to the dearth of subject matter directly pertaining to the life he experienced.

His first volume of poetry was published in 1972. It was entitled *Yakhal' inkomo* (which translates from the Zulu tongue into "the cattle are crying"; the expression is shorthand for the symbolically pregnant notion, "the cattle are crying because of their slaughter at the hands of human beings"). This was followed by *Tsetlo* in 1974, *No Baby Must Weep* in 1975, and *Behold Mama, Flowers* in 1978. He wrote several more works in the 1980s and 1990s, including *Third World Express* (1992), and *Come and Hope with Me* (1994). In this essay I dwell principally on *Behold Mama, Flowers* but also turn briefly to these more recent works.

Dedicated to Steve Biko, *Behold Mama, Flowers* was actually written while Serote was in America, and reflects, to an extent, the tension and despondency of the exile isolated from the coalface. In his Foreword Serote refers to an Osiric myth he learned from Skunder Boghossian, the Ethiopian painter resident in America:

> a man chopped a body many, many times – he chopped this body into many, many small pieces and threw them into the flowing river. When the pieces, floating and flowing, began to dance with the rhythm of the river, a child, seeing this, said, "Mama, look at the flowers!"[2]

---

[2]   Mongane Wally Serote, *Behold Mama, Flowers*, Johannesburg, 1978, 8.

The title reflects a shift in emphasis – from the slaughtering of helpless cattle, as encoded in the title of his first book, we move to redemptive vision within an implicitly violent context. Begun one year before the Soweto uprising, the book encapsulates, to an extent, the new optimism and strength of resistance that accompanied what are known as the Power days, but also the strenuous trials and tribulations along the road to freedom. This bivalence is exemplified in the manner in which the experiencing self is at once devalued, and enshrined in a communal egalitarianism, through the lower-case "i", which is used as personal pronoun throughout. What we gather from the implied semantics of the case is that, despite its divisive nature, oppression promotes unity among those oppressed, although Serote's extended vision in this respect, which incorporates his other works, notably the novel *To Every Birth Its Blood*[3] has been criticized as being too simplistic in the way it presents black unity in purely socialist terms.

Following a complex trajectory, the self of the present poem seems to float down a river of experience, like a piece of body from the myth of Boghossian, which has the potential to be transformed into a flower, if only in the imagination of the perceiver. But near the beginning of the poem, rather than the beautiful flowers of imaginative transformation, we find the parched sunflowers of a late capitalist landscape: these flowers are "neon", like the "rivers", which are flanked by "tall cement trees". Soon after follow images of the bones of slaves, who died in transportation, "screaming bones still chained and bloodstained", and these are juxtaposed with images of men "digging gold beneath the earth", and references to "the chains of the rand" and "the chains of the dollar". In other words, as the juxtapositions make clear, implicated in Serote's critique are both local and metropolitan elements of exploitation, along with recent and ancient examples of imperialist brutality. The poem, then, is a lament for Africa and her exploited peoples, but also a commentary on current universal dehumanizing and destructive trends. A section on blood and tears follows, the first of repeated references to the formulaic trinity of "blood, sweat and tears", which Serote invests with new life. For example, "blood" modulates into "pus", which makes its diseased mark on the women the speaker holds. Then

---

3   Mongane Wally Serote, *To Every Birth Its Blood*, Johannesburg, 1981.

women and blood are closely linked through childbirth, as in earlier
poems, and though Serote empathizes with the agonies of childbirth
and bereavement, he chooses to underscore the resilience of women:
"after mothers weep, they still make love, and bear other / children."[4]
However bleak the present may be, this resilience betokens hope for
the future.

In a new section the river is displaced by a road along which we
find nightmare tableaux from the apartheid years, incorporate
inhuman jail sentences and their impact on wives and children, and the
plight of an old man whose home has been bulldozed down for the
sake of separate "development". In the midst of this landscape the
perceiving consciousness does not simply remain passive. Here and
throughout the poem it interrogates its relationship with the world and
history. The speaker, for instance, now examines the possibility of
forgiveness and the need for the simple rewards of a normal existence,
again conflating the South African situation with disturbing global
trends:

> what does a man want
> to put his life down for a car
> to go to the moon
> i want to walk with ease, laugh and kiss ...[5]

The speaker continues on his visionary journey, hearing footsteps,
seeing "sidewalks" where other journeys have reached their close in
"pools of blood", or "paths" which "seem to vanish into dark
passages". Cognate with the endless flux and reflux of life on the
rivers, roads and paths, is a sense of longing for a distant "home",
which underlines Serote's being in America at the time of writing, but
also suggests the more consuming and fundamental existential
displacement of the non-person as encoded in the poet's lower-case
"i".[6] An apostrophe to Africa at this stage incorporates family figures
– brother, sister, child, grandfather, father. But in present times the
family is the site of pain and disaster, not comfort, and mother Africa
is dogged by nightmare:

---

4   Serote, *Behold Mama*, 12-15.
5   *Ibid.*, 19-20
6   *Ibid.*, 24-25.

> ah, africa, it does matter that you take a look
> and begin to believe that the sahara owns you
> that you own nothing
> behold
> your nightmare grows and grows like waves of the sea.

The image is puissant and terrifying, undercutting the very basis of existence in Africa. As a consequence, her children leave. Serote refers to some of her most gifted absentee children: Coltrane, Eric Dolphy, Miles Davis, Nina Simone, and Miriam Makeba.[7]

Near the conclusion of the poem we find a visionary section on the macabre beginning of Africa, which drops from God's "back pocket" while the Creation is taking place, and is closely scrutinized by the devil, who appears to claim it as his own. But this plunge into the abyss is followed by the section on Skunder Boghossian, exiled from Africa, like Serote, though with his conception of "the continent" intact, along with its implications of a redemptive wholeness.[8] But again, this vision offers no easy end to the quest for liberation, and the conclusion of the poem, which returns to the image of flowers (though now no longer dying), for all its optimism, bears the traces of a continuing journey:

> i can say there is nothing that we know in the end
> i can say, ah
> behold the flowers
> i can say
> your dignity is locked tight in the resting places
> in the places where you shall drink water
> around the fire where you shall laugh with your children
> i can say otherwise
> your dignity is held tight in the sweating cold hands of death
> the village where everything is silent about dignities
> i will say again
> behold the flowers, they begin to bloom![9]

Indeed, the journey over the next twelve years was yet to prove long and dangerous, and close friends would die on the way. After the hardships and the grief, how bizarre, yet how typically South African,

---

7   *Ibid.*, 34.
8   *Ibid.*, 53.
9   *Ibid.*, 60-61.

that Serote's path should take him to the urbane precincts of the University of Natal, a traditionally "white" university, which awarded him an honorary doctorate in April 1991. But he was pleased by this fact, seeing in the occasion not an Establishment flourish incommensurate with raw human experience, and certainly not the end of a journey. For him the event attested to a communal "searching for a way forward" on the part of all South Africans.[10]

This searching is evident in his own recent writing. In *Third World Express* the experiencing self has been restored, through the personal pronoun, to its own rightful and proud uppercase position. (Unforeseen forces and events at work in the country will make of this a temporary gesture, as will be discussed presently.) Serote's search is extended to incorporate others with shared values:

> I know
> there are good men and women –
> in this place
> and in this time the good are there!
> they look you in the eye
> in search
> their faces are like still trees
> and their shoulders are wide open
> they wear tired eyes
> they search and look
> for what we can share
> or for that moment which can make life magic
> for that simple thing
> for that, which can make us us!
> they are black they are white
> they share this earth with us
> and their hearts are not steel
> or gold
> or stone
> but are simple – flesh!
> they are boers and blacks
> women or men ...[11]

Considering his involvement in the struggle (and the losses he suffered because of it), the moderateness of his views is indeed

---

[10]   Duncan Brown, "Interview with Mongane Wally Serote", *Theoria*, 80 (1992), 143.

[11]   Mongane Wally Serote, *Third World Express*, Cape Town, 1992, 4-5.

salutary. His verse embodies reconciliation. But the process of searching in the book is (once more) universal in its concerns, having to do with finding solutions to the continuing violence and poverty not only in South Africa, but the world at large.

He also anticipates, in a visionary manner akin to the Shelley of *Prometheus Unbound*, a change in the consciousness of suffering humanity, where the poor will seek to change themselves, rather than remain the butt of society, where the rich will stop their self-destructive exploitation. The Third World Express would appear to be the medium of change, the means to reaching a new era, whether in Africa, Asia, or Latin America:

> ah my friends
> sometimes I wonder
> when's the express coming
> with its speedy wind it must come
> at night
> in the morning
> it must come
> the Third World Express must come
> at dawn
> in the twilight
> like the wind
> like a river
> like a mad dam.[12]

At once destroyer and preserver (as suggested in the mirror-image of "mad dam"), the Third World Express will exert a pervasive influence – the references to the different elements and times of the day suggest this fact.

Come and Hope with Me is more brooding and disturbed than *Third World Express*. The lower-case personal pronoun is again deployed by Serote, but not as a sign of obliteration or community, rather as a sign of mourning in the face of threats of civil war and the murder of Chris Hani. It is as if unexpected bars to the process of liberation are suddenly erected, and the occasion is cause for further lament. The struggle of self with self in the personal realm, broached in his novel *To Every Birth Its Blood*,[13] now becomes more externalized, as conflict shifts from a unitary common enemy to

---

[12] *Ibid.*, 31-32.
[13] Serote, *To Every Birth*, 281.

power games and destructive situations where inner strengths and resources are necessary, such as the ability to "hope". "Hope", then, becomes a type of transformative tool, a means for achieving a general humanitarian end, rather than a specific, sectarian political end:

> come
> if the truth does stalk us
> we will befriend wisdom
> you and I
> come
> let us return
> come
> come and be with me
> come and hope and dream with me when the dream
> dawns. [14]

If hope is a tool, language is its implement, and, again, Serote would effect transformation through language. His war against apartheid has been a war of words, in the most literal sense, and the world has witnessed that such a war can influence hearts and minds. Serote's words (buttressed – it is true – by his position as British and European cultural attaché for the ANC) spoke to people all around the world, and helped increase the intensity of international pressure on South Africa, pressure so instrumental in local political transformation. Language can help transform the present, and it can also look to the future in order to encapsulate proper responses to that future, as through the word "hope". Serote's is not a shallow hope, but one conditioned by years of struggle, and the successful outcome of that struggle. This hope is contextualized by poetry; put, in other words, into a proper and potent frame, where past and present give impetus to the future, and where the informing power of rejuvenating words (where flowers might displace bloody body pieces) corroborates the fact that history can be cajoled into redemptive directions.

That the whole matter of linguistic intervention in the world of action is more complex and subtle than I have thus far indicated is evidenced in a poem by another South African exile, C. J. Driver. Driver's relation to the political struggle in South Africa, though certainly evident in his writing, does not wholly absorb him as does Serote's, and yet various manifestations of a type of alienation come

---

[14]   Mongane Wally Serote, *Come and Hope with Me*, Cape Town, 1994, 28.

to the fore in his writing, as if corroborating at some inherent level the distinctive perception of an exile. For example, in his "Wilderness: Written on Water", from *In the Water-margins*, he views the difficult relationship between poet and language from a perspective which interrogates the individual input or agency involved in the act of naming, given the autonomous propensities of language:

> We think of something lost
> In writing down
> The flux of time:
> But what completes our thought?
> (The language knows so much beyond oneself)
>
> The thread of meaning lost
> In noting down
> That fleeting time:
> Precise the moment caught
> (The language knows so much beyond oneself)[15]

If the "moment" is "caught", our own understanding plays but a small part in the matter, we "lose" the "thread of meaning" in our act of naming. "Language" – existing apart, never subject to closure (as the brackets help indicate) – "completes our thought" independently of our conscious ability, as if it is a type of universal knowing which transcends our own individual acts of knowing.

But while individual control is questioned by such a perception (where, in effect, the creative "I" becomes exiled from its own utterances), what also emerges from this perception is the positive sense that the capabilities of the self are extended by language. In another South African poet, Lionel Abrahams (who was actually an early and committed champion of Serote), the association between the self and language is less explicit and less troubled, but again linguistic engagement through the shaping lines of poetry has a positive effect on the self's experience of life. In Abrahams' poem "A Dead Tree Full of Live Birds", for example, "moments" are held by the shaping lines "out of time",[16] implying an aesthetic redemption of such moments, which takes us back, at least, to Shakespeare's sonnet 65:

[15] C. J. Driver, *In the Water-margins*, Plumstead, 1994, 47.
[16] Lionel Abrahams, *A Dead Tree Full of Live Birds*, Plumstead, 1995, 8.

> Since brass, nor stone, nor earth, nor boundless sea,
> But sad mortality o'ersways their power,
> How with this rage shall beauty hold a plea,
> Whose action is no stronger than a flower?
> O how shall summer's honey breath hold out
> Against the wrackful siege of batt'ring days,
> When rocks impregnable are not so stout,
> Nor gates of steel so strong, but Time decays?
> O fearful meditation: Where, alack,
> Shall Time's best jewel from Time's chest lie hid?
> Or what strong hand can hold his swift foot back,
> Or who his spoil of beauty can forbid?
>   O none, unless this miracle have might,
>   That in black ink my love may still shine bright. [17]

The lines I am particularly interested in here, as anyone familiar with Heaney's *Preoccupations* will appreciate,[18] are lines 3 and 4:

> How with this rage shall beauty hold a plea,
> Whose action is no stronger than a flower?

The question concerns the devouring "rage" of Time, to which all existence is subject, and against which art (metonymically incorporated in the notion of "beauty") must pit itself. Heaney extends the resonance of "rage", to make it refer to any brutal force in life. In order to "hold a plea" against the "rage" of his place and time, he finds his own "befitting emblems of adversity" (Heaney quotes from Yeats' "Meditations in Time of Civil War"), and in doing so embodies the complex meshwork of demands of his public and private visions, which poets at social cutting edges need to do (but often ignore). Heaney's aesthetic strategy incorporates, it hardly needs mentioning, the reflection of a literal preservation – centuries-old human bodies embalmed by bog juices – of the otherwise momentary flux of history. The significance of this preservation is that these figures relate to the current violence in Ireland, and bring into juxtaposition the earth goddess of the original human sacrifices two thousand years ago, and the nationalist feminization of Ireland (as expressed in the populist images of "Mother Ireland" and "Kathleen Ni Houlihan").

---

[17] Helen Vendler, *The Art of Shakespeare's Sonnets*, Cambridge: MA, 1997, 303.
[18] Seamus Heaney, *Preoccupations: Selected Poems 1968-1978*, London, 1980, 41-60.

Heaney has since sought other means of "holding a plea" against rage. I think, for example, of the crucial organizing image of "Frontiers of Writing", in *The Redress of Poetry*. It is that of five towers – a quincunx of literary towers – by means of which Heaney would "bring the frontiers of the country into alignment with the frontiers of writing", and "attempt to sketch the shape of an integrated literary tradition".[19] The five towers consist of, at the centre, "the tower of prior Irelandness", or the round aboriginal dwelling of the ancients. On the southern point is Kilcolman Castle, Spenser's tower of Anglicization; on the western point is Thoor Ballylee, Yeats' tower of spiritual and magical restoration in the face of English phlegmaticness; on the eastern point we find, of course, Joyce's Martello tower, representing "his attempt to marginalize the imperium which had marginalized him by replacing the Anglocentric Protestant tradition with a newly forged apparatus of Homeric correspondences". Heaney imagines Louis MacNeice's tower at Carrickfergus Castle in the north, and it in a sense subsumes the forces inherent in the other four towers. MacNeice "can be regarded as an Irish Protestant writer with Anglocentric attitudes who managed to be faithful to his Ulster inheritance, his Irish affections and his English predilections". Heaney's sense of political responsibility, his healing vision, his tolerance, his deep humanity, merge in the quincunx, and leave one with an impression of the confluence of life and art, the hope inherent in art, and the fact that poetry really and indisputably matters. Indeed, such is the poet's human canniness and aesthetic strength, that it is almost as if he deploys the rage of political violence to test the credibility of his poetry.

Violence in Heaney's *The Spirit Level*, spills over into public and private spheres, as in "Two Lorries".[20] The poem juxtaposes a remembered scene between the poet's mother and a flirtatious coalman in the 1940s who delivers his load in an old lorry, and the bomb-packed lorry of modern times which shatters a bus station in "Magherafelt". The location was an innocent enough one in the time of the first lorry, but is now made terrible and terrifying by the mayhem. The name "Magherafelt" pulses throughout the poem, like an incantation, or the ticking of an explosive device. But consider the conclusion to the poem, where a dream-image combines the

---

[19] Seamus Heaney, *The Redress of Poetry*, London and Boston, 1995, 199.
[20] Seamus Heaney, *The Spirit Level*, New York, 1996, 17.

tenderness and terror of past and present, and leaves us with
something peculiarly beautiful:

>   but which lorry
> Was it now? Young Agnew's or that other,
> Heavier, deadlier one, set to explode
> In a time beyond her time in Magherafelt ...
> So tally bags and sweet-talk darkness, coalman.
> Listen to the rain spit in new ashes
>
> As you heft a load of dust that was Magherafelt,
> Then reappear from your lorry as my mother"s
> Dreamboat coalman filmed in silk-white ashes.

Political violence is apparent too in a poem dedicated to the poet's
brother, "Keeping Going",[21] where it is a means for testing human
spirit and endurance. The brother's humorous resilience, for example,
is evident in his good-natured parody of a military and populist icon of
the conflict in the North – an Orangeman piper:

> The piper coming from far away is you
> With a whitewash brush for a sporran
> Wobbling round you, a kitchen chair
> Upside down on your shoulder, your right arm
> Pretending to tuck the bag beneath your elbow,
> Your pop-eyes and big cheeks nearly bursting
> With laughter, but keeping the drone going on
> Interminably, between catches of breath.

The "brush" itself becomes one of those Heaneyesque objects that
offers a perspective on to something else, in this case a family past,
when the Heaney farmhouse used to be regularly whitewashed. The
brush in those days performed something of a miracle, and so
encapsulates Heaney's preoccupation with the transformative power
of small things, as the "watery grey" it "lashes" onto the walls, dries
out "whiter and whiter".

    Another modulation takes us to one of the repeated images in this
book, the Homeric blood trench, from which the souls of the dead
drink fresh blood and are given human voice. The tar border to the
house on which the whitewashing is being done is this "freshly

---

[21] *Ibid.*, 13.

opened, pungent, reeking trench", and the ghosts are memories of a
past that Heaney shared with his brother, and which include (in a type
of surrealist setting from *Macbeth*) a mother's warning to her wet-
behind-the-ears undergraduate son about the danger of "bad boys" at
college. This embarrassing warning (a humorous encapsulation of
parental naïvety) modulates shockingly into the scene of contemporary violence which follows, and which involves bad boys indeed. The
casual, relaxed pose of the victim underscores the everyday nature of
the brutality of the vicinity in which Heaney's brother lives. The tar of
the street and the gutter conflate with the tar-strip of the whitewashing
and the blood trench, and the murdered man becomes a sacrificial
victim whose blood (it is implied) only gives voice to the unquiet
ghosts of the struggle, and so perpetuates violence:

> A car came slow down Castle Street, made the halt,
> Crossed the Diamond, slowed again and stopped
> Level with him, although it was not his lift.
> And then he saw an ordinary face
> For what it was and a gun in his own face.
> His right leg was hooked back, his sole and heel
> Against the wall, his right knee propped up steady,
> So he never moved, just pushed with all his might
> Against himself, then fell past the tarred strip,
> Feeding the gutter with his copious blood.

Set against such scenes, his brother's resilience seems all the more
remarkable, but of conclusive redemptive significance in the poem is
the functional object, the brush, which takes within its wholesome
ambit the goodness of utility and the potency of the magic of
transformation:

> I see you at the end of your tether sometimes,
> In the milking parlour, holding yourself up
> Between two cows until your turn goes past,
> Then coming to in the smell of dung again
> And wondering, is this all? As it was
> In the beginning, is now and shall be?
> Then rubbing your eyes and seeing our old brush
> Up on the byre door, and keeping going.

Nicholas Meihuizen

Another "trench" poem is "Damson", which also relies on breathtakingly bold imagistic modulation.[22] The first image of a wound, described with Heaney's usual fresh exactitude, is conflated, disturbingly, with a "packed lunch":

> Gules and cement dust. A matte tacky blood
> On the bricklayer's knuckles, like the damson stain
> That seeped through his packed lunch.

This blood, however, is the result of an honest wound, not of deadening political violence, and the trench scene with its ghosts only serves to underscore the difference between Odysseus, the "sacker", and the present wounded "builder". The stain of his "packed lunch" anticipates the final image of the poem, though it takes this very mundane source of nourishment to the next power. Confronted by the ghosts the builder will:

> Drive them back to the wine-dark taste of home,
> The smell of damsons simmering in a pot,
> Jam ladled thick and steaming down the sunlight.

The imagination picks up on a colour, links it to various things and senses, and displaces the images and materials of violence with those of domestic creation, nutritious, restorative.

The principal focus of "The Swing" is also domestic.[23] Here, a state of grace stems from the sanctuary offered by remembered childhood. The measure of the complex pressures of past, present, and future are recognized and acknowledged by the poem, which chooses to privilege the experiences and sensations of the past, the analogue – it may be – of even a socially responsible art's imperative to suspend the multitudinous tide of experience (including the indescribable violence of Hiroshima) and offer (in a way reminiscent of Shakespeare's "miracle" of "black ink") the glimpse of a tension-free and enduring realm of "beauty":

> To start up by yourself, you hitched the rope
> Against your backside and backed on into it
> Until it tautened, then tiptoed and drove off

---

22 *Ibid.*, 19.
23 *Ibid.*, 58.

As hard as possible. You hurled a gathered thing
From the small of your own back into the air.
Your head swept low, you heard the whole shed creak.

We all learned one by one to go sky high.
Then townlands vanished into aerodromes,
Hiroshima made light of human bones,
Concorde's neb migrated towards the future.
So who were we to want to hang back there
In spite of all?
In spite of all, we sailed
Beyond ourselves and over and above
The rafters aching in our shoulder-blades,
The give and take of branches in our arms.

Nevertheless, while the spirit of the past has its own particular merit, Heaney has also captured in powerfully felt terms the spirit of the act of swinging, the spirit, in other words, of continuing process, which implies a moving "beyond" that past. This movement carries the refreshing aspects of that past, and so proclaims Heaney's own involvement with a type of "hope" regarding the future.

As in Serote, the aesthetic bodying forth of the past fuels an enriched engagement with the future. In fact, each type of spirit portrayed in this book has its own resonance, its own level, and Heaney seems able to take the exact measure of all of them, rendering the title *The Spirit Level* linguistically functional, and not just a verbal shadow of the actual spirit level. This sense of the functional worth of language impresses us most in the presence of Heaney, and makes us value the substantial force of his words. To return to the image of the quincunx of towers, it is as if verbal artefacts have the solidity of towers, and can take their stand in the lived world in a similar manner. The towers, in turn, have a significatory function inasmuch as they suggest psychological attitudes, and ways of ordering and confronting lived experience. Heaney's towers are distinctively verbal, just as his words are distinctively substantial. This is the "frontier of writing" of which he is so aware, presided over by towers that blur the edges between words and things. Further, it is from this level of molten potential that he acts. From here he assumes the profound responsibility to reconcile the forces inherent in each of the towers, an act which we might see, again, as a supreme act of hope for the future of Ireland. He thus helps us to appreciate that Serote's encoding of "hope" (the product of a related "frontier of writing", if we consider the close relation it bears to already-achieved humanitarian ends) is more than just a literary gesture, is closer akin to a similar social responsibility, a responsibility shared by all those who work with, or come under the impact of, language.

HISTORIC OR COMIC?
THE IRISHNESS OF DURRELL'S *ALEXANDRIA QUARTET*

MARY M. F. MASSOUD

In an article entitled "Curate's Egg: An Alexandrian Opinion of
Durrell's *Quartet*", Dr M. Manzalawi of Alexandria University
criticized Durrell's distortion of objective details, in view of all the
linguistic, topographical and historical inaccuracies it contains. He
showed how almost every Arabic word in the *Quartet* has a wrong
form or is misused. He pointed out various errors in topography, such
as placing the desert in the middle of the Delta, and the grotesque
misrepresentations of various facets of Egyptian life such as the
bizarre suggestion that Copts (that is, the Egyptian Christians) regard
the creation of Israel as a boon to Middle Eastern Christians, despite
the fact that quite a number of refugees are themselves Christians.[1]
This article appeared in 1962, soon after the publication of the four
books of the *Quartet* in one volume. From then on critics, both
Egyptian and international, have not ceased to make the same complaint: that Durrell's portrayal is historically inaccurate.[2]

And yet, one may ask, was Durrell really interested in giving a
realistic picture of Alexandria? It seems hardly credible that Durrell,
who (according to his biographers)[3] had lived and worked in

---

[1] M. Manzalwi, "Curate's Egg: An Alexandrian Opinion of Durrell's *Quartet*",
     Etudes Anglaises, 15 (1962), 248-60.
[2] See, for example, Mona Mones, "Limitations in Vision: The Egyptian People in
     Lawrence Durrell's *Quartet*", *Annales of the Faculty of Arts, Cairo University*,
     LVI/3 (1996); Soad Sobhi, "Behind the Dark Velvet Breast of Montaza", *Ahram
     Weekly*, 7-13 July 1994, 11; D. J. Enright, "Alexandrian Nights Entertainments:
     Lawrence Durrell's Quartet", *International Literary Annual*, London, 1961; and
     Roger Bowen's *Many Histories Deep: The Personal Landscape Poets in Egypt
     1940-45*, London, 1995, 164, to mention only a few.
[3] Durrell's official biographers are Ian and Susan MacNiven. Other valuable
     accounts of his life are by Keith Brown, "Lawrence Durrell", in *British Writers
     Supplement I: Graham Greene to Tom Stoppard*, ed. I. Scott-Kilvert, New York,

Alexandria for some time and who had a number of Alexandrian friends, could have committed such grave errors out of mere ignorance, carelessness or dishonesty. Indeed, his own confession (in a prefatory note to *Justine)* of having "exercised a novelist's right in taking a few necessary liberties with modern Middle Eastern History", makes one suspect that he knew better. Was Durrell, then, deliberately throwing dust into the reader's eyes when he twice asserted (in prefatory notes to *Justine* and *Balthazar)* that the city is "real"? And if so, to what purpose?

I should like to suggest that Durrell, the Anglo-Irish novelist, was primarily interested in producing a comedy which (whether consciously or not) is very much in "the Irish comic tradition" (to borrow Vivian Mercier's expression), and that the setting of *The Alexandria Quartet* is no more objectively real than, say, Brobdingnag or Lilliput in Swift's *Gulliver's Travels.*

Irish on his mother's side and English on his father's, Durrell was conscious and proud of the influence of both strands on his way of thinking. As he expressed it in an interview:

> Irish-English? Do I harp on the matter? I keep both because I'm compounded of both. English because I write in it, and language is really nationality. Here, I'm as English as Shakespeare's birthday, and proud of it. Irish now? That means the fire, the hysteria, the mental sluttishness, the sensuality and intuition. Valuable factors I can't deny or do without.[4]

The "story" of the *Quartet,* told in its 1100 pages or so, boils down to a few words: Nessim Hosnani and his wife, Justine, secretly trade in armaments, conspiring with the Jews against the Egyptian royal house. In the end the Hosnani intrigue collapses, Hosnani's riches are sequestered, and the couple is sentenced to house detention. Their friends who, thanks to the city of Alexandria in which they all live, have been "deeply wounded in their sex",[5] break up and leave for Europe. Later, Nessim and Justine also leave for Europe, this time to engage in a political intrigue on an international scale.

1987 and Marc Alyn, *Lawrence Durrell: The Big Supposer*, London, 1973. For the influence of Ireland on Durrell, see Richard Pine, *Lawrence Durrell: The Mindscape*, New York, 1994, Chapter 11.

[4] Lawrence Durrell, "The Kenneller Tape", in *The World of Lawrence Durrell*, ed. H. Moore, Carbondale: IL, 1962, 162-63.

[5] Lawrence Durrell, *Justine*, London, 1957, 14.

This is the skeleton of the work. The *Quartet,* however, has very little to do with politics. Durrell tells us (in his Preface to *Balthazar*) that "the central topic of the book is an investigation of modern love". As such, it is primarily occupied with the amorous relationships of various individuals. As Steiner remarks, "[its] angle of vision is rigorously private. The gusts of political life blow across the scene, but they are not accorded any importance."[6]

Significantly, all the amorous relationships depicted in the *Quartet* are incestuous and adulterous. This, however, is not due to anything in the characters of the individuals concerned, but to the ancient city of Alexandria, from the influence of which none has been able to escape from Cleopatra's day to ours. This idea is stressed again and again in the *Quartet.* On the opening page of *Justine,* Alexandria is described as "the city which used us as its flora – precipitated in us conflicts which were hers and which we mistook for our own". Balthazar speaks of Alexandria as "the city which has everything but happiness to offer its lovers".[7] Nessim asks Clea, "How do you spell love in Alexandria?" He answers his own question: "Sleeplessness, loneliness, *bonheur, chagrin.*"[8] Justine thinks that she and her friends have been "trapped in the projection of a will too powerful to be human ... the gravitational field which Alexandria threw down about those it had chosen as its exemplars".[9] Darley, who feels victimized by it, is advised to leave it.[10] However, even while away from it, Darley is still obsessed by its image[11] and when he returns to it after the war, he notices that it is the same city it has always been: "Alexandria, princess and whore .... She would never change."[12] Throughout the whole of the *Quartet,* we are not allowed to forget this image of the city, or its irresistible hold on its inhabitants. Hardly a single character is able to escape its influence – with the one exception, perhaps, of the "virtuous Semira" who is terribly deformed.

This, then, is the central theme of the work (if one is allowed to simplify). Durrell, of course, has a lot more to say about "modern love". Drawing on Einstein's relativity theory, he gives each amorous

6 George Steiner, "Lawrence Durrell: The Baroque Novel", *Yale Review*, 49 (1960), 494.
7 Lawrence Durrell, *Balthazar*, London, 1958, 21.
8 Lawrence Durrell, *Mountolive*, London, 1958, 194.
9 Durrell, *Justine*, 18-19.
10 *Ibid.*, 230.
11 Durrell, *Balthazar*, 22-23; Lawrence Durrell, *Clea*, London, 1960, 14-15.
12 Durrell, *Clea*, 63.

relationship a number of different interpretations, all of which appear to be equally valid. He also draws on Freud, trying to apply to his lovers the idea that every human being is part male and part female, and that "every sexual act" is "a process in which four persons are involved", as he says in his epigraph to *Justine*. He further complicates matters by adding a symbolical level,[13] and by inter-weaving with his central topic a number of minor ones related to matters of the intellect, politics and religion, all expressed in a most poetical style, and using the "conventions of the psychological novel as a framework".[14] However, stripped of all secondary elements, and reduced to the simplest and most basic rendering, the main theme amounts to nothing but this: that the ancient city of Alexandria is responsible for the incestuous and adulterous relationships of its inhabitants. This, in itself, is a comic idea, since it is a reversal of the actual. In this connection we remember a remark made about British intelligence agent Pursewarden, that he "made a habit of saying the opposite of what he meant in a joking way".[15] This is what Durrell has done. The method is as old as Swift, Durrell's great Anglo-Irish ancestor. If we turn to Swift's *Gulliver's Travels,* we discover that Gulliver's third voyage is a moon voyage. However, instead of Gulliver going to the moon, the moon (Laputa) comes to Gulliver.

D. J. Enright calls Durrell's lovers "a group of over-bred neurotics and sexual dilettantes".[16] If we are to regard them merely on the realistic level, then so they are; and Alexandria can have nothing to do with their inclinations and practices. In fact, we have to agree not only with Newby, but also with a host of other critics who, while highly praising some aspect of Durrell's technique, find that they cannot rationally accept the contents of his work.[17] However, as already

---

[13]   C. Bode, "Durrell's Way to Alexandria", *College English*, 22 (1961), 531.

[14]   G. S. Fraser, *"The Alexandria Quartet*: From Psychology to Myth", in *Lawrence Durrell: A Study*, ed. G. S. Fraser, London, 1973, 114.

[15]   Durrell, *Balthazar*, 111.

[16]   Enright, "Alexandrian Nights Entertainments", 31.

[17]   Manzalawi's criticism of Durrell's distortion of objective details has already been referred to. Gilbert Phelps confesses that "there is no doubt of course as to the frequent brilliance of Durrell's writing: there are some verbal fireworks and an impressive unity of tone is maintained". Nevertheless, he greatly regrets the thinness of the human values in the *Quartet,* declaring that "the novels purport to analyse love, but where", he asks, "are the examples of profound human relationships that alone could support the claim? ... If ever there was a case of 'sex in the head' it is here" ("The Novel Today", in *The Modern Age*, ed. Boris Ford, Harmondsworth, 1961, 491). David Lodge admits that Durrell's original

suggested, Durrell was not interested in a realistic portrayal, but in a comic one.

To carry out his comic purpose, Durrell envisaged a technique which (as he tells us in his 1962 preface to *The Alexandria Quartet*) "was intended as a challenge to the serial form of the conventional novel".[18] The work waso be composed of four parts: in the first three, time would be "stayed" so that three different but equally true views of the same events could be given. In two of these parts the narrator would be a subject since he tells the story himself, but in the third he would become an object, that is to say, one of the characters who are narrated about, and the story would be told from the omniscient novelist's point of view. In the fourth, the characters of the first three novels would move on into the future. In each case the observer would not be situated in the conventional extended time of past, present, and future, but in a new time "which contained all time in every moment of time".[19] This is what Durrell proposed to do, and he artistically carried it out.

The narrator of the first, second and fourth volumes is the Irish protagonist Darley, the "mental refugee" whose "small flat" is shared by Gaston Pomba.[20] Interestingly, he has the same surname as the Irish minor poet George Darley (1795–1846), and is, in Durrell's opinion, "a good honest poet".[21] We must remember that Darley, as Professor Dobree has pointed out, has the same initials as Durrell (L. D. G.) and that he always speaks for the author. The narrator of the third volume is Durrell, the Anglo-Irish creator of Darley, the colonizing white man who looks down on all Egyptian natives, finding no moral integrity in any of them.[22] We might say that these

---

approach and richness of expression have earned him a rank among the great modern masters of the novel, but maintains that his proliferation of sexual aberrations, intrigues and treasons cannot be considered by a rational reader except as an example of the absurd (David Lodge, "Le roman contemporain en Angleterre", *La Table Ronde*, 179 [Decembre 1962], 80-92). For other approaches, see Carol Pierce's recent article "East and West: Current Critical Responses to *The Alexandria Quartet*", in *Confluences XV: Lawrence Durrell*, ed. C. Alexandre-Garner, Paris, 1998, 125-54.

[18] Lawrence Durrell, *The Alexandria Quartet* (with author's Preface), London, 1962, 28.

[19] Lawrence Durrell, *Key to Modern Poetry*, London, 1952.

[20] Durrell, *Justine*, 21.

[21] Pine, *Lawrence Durrell*, 276.

[22] Examples of this attitude abound in *Mountolive*, but see especially, 412, 417, 481, 587-88, 592, 641-42.

two narrators present the two sides of Durrell: the colonized Irish on the one hand, and the colonizing English on the other.

In *Justine,* the first volume of the *Quartet,* Darley, who is now living in retreat on a Greek island, recalls his Alexandrian days and friends, and certain events revolving round his love-affair with Justine, the wife of the rich Nessim. In the second volume, *Balthazar,* Darley is still in his retreat. His version of the story has been corrected by Dr Balthazar, and he realizes that his vision of the story in *Justine* has been only partial. When he re-writes the same experiences in the light of the new knowledge that has come to him, the result is that many of the actions and events of *Justine* acquire a totally new significance since, as Pursewarden says:

> We live lives based on selected fictions. Our view of reality is conditioned by our position in time and space. Two paces east or west and the picture is changed.[23]

In *Mountolive,* the third volume of the *Quartet,* a third version of the story is told. Here, however, Darley becomes an object (*he* instead of *I*), and the same events are retold, but in the third person, and from the point of view of the omniscient author. Objectivity is supposed to be the mode of presentation, but actually it turns out to be another form of subjectivity, that of the author. It is as if Durrell is saying that we can never be sure that anything is objectively real. We are the ones who comprehend what we call "reality", but the very comprehending changes us, and in consequence for us, changes the object we have been comprehending, so that not only does the line between subject and object become blurred, but also the more we know of an event, the less we can determine its cause and effect. Accordingly, the third version of the story, like the other two, is also incomplete and only partly true.

In *Clea,* the fourth volume, Darley who once again becomes narrator, leaves his place of retreat on the island and returns to Alexandria. He visits those of his friends who are still alive, and renews his relationship with them. However, later developments do not resolve the contradictions of the other views, but add to them. Thus the hunt after truth must ever remain fruitless since "at every moment in Time the possibilities are endless in their multiplicity". [24]

---

[23]   Durrell, *Balthazar*, 14-15.
[24]   *Ibid.*, 226.

No wonder that when we have finished reading Durrell's *Quartet* and laid it aside, we do not feel that the questions raised by the work have been resolved. On the contrary, we find ourselves asking numerous questions, but getting no answers for them. No answer is meant to be given, and in this connection we recall a remark made by Justine as she sat before the multiple mirrors at the dressmaker's:

> "Look! Five different pictures of the same subject. Now if I wrote, I would try for a multi-dimensional effort in character, a sort of prism-sightedness. Why should not people show more than one profile at a time?" [25]

Durrell's characters "show more than one profile at a time". This, of course, is a grotesque distortion, but it is *meant* to be so: it is part of a comic technique which, according to Vivian Mercier, is typically Irish.[26]

Vivian Mercier also claims that parody is another characteristic of Irish comic writing.[27] Parody is used with mastery in Durrell's portrayal of Narouz, who has a prototype in the tarot cards, and Scobie whose prototype is found in Greek mythology In *How to understand the Tarot,* Frank Lind explains that it is composed of two separate packs, the Major Arcana and the Minor. Card IX of the Major Arcana bears the figure of the hermit, of whom Narouz is a parody. Like the hermit, Narouz leads a simple, primitive life away from the crowded towns.[28] He has blue eyes, and wears a blue shirt outdoors[29] and a blue cloak indoors.[30] Blue, we notice, is the colour of celestial things with which the hermit is occupied. The picture on the card shows the hermit holding in his right hand a lantern, symbolical of intuition; and in his left a staff, symbolical of divine comfort.[31] Narouz occasionally shows intuition, though in the manner of one possessed.[32] He is also given to wielding a whip sent to him by Sheikh Bedawi from Aswan. The hermit wears a mantle symbolical of "protection from the chill winds of adverse criticism" and of the Adept's concealment of his

---

25   Durrell, *Justine*, 27.
26   Vivian Mercier, *The Irish Comic Tradition*, London, 1991, 68.
27   *Ibid.*, 210-36.
28   Durrell, *Balthazar*, 73-92.
29   *Ibid.*, 68.
30   *Ibid.*, 80.
31   Psalm 23: 4.
32   Durrell, *Balthazar*, 161-64; Durrell, *Mountolive*, 124.

profound knowledge of higher truths from the eyes of the profane".[33]
Narouz wears a moustache and beard in order to hide the ugly split in
his upper lip from the outside world.[34] The blue cloak which he puts
on indoors symbolizes his attempt to hide even from himself his own
frenzied love for Clea,[35] as well as the inability of his brother to
understand his religious fanaticism.[36]

Although his name signifies the breaking forth of divine light
("Narouz" being derived from the word for the Coptic New Year), he
is not, like his tarot prototype, "led by the illumination from the
Divine",[37] but by a diabolical light from Taor, the desert woman saint
who is reported to have three breasts.[38] Significantly, Narouz is
described as speaking with a "diabolical hiss" and praying with
"demonic meekness upon his face".[39] Narouz's fanaticism leads to his
murder. Ironically, he dies under a "Holy Tree" with Clea's name on
his tongue.[40] After his murder, in his attempt to pull Clea with him to
the underworld, he becomes the agent of that death from which Clea
emerges a re-born artist.[41]

While Narouz has a tarot prototype, old Scobie is a parody of
Tiresias, the ancient prophet of Thebes, the man-woman in close touch
with the most potent forces of life. Like Tiresias, Scobie possesses the
gift of prophecy, accurately foretelling Clea's encounter with death
near the island of Narouz.[42] He too has the characteristics of both
sexes; for though he is male, he confesses that he has "tendencies"
which lead him to dress like Dolly Varden, a Waterloo prostitute, in
order to tempt British sailors.[43] Significantly, while Scobie is making
this confession to Darley, the radio of a ship blares out a comic song
about old Tiresias, "the latest jazz-hit to reach Alexandria":

> Old Tiresias
> No-one half so breezy as

[33] Frank Lind, *How to Understand the Tarot*, London, n.d., 39.
[34] Durrell, *Mountolive*, 68.
[35] Durrell, *Balthazar*, 94.
[36] *Ibid.*, 225.
[37] Lind, *How to Understand the Tarot*, 37.
[38] Durrell, *Mountolive*, 255.
[39] *Ibid.*, 33, 34.
[40] *Ibid.*, 307; Durrell, *Clea*, 57.
[41] Durrell, *Clea*, 247.
[42] *Ibid.*, 206-207, 247.
[43] Durrell, *Balthazar*, 41.

Not so free as
Old Tiresias.[44]

After his death, Scobie becomes El Scob (officially enshrined as El Yacoub) who "by sleeping with impotent men regenerates their forces", and who "could also make the barren conceive".[45] On the day when his "Mulid" (or birthday) is celebrated, suppliants stream to his most sacred relic – which, hilariously enough, is a bathtub.

More than two centuries ago, in order to suspend disbelief and to strengthen the illusion of reality in his reader's mind, Jonathan Swift prefaced *Gulliver's Travels* (1726) with a letter "from Captain Gulliver to his cousin Sympson", in which he wrote:

> As to the People of Lilliput, Brobdingnag ... and Laputa, I have never yet heard of any Yahoo so presumptuous as to dispute their Being, or the facts I have related concerning them.

He even went so far as to insert maps showing the supposed positions of these countries.

Why did Durrell so emphatically assert that his Alexandria is "real"? He was simply trying to do what his great Anglo-Irish ancestor had done before him. Roger Bowen, assuming like many others that Durrell intended a realistic portrayal of Alexandria, complains that the city "was not researched afresh in the field".[46] It is clear, however, that Durrell was not, by any means, trying to convey an objective picture of the city. In fact, this would have been quite inconsistent with everything else in the *Quartet* which, as we have seen, is primarily a comedy in the Irish comic tradition.

---

44   *Ibid.*, 44.
45   Durrell, *Clea*, 82-83.
46   Bowen, *Many Histories Deep*, 164.

NOTES ON CONTRIBUTORS AND EDITORS

Donatella Abbate Badin is Professor of English Literature at Turin University. Amongst other things, she has written articles on Kinsella and a book *Thomas Kinsella* (1996). She has also translated *Una Terra Senza Peccato: Poesie Scelte di Thomas Kinsella* (1996), co-editor of *Insulae/Islands/Ireland: The Classical World and the Mediterranean* (1994) and *Sean O'Faolain: A Centenary Celebration* (2001). Her forthcoming book is on Lady Morgan.

Malcolm Ballin is a Research Associate at Cardiff University, specializing in literary journalism. He took his first degree in Cambridge in 1957 and returned late to the academy, completing his PhD in English at Cardiff in 2002. Publications include a chapter in *Sean O'Faolain: A Centenary Celebration* (2001) and an article in *IASIL – 99 – Barcelona, Bells*, 2000.

Patrick Bohan works for the Barcelona-based scientific publisher, Prous Science. He writes regularly for the James Joyce Centre's Bloomsday Magazine. The article in the present publication is part of a larger work entitled *Reading Joyce and Joyce Reading*, for which he was awarded the degree of M.Litt. from University College Dublin in 1999.

Rui Carvalho Homem is Associate Professor at the Faculty of Letters, University of Oporto, Portugal. His major research interests and publications are in Irish studies and English Renaissance studies. He has recently published a new Portuguese translation of *Antony and Cleopatra*, and is currently working on *Love's Labour Lost*. He is also involved in a research project on poetry and the visual arts.

M. Casey Diana, a native of Limerick, is presently a lecturer at the University of Illinois at Urbana-Champaign. Her recently completed Ph.D. was on eighteenth-century British literature, and her research interests focus primarily on the role addiction plays in imperialism. She has published articles on Jane Austen and Lord Byron.

Brian Coates is a Senior Lecturer in English Studies at the University of Limerick. He was joint organizer of IASIL 1998 and is one of the editors of the present volumes. His most recent publication is a chapter on anthropological criticism in *The Cambridge History of Literary Criticism, IX*. He writes and does research on modernism, postmodernism and cultural and critical theory.

Joachim Fischer is Senior Lecturer in German, Joint Director of the Centre for Irish-German Studies and Deputy Director of the Ralahine Centre of Utopian Studies at the University of Limerick. He was joint organizer of IASIL 1998 and is co-editor of the present volumes. His current major research area is Irish-German connections. Among his recent book-length publications are *Das Deutschlandbild der Iren 1890-1939* [The Irish image of Germany 1890-1939] (2000) and *As Others Saw Us: Cork Through European Eyes* (ed. with G. Neville, 2005).

Maurice Harmon is Emeritus Professor of Anglo-Irish Literature at University College Dublin. His books include *Sean O'Faolain: A Life* (1994), *The Dolmen Press: A Celebration* (2002*), No Author Better Served: The Correspondence between Samuel Beckett and Alan Schneider* (ed., 1998) and a translation, *The Colloquy of the Old Men* (2001). He has published two volumes of poetry, *The Last Regatta* (2000) and *Tales of Death* (2001).

Alexandra Hendriok completed her Ph.D. on "Myth and Identity in Twentieth-Century Irish Fiction and Film" at the Open University in 2000. She teaches English Literature and Language at Epping Forest College in Sussex, where she is Deputy Head of the Sixth Form Centre. She continues to work on identity and myth in Irish fiction.

John Hildebidle earned his Ph.D. at Harvard in 1981. For the past twenty years he has taught English, American and Irish literature at MIT. He writes poetry and short fiction. His scholarly books include *Thoreau: A Naturalist's Liberty* (1983) and *Five Irish Writers: The Errand of Keeping Alive* (1989). His current projects include a study of the Field Day Company, and a book-length essay tentatively entitled *Does Poetry Matter?*

Patricia Lynch is a Lecturer in English Studies at the University of Limerick. She was joint organizer of IASIL 1998 and is co-editor of the present volumes. Her specializations are in Irish studies (various periods), post-colonial studies, Hiberno-English in literature, and literary stylistics, and she has published on Maria Edgeworth, Kate O'Brien, Seamus Heaney, John Montague and Roddy Doyle.

Anthony McCann received his Ph.D. from the University of Limerick in 2002. His research interests are intellectual property, popular music, traditional culture, Irish studies, philosophy, social philosophy, education, and critical management studies. He was the Assistant Co-ordinator and temporary Project Co-ordinator of the 1999 UNESCO/Smithsonian World Conference.

Mary Massoud is currently Professor of English and Comparative Literature at Ain Shams University in Cairo, Egypt and was Head of the Department of English at Ain Shams from 1984 to 1990. She has lectured at several universities abroad, and is the author of many books and papers on English, American and Anglo-Irish literary topics. She has edited *Literary Inter-relations: Ireland, Egypt and the Far East* (1995).

Nicholas Meihuizen is a Professor in the Department of English at the University of Zululand, Kwa-Diangezwa campus. His research interests include the epistemically orientated constructions of empire and imperialism as evinced in the poetry of Luis Vaz de Camões, Thomas Pringle and Roy Campbell. His book on mythopoetics in the poetry of W. B. Yeats, *Yeats and the Drama of Sacred Space,* was published in 1998.

Marisol Morales Ladrón is a Senior Lecturer at the University of Alcalá, Madrid, Spain, where she teaches English, Irish and Comparative Literature. Her publications include *Breve Introducción a la Literatura Comparada* (1999) and *Las Poéticas de James Joyce y Luis Martín-Santos* (forthcoming*)*, two co-edited volumes on feminist criticism, and articles on Wilde, Joyce, Yeats, Friel, Bernard MacLaverty and Emma Donoghue.

Kristin Morrison, who wrote her essay while circumnavigating Ireland, is Professor Emeritus in the Irish Studies Program of Boston College. She now lives in Glasgow and continues research while sailing her boat, Run na Mara, off the west coast of Scotland.

Joanny Moulin teaches at the University de Provence, Aix-Marseille. He is the author of *Seamus Heaney: l'éblouissement de l'impossible* (1999), *Ted Hughes: La Langue Rémunerée* (1999) and editor of *Ted Hughes: New Selected Poems 1957-1994* (2000)

Shane Murphy is a lecturer in the Department of English at the University of Aberdeen. He is Irish and Scottish Programme Co-ordinator for the RIISS. His main interests lie in Irish literature, visual arts, and post-colonial fiction. He has published articles on Irish culture and identity, Northern Irish poetry and politics, and Irish drama. Currently he is completing a monograph entitled *Sympathetic Ink*.

Sean Mythen is Chief Executive Officer of Wexford County Enterprise Board, and Secretary of the Byrne Perry Summer School, which teaches Irish history and literature from the eighteenth century to contemporary times. He was conferred with Ph.D. at the University of Ulster in 2003. He is the author of *Thomas Furlong: A Forgotten Wexford Poet* (1998), and is also interested in the works of another Wexford writer, M. J. Whitty.

Taura Napier is currently an Assistant Professor of English at Wingate University, North Carolina. Her specializations are women's autobiography, Irish literature, and post-colonial Literatures. She is author of *Seeking a Country: Literary Autobiographies of Twentieth Century Irishwomen* (2002).

Eugene O'Brien is Head of the English Department in Mary Immaculate College, Limerick, and is also an editor and a member of editorial boards. He has published *The Question of Irish Identity in the Writings of William Butler Yeats and James Joyce* (1998), *Examining Irish Nationalism in the Context of Literature, Culture and Religion* (2002), *Seamus Heaney: Creating Irelands of the Mind* (2002), and many articles.

Thomas O'Grady is Director of Irish Studies at the University of Massachusetts, Boston. His essays on Irish writers have appeared in many journals, including *Éire/Ireland, James Joyce Quarterly, Études Irlandaises, The Canadian Journal of Irish Studies, New Hibernia Review* and *Studies: An Irish Quarterly Review*.

Åke Persson is a Senior Lecturer in English at the University of Trollhättan/Uddevalla, Sweden, having graduated from Trinity College Dublin and Gothenburg University. He has edited *Journey Into Joy: Selected Prose* (of Brendan Kennelly; 1994) and *This Fellow with the Fabulous Smile: A Tribute to Brendan Kennelly* (1996), and is the author of *Betraying the Age: Social and Artistic Protest in Brendan Kennelly's Work* (2000).

Giovanni Pillonca has taught Italian in several universities (Mogadishu, Casablanca, Groningen and Trinity College Dublin) and is presently cultural attaché at the Italian Cultural Institute in Montreal. He has published a number of essays on Irish writers (Joyce, Wilde, Heaney) in academic journals, a book of translations from Derek Mahon's poetry *L'Ultimo re del fuoco* (together with Roberto Bertoni, Turin 2000) and introduced a book of translations from Seamus Heaney's poetry (Turin 2003).

María de la Cinta Ramblado Minero is currently a lecturer at the University of Limerick. She graduated from the University of Huelva and completed her Ph.D. at the University of Limerick. Her research interests include women's writing in Ireland, Spain and Latin America, and autobiography studies, comparative literature and cultural studies. She is author of *Isabel Allende's Writing of the Self* (2003).

Paul Robinson is Professor Emeritus at the University of Pittsburg at Bradford: Pennsylvania, since July 1990. He has retained an interest in Anglo-Irish literature since then, mostly by collecting and reading work by Irish authors.

Klaus-Gunnar Schneider has the following specializations: post-colonialism, and Irish identity. He has a number of articles in journals pertaining to Irish studies.

B. R. Siegfried is Associate Professor at Brigham Young University, Provo, Utah, USA. Her research interests include Irish literary history, Shakespeare, English literary history, sixteenth- and seventeenth-century women writers. She has published a number of articles in these areas, and is currently working on a book entitled *The Literary History of Gráinne Uí Mháille*.

Giovanna Tallone (Ph.D. Florence) is currently attached to the Department of English at Università Cattolica, Milan. Her main research areas are contemporary Irish drama and Irish women writers, and the remakes of Old Irish legends, and she has published on Brian Friel, James Stephens, Lady Gregory, Mary Lavin, Eilís Ní Dhuibhne and Angela Bourke.

Clare Wallace is a lecturer at the Department of English and American Studies at Charles University, Prague. Her research interests include contemporary Irish and British drama, Joyce and literary theory. She has published essays on Patrick McCabe, James Joyce, Marina Carr and recent Irish drama, and is co-editor with Louis Armand of *Giacomo Joyce: Envoys of the Other* (2002).

Hiroyuki Yamasaki is Professor at the Graduate School of Literature and Human Sciences at Osaka City University, Japan. His research interests are in the areas of cultural hybridity in modern Japanese, Irish and British literatures. He is the author of *W. B. Yeats and Orientalism: A Hermeneutical Approach* (1996) and *Others Inside English Literatures: Postcolonialism and Cultural Hybridity* (2002).

Karin Zettl teaches at the Institut für Anglistik und Amerikanistik at the University of Vienna. Her research interests are in gender studies, Irish writing, and post-colonialism.

INDEX